A GUIDE TO
FOREIGN LANGUAGE COURSES
AND DICTIONARIES

Third edition, revised and enlarged

Edited by

A. J. Walford, M.A., Ph.D., F.L.A.

and

J. E. O. Screen, M.A., Ph.D., A.L.A.

GREENWOOD PRESS
Westport, Connecticut

Library of Congress Cataloging Publication Data

Walford, Albert John.
  A guide to foreign language courses and dictionaries.

  First-2d ed. published under title: A guide to foreign language grammars and
dictionaries.
  Includes index.
  1. Language and languages--Grammars--Bibliography.
  2. Encyclopedias and dictionaries--Bibliography.
  I. Screen, J. E. O. II. Title.
  Z7004.G7W3 1978 [P207] 016.415 77-26283
  ISBN 0-313-20100-5

This edition first published 1977 by Greenwood Press, Inc.
By arrangement with the Library Association, London

Library of Congress Catalog Card Number: 77-26283
ISBN: 0-313-20100-5

Typeset in Great Britain
Manufactured in the U.S.A.

10 9 8 7 6 5 4 3 2 1

CONTENTS

INTRODUCTION

The present British interest in foreign languages owes something to the travel habits of our post-World War II affluent society, and something to the universality of radio and television. Moreover, we are now members of the European Economic Community.

In the teaching of modern languages, the classical tradition has in the past been the dominant influence. French is accepted as the second language to be taught in secondary schools. German and possibly Spanish may appear in the upper-school curriculum, and Russian is taught in some schools. This appears to be a regular pattern. As to language-teaching methods, audio-visual aids are now indispensable.

This third edition of the *Guide*, now under a joint editorship[1], provides a running commentary on selected courses, audio-visual aids and dictionaries in most of the main European languages, plus Arabic, Chinese and Japanese. It is intended for teachers, students, graduates taking up a particular language for the first time, scientists (for acquiring a reading knowledge of a language on a minimum of grammar), tourists, business men and librarians (for book-selection and stock revision). Material has been sectionalised according to type and level of user, the most strongly recommended item usually appearing first in each section.

Audio-visual aid sections have been much expanded. On the other hand, monographs on aspects of grammar, etymological and historical language-dictionaries have been generally excluded, together with dictionaries of synonyms and slang. The exceptions occur mainly in the case of the less familiar, and hence less taught, languages about which information may be

---

[1] Dr. J. E. O. Screen has edited the chapters on the Slavonic and Scandinavian languages, Russian, modern Greek, Finnish, Hungarian and Japanese.

particularly difficult to obtain and which are likely to be studied by those requiring more comprehensive guidance.

Prices, usually as of 1975, are given whenever easily ascertainable. When a book is issued in both hardback and paperback formats, the hardback price is given first.

1

GENERAL

Courses & grammars – Dictionaries – Audio-visual aids

Courses & grammars. For A. H. Sweet[1], grammar was not a piece of dead mechanism or a Chinese puzzle of which the parts must be fitted together in accordance with certain artificial rules, but 'a living organism which has a history and reason of its own'. In the more familiar foreign languages writers of grammars have, after years of trial and error, presented linguistic material in a digested and attractive form, with audio-visual accompaniment.

Grammars cover a multitude of forms, from the two-page cards published by Edward Arnold to the four- or five-volume illustrated courses. Some grammars concentrate on a command of the written language; others stress conversation and oral fluency. Some so-called grammars of the 'German in three months' type give no more than a smattering of the language[2]; others, of *la plume de ma tante* type, have stilted and unrealistic examples and exercises; others, again, need to be reinforced by audio aids. We have got beyond the stage when a Spanish grammar for Frenchmen needs only to be translated into English to make it acceptable to Englishmen.

The main points to be considered in selecting a foreign-language course or grammar may be enumerated:

1. Declared purpose. There should be a clear statement of the level or standard and class of user aimed at. How far have these aims been met?

---

[1] On 'Grammar', in *Encyclopaedia Britannica* (11th ed.), v. 12, p. 332.
[2] How long does an adult require to master a foreign language? Much depends on background. Aslib investigation (*The foreign language barrier* (1962), p. 15) found that the maximum amount of tuition necessary for adult scientists to reach a specified standard in Russian was about 200 hours, and the minimum, about 45 hours.

2. Accuracy and general reliability; up-to-dateness (*e.g.*, obser-
   vance of current official rulings on orthography).
3. Presentation. Stress on points of grammar or the modern 'direct
   method', encouraging oral fluency. A four-year course designed
   for 'O' level may run dry of ideas and interesting material in its
   later stages.
4. Systematic and progressive treatment of material (first things
   first: not blinding the student with out-of-the-way vocabulary,
   exceptions to rules, or difficult exercises before he has been
   adequately prepared); comprehensiveness within limits.
5. Interesting material, *e.g.*, lively and up-to-date passages for
   reading, conversation and translation; practical examples and
   situations; numerous and relevant illustrations; adequate range
   of exercises.
6. Aids to pronunciation. Pronunciation based on English-word
   analogy is a very rough-and-ready system. In Italian and Russian, stress must be indicated. If the grammar is a self-tutor, the
   author should state plainly what can and what cannot be
   learned from his book. Thus discs, tapes or cassettes will be essential for cultivating a correct accent.
7. Reference material on the grammar, *e.g.*, verb tables; summary
   of grammar.
8. Detailed subject index to points of grammar covered.
9. End-vocabulary: each way and based preferably on word
   frequency.
10. Typography: clarity; generous type size (*e.g.*, for Cyrillic
    characters); and attractive layout; judicious use of bold type
    and italic.
11. Availability of a key (for self-tuition).
12. Price.

Dictionaries[1]. If we accept the axiom that languages are complex organisms, then the dictionary is obviously at a disadvantage. To quote the Chevalleys[2]: 'Speaking in terms of life, there

---

[1] Recent lists of dictionaries: *Camden Reference Libraries foreign language dictionaries* (London Borough of Camden Libraries & Arts Department, 1974. [iii], 10,
28, 21 pp. *c.* 1750 titles); *Bailey's Technical dictionaries catalogue, 1974* (Folkestone,
Bailey Bros. & Swinfen, Ltd., 1974. 79 pp. *c.* 1200 items, with prices); and the
massive Catalogue of the Translator's Library in the Department of Trade & Industry, London; edited by G. E. Hamilton (Dobbs Ferry, N.Y., Oceana Publications,
Inc., 1975. 3 v. $250) the 3 volumes covering authors, subjects and languages
respectively.
[2] *The Concise Oxford French dictionary*, Introduction, p. v.

is no such thing as a "separate" word. When you speak or write, none of your words stand alone; they derive their form, colour, functions, special meaning or strength from the context. ... A dictionary is like a herbarium. It can only present words in a dried state, and must, for the sake of reference, give them in alphabetical order.' But the dictionary can, with more or less exactness, give the different senses of a word, discriminate between those senses, and enumerate them in order of frequency, with examples.

The main points to be considered in selecting a foreign-language dictionary:

1. Authority of issuing body; reputation of publisher.
2. Aims, as stated by publisher and compiler(s). How far are these met, in practice? Are types of intended user stated?
3. Scope. If a technical dictionary, how far are common words with non-technical meanings included? Are roots and derivatives, colloquialisms and country variations (*e.g.*, Swiss German, Brazilian Portuguese) covered? Number of headwords[1], assuming sub-entries are not being counted separately. Extent of entries: frequency of idioms and sentences illustrating meaning in context: categorisation of nouns, etc. Mini-dictionaries have usually only cheapness and portability to recommend them; they are less legible, have a more restricted vocabulary and tend to give a take-it-or-leave-it equivalent or a string of undifferentiated equivalents. (Polyglot dictionaries, because of the need for compression, are also prone to this weakness.)
4. Arrangement and balance. A–Z order of headwords is not necessarily the best arrangement for a specialised dictionary. A dictionary may be mainly for home-country consumption; the number of pages and pronunciation guides in the two parts of a two-way dictionary will need to be compared. Note the importance of monolingual – possibly illustrated – native dictionaries.
5. Consistency (*e.g.*, a qualifying adjective and its noun should be entered under either (or both) the adjective or the noun, not sometimes one and sometimes the other.
6. Up-to-dateness (particularly applicable to technical dictionaries); in line with current official rulings on orthography. Is

---

[1] In some dictionaries compounds of a headword may be given separate entries, while in others they may be run-on sub-entries. This invalidates entry-word counting except as a very rough comparative check.

a so-called later 'edition' a substantial, re-set revision, or the previous edition plus a small (often overlooked) supplement, or merely a reprint?

7. Aids to pronunciation: use of international phonetic symbols (IPA); indication of stress and syllabification; noting of quality of vowels and sibilants.

8. Indication of gender (omitted in most technical dictionaries), genitive singular and/or nominative plural of nouns, basic verb forms, etc.

9. Appendices: verb and other tables; abbreviations and proper names (if not caught up in the main sequence); conversion tables of weights and measures.

10. Illustrations, particularly if keyed parts are shown.

11. Legibility and ease of reference, usually involving use of bold type, numbering of different meanings/applications of headwords, use of italic for examples of usage, and avoidance of too many symbols and other abbreviations. Whiteness and opaqueness of paper make for legibility, and a stout binding ensures a longer life for the dictionary. Portability, unfortunately for the user, is in inverse ratio to comprehensiveness.

12. Price.

Audio-visual aids. Apart from various publishers' catalogues (*e.g.*, Harrap-Didier's *Audio-visual 1975*, *Linguaphone for languages*, and Tutor Tape Company's annotated lists), there are the invaluable CILT (Centre for Information on Language Teaching and Research) annotated *Recorded and audio-visual materials* lists for Russian, Spanish, Italian, French and German. These are supplemented or revised at intervals.

Other languages. CILT Teaching materials lists are limited to the five languages just given. Nineteen other languages are so far covered in briefer fashion as 'Language and culture guides'. The languages are: Arabic, Bulgarian, Celtic languages (Irish, Gaelic, Welsh), Czech (Slovak); Chinese (Cantonese and Mandarin), Dutch (Afrikaans), Danish, Finnish, Hungarian, Indian languages: Bengali, Gujarati, Panjabi, Hindi, Urdu, Japanese; Modern Greek; Norwegian, Polish, Portuguese; Serbo-Croat, Swedish, Turkish and Swahili. That on Farsl is in preparation. Each costs £0.25. Each *Guide* has sections listing teaching institutions, courses, research, materials (grammars, dictionaries, audio-visual materials) and sources of further information.

Some helpful points concerning the less commonly taught languages are to be found in the papers of a conference arranged by CILT in 1975[1].

A. J. WALFORD
J. E. O. SCREEN

---

[1] *Less commonly taught languages: resources and problems.* Papers from a conference convened in June 1975 (London, Centre for Information on Language Teaching and Research, 1975. 71 pp. CILT Reports and Papers, 12).

2

FRENCH

I think then that it is merely waste of time to learn more than a smattering of foreign tongues. The only exception I would make to this is French.

(W. Somerset Maugham. *The summing-up.*)

Whether or not one agrees with either part of Maugham's statement, French will go on being taught and learned in this country and is likely to remain our most common second language. It follows that there is a wide range of courses, grammars, dictionaries and audio-visual aids devoted to the teaching and learning of French. The items given below are selected because they are recommended (within their limits) and are also (usually) in print.

For some, the formal approach to a language through the conscientious assimilation of the basic rules of grammar may still be the most satisfactory method. Others may prefer the more modern Direct Method approach, whereby the pupil pronounces and writes the word simultaneously, but the teacher uses the foreign language as the medium in which the lesson is taught, instead of English.

As a development of the Direct Method many people, both children and adults, are now learning French and other languages in a language laboratory where students can learn to speak a language quickly and without the agonies which some of us will have suffered through repeated attempts at a difficult pronunciation in a strange language in front of an unsympathetic class. Even so, the language laboratory is more suitable for adults than for children, who need the personality of the teacher to keep the subject interesting.

Where a language laboratory is not available it may still be possible to supplement formal study by use of other audio-visual aids such as discs, tapes and film strips. Records and tapes are now available to accompany a number of courses, – a particularly useful aid to the student trying to learn by himself. But such aids are only 'audio' and not 'visual'. Pupils are dependent on the film-strip for understanding the meaning of the tape. The audio-visual method is particularly useful in schools where the pupils may be unable to tackle the grammatical side of the language.

The best-known audio-visual method of teaching and learning French is the Tavor system. Writing about this in 1962, S. R. Ingram said[1]:

> ... *the aim of the course is to bombard the eye and ear of the pupil with situations which are immediately comprehensible* ... [*and*] *to give the mastery over enough elements of the spoken language to enable them to approach its grammatical study through material which is completely familiar.*

This is a modern recognition of the natural way of learning a language. Audio-visual aids, whether they be illustrations, wall charts, discs, tapes, radio, television or language laboratory drills, supplement and are supplemented by the printed word[2].

COURSES & GRAMMARS

1. For beginners

French in the primary school, by M. Raymond and C. L. Bourcier; edited and adapted by R. P. A. Edwards (Burke, 1964. 4 pupil's books £2.60, and Teacher's manual. £1.50) is designed to enable those aged 7–10 'to express themselves freely in the French language and to understand it'. No better primer exists. It can also be used by adults with no previous knowledge of the language, the Teacher's manual giving it the advantage of a self-tutor. V. 1–2 consist of illustrations only; v. 3, *Je sais lire*, adds

---

[1] S. R. Ingram. "Audio-visual French: the Tavor system." *In* National Committee for Audio-Visual Aids in Education. *Audio-visual aids and modern language teaching: a symposium* (London, N.C.L.V.A.E., 1962), p. 23–24.

[2] I am indebted to Dr. Peter Platt for much of this introduction, largely taken from the second edition of this *Guide* (1967), p. 18–19.

a few simple sentences to illustrations; v.4, *Je lis avec joie*, is made up of reading matter plus some illustrations. Supporting audio material consists of sixteen 7″ discs, 45 rpm.

Pamela Symonds' *Let's speak French* (Oxford University Press, 1962–63. 2 v. (vi, 175 pp.; vi, 229 pp. each £0.75) is well regarded as an oral course for young beginners and the lower forms of secondary schools, in 64 lessons. Each Book has a page of illustrations related to a text, plus sets of questions and suggestions for classroom conversation. The course is amply reinforced by 63 wall pictures (£11.25 + VAT), 19 tapes (5″ reels, $3\frac{3}{4}$ ips, twin half-track. £43.25 + VAT) or 32 C.60 cassettes (£43.25 + VAT). There is also a language-laboratory version (£85 for either 30 tapes or 30 cassettes).

2. For CSE

C. E. Loveman's *A simple French course* (Nelson, 1967–68. 3 v. (xii, 107 pp; x, 141 pp.; x, 158 pp. £1.88) emphasises oral work, with a variety of illustrations, question-and-answer work, stories and dialogues. Each Book has end-vocabularies. Audio material consists of six tapes, 2 per Book (5″ reels, $3\frac{3}{4}$ ips, twin half-track. £12 + VAT); visual, – 6 wall pictures for each of books 1–2. £5.50 + VAT).

In *Le français d'aujourd'hui*, by P. J. Downes and E. A. Griffith (English Universities Press, 1967–72. 4 parts. Pupil's books. £3.35; Teacher's books. £3.75) the text material and the audio-visual aids (filmstrips, dics and/or tapes) can be used independently of each other. Also, Part 4: GCE (Pupil's book. 1969. 144 pp., plus Supplementary booklet. 100 pp. £1.40; 4 tapes: 5″ reels, $3\frac{3}{4}$ ips, twin half-track. £18 + VAT) can be used instead of Part 4: CSE (Pupil's book. 204 pp. £0.95; Teacher's handbook. 1970 v, 40 pp. £0.45; 4 tapes: $5\frac{3}{4}$″ reels, $3\frac{3}{4}$ ips, twin half-track. £22 + VAT).

A. Simpson's *A simplified French course* (Faber, 1953–59. 4 v. 135, 140, 144, 160 pp. £1.55) is written from the point of view of interest rather than academic performance. Thus, it has many helpful illustrations and much interesting information about France and the French. It introduces points gradually in context, and treatment of grammar is fairly comprehensive. There are exercises at frequent intervals throughout. Better used with a teacher than as a self-tutor. A similar emphasis on France and the French way of life is given in *On y a*, edited by A. N. Court (London, Routledge & Kegan Paul, 1974. 5 v. illus. £5.10), which imparts a little French at a time and is suitable as a CSE course.

Cours illustré de français, by Mark Gilbert (University of London Press, 1966–71), also in 5 books, is adapted to both CSE and 'O' level. Books 1–4 (£6.22) are for CSE, with 6 filmstrips and 10 tapes (£45.50). All 5 books cover the 'O' level course, Book 5 comprising a pupil's book (364 pp.), supported by test booklet (£1.40), 2 tapes and one tape of tests (*c.* £11.50 + VAT).

3. For 'O' level

A course that has been produced 'after more research, consultation, try-out and revision than any other French course published in Britain' is the Nuffield Introductory French course, *En avant* (in four stages, for those aged 8–13), and its continuation, *À votre avis* (to be in four stages, for those aged 13–16), prepared by the staff of the French Section of the Schools Council Modern Languages Project. Published by E. J. Arnold (1966–), the course has an attractive profusion of drawings, photographs, maps, crosswords, questions on pictures, drills, narratives, dialogues, graded points in grammar, and songs. Pupil's readers are introduced at Stage 2 and pupil's books at Stage 4. Stage 5 consists of five magazines (*Dans le vent*), a comprehensive teacher's book and two grammars, apart from audio-visual material. A V aids in general cover flashcards, filmstrips, films, and tapes (4″ reels, $3\frac{3}{4}$ ips, twin half-track. Price of complete kits: Stage 1A: £29 + VAT; Stage 1B: £22.75 + VAT; Stage 2: £36.75 + VAT; Stage 3: £46.50 + VAT; Stage 4A: £47.25; Stage 4B: £45.75; Stage 5: £63.70 + VAT; Stage 6: £92.10 + VAT.

À la page, by Denis Grayson (Ginn, 1964–70), is a sound 5-volume 'O' level course, each book having dialogues, narratives, exercises, grammar and chapter vocabularies. Narratives in Book 5 (particularly thorough-going) includes passages from modern French writers. Printed material (£4.81) is supported by 8 filmstrips, 6 discs and 2 tapes (£18.35).

J. R. Watson's *La langue des français* (Harrap, 1963–72. 4 v. (256, 288, 320, 282 pp.); Key to Book 4: *Images et vocabulaires*. £5.20) has well-recorded A/V material (1 filmstrip; 12 tapes. £38.62½), as well as Supplementary oral exercises and structure drills (3 tapescripts: £0.84; 24 tapes: £51). Book 1 now has a pictorial edition (£1.75) and an audio-visual version (tapescripts: £0.40; filmstrips and tapes: £37.20 + VAT). *French: a structural approach*, by C. G. Hadley and B. Howson (Edinburgh, Oliver & Boyd, 1966–70. Books 1–4; Teacher's manuals 1–4 £7.03: 56 tapes: £180) is another four-stage course for 'O' level, the tapes and teacher's manuals playing an essential part. The rate of the grammar assumes an extremely receptive class.

'O' level courses without integrated audio-visual aids may be divided for the sake of convenience into those in 4 to 5 volumes (usually illustrated), and those concentrated into one volume. Among the former, *Nos voisins français*, by L. Tomlinson (2nd ed. Oxford University Press, 1951–63. 4 v. £2.70. Exercises, pts. 1 & 2. £0.40) provides full treatment of grammar, points being introduced naturally and progressively. In essence this course attempts from the beginning to make the student speak and think entirely in French. *Cinq années de français*, by M. Shockett (Cambridge University Press, 1938. 5 v. each £1), too, is based on the Direct Method. V. 5 introduces the subjunctive, and consolidates and prepares for first university examinations. *A modern French course*, by S. M. Smith (University Tutorial Press, 1950–58. 5 v. £2.60) has adequate drill and oral questions, v. 5 being for examination year. C. Hermus's *French* (E. Arnold, 1956–61. 5 v. v. 2–5, each £0.65) has about 140 one-page lessons in each volume. V. 5 is a revision volume by C. Hermus and D. N. R. Lester. (An alternative to it, also by Hermus and Lester, is *French for first examinations* (1956. £0.70), which includes examples of examination questions.)

W. F. H. Whitmarsh's *A graded French course* (London, Longmans, 1965. 4 bks. £2.75), a reprint of the 1947–51 edition, is a good solid course with the virtue of clarity. Book 4 is among the best of the orthodox grammar courses. But the whole lacks the 'spark' and imagination that distinguishes Grayson's *A la page* (see p. 15).

One of the most useful and attractive of single-volume 'O' level courses is *A new French grammar for G.C.E. candidates*, A. H. G. Morle and J. R. J. Jammes (Hutchinson, 1964. Exercises. £0.30; Grammar only. 221 pp. £0.60), although it has no guide to pronunication or end-vocabularies. It would be an excellent course for someone with a working knowledge of French. J. R. Fox's *A School Certificate grammar* (Grant Educational Co., 1946. viii, 244 pp.) also gives a thorough treatment of grammar and is one of the few grammars to have a really good index. D. K. Pryce's *Certificate French* (Harrap, 1967. 398 pp. £1.35) is a four-year course, lessons being followed by a grammar summary, with well-chosen examples. 'A pupil taken carefully through this book would have covered all the points required for a pass at 'O' level, with something to spare' (*Modern languages*, v. 48, no. 4, December 1967, p. 177). Finally, J. E. Travis's *A précis of French grammar* (Harrap, 1939. 176 pp. £0.70) is a straighforward statement of all but the more advanced grammar and is preferably to be used with a teacher.

The 5 books (£3.50) of *Modern method French course*, by E. B. Crampton and others (London, Nelson, 1955–58) cover the ground for 'O' level in books 1–4; book 5 is for those tackling this examination after 5 years. The 5 textbooks are accompanied by 10–4" tapes $3\frac{3}{4}$ ips, half-twin track (£27 + V.A.T.).

'O' level revision. Apart from the revision volume by Hermus and Lester, already mentioned, there is F. Gubb's *Points to watch in 'O' level French* (Heinemann, 1959. 38 pp. £0.25), which deals with pitfalls only and would well suit those with an adequate French vocabulary but a 'rusty' knowledge of grammar. J. N. Muir's *French examination practice* (Blackie, [n.d.]. ix, 118 pp.) affords a very sound résumé of basic points of grammar, with exercises and end-vocabularies. H. F. Collins' *A French manual for the examination form* (London, Macmillian, 1961. ix, 224 p. £0.40) has 23 sections of passages for translation, composition, poems, grammars and exercises, with appended outline of grammar, verb tables and end-vocabularies. *A revision course in French grammar*, by J. P. Bowden (London, Macmillan, 1961. x, 222 p. £0.70), a reprint of the 1943 edition, provides 36 study-units on grammar topics, with adequate exercises and end-vocabularies.

4. Self-tutors; courses for adults

Ideally self-tutor courses should include audio-aids as an integral part. *Everyday French*, by N. Scarlyn Wilson (English Universities Press, 1940. 232. pp. (Teach yourself books). £0.55) has 20 lessons, each with conversation, exercises (with key) and passages for translation, but no end-vocabulary. The supporting tapes (1 tape, 3″ reel, 3¾ ips, and 1 tape, 4″ reel, 3¾ ips, both twin half-track. £3.87½) concern commercial French. T. W. Knight's *Living French* (3rd ed. University of London Press, 1968. 255 pp. £0.75) is primarily for day and evening students in commercial and technical colleges. Each of the 25 lessons has exercises and vocabulary, and revision lessons occur after every 5 lessons. Recorded material consists of 2 tapes (5″ reels, 3¾ ips, twin half-track. £7 + VAT) *or* two C.60 cassettes (£7 + VAT). The course is adaptable for 'O' level revision or as a self-tutor.

Hugo's Simplified system: practical French in three months (3rd ed. London, Hugo's Language Books, Ltd., 1971. 192 p. £0.65) has 2 parts: 1. Grammar simplified. Exercises and vocabularies. Conversation. – 2. Idioms. Reading. Vocabularies. A key to exercises is included. Pronunciation is simulated. However, there is a Hugo's Cassette course in French comprising 4 cassettes (5 hours' play-back) and textbook (*c.* 200 pp.) at £13.20.

One of the best self-tutoring courses without integral A/V aids is Collins' *Cortina French in twenty lessons*, by D. W. Alden (Collins, 1962 (reprinted 1974). 382 pp. £1.95), for beginners. Two chapters concern pronunciation (simulated). Although well illustrated, part of the reference grammar is set in very small type. In the 'Teach yourself' series is the recently published *Essential French grammar*, by S. Resnick (London, Teach Yourself Books, 1975. £0.40), designed for beginners wishing to learn everyday French but having little time to do so. It can also serve as a refresher course. Another handy approach, especially for those who find the formal grammar method difficult, is

H. O. Emerson's *A practical French course* (Hachette, 1962. 3 v.), a three-year course designed for evening, technical and commercial schools. It could also function as a self-tutor. The author was former GCE Chief Examiner.

D. Grayson's *À propos* (London, Ginn, 1956–58. 2 v. each £1) is an attractively illustrated 2-year course 'for adults, specially intended for those enthusiastic but heterogenous groups in evening classes for whom the teacher needs interesting material', – and material which students can on occasion handle on their own. Equally designed for evening classes, *French once a week*, by P. H. Hargreaves and others (Oxford, Blackwell, 1961–70. 2 Books. £0.80), a reprint of the 1961–62 edition, has a total of 40 study-units and aims at a working vocabulary and grammar adequate for everyday French.

5. 'A' level courses

'A' level French course, by D. E. Clayton and J. Cadix (London, Harrap, 1969. 2 v. illus. £2.10) is aimed at students preparing for special GCE examination as well as 'A' level. Each volume is in 5 parts and vol. 2 carries sets of past examination-paper questions.

Post 'A' level French, by John E. G. White and Gill Seidel (University of London Press. 127 pp. £0.95) has 3 sections: A, passages in French, with a variety of topics; B, 'prose'; C, material in French, for analysis rather than translation. According to *Modern languages* (v. 56, no. 4, December 1975, p. 218), it should prove 'very popular in the polytechnics and other establishments of higher learning at which it is aimed, where French is not primarily seen in terms of literature'.

J. E. Mansion's *A grammar of present-day French* (Harrap, 1952. 400 pp. £0.85; with exercises, £1; Key. £0.75) is 'for sixth form pupils and university students studying the *mechanism* of present-day French'. It is praised for its arrangement, treatment and accuracy, in Harmer and Norton's *Manual of modern Spanish. Études supérieures de français*, by J. E. Travis and D. M. Auld (Harrap, 1959–60. 2 v.) has two parts. Part 1 is a course for sixth forms and contains French passage and translations: part 2 is for second-year sixth forms and those taking junior university examinations. V. 4 of J. R. Watson's *La langue des français* (Harrap, 1966. 280 pp.), independent of v. 1–3 ('O' level), is intended for consolidation or for the first year of 'A' level work. Apart from passages for translation from and into French, there are sections for sentences for translation into French, vocabulary difficulties, and a summary of grammar.

6. Reference grammars

A comprehensive French grammar, by L. S. R. Byrne and E. L. Churchill (Oxford, Blackwell, 1966 ed. xxiv, 515 pp. £3.50) is a detailed pre-'O' level reference grammar that makes good use of bold type and has an index. *Exercises and vocabulary* are available (1951. vii, 320 pp.). H. Ferrar's *A French reference grammar* (Oxford University Press, 1955. 352 pp.; 2nd ed., 1973. £0.95) is compiled with 'O' level candidates in mind. It includes exercises and has a detailed index. It can thus be used as a self-tutoring course. The brief *Basic French grammar*, by J. A. Corbett and A. Johnson (London, Murray, 1975. viii, 90 p. £0.60), is a skeleton outline, for rapid reference.

The French reference grammar *par excellence* naturally emanates from France itself. *Grammaire Larousse de français contemporain* (Paris, Larousse, 1964. 496 pp. £29.80) provides a very detailed treatment of the whole of French grammar (units of speech; grammar and syntax; prosody) and has an exemplary index. As such, it would be excellent at university level or for refurbishing a 'rusty' but otherwise good standard of French. Even fuller is M. Grévisse's *Le bon usage de la grammaire français, avec des remarques sur la langue française d'aujourd'hui* (8. éd. revue. Gembloux (Belgium), Duculot; Paris, Hatier, 1964. 1,194 pp. F 39–50; 1968 ed. 1229 p.), primarily for those who have French as their mother tongue. It is a very detailed work of reference (1,072 paragraphs), with profuse examples drawn from French literature as well as from current usage, bibliographies and a full subject index. The section on the preposition alone occupies about 75 pages. A 10th revised edition (viii, 1322 p.) appeared in 1975.

7. Specialist courses

French course for technologists and scientists, by H. S. Jackson and J. Standring (Harrap, 1960. 272 pp. £1) is for sixth-formers studying science, undergraduates taking an examination in scientific French, and others. Grammar, sentences and 167 passages for translation (extracts from French books and periodicals) are supplemented by suggestions for further reading, a French–English vocabulary of some 2,000 words, and an index to grammar. *French for science students*, by A. Kellett (London, Macdonald & Evans, 1976. viii, 184 p. £1.75) has text in English and French and includes answers to exercises.

Business French, by P. H. Hargreaves and others (Alpha Books Agency, 1974. 2 v. £12) is intended for executives in contact with the French-speaking world and includes practice with actual business and social situations, plus a basic business vocabulary, terms and expressions. V. 1 textbook (160 pp. £4) (which carries exercises) is available on 8 C.60 cassettes, single-track, or on 4 reels or 4 C.60 cassettes, twin-track (Tutor Tape Co., Ltd. £20). V. 2 (pattern drills and language-laboratory drill exercises) is available on 25 reels or 25 compact cassettes, single-track (£75), or on 13 reels or 13 C.60 cassettes twin-track (£45; the last reel/cassette on single-track) from the same firm.

An audio-lingual French course for industry and commerce, by Barbara Bishop, is recommended by Tutor Tape Co. for Ordinary and Higher National Diploma courses, secretarial linguist classes, and students for 'A' level who are studying commerce as well as French, among others. The course (textbook: £2.50) is available on 18 reels, L.P. tape or on 18 C.90 cassettes, single-track. (£36).

French correspondence is the concern of *Bilingual guide to business and professional correspondence, French–English*, by J. Harvard and F. Rose. French text by Félix Rose. (Oxford, Pergamon Press, 1965 ix, 140 pp. £3.40), the 9 sections dealing with the layout and contents of a French business letter, business organisation and transactions, money and legal matters, packing, transport and insurance, business relations, inquiry and information, and applications and references. It differentiates between English and American vocabulary and spelling.

G. Duttweiler's monolingual *Dictionnaire pratique de la correspondance commerciale et privée* (Geneva, Éditions Générales S.A., 1967 ed. 406 p. £6.80) has some 2,500 entries under keywords. Also monolingual is *Le français commercial* (Paris, Larousse, 1970. 2 v. £4.10). Vol. 1: *Manuel* includes facsimiles of business documents and letters; vol. 2 *Textes d'étude* has keys to the exercises in the two volumes.

8. Pronunciation. Words and phrases. Usage

Prononciation du français standard: aide-mémoire d'orthoépie à l'usage des étudiants étrangers, by P. R. Léon (revised ed. Paris, Didier, 1969. 186 pp. F 27.40), deals with rules, accepted variants and current trends, plus exercises and keys. Three tapes are available. Two dictionaries, each giving IPA phonetic transcription of c. 50,000 French words, are: *Dictionnaire de la prononciation française dans son usage réel*, by André Martinet and Henriette Walter (Paris, France-Expansion. 1973. 932 pp.), and *Dictionnaire de la prononciation française*, by Léon Warnant (3. ed. Gembloux, Hatier-Duculot, 1968. 654 pp. F 58). While conceding that in France the bourgeois pronunciation of Paris is usually accepted as a standard, Martinet and Walter admit that there is considerable divergence within this framework. Warnant includes a supplementary list of 20,000 proper names and a disc. P. A. D. MacCarthy's *The pronunciation of French* (Oxford University Press, 1975. x, 150 pp. illus. £2.50) has a cassette recording available, to illustrate pronunciation.

Word lists. For younger learners up to the age of 12, Colin Henstock's *A first French dictionary, based on Le français fondamental* (Harrap, 1972. 133 pp. £1.35) has two-way lists, with 2,500 words in each section. The two volumes of *Vocabulaire fondamental illustré*, by A. Kropman and others (Harrap, 1972–74. 2 v. (122, 156 pp. £2.15) selectively cover Le français fondamental, both premier and deuxième degré, arranged in sections by topics. V. 2 provides definitions and examples of increasing complexity. *A classified French vocabulary*, by H.

Howard Baker (Harrap, 1968 (reprint of 1958 ed.). 96 pp. £0.30) is also grouped (34 sections), being designed for use at 'O' and 'A' levels. English translations of French entries are given. G. Gougenheim's *Dictionnaire fondamental de la langue française* (Nouvelle éd. revue et augmentée. Harrap, 1971. 283 pp. £1.15) is, by contrast, a monolingual dictionary, with IPA phonetic transcription of the 3,000 vocabulary of Le francais fondamental premier degré and deuxième degré, with definitions and idioms.

Phrase books for tourists. The Berlitz' *French for travellers* (Rev. ed. 1974. 193 p. £0.60, first published 1970, gives 1,200 phrases and 2,000 useful words; guide to shopping, eating out, tipping, sightseeing and relaxing. The edge-coloured topic sections carry their own vocabularies; there are no end-vocabularies. Simulated pronunciation throughout, but there is a separate 1–33⅓ rpm disc on 1 cassette, at £1.95.

Hugo's *French phrase book* (Revised ed. Hugo's Language Institute, 1971. 192 pp. £0.20), which also adopts simulated pronunciation, group phrases and sentences under ten subject headings.

Usage. For a systematic account of good contemporary usage there is Maurice Grévisse's *Le français correct: guide pratique* (Gembloux, Duculot, 1972. 400 pp. F 24), with examples drawn from literary sources. Two dictionaries of usage deserve mention: *A dictionary of modern French usage*, by H. Bonnard and others (2nd revised ed. Edinburgh, Oliver & Boyd, 1973. viii, 412 pp. £2), first published 1970, is intended for non-native students and teachers of French. Many examples of usage are given (*e.g.*, 4½ pages are devoted to 'Celui, celle'). P. Dupré's *Encyclopédie du bon français dans l'usage contemporain: difficultés, subtilités, complexités, singularités* (Paris, Trévise, 1972, 1972. 3 v. (lxiv, 2,716 pp.) each F 140) is a comprehensive, scholarly work, with 10,000 entries and profuse examples. It discusses questions of French usage that pose problems even to educated speakers of French. It also deals with the use of borrowed words and *franglais*. J.–P. Colin's *Nouveau dictionnaire des difficultés du français* (Paris, Hachette-Tchou, 1970. xiv, 858 pp. F 49), too, has entries A–Z, for 10,000 words and expressions, – those likely to be met with and used in 20th-century fiction, journalism and conversation, with comment on usage according to social conventions and on punctuation, spelling and grammar.

J. Hennebert's *Au lieu de dites plutôt. Le bon usage en exemples pratiques* (Paris, Mercure de France, 1968. 192 pp. illus. F19) has been described as a particularly handy guide for purists, the left-hand page providing the howlers and the right-hand page the correct nuances as used by the true Frenchman. M. and E. Levieux, *Beyond the dictionary in French: a handbook of colloqiual French* (Cassell, 1967. 183 p. £0.80) aims to explain particular French phraseology. Apart from a main French–English section, it has 14 special topical vocabularies, sections on *faux amis*, formal and informal French usage and an English–French cross-reference index.

Les faux amis: des vocabulaires anglais et américain, by M. Koessler (Paris, Vuibert, 1976. 584 p. F120), first published in 1926 and arranged alphabetically under English words, is a handbook for translation work, on the principles of *traduire, c'est trahir.*

AUDIO-VISUAL MATERIAL

(What follows owes a good deal to the CILT (Centre for Information on Language Teaching and Research's *Teaching materials for French. 6. 1A: Recorded and visual courses* (3rd revised ed. November 1973 32, 8 pp. £0.40)). A selection of about half of the 67 items there listed are described below, with a few additions. Details of some A/V courses will already have been given under course books in the foregoing sections.

1. For beginners

Bonjour line (Harrap: Harrap-Didier Audio-Visual Division), used in primary, prep. and middle schools, is in 3 parts. Printed material comprises work and picture books, plus teacher's books. Part 1 (lessons 1–26) comprises 32 filmstrips (31 in colour), £38 + VAT; 9 reels, $3\frac{3}{4}$ ips, single-track (£29 + VAT) and 14 reels, $7\frac{1}{2}$ ips, single track (£20 + VAT). Part 2 (lessons 1–12): 14 filmstrips (12 in colour) (£18 + VAT); 9 reels, $3\frac{3}{4}$ ips, single-track: £20 + VAT; 14 reels, $7\frac{1}{2}$ ips, single-track: £20 + VAT); and part 3 (lessons 13–26): 15 filmstrips (14 in colour) (£20 + VAT), 9 reels, $3\frac{3}{4}$ ips, single-track: £20 + VAT). The vocabulary of *Bonjour line* is mainly based on the some 1,500 words of Le français fondamental, premier degré.

Le français élémentaire: méthode progressive de français usuel, by G. Mauger and G. Gougenheim, with A. Ioannou (Hachette, 1964–67. Debutants: Books 1–2; Teacher's books 1–2. £2.40; six 10″ discs, 33 rpm, £7.60 + VAT; 20 7″ discs; £5.32) is based on line illustrations and aims primarily to teach the spoken word, although writing and reading are introduced as an aid.

2. For secondary school beginners

Pamela Symonds' *Let's speak French* (Oxford University Press, 1962–63. 2 textbooks. £1.50) uses the oral method throughout. A/V aids, issued by Tudor Tape Co., Ltd., consist of 63 wall pictures (£11.25 + VAT) and 19 tapes (5″ reels, $3\frac{3}{4}$ ips, twin half-track: £43.25) or 19 C.60 cassettes (£43.25). The pace of Book 1 (for children 9–12) is slower than most beginners' courses. Book 2 is for those aged 13–16 or for adult beginners.

Bonjour Monsieur Leroux, by Eugene-Pierre Davoust; edited by Gladys C. Loney and Jessie M. McGeorge (Harrap, 1967. Textbook. 198 pp. £1.40) consists of 20 lessons for secondary and adult beginners. The audio material is on 9 7″ discs, 45 rpm: (£7.50). The follow-up course, *Au revoir Monsieur Leroux* (Harrap, 1967. Textbook. 158 pp. £0.70) has 10 lessons, with audio material on 5 7″ discs, 45 rpm (£4.25 + VAT).

Toute le bande (Mary Glasgow (Recordings), Ltd., 1970) consists of 13 teacher's booklets and 13 16 mm. sound colour films, supported by 13 35 mm. double-frame colour strips (£15). The series uses 1,160 different words, 60% being drawn from Le français fondamental, premier degré.

(CSE course with A/V aids are mentioned on pp. 14–15).

3. For 'O' level

The *Longman audio-visual French* course, by S. Moore and others (Longman, 1966–73) is devised for pupils of mixed ability, with the advantage that after Stage 2 there are alternative versions, one for slower and one for faster students. At Stage 1 the approach is basically oral; at Stage 2 writing plays a greater part[1].

Voix et images de France (Harrap: Harrap-Didier Audio-Visual Division, 1967–), also complex in structure, is a full-scale A/V course for adult or secondary school beginners. Part 1 (32 lessons; three-years' work) covers most of the vocabulary of Le français fondamental: premier degré. Details of teacher's material (including filmstrips and tapes), pupil's material (including tapes and discs) and testing materials appear in the Harrap-Didier *Audio-Visual 1975* catalogue, p. 10–11. It is followed by (*op. cit.*, pp. 16–18) *Leçons de transition*, a course of 9 units (about 150 hours of classwork), intended progressively to reduce the student's reliance on the visual for linguistic explanation. It can be used for 'those needing integrated written and oral work for 'O' level courses and stimulating revision for sixth forms; and also for equivalent levels in adult colleges'. Part 2 of the course is in a provisional state (*op. cit.*, pp. 15–16).

Activités, by Vivian Rowe and Stewart Ingram, with Leslie K. Upton (Glasgow, 1966–69. A/V version distributed by Rank Audio-Visual), a two-year course in 4 parts, covers the oral/aural aspects of 'O' level and CSE. Printed material consists of 20 pupil's booklets and 5 teacher's pamphlets (£3.60); audio material: 40 1" discs, $33\frac{1}{3}$ rpm, or 20 tapes (5" reels, $3\frac{3}{4}$ ips, single top track; £81.80).

Several of the school courses already mentioned have A/V aids: those by D. Grayson (*À la page:* filmstrips, discs and tapes, p. 15), C. G. Hadley and B. Howson (tapes, p. 16), E. B. Crampton and others (tapes), P. Symonds (wall pictures and tapes or cassettes, P. 25) and J. R. Watson (filmstrips and tapes, p. 16).

---

[1] Details of prices of the printed and A/V material at the various stages are given in CILT *Teaching materials for French. Recorded and visual courses* (3rd revised ed. November 1973), at entry 46.

4. For adult beginners. Self-tutors

Beginner's French, by J. Harvard (University of London Press, 1960) aims to instil conversational skill and confidence in a comparatively short time. Each of the 14 lessons in the textbook (£0.50) contains a short dialogue, plus fluency lessons and substitution tables. Tudor Tape Co. provide 2 tapes (5″ reels, 3¾ ips. twin half-track) or 2 C.60 cassettes, at £7. *Conversational French* is a follow-on. The textbook (£0.60) has 18 lessons. Tutor Tape Co.'s 2 tapes (5″ reels, 3¾ ips, twin half-track) or 2 C.60 cassettes cost £7. *French at home/Français chez vous*, by H. Appia and J. Guénot (Harrap, 1962. Textbook: xi, 275 pp. £1.65), plus 5 12″ discs (33⅓ rpm. £12.70 − VAT) also has a follow-on, − *Gaspard mon ami* (Harrap, 1966. Textbook: 152 pp. £0.90; discs: 2 12″, 33⅓ rpm. £4.50 + VAT). The intensive PILL 24-hour language course, *The French language*, provides instruction books vocabularies, cards, etc., plus 4 12″ discs (33⅓ rpm) or 3 tapes (5″ reels, twin half-track on cassette) at £38.50.

Two fairly cheap courses are the Reader's Digest's *At home with French*, by R. E. Maddison and A. M. Hall (1968), providing two books (xix, 295, 272 pp., with answers to questions, plus a conversational guide (112 pp.) and 20 7″ discs, 33 rpm, for £13; and the Berlitz self-teaching course in 5 parts (241 pp.), with 5 12″ discs, 33⅓ rpm, at £10.

The more elaborate Linguaphone Institute's *Cours de français* (1971) runs to 3 printed items and 16 7″ discs, and 2 tapes, or 2 cassettes, at £49.50.

Le français par la méthode audio-visual (London, Harrap-Didier Audio-Visual Division, 1961−71), in 2 parts (each of 25 units), with filmstrips, tapes, discs, cassettes and student's books plus a teaching guide, provides enough material for a 4-year non-intensive course for adults, or middle-ability secondary-school students, at £69.80 + £78.30.

5. For tourists

Survival French: a programmed teaching method to simplify language teaching, by A. V. Toutoungi (Euro-Lang Tapes, 1972) is, as the title suggests, a basic course on a French holiday. The instruction booklet (32 pp.) has a 380-word French–English end-vocabulary, amplified by Harrap's new pocket French and English dictionary (525 pp.). Audio-material: 6 tapes (5″ reels, 3¾ ips, single top-track) or 6 cassettes; complete kit: £29.50 + VAT. *Sur la route*, by H. Appia and J. Guénot, edited by J. R. Watson (Harrap, 1968) concerns a hitch-hiking journey in S. W. France and comprises a 160 pp. textbook with key to exercises (£1.05) and 2 tapes (5″ reels, 3¾ ips, twin half-track (£5.50 + VAT). *Destination Paris*, by L. Lanchy (Hachette, 1971) goes further and aims to cultivate listening-comprehension skills as well as conversation. The complete course (textbook viii, 152 pp. £1.15) plus 6 twin-track or 12 top-track cassettes, costs £31.35 + VAT.

6. For advanced level

Actualités français: a complete course for advanced students, by D. O. Nott and J. E. Trickey (English Universities Press, 1971) provides material to GCE 'A' and 'S' level in 2 parts, comprising 2 textbooks (£2.60), 2 tape booklets (£1) and 6 tapes (5″ reels, 3 ips, twin half-track (£35). *Jean Legallois*, by C. A. Milner (Oxford University Press, 1971) aims at developing post-'O' level oral and written skills. The single textbook (xi, 330 pp. £1.50) is accompanied by 16 tapes (5″ reels, 3¾ ips, twin half-track (£8 + VAT). *Voix françaises*, by A. R. Servel and C. I. Königsberg, edited by P. H. Hargreaves, is, on the other hand particularly for post-'O' level students, with emphasis on oral skills. Leonard Hill publish the two textbooks (ix, 368 pp., vii, 135 pp. £1.30 + £0.90), and Tutor Tape Co., the tapes or cassettes (£14).

The elaborate *La France en direct*, by Janine Capelle and others (Paris, Hachette, 1969–72), on 4 levels, takes the beginner to 'A' level in 4–6 years. Levels 1 and 2 have teacher's books (£11.50), pupil's books (£3.25), 44 tapes (£258.90 + VAT), apart from filmstrips and practice discs. Level 3: teacher's book (£4), pupil's book (£2.70), 10 tapes (£73.15 + VAT); Level 4: teacher's book (£1.60); pupil's book (£2.40); 4 tapes (£28.56 + VAT).

7. For business men

Export marketing in French, by J. M. C. Lawler (Intertext books, with Inter'lang, 1972) assumes an 'O'-level or equivalent London Chamber of Commerce conversational ability in French. The textbook (xv, 159 pp. £2.20) is accompanied by 5 tapes or 5 C.60 cassettes from Inter'lang (£19.70) *Business French*, by P. H. Hargreaves and others, is a course for executives in contact with the French-speaking world. The two textbooks (£10) are accompanied by audio material (Tutor Tape Co.) on tapes or C.60 cassettes (£14, twin-track; £20, single-track, for v. 1; £45, single-track, £45; single-track: £75, for v. 2).

Introduction au français commercial, by B. Cresson (Paris, Didier, 1972) claims to be a comprehensive introduction to spoken and written commercial French, giving, for example, specimen *lettres commerciales* on chosen topics and also *exercises de téléphone*. The textbook (144 pp. £1.75) is supported by tapes (£27.50 + VAT) or cassettes (£15 + VAT). This course follows *Introduction au français économique*, also by B. Cresson (Paris, Didier, 1971), with its textbook (£1.60) and 12 tapes (£32.50).

An intensive course of 31 lessons at two levels is available in *French for the businessman*, by F. Lapouille and Gina Butler (Inter'lang, 1967–69). Printed matter (2 textbooks and 1 teacher's manual: £6.50) is accompanied by 60 tapes (£202.80 + VAT).

8. For engineers

Le français pour l'ingénieur, by J. Coveney and J. Grosjean (Paris, Didier, 1971), is designed for students of engineering who have learnt French for a year at university and wish to converse with French-speaking engineers on elementary topics in the field. The course comprises an illustrated *Student's book* (£1.35), a *Teacher's book* (£8.50) and 6 tapes (3¾ ips, twin-track. £38 + VAT).

GENERAL DICTIONARIES

1. Bilingual

The monumental *Harrap's New standard French and English dictionary* is still only half completed. Part one: French–English (revised and edited by R. P. L. Ledésert and Margaret Ledésert. Harrap, 1972. 2 v. (608, 554 pp.), each £8.50) has some 100,000 headwords. It includes many idioms, colloquial and slang words, scientific and technical terms and U.S. variants of British equivalents. A new feature is the substantial list of French Canadianisms, as well as words and expressions used in French-speaking Switzerland and Belgium. The International Phonetic Alphabet is used for pronunciation. The original completed dictionary, by J. E. Mansion, appeared in 1934, with supplements in 1950, 1955 and 1961. It is a drawback that the English–French volumes are not due for completion before 1978, and the contents will, naturally, be more detailed and current than the corresponding French–English volumes (which have occasionally already been criticised for lack of up-to-dateness).

Meanwhile we have the completely revised edition of *Harrap's New shorter French and English dictionary* by the same editors; revised by M. Ferlin and P. Forbes (Harrap, 1967, reprinted with corrections and additions, 1972, xvi, 645, 860 pp. £4.50). Part 1: French–English has 41,000 headwords; part 2: English–French, 56,000 headwords. First published in 1940, it is an admirable first choice for home and school use. French Canadianisms and U.S. idioms are also featured. The two-volume edition costs £3.50 per volume.

Comparable in size to the *Harrap's New standard dictionary*, though not in up-to-dateness, is *Dictionnaire anglais–français et français–anglais*, by Ch. Petit (2. éd. Paris, Hachette, 1963. 2 v. (xviii, 1418 pp.; xvi, 1380 pp.). *Dictionnarie moderne français–anglais, anglais–français*, by M. M. Dubois (Paris, Larousse, 1960. xvi, 768 pp.; xvi, 752 pp. F 55.60) has *c.* 35,000 headwords in each part, with phonetic pronunciation and U.S.

as well as British usage. Included are 27 word-lists and illustrations with keyed parts.

Cassell's New French–English, English–French dictionary,
completely revised by Denis Gerard, with Gaston Dulong and
others (8th ed. Cassell, 1968. xvi, 762 pp, 655 pp. £2.80) is a
cheap, popular dictionary that is reprinted annually with some
additions. It includes French–Canadian usage and gives
phonetic pronunciation, with appendices of abbreviations, verbs,
etc. Of the small French and English dictionaries published in
Britain, mention must be made of *Langenscheidt's Standard
dictionary of the French and English languages* (Nouv. éd. par
J. Bell. Paris, Garnier, 1968. x, 440 pp., viii, 480 pp. F10), with
its illustrated supplement showing keyed parts of a motorcar,
aeroplane, TV set, etc., for students and teachers of French
between 'O' level and first-year university. The neatly produced
The concise Oxford French dictionary, by A. and M. Chevalley
(Oxford, Clarendon Press, 1958. xx, 895, 12 pp. £2.50), which
has c. 40,000 headwords and aims at being a companion to *The
concise Oxford dictionary of current English*. IPA phonetic
transcription of French headwords is given, plus 12 pages of
line-drawings, showing keyed parts of a motorcar, etc. The companion volume to Chevalley, and also available bound with it at
£2.50, is G. W. F. R. Goodridge's *A practical French–English
dictionary for English–French-speaking countries* (Oxford,
Clarendon Press, 1940. vi, 295 pp. £1). *Langenscheidt's Shorter
French dictionary* (Hodder & Stoughton, 1973. 640 pp. £0.85),
with 38,000 entries, has very good value and is praised in *The
incorporated linguist* (v. 12, no. 3, July 1973, p. 54).

Of the Canadian French dictionaries, the two-way
*Everyman's French–English, English–French dictionary, with
special reference to Canada*, by Jean-Paul Vinay and others
(Dent, 1962. xxvi, 862 pp. £3.50), prepared at the Lexicographic
Research Centre, University of Montreal, aims to provide a dictionary of 'the current, living language' and has 20–25,000
headwords in each part. H. Carbonneau's *Vocabulaire général:
glossaire anglais–français* (Ottawa, Secrétariat d' État, Bureau
de Traductions. Centre de Terminologie, 1972. 3 v. (*c.* 1250
pp.) has some 100,000 headwords and includes a wealth of
idioms.

2. Monolingual

The French take a particular pride in the clarity and precision of their language, and for the advanced student there is no lack of multi-volume dictionaries.

Paul Robert's *Dictionnaire alphabétique et analogique de la langue française. Les mots et les associations d'idées* (Paris, Société du Nouveau Littré, 1970. 6 v.) and its *Supplément* (Redaction dirigée par A. Rey et J. Rey-Debove. 1970. xxi, 514 pp. £60, the set) heads the list. Robert's premise – like Chevalley's – is that a word is not defined completely by its etymology, its grammatical classification and its meaning in its various uses, but that it only takes on its full value in its relationship to other words. The dictionary gives comprehensive coverage of the French language, from Villon to Camus, showing etymology, pronunciation, analogies, antonyms, synonyms, grammatical difficulties, word history (from the date of first usage) and copious quotations, making extensive use of examples drawn from the works of recent and contemporary writers. 'Le petit Robert', with the same title (10. éd. Paris, Société du Nouveau Littré, 1972. 2,000 pp. £6) has 54,000 headwords, with quotations reduced by some 50% and slighter treatment is given to etymology. 'Petit Robert II' (1970. 1,967 pp. F102) adds coloured illustrations and maps. For desk use, – the *Micro-Robert* (Harrap, 1972. 1,332 pp. £2), with 34,000 headwords, and *Micro-Robert en poche* (2 v. £1.50), with 30,000 headwords, and particularly designed for the non-French student.

Three volumes of *Trésor de la langue française. Dictionnaire de la langue du XIXe et du XXe siècle* (1789–1960), edited by P. Limbs (Paris, Centre National de la Recherche Scientifique, 1972–75. F200; F200; F250) have so far appeared, reaching only the word 'BADIN'. The remaining 12 or so volumes will appear at the rate of 3 per year. Each headword is given extended definitions, with quotations, pronunciation, orthography, etymology and historical treatment on an ample page. It is highly praised in *T.L.S.* (no. 3821) 30th May, 1975, p. 589), which does, however, note the reduction in the number of quoted examples in v. 3. Four volumes have been published of the *Grand Larousse de la langue française en sept volumes* (Paris, Larousse, 1971. each v. F 155). V. 4, covering IND–NY, covers pages 2,623–3,697, and has some 15,000, usually lengthy, entries. Synonyms and antonyms are given, with many quotations (but lacking exact references), and pronunciation. Grammatical and linguistic articles (*e.g.*, on the alphabet) are a feature. V. 1 has a lengthy section (p. xci–cxix) which is a bibliography of material used for the historical aspects of the language.

Dictionnaire Bordas. Dictionnaire du français vivant, edited by M. Davau and others (Paris, Bordas; London, Harrap, 1972. xviii, 1,338 pp. £3.95) is aimed specifically at the student. It has 34,000 headwords, gives phonetic pronunciation, examples of use, synonyms and antonyms, and a wealth of appendices (including one on Belgium, Canadian and Swiss words and expressions. The *Larousse Dictionnaire du français contemporain* ([1971]. xxii, 1,224 pp. F59), edited by J. Dubois and others, is comparable.

The *Petit Larousse*, with annual editions (1975. 1,799 pp. F62.80) and first published in 1856, is by far the best known of the one-volume French encyclopaedic dictionaries. It has two main sequences: the dictionary itself, with about 70,000 headwords and an encyclopedia of proper, geographical, etc. names. Illustrations number about 5,000 and appear in margins; maps, – about 250, plus an atlas. There is a *Petit Larousse en couleurs* (1972. xvi, 1,664, 10 pp. F 115.60), and also a version in which dictionary and encyclopaedia appear in one sequence, – *Pluridictionnaire Larousse* (xxiii, 1,470 pp. F59). The *Dictionnaire usuel Quillet–Flammarion par le texte et par l'image,* redigé par Pierre Goan (Paris, Flammarion, 1960. 1,458 pp. F45) also combines dictionary and encyclopaedia in one sequence, with clear definitions, but illustrations are fewer than and inferior to those in the *Petit Larousse*. Again, there is a version in colour, – *Dictionnaire usuel en couleurs* (1964. 1,708 pp.).

The recent *Lexis: dictionnaire de la langue française* published by Larousse (1975. lxxix, 1,905 pp. £15.90) is a dictionary proper. It has entries for more than 70,000 terms and is praised in the *T.L.S.* (no. 3,863, 26th March 1976, p. 336) as an all-purpose working tool that is 'probably the best one-volume French dictionary in existence'. A grammar is appended, and the layout makes for easy use.

To keep track of new words and other linguistic developments, the Conseil International de la Langue Française is publishing *La banque des mots*, a semi-annual review of French terminology (Paris, Presses Universitaires de France, [1971?–]. According to *Bibliography, documentation, terminology* (v. 14, no. 1, January 1974, p. 35), Issue 5 (1973) has contributions on neologisms, terminology, authority, and technical glossaries.

TECHNICAL & COMMERCIAL DICTIONARIES

Technical dictionaries

Up-to-dateness is a pre-requisite, and the searcher may well find his answer in *Harrap's New standard French and English dictionary. Part 1: French–English* (1972. 2 v.), already discussed above, or in such French encyclopaedias as the *Grand Larousse encyclopédique en dix volumes* (1960–64. F1,908) and its two supplements, to date (F196.20 + F208).

Strictly devoted to technology is *Dictionnaire des techniques* (Bordas, 1971. 1,034 pp. F110), headwords being explained in detail, with photographs and diagrams. G. Malgorn's *Lexique technique anglais–français: machines-outils, mines, moteurs – combustion interne, aviation, électricité, TSF, constructions navales, metallurgie, travaux publics, commerce* (5. éd., revue et corrigée. Paris, Gauthier-Villars, 1965 (and reprints). xxxiv, 493 pp. £9.80) has about 12,000 headwords (with compound words subsumed) and abbreviations. The companion volume is: *Lexique technique français–anglais* (4. ed. 1956 (and reprints). xxviii, 475 pp. £9.80). F. Cusset's *Vocabulaire technique, anglais–français, français–anglais: électricité, mécanique, industries extractives et annexes, métallurgie, sciences* (8. éd. Paris, Berger-Levrault, 1968. 434 pp. £7.60) has some 7,000 headwords in each part.

More extensive, but more dated are L. de Vries'

French–English science dictionary, for students in agricultural, biological and physical sciences (3rd ed. New York, McGraw-Hill, 1962. ix, 655 pp. $10.50), with about 48,000 headwords[1] and J. O. Kettridge's *French–English and English–French dictionary of technical terms and phrases* (Rev. ed. Routledge & Kegan Paul, 1969–70. 2 v. (xvi, 1,156 pp.). £9), with translations of 100,000 terms and phrases in all. J. G. G. Belle-Isle's *Dictionnaire technique général: anglais–français* (Quebec, Bélisle, 1965. 516, 4 pp. Can. $12) is one-way only, but it does include U.S. and Canadian variants.

Commercial dictionaires (see also 7. Specialist courses, p. 21).

Well spoken of by translators, the *Delmas dictionnaire des affaires, anglais–français, français–anglais/Business dictionary, English–French, French–English*, by G. Anderla and G. Schmidt-Anderla (Harrap, 1972. x, [1], 587 pp. £12) is relatively up-to-date and has about 35,000 entries in each part. 'Business' is broadly interpreted, to include aspects of law, statistics and management systems, as well as words in common use. U.K. and U.S. terms are differentiated. Headwords and sub-entries (given separate entry lines) are capitalised, making for greater clarity. There is a lengthy two-way appendix of abbreviations. J. V. Servotte's *Dictionnaire commercial et financier, français–anglais, anglais–français* (Brussels, Marabout Service, 1950. 446, [1] pp. £2.30) is basically a French–English dictionary (30,000 entries and sub-entries), with an English index of about 7,000 words. J. O. Kettridge's *French–English and English–French dictionary of commercial and financial terms, phrases and practice* (Revised ed. Routledge & Kegan Paul, 1969. xii, 655 pp. £3.50) has *c.* 12,000 headwords in each part and includes many commercial phrases. The two addenda should not be overlooked. Also two-way are Henri van Hoof's *Economic terminology, English–French; systematic and alphabetical vocabulary, with exercises* (Paris, Dunod, 1967. 770 pp. £7), and the *French–English and English–French*

---

[1] A 4th ed., entitled *French–English science and technology dictionary*, was published in May 1976, at $14.95.

business dictionary, by M. Péron and W. Withnell (Paris, Larousse, 1968. 2 v. xii, 230 pp.; xvi, 246 pp. £6.25).

Lexique de l'anglais des affaires, by Ivan de Renty (Paris, Librairie Générale Française, 1973. 320 pp. (Le livre de poche). F5.80) covers 8,000 terms and expressions in 3 sections (*e.g.*, correspondence, banks, international trade, legal matters, commercial and financial abbreviations), with English and French columns adjacent. *Dictionnaire économique et financier*, by V. Bernard and others (Paris, Éditions du Seuil, [1975]. 1,168 pp.) is up-to-date but monolingual.

Bibliography

The *Teaching materials for French* lists published by CILT (Centre for Information on Language Teaching and Research) are worth enumerating for their comparative up-to-dateness and comprehensiveness (although section 6.7: 'Vocabularies' does not cover the larger dictionaries):

6.1A:	Recorded and visual courses 3rd rev. ed. 1973. £0.40.
1B:	Recorded and audio-visual supplementary material. 2nd rev. ed. 1972. £0.20.
2/5:	Textbooks and grammars. 1976. £0.60.
4A:	Books for conversation, comprehension, composition, translation. 1972. £0.20.
4B:	Pictorial readers, classroom magazines, books with games and puzzles, playlets, songs. 1973. £0.25.
6A:	Readers in graded series. 1973. £0.30.
6B:	General readers. 1974. £0.25.
6C:	Background readers. 1974. £0.25.
7:	Vocabularies. 1975. £0.30.
11:	Primary school French. 2nd rev. ed. 1972. £0.25.

Free CILT material is available in its *Information guides* (5: Sources of visual and audio aids: French; 10c: Information for teachers of French-organisations and centres) and *Selected reading lists* (7: French-description of the languages and usage; 19: French cultural guides).

3

ITALIAN

by F. S. STYCH, M.A., Ph.D., F.L.A.

INTRODUCTION

Since the last edition of the *Guide* appeared (1967) there has been no particularly important grammar published in English and we still await Professor Griffith's reference grammar. In particular there is little sign of the grammars designed for learners at different levels and for different puposes for which teachers of Italian have been pressing for some years. There are however some useful grammars in Italian and some useful new works in English among teaching aids, notably H. W. Smith's *Using Italian* and *Advanced Italian* by R. N. L. Absalom and S. Potestà. New dictionaries are relatively more numerous and include the new Harrap-Sansoni, *The Concise Cambridge* and those of Ragazzini (with the abridgement of it by Biagi), Tedeschi and Rossi Fantonetti, and Zanco and Caliumi.

The greatest development however has been in the field of recorded and audio-visual materials, either published as the basis of a course, albeit with accompanying textbooks or pamphlets, or as adjuncts to grammars published in book form. They include several BBC courses, M. Tyler's *Introductory Italian course*, the *A–LM Italian*, the *World of Learning Italian Language* and tapes for Dr. Speight's *Teach yourself Italian* and Valgimigli's *Living Italian*. The *Méthode audio-visuelle d'italien* of Cernecca and Jernej has film strips as well as tapes.

In the following survey books based on BBC courses and published without records or tapes have been excluded.

Some Italian prices have been estimated in the absence of firm information.

TEXTBOOK COURSES & GRAMMARS

General courses for schools up to 'O' and 'A' level

The most complete and scholarly work of this kind remains Prof. J. F. Jones's *Modern Italian grammar* (London, University of London Press, 1976. 390 pp. plates, map. £1.15, sewed) which is suitable for a beginners' course and also as a standard grammar for more advanced students. It aims to deal with modern, conversational, rather than literary or commercial Italian. The main structure of the grammar is set out in the first 25 lessons and finer points, such as the use of the subjunctive, are left until later. Students should acquire an active vocabulary of 2,000 words and a passive one of 3,200. Stress is marked where it is unusual but the quality of e, o, s and z is not. Exercises consist of passages for reading and for translation into Italian. Irregular verbs and a list of transitive verbs taking *essere* are given in an appendix. There is a vocabulary and a bibliography. The pages are a little full but presentation is economical and attractive.

The only remotely comparable work at a similar price is *Italian made simple*, by E. Jackson and J. Lopreato (London, W. H. Allen, 1968. 358 pp. paperback, £1) a fairly conventional grammar in a large format and with a slight American flavour, although not enough to rule out its use in this country. C. A. McCormick's *Basic Italian grammar* (London, Harrap, 1962. 292 pp. £1.10) cuts some corners but is otherwise good. It has grammar, reading passages, exercises and verb tables. It marks stress and also quality of e, o, s and z. The print is rather small. More expensive is G. Milesi's *Italiano vivo* (London, Harrap, 1966. 484 pp. £1.70; Key 1967. 108 pp. £1.45) which has grammar and exercises in long lessons, with much practice material. It has verb tables and is good on idioms but is to some extent simplified. A group of American works are considerably more expensive or else partial in coverage. V. Cioffari's *Italian review grammar and composition with everyday idiom drill and conversation practice* (Boston, Heath; London, Harrap. 1950. 308 pp. illus., map. £2.95) is intended as a U.S. high-school course and has 40 lessons with reading passages and exercises for translation both ways, compared with Jones's for translation into Italian only. The quality of e, o, s and z is not marked but there are verb tables. J. L. Russo has four textbooks in print, all designed for first- or second-year class use. The *Practical Italian grammar* (London, Harrap, 1941. xiv, 342 pp. illus., map. £1) is a basic two-year course of 50 lessns, selective in nature and designed for maximum simplicity and clarity. There are substitution and completion exercises and passages for translation both ways and oral drills. Drawings with special vocabularies are included for direct-method teaching. There are verb tables and a general vocabulary both ways. Quality of e and o is shown. The American origin of the work is sometimes apparent in the vocabulary. Separate first and second year courses are provided by the *Primo corso italiano* (Boston, Heath, 1960 xxii, 389 pp. illus. £2.60) with 28 lessons and vocabulary both ways, quality of e, o, s and z being marked, and *Secondo corso italiano* (Boston, Heath, 1961. xxii, 417 pp. illus., map £3.10) of similar type. *Present day Italian* (Boston, Heath; London, Harrap, 1947. xvi, 501 pp. illus. £3.20) is again on a similar plan, consisting in this case of 42 lessons and 7 review lessons, equally divided to cover two sessions. A third section contains dialogues and letters. The illustrations are good and the type large and clear. Stress and the quality of e, o, s and z is marked. An appendix gives verb conjugations and a list of personal pronouns, and there is a vocabulary both ways.

Courses for adults and self-study courses

The most formal work under this heading is *Italian for you: a practical grammar*, by D. Lennie and M. Grego (3rd ed. London, Longmans, 1966. xix, 321 pp. limp, £1.10) intended for university and evening class students. Contents include exercises and practice material including passages for translation both ways. There are verb lists including use of prepositions, and specimen letters. Stress and the quality of e and o are marked, s and z are not marked.

Smaller but reasonably complete and most reliable is Dr. K. Speight's *Teach yourself Italian*. (2nd ed. London, English Universities Press. 1962, reprinted 1973. x, 278 pp. £0.50.) Part

1 consists of 30 lessons, containing grammar notes, vocabulary and passages for translation both ways. Quality of e, o, s and z is marked. Part 2 consists of a key and notes. An appendix gives some help with pronunciation, accents and syllabification and lists common irregular verbs. An Italian–English vocabulary of about 2,000 words shows commonly used prepositions after verbs and adjectives. Two tapes are now available to supplement the book, one on pronunciation (3″ reel, 3¾ ips £1.75) and the other of exercises (4″ reel, 3¾ ips. £3).

Very suitable for adult beginners, especially for travel purposes, is M. Valgimigli's *Living Italian* (London, University of London Press. 2nd ed. 1968, etc. 254 pp. illus., map. £0.75; paperback, £0.65). Again there are 30 lessons, intended to cover one year's work. Lessons consist of grammar, vocabulary, reading passages and exercises including translation both ways. The quality of e, o, s and z is not marked but stress is, except in *piane*. There are vocabularies both ways and verb tables. There are puzzles and word games, and sections 2 and 3 are concerned with a 'Journey to Italy', with accent on travel and short descriptions of places. Layout is clear and attractive. This work is perhaps better suited to class use, with older and less academic students, and Speight for more academic beginners working alone. There are tapes to supplement the text (4 × 5″ reels, 3¾ ips. £10 + VAT).

Collins' *Italian in 20 lessons* by M. Cagno (London, Collins, 1954 and reprints. 352 pp. illus. £1.95) seems to be designed to teach a conversational rather than a reading knowledge. The first 16 lessons consist of vocabularies and dialogues with grammar relegated to footnotes. Stress is indicated. A 'reference grammar' at the end is arranged by grammatical categories. Irregular tenses of irregular verbs are listed and there is a vocabulary both ways. A. L. Hayward's *Colloquial Italian* (New ed. London, Routledge, 1969. sewed, £0.70) is elementary and selective. There is a brief pronunciation guide, but stress and quality of e, o, s and z are unmarked. There are 12 lessons with grammar, vocabulary, conversational material and reading passages and the work could be used as a crash course for the spoken language. Similar in type is N. Hilton's *Italiano parlato* (London, Longmans, 1965. [7], 120 pp. illus., map, plan. limp,

£0.85) in 14 lessons. Hugo's *Italian in three months* (rev. ed.
1969. 210 pp. £0.50) is more substantial but would be fairly
heavy going for a student working alone. *Beginner's Italian: an
introduction to conversational Italian*, by O. Negro and J. Harvard (London, University of London Press. 2nd ed. 1969. 112
pp. £0.40) has a brief introduction on pronunciation and 16
lessons, consisting of dialogue and practice with grammatical
notes. There are translation exercises at the end and grammar
drill. The illustrations are effective. This again might make a
useful crash course. Accompanying tapes are obtainable (2 × 5"
reels, 3¾ ips. £7 + VAT, from Tutor Tape, 2 Replingham Rd.
London, S.W.18). S. X. Piazza's *Italian in 39 steps: an easy introduction, etc.* (Kingswood, Surrey, Elliot. 1965. 126 pp. tables.
£1) is intended for tourists and is quite sound within its avowed
limitations, but too selective and superficial for other purposes.
Vellaccio and Elston's *Let's talk Italian: a new approach to conversation and reading* (London, University of London Press,
1972. 192 pp. illus. £1.60) with 26 lessons, passages for reading,
conversations on themes such as the use of the telephone and
driving a car, vocabulary and idioms, also seems to be designed
for tourist use.

Courses for Specialists

Only one of these has been noted, the *Italian for commerce* of
Julian Popescu (Oxford, Pergamon, 1968. xviii, 143 pp. illus.
£2.60). This has translation, composition and reading exercises,
plus a list of abbreviations, a bibliography and a vocabulary.
Chapters are on various topics, such as, Book-keeping, Insurance, Banking, Shipping, Companies and the Stock
Exchange, Commercial correspondence, etc. and there is one on
translation techniques.

Reference Grammars and Grammars in Italian

There are several good reference grammars available which
are more likely to be of use to teachers than to students, but as
yet none in English. F. B. Agard and R. J. Di Pietro's *The grammatical structure of English and Italian* (Chicago, University of

Chicago Press, 1965. 91 pp.), which deals with parts of speech and phrase structure, is interesting but of little practical value from the point of view of learning the language. Much more useful is *La struttura della lingua italiana: grammatica generativo-trasformazionale* of Norma Costabile (Bologna, Pàtron, 1967. vii, 211 pp. about £3), on Chomskian principles. While appealing mainly to teachers this work could be consulted with profit by more advanced students. It is provided with a list of symbols, a repertoire of formulae and a bibliography. The so-called index is no more than a contents list. Also useful as a reference grammar for English teachers and students of Italian is U. Panozzo and D. Greco's *Struttura della lingua italiana: grammatica, sintassi, stilistica per il primo ciclo delle scuole medie superiori* (Florence, Le Monnier, 1974. about £4). R. A. Hall's *La struttura dell'italiano* (Rome, Armando, 1971. 431 pp. about £5), which applies generative-transformational methods to descriptive grammar, was not particularly well received but has apparently been found useful as a reference grammar by some teachers, as has also the *Grammatica trasformazionale italiana* of M. Medici and R. Simone (Rome, Bulzoni, 1971 (*Pubblicazioni della Società di Linguistica Italiana 3*) about £2).

Two new grammars in Italian for foreign students have been produced in connection with the courses at the Università Italiana per Stranieri at Perugia. *La lingua italiana insegnata agli stranieri* (Florence, Le Monnier for the Università Italiana per Stranieri, [1974]. about £2.25) has rules and exercises and there is an associated *Vocabolario minimo* by Baldelli and A. Mazzelli, containing 1,741 words, the use of which is exemplified. K. Katerinov's *La lingua italiana per stranieri* (Perugia, Guerra. 2nd ed. 1974) is in three parts 1 *Corso elementare*, based on 1,500 most used words (about £2) and 2, *Corso medio* and 3, *Corso superiore* each based on a vocabulary of 3,000 words (about £1.50 each). Each course has lessons, exercises and key. An associated pamphlet *Note didattiche* (1974) outlines the methodology of the course, which is used at the University for Foreigners at Perugia. Another Italian grammar for foreigners which can be recommended is *La lingua italiana per stranieri: metodo teorico-pratico per l'apprendimento della lingua italiana* (Milan, Mondadori. 30th ed. [1970]. 288 pp. about £1.50). This has grammar, reading passages, vocabulary and idioms and marks stress of non-*piane*.

Aids to Learning

Before passing on to Recorded and Audio-visual courses and aids it may be well to notice three supplementary works which have much to offer to the student who has reached the stage of translating difficult connected passages. The first of these is H. W. Smith's *Using Italian* (London, Pitman, 1972. ix, 259 pp. £2.25) consisting mainly of idioms, classified by subject and also presented alphabetically, in English and Italian, together with hints on translation and passages to be translated. The other two are R. N. L. Absalom's *Passages for translation from Italian* (Cambridge University Press, 1967. xxvi, 118 pp. £1.90; £0.85, sewed), which really tests ability to put difficult Italian passages into good English, and Absalom and S. Potestà, *Advanced Italian* (Cambridge, Cambridge University Press, 1971. viii, 152 pp. £1.30) containing 60 graded passages from contemporary non-literary sources with notes and exercises based on them. This work is specially designed for use in courses for A-level syllabuses which lay more emphasis on the non-literary use of language.

RECORDED & AUDIO-VISUAL AIDS

N.B. Courses which consist mainly of a textbook for which tapes have been provided *as an adjunct* have been included in the appropriate category above, where details of the tapes will also be found. On the other hand courses which involve the use of audio-visual materials *as an essential feature* have been included in this section in spite of the fact that they may include a substantial printed volume.

The following are *not* ranked in order of preference as the books and films have not been seen and the tapes or records heard in every case. The well-tried *Linguaphone corso d'italiano* by R. Anzilotti *and others* (London, Linguaphone Institute

[196?]). Complete course, £29.50. Course and practice material
(5 records *or* 1 cassette, £35.50) consists of a textbook of 150
pages with illustrations and maps; a vocabulary of 131 pages;
explanatory notes (150 pages); a student's instruction booklet of
22 pages, and 16 × 7″ records (45 rpm) *or* 2 × 5″ reels of tape
(3¾ ips) *or* 2 × C.60 compact cassette tapes (1⅞ ips). The
speakers are all Tuscans, which means the student will hear a
good accent from the start.

Parlate con noi. Italiano 1: an Italian course for beginners
(Longmans, 1971–3) Part 1 is intended for 6th form or adult
beginners and consists of 48 lessons through pictures and
dialogue. Labelled drawings and visual cues stress points of
grammar. Exercises are in the workbook (Student's book. 176
pp., Grammar summary and vocabulary. £0.95; Student's
workbook 89 pp. £0.45; Key. 31 pp £0.50 2 × 5″ reels tape (3¾
ips. £6.50 + VAT). Part 2, in three sections, leads to aural and
visual comprehension. Section 1 of 23 dialogues (6 on tape) is
about a visit to Rome. Section 2 of 29 passages (13 on tape) illustrates Italian life under headings such as *Paese*; *La famiglia*;
La stampa. Section 3 consists of 35 passages (12 on tape) concerning regional life as seen by contemporary authors. There are
also 8 extracts from opera libretti which seems a very odd
choice in view of the peculiar language in which these are
written. There are a vocabulary and verb tables. Stress and
pronunciation are indicated. (Student's book 257 pages, por-
traits, photographs, maps and drawings. £1.25, paperback;
Student's workbook £0.45; 2 × 5″ reels tape (3¾ ips) £7 +
VAT).

The *Harrap–Didier audio-visual Italian course* by D.
Cernecca and J. Jernej (Paris, Didier; London, Harrap.
1965–72) is in two parts, each consisting of 25 lessons. Part 2 is
suitable for adults as well as schools up to 'O'-level. Part 1 consists of a Teaching guide (viii, 125 pp.) £1.65; Student's book
(107 pp.) with illustrations, some coloured), £1.65; 25
Filmstrips, some in colour, £61 + VAT, replacements, £2.50
each + VAT; 12 × 5″ reels (3¾ ips), £30 + VAT. Part 2 consists
of a Student's book (120 pages with illustrations), £2.15; 26
Filmstrips (13 black and white, 13 coloured), £40 + VAT; 11 ×
5″ reels tape (3¾ ips), £33 + VAT.

Ciao bambini! by S. Chiarini, edited by M. McAllister (European Schoolbooks, Ltd. 122 Bath Road, Cheltenham GL53 7JX. 1966) is intended for children in primary schools and consists of a Textbook (85, xv pp. with coloured illustrations and a vocabulary in five languages), £1.25 *or* £0.75, each for 10 or more copies; Teaching notes, and 5 × 7" records (33⅓ rpm). Book and records with teaching notes, £3.12.

J. Cremona's *Si dice così, This is how we say it.* (BBC, 1968) was written for a television programme for adult beginners, of which each part was to be seen twice, and is based on substitution drills. Textbook 1 (111 pp., illustrated) of 15 lessons has a grammar summary and glossary; paperback, £0.25; 2 × 12" records (33 rpm) £0.99 each. Textbook 2 of 11 lessons (96 pp., illustrated) has similar features and also costs £0.25. An accompanying record costs £0.99.

Italiano: AAC sistema d'insegnamento (Zurich, Philips. 1969) UK distributors ESL (Bristol) Ltd. St. Lawrence House, 29–31, Broad St, Bristol BS1 2HF) is based on *Language through pictures,* by I. A. Richards and others. It consists essentially of line drawings, with printed comments in Italian which are also recorded on tape. Grammar is to be deduced. There are test sequences, with specimen answers, and a vocabulary. The paperback textbook (274 pp., illustrated) and 12 cassettes complete, £32.20 + VAT *or* with mini language laboratory (tape recorder and accessories), £96 + VAT.

The A-LM Italian (New York, Harcourt, Brace, 1961) of the Modern Language Materials Development Center is in two parts, each intended for one year of an American college course. The approach is purely aural at first, leading to reading and writing at a later stage. Level one consists of a Teacher's manual (VII, 120 pp.). £0.40. 15 Student booklets, £1.10, and 15 × 12" records (33⅓ rpm) £15 + VAT plus 14 optional practice records (7" 33⅓ rpm), £2.60 each + VAT *or* 36 × 7" reels of tape (7½ ips), £43.20 + VAT. There are also optional tests available at 20p. Level two consists of a Teacher's manual (vi, 134 pp.) 35p.; Student's textbook (viii, 290 pp., with illustrations, maps, vocabulary and index) £1.45, 9 optional practice records (7" 33⅓ rpm) *or* 41 × 7" reels of tape (7½ ips) £50.40 + VAT.

H. Shankland and E. Mussi's *Amici, buona sera!* (BBC, 1969)

208 pp. illus., maps. £0.45 (Further education series) has 2 ×
12″ records (33⅓ rpm) £0.99 each. The course is intended for
adult beginners and consists of 30 dialogues, exercises, grammar
notes and a glossary. It covers shopping, travel and the like and
teaches use of the indicative tenses except the *passato rimoto*.
The conditional is briefly touched on.

The excellent *Introductory Italian course*, by Maud Tyler
(1971). is obtainable from the author at 5, Brookside, Cambridge. It consists of 33 lessons designed to teach vocabulary of
1,800 words, while grammar rules are learnt by the direct
method from the dialogues. There are substitutional exercises, a
vocabulary, list of irregular verbs and index. The tapes can be
used for repetition, reading aloud, comprehension and substitution exercises. Volume 1 (v, 160 pp.), volume 2 (160 pp.), £1.50;
16 tapes (3¾ ips). £4, *for hire only.*

*The World of Learning PILL course (Language learning: the
Italian language,* developed by Brian Dutton (World of Learning, 359 Upper Richmond Rd. W.S.W.14) consists of three
cassettes *or* double-sided records with three bands to each side,
three main booklets covering the contents of these, a booklet
giving the full text of each band, an introductory booklet, a test-
book to be filled with the answers to exercises and sent in for
comments by a tutor, vocabularies, for each room of the house,
the office, restaurant etc. and topics such as the body, sport,
clothes, the doctor etc., also a guide to Italy with a
businessman's vocabulary. The course consists of twenty-four
hours of work intended to be spread over about a month, but it
may be taken more quickly or, of course, repeated. It is very
thorough as far as it goes and should give a good conversational
grasp of the indicative tenses and of basic constructions, even to
those with little flair for languages. Some corners are inevitably
cut and there is some over-simplification, but the course is well-
suited to the intending holiday-maker or to the businessman
seeking a crash course. There are a few misprints and one of
these, followed by a speaker in one of the conversations, leads to
her saying the opposite of what was intended. There are several
with slightly different pronunciations, which could be useful to a
student about to visit Italy alone for the first time. The
recommended retail price of the course is £35.50 (£32.95 to

libraries). Libraries may also acquire three separate packs at £11.40 each and additional records and extra booklets at discount of about ⅓.

DICTIONARIES

Dictionaries: General, bilingual. Larger works.

The largest bilingual dictionary available is the *Sansoni–Harrap Standard Italian and English dictionary* edited by V. Macchi and others (Florence, Sansoni; London, Harrap, 1970–76: Italian–English. 2 vols. £17 each, English–Italian. 2 vols. £20 + £25). Part 1 contains more than 100,000 headwords, often with many derivatives, compounds, phrases etc. Stress and the quality of e o s and z are marked. The dictionary includes Americanisms. The preface explains the formation of diminutives, augmentatives, pejoratives and so forth and gives irregular forms and tenses of verbs. The prepositions taken by verbs are noted. There is a list of geographical names. Part 2 is similar in size and make up. Some words in one part are not to be found in the other and this is the case in both directions, but the standard of the dictionary is high and the number of words listed very large.

The Cambridge Italian dictionary, General editor, Barbara Reynolds. Vol. 1: Italian–English (Cambridge, Cambridge University Press, 1962. xxxi, 900 pp. £14) is based on the much older work by Hoare but has been thoroughly revised by a team of subject experts. It gives English equivalents, not definitions. Words are qualified as colloquial, poetic and so forth and obsolete words are marked. Words peculiar to Tuscany are noted but some local words, e.g. names of fishes, have been omitted. Proper names are included. There are 45–50,000 headwords, with many derivatives, inflected forms, phrases, etc. arranged under them. Some translators have complained of difficulty in finding the required phrase in long entries. Stress is marked and so is the quality of e, o s and z, as well as the pronunciation of g before li where this is as in English. Abbreviations, conjugations and the use of prepositions with verbs are given in separate tables.

G. Ragazzini's *Dizionario inglese–italiano, italiano–inglese* (Bologna, Zanichelli. 1973. about £6 or £7, according to binding) marks stress and the quality of e o s and z and lists a large number of headwords, under which the arrangement and the examples of usage are said to be excellent. One reviewer hailed it soon after publication as the best dictionary available for students when price is taken into consideration.

The *Grande dizionario inglese–italiano, italiano–inglese*, of M. Hazon (Milan, Garzanti. 19th ed. 1973. 2 v. £10) has about 55,000 and 65,00 headings in the respective volumes. It is up-to-date, though not always correct, and indicates stress and the quality of e and o. There are abbreviations both ways, Italian proper names in the main sequence, English proper names, weights and measures, verbal constructions etc. It is no doubt intended primarily for Italians but very useful in this country. The English–Italian part is said to be better than the Italian–English.

The *Nuovissimo dizionario italiano–inglese, inglese–italiano* (Milan, Ceschina, 1967. xi, 2388 pp. about £7) marks stress and the quality of e and o. It deals with idioms and has an appendix of symbols and acronyms.

Cassell's Italian–English, English–Italian dictionary ed. by P. Rebora and others (London, Cassell. 1971. xxi, 1096 pp. £2.80) has about 55,000 words and phrases in the Italian–English section and about 40,000 the other way. Both parts have appendices of neologisms, Americanisms and new and additional meanings. Stress is given for non-*piane* but difference of sound in e and o is supposed to be marked only where there is possible ambiguity. It is marked in the case of *pésca, pèsca* but not in *aréna, arèna,* or *tócco, tòcco,* although this is given as an example in the preface. Older words, many synonyms and variant spellings are omitted. Not all *faux amis* and traps have been avoided. A good dictionary for non-academic purposes and good value for money.

G. Orlandi's *Dizionario italiano–inglese e inglese–italiano: voci dell'uso corrente e familiare e della lingua classica; termini commerciali, scientifici, tecnici, americanismi, voci del gergo* (Milan, Signorelli: London, Bailey, 1972. 2,130 pp.) has about 100,000 words Italian–English and 50,000 in reverse. Stress and the quality of e and o are marked. A useful one-volume dictionary.

The *Dizionario italiano–inglese, inglese–italiano, ecc.* of N. Spinelli (3rd ed. Turin, Società Editrice Internazionale: London, Bailey, 1955. about £15.50) has about 40,000 words Italian–English and about 55,000 the other way Stress and the quality of e and o are marked. There are geographical and proper names both ways and English abbreviations. It is still very expensive in comparison with other works which give more information and, despite its claim to be *interamente rifatta*, this edition shows few changes or additions since the 2nd ed. of 1930.

Dictionaries: General, bilingual. Medium-sized and smaller works

The *English–Italian, Italian–English dictionary* of G. Ragazzini and A. Biagi (London, Longmans, Bologna, Zanichelli, 1973. xxii, 1,200 pp. paperback, £2.50) is an abridgement of Ragazzini, having about 35,000 entries each way. It marks stress in non-*piane* and the quality of e o s and z. It is a very good buy at the price and perhaps rates as the best dictionary of its size available.

The *Concise Italian dictionary*, edited by Barbara Reynolds (lxxvii, 792 pp. Cambridge, Cambridge University Press, 1975. £7.50; paperback, £2.50) has about 17,000 words in the Italian–English part and about 25,000 in the English–Italian. It contains a concise grammar, tables of verbs both ways, use of prepositions with Italian verbs and abbreviations. It marks stress in non-*piane* and the quality of e o s and z.

The *Compact English–Italian dictionary. Piccolo dizionario italiano–inglese* (London, Harrap, 1970. £1.05) has about 25,000 words each way and marks stress and the quality of e and o.

The *Dizionario moderno inglese–italiano, italiano–inglese* of A. Tedeschi and C. Rossi Fantonetti. 2nd ed. Milan, Mondadori. 1970. 1,120 pp. about £3) has about 50,000 words each way. It marks stress and the quality of e and o.

J. Purves' *A dictionary of modern Italian: Italian–English,*

English–Italian (London, Routledge, 1953. xxviii, 833 pp. £2.50) is still a very good small dictionary and still not bad value in spite of having quadrupled in price since our last edition. It has an introductory guide to pronunciation, paradigms of regular and auxiliary verbs and irregularities of irregular verbs. The Italian–English section has words and phrases listed under 14,500 main headings, the English–Italian section has 13,500 main headings and a list of proper names. Stress and the quality of e o s and z are marked.

The *Contemporary Italian dictionary*, edited by I. May and I. S. Stott (London, Collins, 1970, reprinted 1974. 462 pp. £1.25) has about 18,000 words Italian–English and 21,000 English–Italian. It has an outline of Italian grammar and lists of verbs and abbreviations and stress and the quality of e o s and z are marked. This also is quite a good small dictionary and good value for money.

M. Hazon's *Italian–English, English–Italian dictionary. Edizione pratica scolastica.* (7th ed. Milan, Garzanti, 1968. £5.10) is a smaller version of the larger Garzanti dictionary. It marks stress and the quality of e and o. The English–Italian section is better than the Italian–English. The *Nuovo Hazon Garzanti dizionario inglese–italiano, italiano–inglese* (Milan, Garzanti, [1960]. 1,700 pp. 32 pp. of keyed illustrations) is intermediate in size between the other two.

A short Italian dictionary (Cambridge, University Press, 1926 and reprints. 2 vols. in 1. £4) is based upon Alfred Hoare's larger work. It contains about 18,000 headwords each way with many inflected forms, phrases and so forth under each entry. Stress is marked 'where it seems desirable' and the quality of e o s and z is marked. There are notes on difficult verbs and a table of words which may be followed by an infinitive. The content is rather literary and old-fashioned but the standard is high and the work is useful for the student of the Italian classics.
is high and the work is useful for the student of the Italian classics.

The *Duden italiano, dizionario figurato* (2nd revised ed. Novara, Istituto Geografico De Agostini; London, Harrap, 1964. 672, 134, 128 pp. pl., some col. illus. £5.70) is based on the German *Duden*. It follows the well-known Duden principle of illustrating words pictorially instead of defining them. 25,000 words and drawings are included and indexed both ways. Subjects such as mythology are included but abstract terms obviously cannot be illustrated. The work is particularly valuable for technical subjects of all kinds.

Dictionaries: General, monolingual

The largest of these is the *Grande dizionario della lingua italiana* of S. Battaglia (Turin, UTET, [1961–]. about £15 per vol.), which is however still in progress, having reached the middle of the alphabet. It is a well-produced, scholarly work, of similar type to the NED, but the quotations are not dated. Cumulative fascicules, of which Nos. 1–8 had appeared by 1974, are, however, giving precise references to the authors cited. Etymologies are given and some dialect words are included. Research for the dictionary is going on at Florence and Padua.

Next in size is N. Zingarelli's *Vocabolario della lingua italiana* (10th ed. Bologna, Zanichelli, 1970. about £8) which has been re-edited by a team of experts and contains 118,000 words. It marks stress and the quality of e o s and z.

The next largest are five dictionaries of roughly equal size. The first of these is G. Devoto and G. C. Oli, the *Dizionario della lingua italiana* (Sesta ristampa Florence, Le Monnier, 1975. about £11) which has about 63,000 headings and contains illustrations in the text, some of the Duden type. The stress is marked but not the quality of e o s and z. An alternative at the same price is the *Modernissimo dizionario illustrato* (Novara, Istituto Geografico De Agostini. about £11). This is in two parts 1 *Lingua* and 2 *Arti, scienze, storia, geografia*. There are coloured plates and illustrations in the text, some of Duden type.

Cheaper than these is the *Dizionario Garzanti della lingua italiana* (Milan, Garzanti, 1965. xvi, 1,990 pp. 1,500 illus. 55 tables. about £5), which contains about 60,000 main entries. There are contributions by over 60 specialists. Etymologies are given and stress is marked in difficult cases, while the quality of e o s and z is indicated. Many of the illustrations are of Duden type and tables group together words with related meanings. A small dictionary, published with the same title in 1963, is intended for school use. It has 994 pages, 1,300 illustrations and contains 42,000 entries. There are supplements for Italian proper names, place names of Italy and correct usage. It is edited by M. Hazon and costs about £1.50.

Rather more expensive is the *Novissimo dizionario della lingua italiana* of F. Palazzi (3rd ed. Milan, Ceschina; London, Bailey. 1969. illus. and coloured plates. £6.20) which has 60,000 entries arranged in three columns. It includes etymology, phraseology and synonyms. An appendix gives proper names, abbreviations and geographical adjectives.

C. Passerini Tosi's *Dizionario della lingua italiana*. (Milan, Principato 1969. xii, 1,744 pp. col.pl.illus.(some of Duden type). £6.50) is similar in price to Palazzi but is a new work. It contains about 75,000 words and marks the quality of e o s and z. It includes a small section on synonyms.

A. Gabrielli's *Dizionario linguistico moderno: guida pratica per scrivere e parlare bene* (Milan, Mondadori, 1956. 5th reprint, 1969. 1,192 pp. paperback, about £4) suggests equivalents for foreign words imported into Italian and for unnecessary neologisms. It marks the quality of e and o gives rules for surd or sonant s. The Florentine and Roman pronunciations are indicated for many words with z. There is a bibliography. Part 1 gives grammatical rules and difficult constructions, dialect forms, stylistic rules, metrical rules and forms, etymology and the pronunciation of common foreign words. Part 2 is a dictionary with spelling and pronunciation but no definitions. There are lists of geographical adjectives, feminine, plural and comparative forms and also verb tables. The use of *essere* and *avere* is explained and a number of difficult constructions which are not usually covered.

Synonyms and antonyms are covered by Gabrielli's *Dizionario dei sinonimi e dei contrari: analogico e nomenclatore* (Milan, Istituto Editoriale Italiano 1967 and reprints. 866 pp. col.pl.illus(some of Duden type)).

There is an excellent etymological dictionary in C. Battisti and G. Alessio *Dizionario etimologico italiano* (Florence, Giunti – Barbèra, 1948–57. 5 v. about £25) published under the auspices of the Istituto di Glottologia of the University of

Florence. This gives etymologies, dates of introduction into the language, variants and parallels or cognates in other languages. It includes many scientific and technical terms for which alone it is most useful, and dialect words. A series of *Aggiunte e retrodatazioni* began publication in 1964.

Dictionaries: Commercial

G. Motta's *Dizionario commerciale, inglese–italiano, italiano–inglese: economia–legge–finanza.* (Milan, Signorelli, 1961, reprinted 1966. x [1], 1,051 pp. about £3.50) devotes, for example 2½ columns to the entry 'account', 2 columns to 'stock', 1⅔ columns to *'mercato'*. The stress of Italian words is not shown. There are about 15,000 entries each way, and the work is evidently intended mainly for Italian users.

The *Dizionario inglese–italinao, italiano–inglese con glossario bilingue di economia e organizzazione aziendale* (Bologna, Zanichelli; Milan, Etas–Kompass, 1966–7. xxx, 2,036, iv pp.) is basically the Ragazzini dictionary with a commercial supplement which occupies pp. 1,865–2,036. About 48,000 words are covered in the English–Italian section and 53,000 in the Italian–English. The work is a team effort. There are lists of abbreviations, proper names, parts of irregular verbs, monetary system, temperature scales and so forth.

N. Spinelli's *Dizionario commerciale: italiano–inglese, inglese–italiano. Terminologia commerciale, contabile, economica, finanziaria, giuridica.* 1957 ed., reprinted 1961, con un Appendice a cura del prof. dott. Giuseppe Motta (Turin, Lattes; London, Bailey. vii, 464, 683, 138 pp. about £3) was first published in 1917 and has about 12,000 entries in the Italian–English part and 17,000 in the English–Italian part of the main sequence. There is a supplement of 138 pages covering both parts. The stress of Italian words is not shown. 4 columns are devoted to the entry 'account' and 2 to *'mercato'*.

Dictionaries: Technical

There are three bilingual technical dictionaries available. That of S. Gatto, *Dizionario tecnico scientifico illustrato, italiano–inglese, inglese–italiano* (Milan, Ceschina, 1960. xxii, [1], 381 pp. illus. about £3.50 bound, or £2 paperback) has the most headings: about 75,000 and 60,000 in the two parts respectively. Terms are categorised, there are separate entries for compounds and references from the second part of compound words (*e.g.* 'brake', see also 'air-'). The illustrations are very small and occur about one per page. There is a bibliography of 40 items.

Smaller, but an excellent translating dictionary, with compounds and extensions of entries indented to allow of easy reference, is the *Dizionario tecnico, italiano–inglese, inglese–italiano* of R. Denti (Milan, Hoepli. 6th revised and enlarged ed. 1965. xiv, 1,307 pp. about £5.50). The two parts of this have about 35,000 and 50,000 entries respectively. Stress and pronunciation are not shown but the gender of Italian words is given. Technical terms are categorised, *e.g.* '(auto)' and '(aereo)'. There are appendices of technical abbreviations, conversion factors, tables of Anglo–American and metric measures and a table of elements.

G. Marolli's *Dizionario tecnico, inglese–italiano, italiano–inglese* (10th revised and enlarged ed. Florence, Le Monnier. 1972. xxii [1], 4, 1621 pp. illus. about £16.50) shows stress but not genders. It categorizes technical terms and there are about 30,000 and 20,000 words in the two parts respectively. There is an appendix of 39 folding outline drawings (*e.g.* of an atomic power station, with 91 keyed parts). There are conversion and other tables. The layout is less good than in Denti, which is a better bargain.

4

SPANISH

Spanish is spoken by over 200 million people, ranking after Chinese, English, Russian and Hindi among the world's languages. In Britain it is taught in schools as, possibly, a third language or as an alternative to German for those who wish to take up commerce. Trade in Latin America, we are reliably informed[1], is hardly possible without a knowledge of Spanish (or Portuguese, for Brazil), 'and the Spanish-speaking world demands more and more to be addressed by foreign business men in its own language'. Probably what commends Spanish as a foreign language to the student are the comparative simplicity of pronunciation, spelling and elementary grammar.

COURSES, GRAMMARS

1. For beginners

A first Spanish book, by W. W. Timms (Longman, 1963 (reprint of 1957 ed.). x, 190 pp. illus. £0.50) consists of 15 lessons and is for class use, for young beginners. It provides a lively oral approach and has plenty of useful and interesting exercises (about 12 per lesson). Together with *A second Spanish book* (Longman, 1965 (reprint of 1958 ed.). x, 238 pp. illus. £0.50), this volume aims to provide a three-year study of Spanish for 'O' level. The topical end-vocabulary is Spanish–English only, whereas *Principios de español*, by J. E. Travis, and others (New ed., rev. Harrap, 1963–64 (reprint of 1956–58 ed.). 2 v. illus., maps. £1.45) has two-way and fuller end-vocabularies. *Principios*, first published in 1935–36, has 25 and 15 lessons respectively in its two volumes and is for class

---

[1] British Institute of Management. *Languages for managers* (1969), p. 2.

use over a two-year period. It has adequate reading matter, exercises and drill in each lesson.

Beginner's Spanish, by J. M. Pittaro and A. Green (Harrap,
1932. xvi, 501, ii, 30 pp. illus., maps. £1.50) aims to provide a
comprehensive 'elementary course comprising two to four
terms'. Of the 56 lessons, 10 are devoted to the subjunctive.
Again, there are plenty of exercises, questions, conversation. To
the two-way end-vocabularies is added an index to grammar.

Adult beginners may prefer J. W. Barlow's *Basic Spanish*
(Bell, 1965 (reprint of 1939 ed.). xii, 208 pp. maps. £1), which
does devote its 25 lessons to basic usage. Each lesson has
reading passages, questions, exercises and Spanish–English
word-list. Short two-way end-vocabularies and an index to
grammar.

2. Self-tutors

N. S. Wilson's *Teach yourself Spanish* (English Universities
Press, 1962 (reprint of 1939 ed.), xiv, 242 pp. £0.40), an elementary self-tutor in 30 lessons, leading up to the subjunctive, has
the advantage of tape-recorded Spanish exercises (1 tape. 4″
reel. 3⅜ ips; twin half-track. £3.00). The textbook has grammar,
exercises and sentences each way, working up to connected
passages, with a table of common irregular verbs and
Spanish–English vocabulary only. It is continued in L. D.
Collier's *Teach yourself everyday Spanish* (English Universities
Press, 1967 (reprint of 1957 ed.). viii, 232 pp. maps. £0.60),
which comprises 20 lessons, with key to exercises and connected
passages, but no vocabulary. The recorded material consists of
1 tape (4″ reel. 3¾ ips, twin half-track. £2.50).

El español práctico, by J. P. Fitzgibbon and J. Roldan
(Harrap, 1964. viii, 338 pp. illus. £1.25) is also supported by
recorded material, for all reading passages (4 discs. 10″. 33⅓
rpm. £9.00 + VAT). Its 53 lessons provide enough material for
a two-year course, at least. Keys are given to all exercises. According to *Modern languages* (v. 45, no. 3, September 1964, p.
127) the course is up-to-date, with idiomatic Spanish and interesting material on Spain and the Spanish way of life; well illustrated. Dialogue is used for the reading passages.

Español rápido, by P. M. H. Quinlan and W. V. Compton; edited by P. J. Hargreaves (Rev. ed. Leonard Hill, 1970. x, 170 pp. £0.80), first published in 1966, is an attractively produced paperback crash-course for mature beginners. Each of the 20 lessons in part 1 (on the elements of Spanish) consists of pronunciation exercise, reading passage, vocabulary, grammar and Spanish-into-English exercises. Part 2 has two series of test papers; Spanish–English end-vocabulary and index to grammar. Also edited by P. J. Hargreaves is *Spanish once a week*, by N. Clegg and P. K. Caldwell (Oxford, Blackwell, 1971. x, 131 pp. £0.60), a short course of 20 lessons, with two-way vocabularies.

By its nature, a self-tutor should be armed with a key to exercises or at least translations of sentences or passages in the language studied. *Spanish in twenty lessons*, by R. Diez de la Cortina (152nd ed., revised. New York, Cortina, 1966. 406 pp. illus.) has 20 lessons, each with topical vocabularies and conversational sentences (each translated, with pronunciation), plus five sections on basic grammar; Spanish–English vocabulary only. W. R. Patterson's *Colloquial Spanish* (4th ed., revised and brought up to date by G. H. Calvert. Routledge & Kegan Paul, 1963. x, 145 pp. £1.00; £0.45) is a 12-lesson course for beginners, concentrating on basic grammar, vocabulary and conversation; the Spanish stories have English translations. Hugo's Lanuage Institute's *Spanish self-tuition in three months* (containing *Spanish grammar simplified* ... and *Spanish coversation simplified* (The Institute, 1969. 96, 48, 28 pp. (£0.65; £0.50) has a key to exercises. Its 26 lessons conver grammar, exercises and vocabulary. Drawbacks are the paucity of connected passages and the simulated pronunciation, although there is a Hugo's cassette course in Spanish comprises 4 cassettes (5 hours' play-back) and textbook at £13.20. Hugo's is intended for tourist, not the serious student, whereas Charles Duff's *All purposes Spanish for adults* (Revised ed. English Universities Press, 1965. 296 pp. £0.75) is for the strong-willed student. In its 15 lessons the user is encouraged to use Spanish in real-life situations and he is introduced to the Spanish classics. The classified vocabulary (3,500 words) has three main parts: indispensable words; essential words; and reading vocabulary.

3. Courses for 'O' level

(a) Courses without audio-visual aids

A reliable 3-year course in three volumes is published by
Harrap. The first book, *Nos ponemos en camino*, by E. L. Dean
and M. C. M. Roberts (Harrap, 1966 (reprint of 1956 ed.). 225
pp. illus. £0.65) is for third-form beginners. The 20 lessons cover
vocabulary, grammar and a variety of exercises, with two-way
end-vocabularies. Its sequel, *Sequimos adelante*, also by Dean
and Roberts (Harrap, 1964 (reprint of 1957 ed.). 288 pp. illus.
£0.75) has a similar pattern. 20 lessons contain reading matter,
questions, grammar and numerous exercises, with verb tables
and two-way end-vocabularies. For 'O'-level examination year,
– *A comprehensive Spanish course for first examination*, by
P. W. Packer and E. L. Dean (2nd ed., revised. Harrap, 1966
reprint of 1962 ed. 226 pp. £0.76). Part 1 has 35 sections, each
with a Spanish passage and questions in Spanish; English, for
translation; and subjects for free composition. Part 2 (19 sections) covers grammar, with exercises. Part 3 (14 sections) deals
with verbs and has practice sentences. Appendix of School Certificate examination questions; two-way end-vocabularies. A key
(54 pp.) is available, at £0.40.

J. C. Pride's *School Spanish course* (Rev. ed. University
Tutorial Press, 1975. viii, 354 pp. illus. £1.35), first published
1968, is for pupils who have 1–2 years in which to study for 'O'
level. The 45 lessons carry a revision lesson after each 5 lessons,
the subjunctive being introduced from lesson 18 onwards. The
text is supported by verb tables, two-way end-vocabularies and
an index to grammar. According to *Modern languages* (v. 49,
no. 3, September 1968, p. 139), 'this is a textbook which should
soon find a place in many grammar schools, further education
establishments and adult education classes'.

For the final year of preparation for 'O' level, there is a choice
between *A simpler Spanish course for first examinations*, by
W. W. Timms and M. Pulgar (Longman, 1966 (reprint of 1962
ed.). viii, 326 pp. £0.68; Teachers' book,. viii, 95 pp. £0.53),
Essential Spanish, by H. Lester and V. Terrádez (2nd ed.
University of London Press, 1968 (reprint of 1960 ed.). 254 pp.
£0.65), and M. C. M. Roberts' *El español vivo: Spanish for the*

CSE and for general colloquial practice (Harrap, 1970. 233 pp. illus. £1.10).

B. J. W. Hill's *A Spanish course* (London, E. Arnold, 1975 (reprint, with corrections and additions of, 1952 ed.). 391 pp. illus. £2.25) covers rather more than 'O' level requirements and is 'primarily for those who take up Spanish at the age of sixteen or a little later'. The 45 well-constructed lessons embrace exercises, drill and connected passages for translation, with two-way vocabularies and an index to grammar.

(b) Course with audio-visual aids

Living Spanish, by R. P. Littlewood (University of London Press, 1964 (reprint of 1949 ed.). 320 pp. illus. £0.75; £0.65) is 'intended primarily for students in commercial and technical institutions and private students preparing for the more elementary examinations of such bodies as the Royal Society of Arts or the Institute of Linguists. It is equally suitable for older students in secondary schools'. It has 25 chapters, plus 5 recapitulations; two-way end-vocabularies. Recorded materials consist of 4 tapes (5″ reels, $3\frac{3}{4}$ ips, twin half-track) or 4 casettes £9.00 + VAT; language laboratory tapes: 25 tapes, 5″ reels, $3\frac{3}{4}$ ips, single top track; or 25 casettes. £40.00 + VAT.

Present-day Spanish, by J. R. Scarr (Oxford, Pergamon Press, 1966–7. 2 v. (xvi, 219 pp.; viii, 266 pp. £2.50; £1.30) provides an intensive two-year course on orthodox lines, for 'O' level. Formal translation from English starts with v. 1, lesson 1, and there is an abundance of exercises in forbiddingly small print. V. 2 includes a very full grammatical summary and end-vocabularies, as well as an index to grammar. Recorded materials consist of tape (readings and conversations), 5″ reel, $3\frac{3}{4}$ ips, twin half-track (£7).

4. Advanced courses

R. P. Littlewood's *Further living Spanish* (University of London Press, [1965]. 384 pp. illus., map. £0.70), is mainly for 'A' level candidates and would also be valuable for first-year university students, especially in the revision of grammar, which occupies the second half. Chapters 18–32 enterprisingly concentrate on aspects of Latin America. Praised in *The incorporated linguist* (v. 5, no. 4, October 1966, pp. 120–1), it incorporates the then latest Academy pronouncements on grammar and spelling. Two-way end-vocabularies.

K. L. J. Mason's *Advanced Spanish course* (Oxford, Pergamon, 1967. viii, 377 pp. £2, £1.25; Key. viii, 101 pp. £0.90) is a very good, comprehensive course for post-'O' level students, in 5 parts, with numerous passages and sentences for translation from and into Spanish. Part 5 consists of 150 pages of grammar, giving the student all he needs to take him well beyond 'A' level. According to *Modern languages* (v. 48, no. 4, December 1967, p. 181), this course 'will become a standard text-book for 'A' level students for many years to come'.

Like Mason, *Advanced Spanish course*, by W. W. Timms and M. Pulgar (Oxford, Pergamon, 1971. xiv, 279 pp. £1: Key. [x], 69 pp. £1), has the advantage of a key to exercises and passages for translation from English. A sequel to their *A simpler Spanish course for first examinations* (see p. 58), it is intended for those preparing for 'A' level and similar exams.

H. Ramsden's *An essential course in modern Spanish* (Harrap, 1975 (reprint of 1959 ed.). 416 pp. £2.25) is primarily 'for University students who offer Spanish as one of the Intermediate subjects'. Its 25 lessons, plus 8 review and development sections, offer plenty of drill and exercises (with key), including verb tables, two-way vocabularies and index to grammar. Highly recommended, it was used as a model for Willis's *An essential course in modern Portuguese* (q.v.).

5. Reference grammars

One expects of a reference grammar that it should be detailed, giving – in the case of Spanish – full treatment to the verb. Examples of usage should be copious, drawn from both classics and everyday Spanish. Two-way vocabularies should be extensive, with an index to the grammar concerned. A bibliography would also be of help.

A manual of modern Spanish, by L. C. Harmer and F. J. Norton (2nd ed. University Tutorial Press, 1966 (reprint of 1957 ed.). xii, 623 pp. £1.45), first published in 1935, fulfills most of these criteria. Pages 100–387 concern the verb; many examples are drawn from classical and contemporary Spanish writers (about 200 citations alone from chapter 30, 'The infinitive (continued)'. The index to grammar is supplemented by references to chapters and paragraphs of the text in the two-way vocabularies. Only 1½ pages, however, are devoted to pronunciation. M. M. Ramsey's *Textbook of modern Spanish* (Revised ed., edited by R. K. Spaulding, New York, Holt, [1967] (reprint of 1956, ed. xix, [1], 692, xvii pp. $10.95) too, has, several thousand examples of idioms, 24 pages on orthography and pronunciation, an index to grammar and a bibliography of 'useful works of reference'. But instead of two-way end-vocabularies there are lesson vocabularies.

The authority on current usage is the Real Academia Española's *Gramática de la lengua española* (Nueva ed., reformada de 1931 y apendice con las nuevas normas de prosodia y ortografía declaradas de aplicación perceptiva desde 1.° de enero de 1959. Madrid, Espasa–Calpe, 1959. 542 pp.), first published in 1879. The four parts deal with word-formation, syntax, pronunciation and orthography. Copious examples are given and an analytical subject index is appended.

6. Pronunciation. Phrase books. Word lists[1]

Spanish pronunciation illustrated, by J. P. Fitzgibbon and Jillian Norman (Cambridge University Press, 1963. 64 pp. £0.25) is an attractive short guide to pronunciation of vowels, consonants, etc., with amusing drawings.

Phrase books for the tourist are numerous. Three may be singled out, all pocket-sized.

The Berlitz *Spanish for travellers* (London, Berlitz, 1974. £1.95) provides 2,000 useful words and 1,200 phrases with a guide to shopping, eating out, tipping, sightseeing and relaxing. Pronunciation is simulated throughout, but a 33⅓ rpm disc, or a cassette, is available at £1.95.

---

[1] *Teaching materials for Spanish: supplementary material* 2nd revised ed. (Centre for Information on language Teaching and Research, 1974. 8 pp. £0.25) is a lengthy annotated list of items on these subjects.

Spanish phrase book, by M. V. Alvarez and Jillian Norman (Harmondsworth, Penguin, 1968. 198 pp. £0.30), like the companion *French phrase book*, has notes on simulated pronunciation, essential grammar, grouped phrases covering everyday contingencies, and a 1,500-word English–Spanish vocabulary. *Latin American phrase book*, by D. S. Gifford and Carlos Reyes Orozco (Collins, 1969. 144 pp. £0.35, £0.25), also deals with topics of concern to the tourist and has a Spanish–English vocabulary of about 700 words, in addition to an English index of words.

Special mention should be made of *Beyond the dictionary in Spanish: a handbook of everyday usage in Spain and Latin America*, by A. B. Gerrard and J. de Heras Heras (Rev. ed. Cassell, 1972. xxi, 226 pp. £2.10), first published in 1963. The aim stated in the latter is to bridge the gap, for the Englishman, 'between the written word, as acquired from grammar books, and the living Spanish as spoken by a native'. The 1973 edition includes a Spanish–English dictionary, with commentary; special vocabularies; topics; and an English–Spanish cross-reference index.

The most common Spanish words and idioms, by H. J. Russell (2nd ed., revised and enlarged. Oxford University Press, 1946. 55 pp. £0.45), first published 1937, has a Spanish–English vocabulary of about 2,500 words, graded in five lists according to word frequency.

AUDIO-VISUAL MATERIAL

The following, a selection of British items from CILT's *Teaching materials for Spanish: recorded and audio-visual materials* (5th revised ed., 1973. 12, 3 pp. £0.25), are listed in descending price-order.

So far four stages have been completed of the *Adelante* course for secondary schools. Stages 1 and 2, prepared by the Spanish section of the Nuffield Foreign Language Teaching Materials Project (Macmillan Education, 1967–69. Stage 1: £44 + VAT; Stages 2a, 3b: £46.75 + VAT; £39.15 + VAT) consist of 38 units. The complete kit includes filmstrips, tapes, flashcards, posters, etc., plus teacher's books, readers and workbooks. Stages 3 and 4 have been prepared by the Spanish section of the Schools Council Modern Languages Project (E. J. Arnold, 971–72. Stage 3: £33.02 + VAT; stage 4: £41.40 + VAT). Text matter takes the form, in stage 3, of a magazine, *Pegaso* (10 issues), plus 4 readers, a grammar book and teacher's book. At stage 4 there is a pupil's book (*Zarzuela*) and a teacher's book. These are accompanied, at stage 3, by 10 filmstrips in colour on the regions of Spain, plus dialogues on 5 tapes (5″ reels, 3¾ ips, twin half-track); and at stage 4, by 14 filmstrips in colour on life in Spain and Spanish America, plus 6 tapes (5″ reel, 3¾ ips, twin half-track). The four stages bring the pupil up to 'O' level. According to *Modern languages* (v. 55, no. 4, December 1974, p. 204), the most commendable feature of *Adelante* is that 'it has all along been aimed particularly at the average and rather below-average pupil'.

The *Ealing course in Spanish*, produced under the direction of Philip Lock (Harlow, Longman, 1970), is, by contrast, for the able, mature student. It was first issued in 1967. Text matter consists of two books (36 units), each £1.35. This is for use with 22 filmstrips in colour, plus 25 tapes (texts) and 13 other tapes (drills), each 5″ reels, 3¾ ips, single top track.

Language laboratory pattern drills in Spanish: basic series, by R. P. Overy (Pitman, 1970) provides the text of the drills in 3 parts (42 lessons), at £1.25, and 20 tapes (recordings by native speakers) (4″ reels, 3¾ ips, twin half-track) at £60.00 + VAT.

The Linguaphone Institute provides two courses, one for Castilian Spanish and the other for South American Spanish. The former, *Curso de español*, is for beginners. Printed matter comprises 50 lessons (conversations, vocabularies and notes; Recorded materials consist of either 21 7″-records, 45 rpm, or four tapes (5″ reels, 3¾ ips, twin half-track) or 4 standard play compact cassettes, at a total cost of £49.50. The Spanish American course, also £49.50, has recorded material on records or cassettes only.

The PILL (Programmed Instruction Language Learning) course: *The Spanish language*, by B. Dutton and Gordon Rayment Programmes (World of Learning, 1966. £39.50) consists of text matter (basic grammar: vocabulary of c. 800 words, tests, etc.) and has recorded material on either three 12″ 33⅓ rpm records, or two tapes (5″ reels, 3¾ ips, twin half-track) or two cassettes.

El español hablado, by Hans Buisman and Alejandro Larona (Visaphone, 1964) provides an illustrated textbook with 60 short lessons, plus English translation and grammar book, and either 12 7″-records, 33⅓ rpm, at £11, or plus 3 tapes (5″ reels, twin half-track) at £11.50.

The BBC's *Vamos a ver* (1966) provides Spanish for beginners in 20 lessons, based on a narrative story first televised on BBC1 in 1967 and repeated in 1969. Text matter consists of the lessons, with grammar notes and vocabularies (176 pp. £0.40) and two 12″ LP records, 33⅓ rpm, each £1.05. Another BBC publication, *Zarabanda* (1971) has a textbook, with dialogues, vocabulary, grammar, drills and exercises (£0.55), recorded on two 12″ records, 33⅓ rpm., each £1.75. Alternatively, the textbook can be supported by teacher's notes, 100 colour slides and four tapes (5″ reels, 3¾ ips, twin half-track), at £31.50. A third BBC course, *Tal como es,* by Anne E. Ife (1972) is designed to follow on from *Zarabanda* and consists of 20 units in 2 books (interviews, vocabularies, grammar and exercises), each £0.35. Two 12″ records, 33⅓ rpm complement the text, each at £1.05.

Several of the school courses already mentioned are supported by recorded materials – those by L. D. Collier (tapes), J. P. Fitzgibbon (records), R. P. Littlewood (tapes or cassettes), J. R. Scarr (tapes) and Scarlyn Wilson (tapes).

GENERAL DICTIONARIES[1]

1. Bilingual

As a general-utility dictionary, *Collins' Spanish–English, English–Spanish dictionary,* compiled by Colin Smith in

[1] Criteria for foreign-language dictionaries have been enumerated in chapter 1. They include: accuracy, up-to-dateness, number of headwords, provision of aids to pronunciation and stress, inclusion of verb tables (at least), legibility plus portability, and reasonable price. In the case of Spanish and English dictionaries, Spanish–American vocabulary (preferably by country), and British and US usage, should be differentiated.

collaboration with N. B. Marcos and E. Chang-Rodriquez (Collins, 1971. xxxviii, 602, 640 pp. £4.50; £5.50, with thumb index), has much to recommend it. Each part has some 30,000 headwords. It features current idioms, stressing high-frequency words, and covers Spanish–American Spanish and North American English, as well as slang. 'My aim,' states Colin Smith, 'was to make a dictionary of modern current English and Spanish which ... should embrace no more than the typical *parole* or personal language of the average educated English speaker of 1970 and that of the corresponding speaker of Spanish'. E. M. Martínez Amador's *Standard Spanish–English dictionary*, and *Diccionário inglés español* (4. ed. Barcolona, Sopena; London, Bailey Bros. & Swinfen, 1958. 2 v. (2,166 pp.).) is another good two-way general dictionary, particularly rich in idioms and synonyms. Each volume has more than 60,000 headwords, including Latin–American.

The larger bilingual dictionaries extend their coverage to scientific and technical terms. *Appleton's New Cuyás English–Spanish and Spanish–English dictionary*, by Arturo Cuyás (5th ed., revised and enlarged. New York, Appleton, 1972. xxx, 689 pp.; xvi, 589 pp. $8.95), with some 130,000 entries in all, is essentially a detailed bilingual dictionary giving equivalents. (*Cassell's Spanish–English, English–Spanish dictionary*, by E. A. Peers and others. (6th ed. Cassell, 1962. xiv, 1,477 pp. £2.80) has annual new impressions that show few signs of extensive revision. It has been criticised[1] for owing 'more to Cuyás than it should'. Neither dictionary provides International Phonetic Alphabet (IPA) pronunciation for Spanish entry-words.

Simon and Schuster's International dictionary: English/Spanish, Spanish/English, edited by Tana de Gámez (New York, Simon & Schuster, 1973. xviii, 1,603 pp. $10.95), containing 200,000 entries in all, has poor typography but is up-to-date, has clear definitions and is reasonably priced.

The *Vox shorter Spanish and English dictionary*, edited by Bibliograf SA (Harrap, 1972. xxi, 1,416 pp. £3.90), with

---

[1] *Library journal*, v. 85, no. 4, 15th August 1960, p. 2805.

100,000 entries, has, like Cuyás, numbered applications of usage. One critic has stated that, 'Were it not for Smith ... [it] might stand comparison with most other single-volume dictionaries'. *Nuevo diccionario general inglés–español, español–inglés*, by U. di Benedetto, and other (Madrid, EDAFE, 1966. liv, [1], 1,495 pp; 18 1, 1,300 pp.) has some 100,000 headwords in each part and is intended primarily for Spaniards.

While conceding that Martínez Amador is much richer in ideas and Raventós (see below) more careful in distinguishing differences, the reviewer in *Modern languages* (v. 38, no. 3, September 1957, p. 118) considers that E. B. Williams' *Holt Spanish and English dictionary* (expanded ed. London, Nelson, [1974]. xvi, 621 pp.; lxv, 623 pp. £4.20) is very good 'as a practical guide of contemporary language, especially the scientific and technical'. It has some 115,000 entries in all. There is no IPA pronunciation for Spanish entry-words.

Of the shorter bilingual dictionaries, Margaret H. Raventós' *A modern Spanish dictionary* (English Universities Press, 1953. xx, 494, [5] pp.; 495–1,230 pp.), with 60,000 headwords in all, and many idioms and appendices, is recommended for sixth-form and university English-students of Spanish. It does not extend to Latin–American usage. On the other hand, *The University of Chicago Spanish dictionary: a new concise Spanish–English and English–Spanish dictionary of words and phrases*, compiled by Carlos Castillo and Otto F. Bond (Revised ed. University of Chicago Press, 1972. xlvi, 202 pp.; xii, 233 p. $9.50), first published in 1948, emphasises Latin American usage. Each part has some 15,000 headwords. There is no IPA pronunciation for Spanish entry words. *Langenscheidt's Standard dictionary of the English and Spanish languages*, by C. C. Smith, G. A. Davies and H. B. Hall (Hodder & Stoughton, 1966. 533, 474 pp. £2.40) is a cheap, reliable dictionary with some 15,000 headwords in each part, plus IPA pronunciation, syllabification and category symbols.

Duden español. Diccionario por la imagen (Mannheim Bibliographisches Institute; Harrap, 1963. 672, 111, 128 pp. £6.25) breaks new ground in providing 368 drawings, grouped by subject on verso pages, with numbered Spanish terms on pages facing, supported by Spanish and English indexes to the

25,000 terms. It is a valuable visual aid for learning and recognising grouped Spanish nouns.

2. Monolingual

Of the Spanish encyclopaedic dictionaries, pride of place must go to *Larousse universal diccionario enciclopédico en seis volúmenes. Adaptación hispanoamericano del 'Nouveau Larousse universel'* (Paris & Buenos Aires, Larousse, 1968. 6 v. illus.).

Apart from width of scope and 3,500 enlivening illustrations and coloured maps, its 2,000 pages include scientific and technical terms, as well as Latin American vocabulary. Quotations are given for rarer words and idioms. The single-volume *Pequeño Larousse ilustrado*, by R. G. Pelayo (Buenos Aires & Paris, Larousse, 1964. Rev. ed., 1974. viii, 1,663 pp. illus., maps. F53.95), based on *Petit Larousse*, has some 60,000 entries in dictionary and encyclopaeida sections, with 5,000 illustrations and maps. (The version with illustrations in colour – *Pequeño Larousse en color* – costs F112.25.) *Diccionario manual Sopena y enciclopedico e ilustrado* (Barcelona, Sopena, 1962. 2 v. (2,320, cxxxiv pp.) has a single sequence of entries, with more than 6,000 illustrations and maps. Parts of illustrated objects are helpfully keyed (*e.g.* the horse: 51 parts).

The (Real) Academia Española's *Diccionario de la lengua española* (19th ed. Madrid, Espasa–Calpe, 1970. xxiv, 1,424 pp.) is the authority for current Spanish usage, as well as for etymology. It is rich in examples. The Academy's *Diccionario manual e ilustrado de la lengua española* (2. ed. Madrid, Espasa–Calpe, 1950. ix, 1,572 pp.) is based on the 16th and 17th editions of the Academy's *Diccionario de la lengua española* and has some 4,000 illustrations, being superior in this respect to *Vox: diccionario general ilustrado de la lengua española* (2. ed., corr. y notablemente ampl. por D. Samuel Gili Gaya. Barcelona, Spes, 1953. xxxix, 1,815 pp.).

Spanish usage is thoroughly covered in Maria Moliner's *Diccionario de uso del español* (Madrid, Gredos, 1966–67. 2 v.); it has *c.* 40,000 headwords and is intended for non-Spanish speaking students of the language. Manuel Seco's *Diccionario de dudas y dificultades de la lengua española* (4. ed. Madrid, Aguilar, 1966. xx, 516 pp.) treats points in grammar, punctuation and spelling, as well as the Academy's rulings and American Spanish usage. In *Diccionario de Mejicanismos razonado* (Mexico, Porrua, 1959. xxiv, 1,197 pp.) comparison is made with usage in other American countries.

TECHNICAL & COMMERCIAL DICTIONARIES

3. Technical dictionaries

Specialised Spanish-and-English dictionaries are numerous. A handy list of 74 such dictionaries appears in the Canning House Library's *Portuguese and Spanish dictionaries* (The Luso-Brazilian Council, 1971. [iii], 22 pp.). It includes multilingual special dictionaries. Some of the best known are considered below.

Castilla's Spanish and English technical dictionary (3rd ed. Routledge & Kegan Paul, 1958. 2 v.) (v. 1: English–Spanish. xi, 1,611 pp.: *c.* 150,000 headwords; v. 2: Spanish–English. 1,137 pp.; *c.* 120,000 headwords) concentrates on engineering technology. In comprehensiveness it is second only to the three technical volumes of Lewis L. Sell – *English–Spanish comprehensive technical dictionary* (New York, London, McGraw-Hill, 1944. xii, 1,478 pp. $35; £14; *Section* 2. 1958 [3]. 1,079 pp. $35; £14), and *Español–inglés diccionario técnico completísimo* (New York, International Dictionary Co., 1949. xi, 1,706 pp. £16). These three bulky volumes claim to contain 525,000, 400,000 and 700,000 technical terms – not headwords, but entry-words plus equivalents. They include Latin American terms and differentiate between British and American English. The layout is daunting, entries being set solid, with little type-variation.

Chambers diccionario tecnológico, español–inglés, inglés–español ... dirigido por C. F. Tweney y L. E. C. Hughes. La traducción española ... dirigida por Carlos Botet (Barcelona, Omega, 1974. xv. 1,227, 287 pp.) is basically a translation of *Chamber's Technical dictionary* (which defines and categorises *c.* 60,000 scientific and technical terms). Entries include English translation of entry-words, and an English–Spanish dictionary of equivalents is appended.

More specialised are the companion volumes by Morris Goldberg – *Spanish–English chemical and medical dictionary* (New York, McGraw-Hill, 1952. viii, 609 pp. $17.50) and *English–Spanish chemical and medical dictionary* (New York, McGraw-Hill, 1947. ix, 692 pp. $15). The two parts comprise 30,000 and 35,000 headwords respectively, with definitions following equivalents.

4. Commercial dictionaries

Up-to-dateness is an important in this field as in the technical. A. F.-S. Giraud's *Diccionario comercial español–inglés, inglés–español. El secretario* (Nueva ed., revisada y ampliada. Barcelona, Editorial Juventud, S.A., 1965. 158, 137 pp. $9.95), first published in 1940, has some 4,000 headwords in each half. Particular attention is given to terms and phrases used in commercial correspondence. G. R. Macdonald's *Spanish–English and English–Spanish commercial dictionary* (5th ed., revised and enlarged. Pitman, 1944. xiv, 950 pp.) has no less than some 20,000 headwords in each part, being by no means confined to commercial terms; but it is rather dated. M. Moreno Pacheco's *Economic terminology, English–Spanish* (Munich, Hueber, 1967. 480 pp. DM24.80) has the advantage of both systematic and alphabetical vocabularies, plus translation exercises, and English and Spanish indexes, each with *c.* 6,000 entries.

Spanish commercial correspondence is covered in *Bilingual guide to business and commercial correspondence* (Spanish–English), by J. Harvard (Oxford, Pergamon Press; 1970. xiii, 224 pp. £3.80; £2), and *Manual of Spanish commercial correspondence* by, G. R. Macdonald (5th ed. London, Pitman, 1965. xii, 348 p. £0.50).

5

PORTUGUESE

Portuguse is rarely taught at secondary-school level in Britain. Full-time courses are, however, available at 23 universities, 5 polytechnics and 4 technical and other colleges.[1]

There are comparatively few Portuguese grammars, and such audio-visual aids as exist have particular relevance.

COURSES, GRAMMARS

1. For beginners

Colloquial Portuguese, by Maria Emilia de Alvelos Naar (2nd revised ed. Routledge & Kegan Paul, 1972. viii, 184 pp. £1.60; £0.85) provides the basic grammar, plus exercises and conversation, enabling the student, tourist or business man 'to learn and understand normal Portuguese, which is fast and full of contractions and liaisons', according to Tutor Tape Company's list of 'Miscellaneous recordings'. It is also used for first-year students in the Portuguese Language Committee's evening-classes at Canning House, London. Brazilian words and expressions are footnoted. Based on *Colloquial Portuguese* is a two-hour tape-recording by five members of the BBC Portuguese Section (two 5″ reels (£9.25) or two C.60 cassettes (£8.40), twin track. Tutor Tape Co., Ltd., 1972). Accompanying grammar and conversation drills – *Portuguese language laboratory exercises* – are also available from Tutor Tape Co. (six 5″ reels (£17.05) or six C.60 cassettes, (£15.50 single-track).

Alexander da R. Prista's *Essential Portuguese grammar* (New York, Dover; London, Constable, 1966. vi, 114 pp. £1.05) keeps strictly to its title: considerable space is devoted to the

---

[1] Centre for Information on Language Teaching and Research. *Language and culture guides. 15: Portuguese.* 1975, p. 1.

verb and there is an index to the grammar, but there are no hints on pronunciation and no end-vocabularies. It is therefore essential to use the book in conjunction with the Dover *Listen and learn Portuguese A/V course* (see page 73).

2. For more advanced users

R. C. Willis's *An essential course in modern Portuguese* (2nd revised ed. London, Harrap, 1972. 528 pp. £2.70) is a reliable course in 40 lessons, each consisting of grammar, vocabulary and exercises. First published in 1965, it aims to meet a long-standing demand – 'the need for an adult, reasonably detailed and up-to-date teaching grammar of the Portuguese language'. As such, it is primarily for first-year university students with no previous knowledge of Portuguese. Modelled on Ramsden's *Essential course in modern Spanish*, it has two-way end-vocabularies and an index to grammar. The two appendices deal with regular verbs and 'The Portuguese of Brazil'.

3. Self-tutors

J. W. Barker's *Teach yourself Portuguese* (New ed., edited and revised by L. Stringer. London, English Universities Press, 1962. 196 pp. £0.45) consists of 28 lessons (exercises; sentences, each way; conversation, reading and some correspondence. Matters of special difficulty, such as the personal infinitive, pronoun object and sequence of tenses, are fully dealt with. The end-vocabulary is Portuguese–English only.

Spoken Portuguese: basic course, by Margarida F. Reno and V. Cioffari New ed. (Boston, Mass. Heath, 1973. 2 books. $15.50) occupies 30 lessons (Book 1: units 1–12. $7) is thought highly of by the Modern Language Association of American (MLA *Selective list*, p. 70). It has the advantage of being accompanied by 6–12" LP $33\frac{1}{3}$ rpm records. The Record course, plus Book 1, costs $55. The alternative cassette course (Book 1 & 4-C.60 twin-tract cassettes) costs $65; the cassettes are also available separately at $60.50. Suppliers: Spoken Language Services, Ithaca, N.Y.

The Berlitz *Portuguese for travellers* (London, Berlitz, 1974.

£1.95) provides 2,000 useful words and 1,200 phrases, with a guide to shopping, eating out, tipping, sightseeing and relaxing. Pronunciation is simulated throughout, but a 33⅓ rpm disc, or a cassette, is available at £1.95.

4. Reference grammars

Of the grammars in Portuguese, *Gramática portuguêsa*, by J. Pereira Tavares (Lisbon, Livraria Sá da Costa, 1960. 272 pp.), used in Portuguese schools, has three parts, covering phonetics, morphology and syntax. Many examples of usage are drawn from classical and contemporary authors. There is an index to grammar. An up-to-date and recommended Portuguese grammar for Spanish-speaking students is *Gramática portuguêsa*, by P. V. Cuesta and Mendes da Luz (Madrid, Editorial Gredos, 1971).

5. Brazilian Portuguese grammars

M. de L. Sá Pereira's *Brazilian grammar* (Boston, Heath, 1948. 403 pp. illus., maps.) is 'primarily intended for students of Portuguese interested in Brazil'. Its 35 lessons (each of two 50-minutes periods) are essentially for class-room work; exercises cover drill, translation, reading and questions. The many examples of usage make it valuable also as a reference grammar.

P. C. Rossi's *Portuguese, the language of Brazil* (New York, Holt, Rinehart, Winston, 1945. 377, lxxxv pp. $5) is another general reference grammar, with reading passages (plus phonetic transcription) and realistic dialogues. Appendices, on modern spelling and accentuation, are particularly clear and complete. There are two-way vocabularies and an index to grammar.

6. Commercial correspondence

W. N. Cornett's *Portuguese commercial correspondence and technicalities, etc.*, revised in conformity with the official Portuguese orthography by Professor J. Teixeira (Hirschfeld, 1949, vi, [1], 176 pp. £0.25), deals with 28 topics, from 'opening phrases', 'closing phrases', 'abbreviations' to 'money, weights and measures' and 'commercial products'. It gives examples of letters, usually in Portuguese, accounts forms and commercial documents, plus vocabularies.

AUDIO-VISUAL COURSES

The *Didier audio-visual Portuguese course*, by O. Baranda, and others, consists of a student's book (105 pp. £2.80) and filmstrip, and 4-C.60 twin-track cassettes (£12 + VAT). It is based on the 'structuro global' method of language teaching originally developed at the CREDIF (Centre de Recherche et d'Étude pour la Diffusion du français). The book consists of frame-by-frame reproductions of the filmstrip pictures, with their accompanying dialogue. A/V material is in 25 units.

Listen and learn Portuguese (New York, Dover: UK distributor: Constable) consists of 3-12" discs, 33⅓ rpm, and a manual ($8.95). The manual contains all the material recorded, plus subsidiary vocabulary and full index.

The Linguaphone home-study course, *Portuguese*, comprises textbooks and 4 standard-play compact cassettes (5" reels, 3¾ ips, twin-track) and costs £49.50.

The two-hour tape-recording that goes with *Colloquial Portuguese*, by Maria Emilia de Alvelos Naar, and the record or cassette course accompanying Reno-Cioffari's *Spoken Portuguese: basic course* have already been mentioned, on p. 70.

GENERAL DICTIONARIES[1]

1. Bilingual

Novo Michaelis dicionário ilustrado (São Paulo, Edições Melhoramentos; Wiesbaden, Brockhaus, 1958–61. 2 v. v. 1: Inglés–Português. xxxii, 1,123 pp.; v. 2: Português–Inglés. li,

---

[1] The Canning House Library's *Portuguese and Spanish dictionaries* (1971) lists 29 general and 43 special Portuguese dictionaries, entries for recommended items being asterisked.

1,320 pp each $8) has about 60,000 headwords in each volume, with more than 4,000 illustrations in all. The English–Portuguese volume is considered by the Modern Language Association of America to be by far the best dictionary in the market. The dictionary includes Brazilian Portuguese as well as both British and American English. But there is no guide to pronunciation.

As a Portuguese–English dictionary, M. M. Texeira de Oliveira's *Dicionário moderno português–inglês* (Revisto por Colin M. Bowker [and others]. Lisbon, Gomes & Rodrigues, 1954. 1,304 pp. £2.00) has much to commend it, being one of the fullest Portuguese–English dictionaries and particularly rich in idioms. Complementary to it in this respect is Armando de Morais' *Dicionário de inglês–português* (Oporto, Porto Editôra, 1966. 1,492 pp.), equally comprehsnsive and more up to date. Morais has revised J. Albino Ferreira's *Dicionário inglês–português, português–inglês* (ed. escolar. Oporto, Barreira, 1953–54. 2 v. in 1 (886, 896 pp.), a standard shorter two-way dictionary with *c*. 50,000 headwords. It includes Brazilian and technical terms.

The revised edition of James L. Taylor's *A Portuguese–English dictionary* (Stanford, Calif., Stanford University Press, 1970. xx, 655 pp. $15) claims to have *c*. 60,000 headwords. But, as compared with the first (1959) edition, it adds a mere 25–30 new entries, some 800 revised and expanded definitions, and some corrections. Taylor has no guide to pronunciation, whereas the comparable *New Appleton dictionary of the English and Portuguese languages*, by A. Houaiss and C. B. Avery. (New York, Appleton-Century-Crofts: Meredith, 1967. 2 v. xx, 636 pp.; xx, 665 pp. $11.75), provides IPA pronunciation and is two-way (with *c*. 60,000 headwords in each part), emphasising Portuguese 'as it is written and spoken in Brazil'.

The recent *English–Portuguese–English dictionary* is edited by Hygino Aliandro (São Paulo, Editorial McGraw-Hill, 1972. 2 v. (653 pp.; 496 pp. each £2.40). It has an American–English flavour, with *c*. 20,000 headwords in each part. Pocket-sized and plentiful in idioms, it would be a profitable purchase for the tourist or business man.

Cassell's Portuguese and English dictionary (incorporating Brazlian usage) is being compiled by R. C. Willis, and others.

2. Monolingual

The authoritative work is the *Grande dicionário da lingua portuguêsa* (10. ed., corrigida, multo aumentado e actualizada. Lisbon, Editorial Confluência, 1949–59. 12 v.), with copious apt quotations. V. 12 includes a summary of Portuguese grammar and a dictionary of names.

Candido de Figueiredo's *Dicionário da lingua portuguêsa* (10. ed. Lisbon, Bertrand, 1968 (reprint of 1949–50 ed.). 2 v. (1,341, 1,347 pp.) is particularly valuable as an etymological dictionary; it is also well stocked with quotations. *Dicionário de lingua portuguêsa ortoépico, ortográfico e etimolójico. Elaborado em rigorosa conformidade com as bases do Acordo ortográfico luso-brasileiro de 1945* (Oporto, Porto Editôra, (195–?]) is considered authoritative of its kind.

Brazilian Portuguese.

Two of the larger Brazilian Portuguese dictionaries are of first importance – the *Novo dicionário brasileiro Melhoramentos*, by Adalberto Prado E. Silva, and others (16. ed., revista: São Paulo, Melhoramentos, 1970. 5 v.), with illustrations; and the *Dicionário da lingua portuguêsa, elaborado ... a fin de ser submetido à Academia para as devidas alterações*, by A. Nascentes (Rio de Janeiro, Acaderria Brasileira de Letras, 1961–67. 4 v.).

Two manageable single-volume dictionaries are *Pequeno dicionário da lingua portuguêsa*, by Hildebrando de Lima and Gustavo Barroso (10. ed. Rio de Janeiro, Editôra Civilização Brasileira, 1961. 1,287 pp) and, modelled on the *Nouveau petit Larousse*, Jaime de Séguier's *Dicionário prático ilustrado. O pequeno Larousse português* (3. ed. Oporto, Lello & Irmão, 1964. 1966 pp. illus.; 1967 ed. [xii], 2,023, [3]p.), which has c. 100,000 entries and 6,000 illustrations.

TECHNICAL & COMMERCIAL
DICTIONARIES

Technical. Most of the general technical dictionaries are either English–Portuguese or else polyglot. The former include: *Dicionário de têrmos técnicos inglês-português*, by E. E. Fürstenau (Rio de Janeiro, Carneiro, 1974. 2 v. (1,158 pp.). £28); *English–Portuguese technical and idiomatic dictionary*, by Benjamin B. Fraenkel (Rio de Janeiro, Ediex Gráfica e Editôra, [1969). 471 pp. £8); and L. L. Sell's *English–Portuguese comprehensive technical dictionary* (New York & London, McGraw-Hill, 1953. iv, 1,168 pp. £23.30), which claims to have definitions of over 500,000 English technical works and expressions.

Dicionário de têrmos técnicos, by N. A. Buzzoni, and others (Lisbon, LI-BRA, (1968). 383 pp.), a strictly technical English–Portuguese dictionary, forms vol. 3 of the 4-volume *Grande dicionário*, by A. Cardoso Câmara, and others. (Vols. 1–2, non-technical, cover Portuguese–English (*c.* 30,000 headwords and English–Portuguese respectively: v. 4 – English verbs.)

Polyglot technical dictionaries include the six-language *Dicionário técnico polyglota: português–espanhol–francês–italiano–inglês–alemão–latim*, by M. F. da Silva de Medeiros (Lisbon, Gomes & Rodriques, 1968. 3 v. (xlvii, 4,410 pp.); 5 index vols. £60 + £55); and F. J. Buecken's *Vocabulário técnico: português–inglês–francês–alemão* (4. ed. São Paulo, Edições Melhoramentos [1967]. 600 pp.).

A two-way dictionary is *Technical dictionary, English–Portuguese and Portuguese–English*, compiled by A. Araújo (Rio de Janeiro, Livraria Freitas Bastos SA, 1964. 2 v. (616, 495 pp.).

Commercial. For Portuguese into English, these include: *Portuguese–English commercial and industrial phraseology*, by H. J. da S. Queiroz (distributed by Bailey Bros. & Swinfen, Folkestone, 1963. 2 v. £60) and J. Knox's *Dicionário de econômica, finanças, sociologia, comércio e relaões sindicais/Portuguese–English dictionary of economics, finance, sociology, commerce and labour relations* (Rio de Janeiro, Livraria Freitas

Bastos SA, 1968. xiv, 191, 76 pp.); and for English–Portuguese, *Dicionário inglês–português para economistas, elaborado para o escritório técnico de estudos econômicos do Banco do Nordeste do Brasil SA,* published the same firm (1960. 458 pp.). M. M. Netto's *Vocabulário de intercambio comercial* (Rio de Janeiro, Editôra Civilização Brasileira, 1961. 251 pp.) is a two-way commercial dictionary.

6

GERMAN

by MRS. MARGARET LODGE, B.A.

Since the previous edition of this *Guide* (1967), the researches into linguistic methods and the psychology of learning, coupled with secondary school reorganisation, increased foreign travel and interest in Germany, have released a real landslide of courses aimed at every conceivable level of intelligence and learning situation. No longer are pupils tied to grammar primers thinly disguised by artificial purpose-written reading-translation passages describing 'German life', but can have at their disposal the full range of media through which to absorb, almost by osmosis, living colloquial German with a useful vocabulary and a practical awareness of its grammar and syntax, ideally, at least. For, whereas a set of traditional textbooks would cost a school some £25 per class, the complete audio-visual outfit runs into three figures: a daunting prospect for schools everywhere facing severe cuts in staffing as well as financial resources. Nor has Britain's entry into the European Community provoked an appropriate realisation, let alone official policy, as to the need for wider language skills. Despite the fact, too, that apart from the recognised German-speaking countries of Austria and Switzerland, German is a kind of lingua franca in Scandinavia and in East European countries, from Russia to Turkey, and further afield, it is in most schools still a minority language compared to French, at least where financial and material resources are concerned. However, the encouragement offered to less able learners by the CSE and gradually relaxing 'O' Level examinations is echoed in the many attractive courses now available, together with a plethora of readers, magazines, discs and other supplementary materials, too many even to list here.

In compiling this bibliography it has been a case of being spoilt for choice, 'wer die Wahl hat, hat die Qual', especially

among the many and varied courses pouring in from the Hueber
Verlag and other German publishers, so only brief mention, if
any, has been made of the older and more traditional courses,
for which however, there is still some call, not only in the few
surviving traditional schools where German is confined to two
or even one year before 'O' Level, but by adults and home
learners who want to consolidate 'tourists' German'. Moreover
the dividing line between text-book and audio-visual courses is
not often clear, since many books of texts can be used independently of all the other aids – as, in view of the cost, they
frequently have to be. This applies to some reference grammars
which also have audio adjuncts. As to specialist material (for
scientists, businessmen, etc.) this again is often covered in some
of the courses geared to adults or Further Education classes, or
helped by smaller vocabulary lists. Altogether, the approach to
lexicography shows similar changes, and the encyclopaedia-type
of dictionary, from the *Kinder-Duden* to the *Sprachbrockhaus*,
is gaining ground, while smaller works concentrate on individual
aspects such as word-formation, colloquial style or synonyms.

COURSES & GRAMMARS

For beginners

Komm Bitte! by Hermann Schuh (London, European
Schoolbooks, 1973. Lehrerhandbuch. 268 pp. £4.65; Wand-
bilder and Masken: 86 pictures and 12 masks, b/w $11\frac{1}{4}'' \times 8\frac{1}{4}''$.
£8.60; Szenen aus dem Alltag: $4\frac{1}{4}''$ tape, 17 minutes. £4.50;
Schreiben: workbook: 68 pp. £1.35; Leseheft 1, 2, & 3: each *c.*
80 pp. £1.55; Texte aus den Lescheften: 5" tape, 24 minutes.
£5.30. Bild & Wort, ein Bildwörterbuch. 144 pp. £2.10) was first
designed as an intensive course for children of *Gastarbeiter*. But
it could be used in primary schools or with mixed ability first-
year beginners. Via the teacher's book it introduces 250
vocabulary items and the chief structures, first purely orally and
then proceeding rapidly to reading and writing, listening comprehension and games. The *Bildwörterbuch* exploits and
expands this *Kernkurs* but, thanks to its many clear, simple and

amusing line-drawings, it could be used independently to supplement any course.

For CSE

A. Cockburn's *Practice in German for the CSE* (London, Harrap, 1972, 136 pp. £0.70) is the first and so far only book to offer varied practice and training for CSE requirements only. Its 7 sections contain: (1) 15 passages for aural comprehension, with 10 questions; (2) 20 German passages for written comprehension; (3) 20 dictation passages; (4) titles, topics and 6 sets of picture stories, with vocabulary notes for composition; (5) 15 passages for translation into English; (6) 15 passages, each with multiple-choice questions; (7) 235 questions on various topics. There is a German–English summary-vocabulary for the translation and written comprehension sections. Also suitable for 'O' level classes.

An agreeable runner-up to the bare realities of Cockburn's Practice in German is *Die Familie Neumann*, by Evelyn M. Dodkins (London, Macmillan, 1967. xviii, 141 pp. £0.60), a beginner's course leading to CSE, beginning with a useful short teacher's guide. Each lesson is entirely in German, with line drawings followed by exercises on points of grammar and questions on the text. Songs and suggestions for games, then a handy summary of grammar and 'How the language works', with helpful drawings explaining the German examples. A German–English end-vocabulary of *c.* 1,000 items.

Jack Stevenson's *Ich Kann's! An illustrated German course* (London, Bell, 1974–75. Book 1: 123 pp. £1.60; Book 2: 140 pp. £2.25) is a sensible, well-graded guide through the first years of German. It is suitable for mixed abilities, presenting limited material – about 8 items per lesson – and ample revision. The teaching situations are simple and rational, without too many texts, rules or exercises, but with plenty of scope for developing comprehensive conversation and personal situations. Book 2 demonstrates the meaning and function of language in each chapter without grammar explanations, but there is a 24-page grammar section and an index of grammar covered under chapter headings.

Moderner Deutschkurs, edited by Eie Ericson and Christina Eisenberg; [English version] edited and adapted by Donald F. Macgregor and Alexander Mackenzie (Edinburgh & London, Chambers, 1970), first appeared in Sweden as the *Fünf–Länder Kurs*, and in its English adaptation is suitable for pupils of all abilities. It is attractively set out, with clear illustrations and grammar presented on a structural basis. (Book 1. Wir fangen an: 140 pp. £0.95; Übungsheft: 46 pp. £0.30. Book 2. Die Sondermarke: 100 pp. £0.75; Übungshefte: 109 pp. £0.40. Book 3. Wir gehen weiter: 140 pp. £0.80; Übungsheft: 110 pp. £0.40. Book 4. Wir sind soweit, and Übungsheft – in preparation). From Book 2 a more continuous theme is introduced to maintain interest and application despite mounting linguistic difficulties. Each lesson has its own list of words and expressions; in Book 1 the genders are introduced in 3 colours. Each volume has its grammar summary and ample German–English end vocabulary. The Übungshefte include mini-crosswords and other puzzles and guessing games, as well as the usual structural and completion exercises. (Book 3 was not available for examination.)

E. Orton's *Auf Deutsch, bitte!* (London, Harrap, 1966. 2 v. v. 1 (reprint of 1959 ed.). 138 p. £0.60; v. 2 (reprint of 1963 ed.). 142 p £0.60) is aimed at pupils in comprehensive and secondary modern schools. It presents the minimum of grammar as such, preferring constant reptition of structural forms. Texts mostly in dialogues, giving a lively impression of German life, with many oral and written exercises, including dictations based on reading matter, and a few translations to give a sense of achievement. Based on an English boy's visit to Germany, it gives letters, games, competitions, humorous and factual illustrations, and 'Spike's Germany diary', for quick reading.

For 'O' level

A well-established course that could be described as the definitive series of immense value to teacher and pupil alike is *Deutsche Sprachlehre für Ausländer*, by Heinz Griesbach and Dora Schulz (Munich, Hueber; London, European Schoolbooks, 1968, first published 1929). (One-volume edition: Textbook. 264 pp. £2.20; Teacher's book. 84 pp. £1.05; German–English glossary. 72 pp. £0.79; Reader. 67 pp. £0.87; Schülerheft (contrastive grammar German–English): 77pp £1.12; 3 gramophone records, containing texts from the first 30 lessons. £3.90; 4 tape-recordings, containing the 44 texts of the textbook, and pronunciation exercises. £51.75; Sprechübungen. 9 single-track tapes. £112.50; Dikattexte 1. 47 pp. £0.48; Diktattexte 2. 47 pp. £0.58; 1 tape-recording to Dikattexte 1. £14.15; 2 Tape-recordings to Dikattexte 2. £22.95.) (Two-volume edition: Textbook. 150 pp. £1.55; Teaching supplement, phraseological glossary, key. 139 pp. £1.05; 2 tape-recordings, containing reading texts and exercises from the textbook. £18.90; Sprechübungen. 5 tapes. £52.50; Textheft zu den Sprechübungen. 180 pp. £1.05). This course is designed to introduce the student rapidly to oral and written fluency, whatever the length of time available. The 26 lessons (31, in the 2-vol. edition) consist of reading passages, wordlists, grammar explanations, exercises and passages of wider background interest; structure drills encourage oral fluency, and revision is constant. The somewhat traditional exercises and lengthy chapters are enlivened by attractive illustrations, clear examples and diagrams. The end-index contains individual words and grammar points, with references to the lesson where they occur. Could be used in schools beyond 'O' level, or in further education or other intensive courses for adults.

Brangwyn Jones's *Lustiges Lernen* (London, University of London Press, 1965–67. Part 1: Es geht los. 89 pp. £0.50; Part 2: Es geht weiter: 182 pp. £1.10; Part 3: Am Ziel. 142 pp. £1.05) is an originally designed course attractive to less able pupils but containing full instruction to 'O' level. Quarto format (but too lightly bound to last), typescript and free-style lettering, humorous line-drawings, lavish photographic illustrations. Many grammar summaries throughout the text and at the end; even the subjunctive gets full treatment, but a lively picture of contemporary German life and popular topics (cars, football, food) emerges. Few exercises or comprehension questions in the text and no end-vocabularies, so that more work is required from teacher and pupils to consolidate and record items covered.

Simpler German course for first examinations, by A. and L. J. Russon (London, Longmans, 1969. 313 pp. £0.83), first published 1955, is a thorough and systematic grounding for 'O'-level pupils. It deals first with grammar, plus many examples, followed by groups of English sentences for translation as exercises in grammar. Section 3 gives English prose passages for translation, with many footnotes or back-references; section 4, some hints on free composition. Sections 5 and 6 contain German prose passages, adapted from Goethe, Schiller or Fontane, for translation, or comprehension question in English and German. Lists of grammar examples and wordtopics go far beyond the usual requirements of this stage, while the end vocabularies (*c.* 2,500 German–English, and *c.* 1,000 English–German items) again have many omissions. L. J. Russon's *Complete German course for first examinations* (London, Longmans, 1965. 369 pp. £0.90), a reprint of the 1953 edition, is the complete grammar course of which the previous course is a somewhat simpler form. It is modelled on Whitmarsh's French courses and offers wider – though no more modern – material and exercises. Well beyond 'O'-level requirements. A. and L. J. Russon's *A first German book* (London, Longmans, 1965. 220 pp. £0.50), a reprint of the 1959 edition, and *A second German book* (reprint of the 1961 ed. 272 p. £0.57) form a dry, intensive course to cover work up to 'O' level, with fast progression in reading matter, grammar and vocabulary, not helped by poor illustrations and humdrum topics. Restricted grammar summary but useful indexed references; incomplete two-way end-vocabulary. Possibly of use in two-year courses.

David Shotter's *Deutscher Sprachkurs* is a 3-volume course with audio-visual aids (Heinemann, 1973. Vol. 1. *Biberswald*: Teacher's book. 73 pp. £1; Pupil's book. 181 pp. £1; Overhead projector transparencies. £25 + VAT; 4-5″ tapes. £16 + VAT; texts of taped exercises and dialogues. 93 pp. £1. Vol. 2. *Unterwegs*: Pupil's book. £1.75; Teacher's book; 5″ tapes; overhead projector transparencies: texts of taped exercises and dialogues. Vol. 3– in preparation). This is a course suited to all abilities that will take students to 'O' level and beyond. The continuous theme is based on two families with teenage daughters, one a student and one at work, presented orally for listening and understanding, then speaking, reading and writing. Clear illustrations act as aids to vocabulary, items of which are explained and listed in each section, followed by repetition and rewording exercises, later progressing to letters and compositions. Although there is a clear comprehensive grammar summary at the end of each book, followed by a German–English vocabulary, there is no indication as to where grammar items, and structures are introduced in the course, nor does the material in each section make this clear, so the Teacher's book seems essential. The tapes include language-laboratory type exercises and conversation; the quality and choice of voices is variable but there are some interesting background noises. The transparencies consist of vocabulary strips with 4 overlays, presenting key situations in the book and more scope for exploiting the material.

Also in 3 volumes with audio-visual aids in *Wir lernen Deutsch*, by N. Paxton and R. J. Brake (London, English Universities Press, 1970–72. Pupil's book 1. 92 pp. £0.90; 5-5″ tapes. £5 + VAT; Pupils' book 2. 94 pp. £0.90; Teacher's hand-book. 60 pp. £1; 6 colour filmstrips. £3 + VAT; 5-5″ tapes. £5 + VAT; Pupils' book 3 126 pp. £0.85; Teacher's handbook. 32 pp. £0.85; 1-5″ tape. £6 + VAT). It is an attractively presented yet intensive course suited for higher ability pupils and adults. Vocabulary is introduced at 30 words a lesson in parts 1 and 2, 60 per lesson in part 3, totalling 2,800. General theme is of a German family in Essen, with many good photographical and linear illustrations, the latter to reinforce the audio-visual material, without which, however, the books could also be used. Texts are followed by completion and substitution exercises; part 3 offers topics and regular revision exercises for grammatical points. The Teacher's books to part 1 and 2 give hints on exploitation of material; part 3 helps with aural composition.

Similarly titled, *Wir lernen Deutsch. Unterrichtswerk für den Deutschunterricht im Ausland*, by Gerhart Mahler and Richard Schmitt (Frankfurt am Main, Diesterweg, 1964. Band 1. 228 pp. £1.52; Beiheft für die englische Sprache. 140 pp. £0.99. Band 2. 176 pp. £1.52; Wortschatz English zu Band 2. 56 pp. £0.59) is an attractively illustrated basic course written in German. Its supplements for English users include grammar, word-list and indexed references.

Roland Schäpers' *Deutsch 2000. Eine Einführung in die moderne Umgangsprache* (Munich, Hueber; London, European Schoolbooks, 1972) is a 3-part monolingual course designed for adults studying for the Zertifikat Deutsch als Fremdsprache by the Deutsch Volkshochschulverband, in collaboration with the Goethe Institet). (*Erste Unterrichtsstufe*. Lehrbuch Band 1. 168 pp. £1.75; Tonbänder: Sprechübungen 1. 7-5″ reels, 6¼ hours. £31.25; Asbeitbuch 1. 103 pp. £1.40; Lehrerheft. 76 pp. £0.78; Graded German reader 1. 52 pp £0.78; Tonband 1 (complete recording of text in pupil's book. £5.25, or cassettee; Filmstreifen. 8 b/w reproductions of illustrations to first 8 lessons of pupil's book. £15.05; Textheft. Sprechübungen 1. 168 pp. £1.25; Glossar Deutsch–Englisch 1. 48 pp. £0.74. *Zweite Unterrichtsstufe*. Lehrbuch Band 2. 168 pp. £1.95; Tonbänder. Sprechübungen 2. 8-5″ reels. 7¼ hours. £36.25; Textheft. Sprechübungen 2. 164 pp. £1.45; Glossar Deutsch–Englisch 2. 64 pp. £0.78. *Dritte Unterrichtsstufe*. Lehrbuch Band 3. 144 pp. DM.12. Lehrerheft. 56 pp. DM.4.) Apart from the pupil's text-book this includes optional materials like a workbook, glossary, tapes and filmstrips – although the course could be used quite effectively without these. The language presented is derived from various authentic sources rather than being purpose-written to illustrate a large variety of stimulating topics, with many lively line-drawings and relevant colour plates and maps. The course is based on but not restricted to a minimum vocabulary of 2,000 words and structures. The Glossary is not arranged alphabetically but in sections corresponding to each lesson, and it amply illustrates shades of meaning. The exercises after each lesson are varied and stimulate fluency in writing and speech. The subject-matter of all 3 stages is highly topical and conducive to interesting oral discussion as well as to free or 'guided' com-position. Vols. 2 and 3 would be valuable aids to 'A' level work, v. 3 also giving broad cultural-historical background.

Deutsch für die Mittelstufe, by Klaus Adler and Benno Steffens (Munich, Hueber; London, European Schoolbooks, 1974. Texte und Übungen. 260 p. £3.70; Arbeitsheft. 120 pp. £1.70; Lösungen und Transkriptionen and tape-recordings in preparation) is intended for students at school or business who have completed the three parts of *Deutsch 2000* (see foregoing paragraph), but it can be used independently. It aims to provide situations typical of a visit to Germany, using 7 *Reihen* from which are developed questions on the text, discussions and exercises to consolidate and develop vocabulary and grammar, with charts and drills on structures and comprehension. Each basic text is supported by many good and varied illustrations, advertisements, menus, maps, etc., and by full notes on Germany's past and present.

German for the Vth form, by E. A. W. Pritchard (London, Bell, 1975. 262 pp.) is a useful little course aimed at all abilities, with a personal touch in sections entitled 'How to answer questions', using pictures, 'How to do well with your essays', 'How to do well in the oral test', using pictures and role–play situations. Grammar is not stressed, but there is a reliable grammar section of 45 pages, with 15 pages of exercises, covering verbs, word order, nouns and pronouns, cases, adjectives, illustrated by useful phrases (the passive is done by identification exercises); all with cross-references. Written work includes letters, 'directions for use' as regards style, and there are passages from various examination boards as well as topical and anecdotal texts culled from good contemporary writers. German–English vocabulary of *c.* 2,500 items.

From the German Democratic Republic comes the Herder Institut's *Deutsch, ein Lehrbuch für Ausländer* (Leipzig, VEB Verlag Enzyklopädie, 1970. Vol. 1. 616 pp. £1.50; vol. 2. 222 pp. £1.10; vol. 2A. Texts and exercises. 452 pp. + Word List. £1.45). The plain binding and poor paper belie the quality of the contents, a thorough and comprehensive course to meet all requirements. There are few line or photographic illustrations, but the use of coloured lettering makes syntactical and structural points clear. The textual matter in vols. 1 and 2 deals with most everyday and family situations, with the – to us – added piquancy of the DDR flavour, as seen also in the 3 maps and 3 of the 6 songs at the end of the book, which also includes an indexed word-list. Vol. 2A deals with specialised texts such as physics, mathematics, chemistry, biology, and their relationship with industry. The course is introduced by a short teacher's guide which can be supplemented by the *Schlüssel*.

Two courses on traditional lines are those by Baber and Savigny. D. C. Baber's *Mach mit! A German course to 'O' level* (London, Nelson, 1968–71. 3 v. vol. 1. 182 pp. £0.70; vol. 2. 244 pp. £0.90; vol. 3. 300 pp. £1) is somewhat enlivened by b/w illustrations and a few good photographs, poems and songs. The usual grammar instruction and drills in the usual guise of life with a German family. Book 2 introduces translation into German; Book 3 has translation passages from 'O'-level papers. Maps on end-papers; each volume has a grammar summary, word-lists for each chapters, and a German–English end-vocabulary. W. B. Savigny and W. C. Mitchell's *Frisch auf! A German course for the 'O' level examination* (London, Harrap, 1967. 236 pp. £0.75), a reprint of the 1959 edition, is a traditional book for able pupils on short courses, giving a grammar summary, graded exercises and prose passages for translation from and into German and for comprehension. There are also dictation passages and suggestions for free composition, and a two-way end-vocabulary.

A. S. McPherson's *Deutsches Leben* (Revised ed. London, Ginn, 1966. Part 1 (reprint of 1956 ed.). 205 pp. £0.53; Part 2 (reprint of 1961 ed. 272 pp. £0.70; Part 3 (reprint of 1965 ed. 288 pp. £0.75). Despite updating with some quite attractive contemporary material, especially in Part 3, this course is possibly still too academic for wider abilities in comprehensive schools, particularly in competition with newer purpose-compiled courses. Part 1 introduces 4 new Lesestücke and a new way with noun plurals; part 2 is completely rewritten and well illustrated, while part 3 introduces writers like Brecht, Böll and Morgenstern. Each part has a German–English vocabulary, and parts 2 and 3 also an English–German vocabulary. There are also maps as end-papers.

E. A. Greatwood's *School German course* (London, University Tutorial Press, 1969. 390 pp. £0.85), a reprint of the 1959 edition, is not often found in schools, except where 'O' level German is crammed into 2 years or even 1 year. Grammatically thorough and sound. The German texts, though still abounding in errors, cover the usual everyday topics, and provide grammar and vocabulary exercises and suggestions for essays. No grammar summary, but an index, notes on declensions and word order, plus verb lists. German–English end-vocabulary of *c.* 1,600 items.

Self-tutors; courses for adults

W. E. Anderson's *Das schöne Deutschland*, 1 & 2 (London, Harrap, 1956, reprinted 1967. Part 1: 204 pp. £0.65; part 2: 192 pp. £0.65) is intended for adult beginners or those with some knowledge of German. It contains a thorough grounding in syntax and grammar, embedded in lengthy texts dealing with typical tourist situations and relevant idioms. Book 2 consists of a scenic tour of Germany, with photographic illustrations. Each volume comprises 20 lessons. (The same author's *Aufenthalt in Deutschland*, 1 & 2 (London, Harrap, 1949 (recently re-issued). Part 1: 191 pp. £0.60; part 2: 166 pp. £0.60) is still a widely-used cram-book, with sparse and artificial reading and translation matter replete with grammar examples. Traditional grammar drills and ample revision material.)

All-purpose German for adults, by Charles Duff and Paul Stamford, is sub-titled 'A comprehensive course on modern lines designed for beginners and others; for self-tuition or classes, and graduated progressively to university standard (2nd revised edition. London, English Universities Press, 1966. xviii, 19–375 pp. £0.65 paperback reprint of 1967 ed.). Part 1 is a graded introduction to grammar and basic vocabulary, using purpose-written texts or extracts from *Til Eulenspiegel*, with line-by-line translations. Part 2 continues similarly using longer continuous translated reading matter. The book ends with a verb list and a German–English vocabulary of *c.* 300 items. Another useful comprehensive course, especially for self-tuition and evening classes, is *German made simple*, by E. Jackson and A. Geiger (London, W. H. Allen, 1968. 273 pp. (Made simple books). £0.95). 43 graded lessons on everyday topics (including climate, cinema, history, geography, cooking and business), followed by an English translation, a German–English word-list, grammar notes, questions and exercises. At the end, a key, a German–English vocabulary of *c.* 1,300 items and an English–German one of *c.* 700 items.

Still the outstanding and most popular beginners' book for evening classes or older beginners is Magda Kelber's *Heute Abend* (London, Ginn, 1948–49, revised 1964–66. Book 1: 304 pp. £0.80; book 2: 472 pp. £1.25; Book 1 Supplementary exercises: 111 pp. £0.38). It starts with long reading texts, in order to strike a balance between grammar and conversation, and the matter, on the usual topics, is easily remembered, being often in rhyming couplets. Humorous illustrations, proverbs and songs abound. Book 1 ends with grammar revision, weights and measures, and a two-way vocabulary of 1,500 and 1,700 items. Book 2 is on similar lines but includes long extracts from German novels, poems, plays and letters. It ends with a German–English vocabulary of *c.* 4,800 items and an English–German of *c.* 1,070. The Supplementary exercises give grammar drills based on Book 1 and, as it provides a full two-way vocabulary, could be used with other textbooks.

Heinz Griesbach and Dora Schulz's *Ich spreche Deutsch: eine zuverlässige Anleitung* (Munich, Hueber, 1965. 160 pp. £0.97) has the advantage of accompanying tapes, obtainable only from Germany. Not as extensive as the Audiovisueller Lehrgang of the same name (q.v.), it aims in 25 lessons at an introduction to German without formal grammar, to link possibly with later studies such as *Deutsche Sprachlehre für Ausländer* (see p. 81). Each lesson has a short introduction, a brief dialogue, a list of new vocabulary with examples of use, and a few completion or substitution exercises. Separate end-glossaries in English, French and Spanish, plus a short German index. Intended more for adults and home study than for schools.

Hans Schulz and Wilhelm Sundermeyer's *Deutsche Sprachlehre für Ausländer* (first published 1929. Munich, Hueber. 288 pp. (£1.80) is not a short version of the course of the same name by Griesbach and Schulz (see pp. 81–2), but a separate publication. Intended for adults with some previous knowledge of German which they want to improve quickly, it offers in its first part, 'Vorstufe – zur Wiederholung', a basic grounding of grammar and vocabulary. The second part, 'Grammatik und Übungen', covers main points of morphology and syntax, word formation and spelling, and ends with a verb list, tables of weights, measures and coins, and an index.

A traditional intensive course suitable for adults or grammar-school pupils on 2-year courses is J. A. Nicholson's *Praktisches Deutsch* (London, Harrap, 1966–67. 2 v. Vol. 1 (reprint of 1958 ed.): 198 pp. £0.70; vol. 2 (reprint of 1960 ed.): 303 pp. (£0.75) gives in both volumes ample grammar explanations, word-lists, exercises, dictation and reproduction passages, indexes and appendixes. Robert L. Politizer's *Reading German fluently* (Englewood Cliffs, N.J., Prentice-Hall, 1969. 328 pp. £2.90) aims to give practice in quick recognition of structures by means of completion and other exercises containing the elements of grammar. 30 lessons in 5 sections, reading passages illustrating grammar points and exercises. End verb-lists and a German–English vocabulary of 1,700 items. This course is useful for private study and can be supplemented by Politizer's *Speaking German* (328 pp. £3.25), on similar lines and including aural comprehension.

For higher-ability pupils or adults there is a thorough, fast-moving course in L. Stringer's *A first German* (London, Teach Yourself Books, 1969, reprint of 1966 ed. 180 pp. £0.45. Reader: 117 pp. £0.40). Its amusing drawings and practical hints thinly disguise an intensive grammar course of 30 lessons, each starting with grammar points and a word-list, followed by traditional exercises and translations, and an end-vocabulary (German–English) of *c*. 450 words. Key to exercises. The reader can be used less as a supplement than a continuation, as it concentrates on basic and combined patterns of sentence construction, as an aid to comprehension and style. Excerpts include conversations, scientific and journalistic writing, SF and poetry, as well as contemporary fiction.

Suitable for further-education classes and more formal courses, Ekkehard Müller's *Menschen um Müller: lustiger Wiederholungskurs* (Stuttgart, Klett; London, European Schoolbooks, 1971. 79 pp. £0.78; 5″ tape or cassette. £4.45 + VAT) is a lively topical revision course, based on *c*. 1,000 words, and basic grammar and syntax. There is a grammar index and a few exercises per item. 23 of the texts are recorded. *German once a week*, by H. Eichinger, M. Grinvalds and E. Baryon (Oxford, Blackwell, 1968–69. 2 v. Book 1 (1969). 127 pp. £0.40; book 2 (1968). 130 pp. £0.40) is also intended for adult students in further-education classes, but it could be used by more advanced school-pupils. A thorough course, traditional in material and presentation, with scope for written and spoken exercises, revision and learning by heart. Lists of verbs and German–English vocabularies. (P. Prager asserts that his *German dialogues for adult beginners* (Oxford, Blackwell, 1963. 35 pp. £0.40) provides suitable supplementary material for reading and oral work.)

Sprich mal Deutsch! by W. Rowlinson (London, Oxford University Press, 1967–69. 3 v. Part 1. 188 pp. £0.80; part 2. 206 pp. £0.85; part 3, 208 pp. £0.85) has drawbacks. Recorded material for each part offers the same matter – part-readings of the texts, selected exercises from the book – on single or twin-track tapes for class or laboratory use, or on cassettes or disc. Quality of recordings and the smudgy drawings in the text are not attractive or stimulating enough to qualify this course as 'audio-visual', and one can only account for its presence in so many schools by the assumption that it was the first to make this claim on the British market at a reasonable price. Pupils of all abilities and also teachers find its presentation of vocabulary and grammar confusing, its two-way end vocabularies incomplete and the grammar summaries inadequate.

Another course by Heinz Griesbach – *Deutsch mal 3* (Berlin, Langenscheidt, 1974. 3 v. DM.15.40) – is intended for evening classes, emphasising the development of listening and reading skills, oral and written use of the language, 'ohne theoretische Grammatik'. Lernstufe A consists of Lernbuch, Lernheft, Glossar, Sprechübungen, Lösungsheft. B: Übungsbuch. C: Gesprächsheft. D: Lesehefte. By judicious mixing, the student can aim at (a) a basic course, (b) Zertifikatdeutsch als Fremdsprache, (c) conversation course, (d) reading course, or a comprehensive course for more intensive study. Records, cassettes and visual material are also available. Lehrstufe 1 contains 875 lexical items and a formidable amount of grammar. Scope for oral work is more for repetition than original expression.

Deutsch für Sie, by Ursula Förster and Heinrich Gertraud is in 3 volumes (Leipzig, VEB Verlag Enzyklopädie, 1969. Textbook. 264 pp. £1.80; Beiheft: Erläuterungen, Schüssel,

Wörterverzeichnis. 77 p. £1.80; junterrichtshilfen. 162 pp.
£0.60). Despite its appearance, earnest approach and lengthy
lessons, this is a not unattractive all-purpose course for self-
study and intensive work, as well as for more leisurely class-
work. Each of the 24 lessons starts with a dialogue on basic
texts on general topics, followed by exercises and model
sentences to illustrate grammatical points, all presented in German only. The *Beiheft* lists all new words and expressions, with
grammar explanations in German, French and English, for each
lesson, and a German word index referring to the lessons in
which the words first appear. The teacher's book is helpful but
not essential.

How to read German: a short cut for non-linguists, by M. H.
Law (London, Hutchinson Educational, 1964. 252 pp. £0.90) is
a pleasant introduction to well-written contemporary prose on
practical topics, the first 8 passages having English translations.
Part 1 has 21 chapters and 4 revision lessons, also grammar and
vocabulary building. Part 2 gives weights and measures, abbreviations and grammar summaries, with vocabulary building.
Part 3 gives graded supplementary reading passages and ends
with a verb list and a German–English vocabulary of *c.* 3,750
items.

Und so weiter, by C. Keith Butler (London, Pitman, 1967.
170 pp. £1) is intended for evening classes and technical
colleges, aiming at written and spoken fluency. Each chapter introduces vocabulary via pictures (totalling *c.* 1,000 items). Simple consolidating grammar exercises; an end-word-list, German–English, and a grammar summary with clear chapter
references. *German for business studies*, F. Kershaw and S.
Russon (London, Longmans, 1971. £0.80) contains German
texts on all aspects of business, economics and industry, as well
as some general topics, including 4 on the DDR and 2 on Berlin.
Many comprehensive questions, and for each passage there is a
general question for discussion or essay writing. An excellent introduction and a German–German glossary of commercial
terms.

*A course in scientific German: German for technicians and
scientists*, by Hans Meinel (Munich, Hueber; London, European
Schoolbooks, 1974. 248 pp. £4.65) is based on the ideal of

passive mastery of German by means of 41 extracts: 24 main texts faced by grammar explanations, and 17 supplementary texts for practice and reproduction. There are also verb lists and a bibliography; the grammar and specialised vocabulary are explained in English.

Advanced courses

Advanced modern German, by F. Kellet (London, University of London Press, 1964. 446 pp. £1.40; Specimen German translations. 1965. 64 pp. £0.32) usefully bridges the gap between 'O' and 'A' level German, as its reference grammar contains much basic material and good notes on vocabulary and idiom. Its independent sections also include 70 prose passages for translation into German and 80 for translation into English; poems for appreciation, 15 essay subjects and outlines, German–English vocabulary of 2,300 and English–German vocabulary of 1,300 items. (The German translation of the 70 prose passages is available to teachers only.) W. B. Savigny's *A sixth form German course* (London, Harrap, 1965 (reprint of 1962 ed.). 276 pp. £0.90) is a useful book, starting with a grammar survey, with many idiomatic examples followed by revision exercises. There are 45 passages from modern English authors on contemporary topics, for translation into German and 45 modern German prose-passages, as well as some modern poetry for appreciation. The problems of essay writing are discussed and 45 titles suggested. The two-way end-vocabulary totals some 2,000 items.

Heinz Griesbach's *Deutsch für Fortgeschrittene* (Munich, Hueber, 1971; London, European Schoolbooks, 1974) is a series intended for advanced students (Moderne Welt 1. 124 pp. £1.45; Moderne Welt 2. 133 pp. £1.65; Ernste and Heitere Erzählungen. 122 pp. £1.65; Humor and Satire. 111 pp. £1.65; Sprachheft 1 (oral practice for grammar, functions and sentence structures). 174 pp. £2.25; Sprachheft 2 (in preparation); Deutsche Grammatik im Überblick (tables, lists and revision). 130 pp. £1.75). By means of texts and exercises dealing with the modern world – literature, business, politics, technology – the student is encouraged to discuss and express himself in speech and writing. Questions after each text consolidate comprehension; further exercises encourage the use of specialist vocabulary by restating information. The Sprachhefte provide flexible syntactical and semantic angles; the grammar book contains rules and tables, with plenty of examples, also conjugation and declension tables, alphabetical lists, sentence structure and word order.

Advanced German course, by A. and L. J. Russon (London, Longmans, 1965. 426 pp. £1.25; Key to part 3 of textbook. 96 pp. £0.75) is geared to 'A' and 'S'-level work, an intensive course concentrating on literary rather than colloquial language. The first section, 'Grammar and syntax' (118 pp.) lists the points relevant to the 120 English prose-passages of section 3, as well as the exercises of section 2, with copious footnotes for back-reference. The following 145 German prose and 40 German poetry passages, the 125 essay-suggestions are supported only by an inadequate end-vocabulary. Many of the 41 German prose and 39 verse passages for 'comment and appreciation' are unidentified.

E. P. Dickens' *German for advanced students* (London, Oxford University Press, 1966. 320 pp. £1) is a graded 3-year course for 'A' and 'S'-level students. Part 1 offers 18 historical and political as well as cultural topics, serving grammar points and giving 2 relevant German passages from contemporary authors, 1 English passage, 8 English sentences for translation, suggestions for essays and discussions, and 2 non-grammar revision exercises. Part 2 gives prose passages and poems for translation into English and German, also essay subjects and a grammar section with textual references. Part 3 contains German prose passages and poems for comprehension and criticism, and some English passages for translation. No end-vocabulary but ample footnotes and topical vocabulary guides, especially in part 1.

Hilmar Kortmann's *Richtiges Deutsch* (Munich, Hueber; London, European Schoolbooks, 1973. 92 pp. £1.55; Key 44 pp. £0.78) is a series of written exercises on grammatical structures for university or college of education students. Each chapter has grammar notes, a text for analysis, and exercises of the gap-filling or replacement kind, as well as objective tests, but the range of topics is too narrow for background work. An index states the standards of difficulty. K. C. Horton's *German stylistic exercises* (London, European Schoolbooks, 1968. 49 pp. £0.35) aims to familiarise post 'O'-level students with common verbs, adjectives and nouns followed by prepositions. Additional verbs, etc. are listed and consolidated by means of completion and translation exercises, ingenious and amusing dialogues.

REFERENCE GRAMMARS

Of the elementary-to-intermediate reference grammars, J. A. Pfeffer's *German review grammar* (Boston, Mass., Heath, 1961. xii, 270 pp. illus) has several points in its favour. It is a systematic and thorough first grammar, backed by exercises, reading matter, questions and idioms.

Reference grammars should be well indexed, and this certainly applies to F. Clarke's *German grammar for revision and reference* (London, Bell, 1966. vi, 234 pp. £0.60), a reprint of the 1936 edition, and thus the German is in Gothic type. It is useful for pupils during 'O' level year; and the same is true of J. A. Corbett's *Essentials of modern German grammar* (London, Harrap, 1965. 270 pp. £0.75), a reprint of the 1948 edition, first published in 1935, and again the German is in Gothic type. Corbett is sufficiently updated to be still of value to 'O'-level students and beyond, and it is particularly helpful on differences in usage in German and English, C. B. Johnson's *Harrap's new German grammar; based on 'Harrap's modern German grammar' by W. H. van der Smissen and W. H. Fraser* (London, Harrap, 1971. 374 pp. £1.75) could be used for post 'O'-level work. It has more helpful illustrations than the van der Smissen and Fraser, without exercises and reading extracts. Examples are updated, and there are clear glossaries and explanations.

Of the slighter 'O'-level-revision reference grammars, H. G. Atkins' *Skeleton German grammar* (London, Blackie, 1970. 87 pp. £0.69), a reprint of the 1957 edition, still meets most needs. It provides a reliable basic grammar summary, using red type to emphasise points, exceptions, etc. J. E. Clapham's *Basic Ger-*

man grammar (London, Murray, 1971. 64 pp.) is another handy 'O' level revision summary fully contents-listed but without an index. Even more concise is *The fundamentals of German grammar on one card*, by G. A. Wells and B. A. Rowley (London, Arnold, 1963. £0.30), which reduces the essentials for revision – mainly declensions and conjugations – to the two sides of a 9″ × 12″ card, in very small type.

Mainly for sixth form university and teacher's use, A. E. Hammer's *German grammar and usage* (London, E. J. Arnold, 1971. 436 pp. £4.50, hardback; £2.95, paperback) is rich in examples and has a helpful index. A. K. Tyrer's *A programmed German grammar* (London, Methuen, 1965. 2 parts. 228 pp.; 160 pp. each £0.65), also a revision grammar, is less helpful in examples.) Herbert Lederer's *Reference grammar of the German language*; based on 'Grammatik der deutschen Sprache', by Dora Schulz and Heinz Griesbach (New York, Scribner's, 1969. 709 pp. £6.50, hardback; £4.50, paperback) is an adaptation of the German original, for American users. It emphasises parallels and contrasts between German and English, with added original matter and some omissions; some sections are rewritten in the light of more recent linguistic research. This is a thorough, comprehensive study, for university use. Frederick J. Stopp's *A manual of modern German* (London, University Tutorial Press, 1966. 619 pp. £2.10), a reprint of the 1960 edition and first published in 1957 is more valuable to university students as a reference grammar than as a course book. A thorough and scholarly work, its exercises consist mainly of disconnected sentences rather than passages, and there is no reading material. Part 1 contains two-way vocabularies; part 2 develops earlier material. The 5 appendices include verb lists and German grammatical terms; grammar points are numbered, with cross-references, and include subjunctive, and idiomatic uses of preposition. For experienced and dedicated linguists only.

Reference grammars published in German are particularly valuable. Hans Glinz's *Deutsche Grammatik 1* (Frankfurt an Main, Athenäum, 1970–71) is a guide for teachers and students alike, for reorientation and classroom presentation of grammar in the light of the linguistic theories, based on modern texts – from newspapers to Enzensberger. Selected passages could be used even for 'O'-level pupils on a comparative basis. Lack of an appendix or index is a drawback. Glinz's *Linguistische Grundbegriffe* (Athenäum, 1970–71) provides selected texts for operational analysis and independent study.

Deutsche Wirtschaftssprache für Ausländer, by Franz Bäumchen (Munich, Hueber/European Schoolbooks, 1973. 260 pp. DM.18.50) is intended for those already familiar with economic terms in their own language, and 6th form-level German. Each of the 19 chapters is divided into 3 sections of material presentation, the last usually in the form of business letters and comprehension passages. Grammar treatment is based on Schulz-Griesbach terminology. 85 pages of *Wörterverzeichnis*; also verb groups and examples. A sequel is: Lechner, Manfred. *Deutsche Grammatik in Sprechsituationen* (Munich, Hueber/European Schoolbooks, 1974. Textheft: 103 pp. £1.12; Tonbandübungen: 6 tapes; 215 minutes. £57).

Duden. Grammatik der deutschen Gegenwartssprache, edited by Paul Grebe and others (2., vermehrte und verbesserte Aufl. Mannheim, Bibliographisches Institut: London, Harrap, 1966. 774 pp. £3.20) is an extremely useful reference work for advanced students, with a particularly helpful 'Wörtregister und Register für Zweifelsfragen'. *Grammatik der deutschen Sprache*, by Dora Schulz and Heinz Griesbach (Neubearb. von H. Griesbach, Munich, Hueber; London, Longman, 1972. 475 pp. £1.75), referred to above (under 'Lederer') is a standard reference work for 'A' level and beyond, complete with word and content indexes.

Finally in this group – *Inhalte und Ausdrucksformen der deutschen Sprache. Lehrgang für Ausländer mit Vorkenntnissen der Elementargrammatik*, by Alfred Hoppe (5 Aufl. Frankfurt am Main, Diesterweg. 156 pp. DM.6.60), for advanced and dedicated students. All explanations are in German, with 211 Übungen illustrating morphology and syntax, while the study of grammar is linked to word-formation. Plenty of diagrams and illustrations.

Special points in revision. Sentence structure is dealt with in E. Orton's *Sprich mit! Deutsche Strukturen* (London, Harrap, 1972. 80 pp. £0.50), and in *German structure drills*, by J. C. Sager (London, Pitman, 1967. 228 pp. £1.75). For revision of verbs – *German verbs simplified: rules on the formation of tenses; tables for reference* (London, Hugo's Language Institute, 1969. 32 pp. £0.20), a helpful reference book and list. A basic vocabulary of 2,000 words is provided by H. Schuh's *2000 Wörter Deutsch und was man damit machen kann* (London, European Schoolbooks, 1974. 93 pp. £1.90. Lehrerhaft: 62 pp. £0.93), while *German vocabulary in context*, by A. and J. L. Russon (London, Longman, 1970. 86 pp. £0.35) offers 'a progressive vocabulary for conversation and free composition.'

Beyond the dictionary in German: a handbook of colloquial usage, by B. Anderson and M. North (London, Cassell, 1968. 171 pp. £0.80) is a handy revision book for pre- and post-'O'-level students. It has notes on pronunciation, current usage, verbs and compound nouns, an alphabetical word-list with helpful examples: also, 'false friends', journalese and handy tourist-type expressions, and an English–German cross-reference index.

Drills, exercises and tests are the subject of: G. J. W. Lawson's *Language laboratory pattern drills in German: basic series* (London, Pitman, 1966. 120 pp. £1.50; tapes available), and *Language laboratory pattern drills for beginners*, by A. and L. J. Russon (London, Longmans, 1969. 74 pp. £0.50; tapes available); H. N. Winter's *Fluency in German* (London, Longmans, Green, 1964. 2 v. each 124 pp.), with hundreds of exercises on grammar and vocabulary, but no key; and *Wörter zur Wahl*, by Ferenbach and Schüssler (European Schoolbooks, 1974. 160 pp. £1.95)– for the objective comprehension tests now introduced by many examining boards, for 'O' level, CSE and beyond.

RECORDED & AUDIO-VISUAL AIDS

For beginners

Grüss Gott, Liebe Kinder! Schallplatten Deutschkurs für Kinder, by Hartwig Löffler (European Schoolbooks, 1969. Notes and suggestions for parents and teachers. p. 4; with Pupil's book 86 pp. Complete with 5–7″ tapes or cassettes. £5.25) is for younger children at home or in primary school. The sequel is *Guten Tag, Jungen und Mädchen! Kleiner Deutschkurs mit Schallplatten für Kinder. Mittelstufe* (European Schoolbooks, 1969. Pupil's book, notes and 8-7" tapes or cassette. £6.75), with text mainly in dialogue form.

Los! by Rosemary Davidson and Marianne Calmann, with S. R. Ingram (Ingram, 1964. Teacher's notes; 30 working scripts and 15-7" discs per year; £8.00 per year + VAT; scripts separately, £3.75 per year (10 copies each of 30 scripts)) is a 2-year course for young beginners, 30 lessons a year. Discs are accompanied by weekly working scripts full of lively drawings, games, songs and things to do. An encouraging start for lower abilities and in the primary school.

Ich Spreche Deutsch: ein audiovisueller Lehrgang, by Heinz Griesbach and Dora Schulz (Munich, Hueber, 1966; Interbook. Teacher's guide, gratis; Textbook. 1973. 83 pp. DM.13.40; Glossar, Englisch. 12 pp. DM.4.80; 24 filmstrips (DM.296) or 457 slides (DM.420); 2-4" tapes (texts). DM.96; 4-6" tapes (drills). DM.220) is for all-ability secondary-school beginners, perhaps a little too elaborately set out and too many structural drills. Filmstrip pictures are also in the textbook. *Deutsch für Dich*, by H. Eckes (Munich, Hueber, 1974. Textbook. 118 pp. £2.38; Lehrerheft. £0.59; 74 flashcards. £9.90 + VAT; 1 tape, 47 minutes £10.90 + VAT. Transparencies for overhead projector and other material – in preparation) is aimed at children of Gastarbeiter in Germany. It could also be of benefit to primary school or mixed ability beginners, as the material and approach are attractive, non-dogmatic and conversational.

Frisch begonnen. German for beginners, by Stephen Kanocz (2nd ed. London, BBC, 1969. Teacher's notes, 1–10, plus 2–5¾ tapes. £10 + VAT; Teacher's notes, plus 2-5¾" tapes. £10 + VAT; Leseheft 1-10. 16 pp. £0.05; Lesebuch. 64 pp. £0.25; 20 colour filmstrips, lessons 1–10, 11–20, each set £11 + VAT; 30 colour flashcards each for lessons 1–10, 11–20. £3.50 + VAT; 2-5¾ tapes (exercises) each £2.61 + VAT). A popular and successful course (despite fairly intensive grammar and 1,400 high-frequency word vocabulary), adaptable to lower-ability pupils, though better suited to the first 3-5 terms of a grammar-school beginner's course. Thorough practice of listening, comprehension and speaking skills. The subject matter is homely but attractive and varied.

Longman's Audio-visual German. Stage 1 ('Herr Körner und seine Welt', by C. C. B. Wightwick and H. W. Strubelt. Pupils' book. £1.25; Teacher's book. £2. 8-5″ tapes. £31.50 + VAT; Wall pictures. *c.* £6 + VAT) is based on the familiar material of home, food, clothes, shopping and post, with entertaining text illustrations. No English is used except in the Kurze Grammatik at the end, with a German–English end-vocabulary of *c.* 1,250 items. It begins with 4 oral series, using the wall charts and introducing basic nouns, verbs and cases. The next 11 units gives longer reading passages and dialogues, followed by multiple choice comprehension tests, language, drills and lists of new words and expressions. Interspersed Abzählreime, Sprichwörter, Ausrufe and a poem by Morgenstern. Symbols at the top of each exercise guide the pupil and teacher as to the use of tapes and other aids, without which, however, the course could be used quite effectively. The tapes are of average quality and by native speakers; transcripts are in the teacher's book. Suitable for beginners of all abilities.

For 'O' level

Ealing course in German, by Una McNab, and others (London, Longman, 1969. Complete course. £42.50; Textbook (parts 1 and 2. 520 pp.). £3.80, or in 2 parts each £1.90; 5 colour filmstrips. £11.25 + VAT; 15-5″ tapes. £60 + VAT; 15-5″ tapes. £60 + VAT) is a thoroughly up-to-date course. It is set out in 38 Abschnitte, each providing a situation in dialogue form, preceded by an English explanation and followed by intensive question-and-answer drills. Each Abschnitt is followed by a Lesestück on wider aspects of German life. Many pictures and maps, as well as filmstrips. Detailed grammar work, with many examples, figures in the units. Basic end-vocabulary. Suitable for tourists and businessmen as well as advanced school and college students.

Vorwörts. Schools Council German course. Prepared by the German section, Schools Council, Modern Languages Project (London, E. J. Arnold, 1968–73) is in 4 stages, bringing the course to examination standards. *Stage 1A* (units 1–10. 1968.

Complete set. £41.49 + VAT) and *Stage 1B* (units 11–20. 1969. Complete set. £47.69 + VAT) contain work for the first year, emphasising listening and speaking, reading and writing, in groups and individually, based on life with a Hamburg family. *Stage 2A* (units 21–30. 1969. Complete set. £49.42 + VAT) and *Stage 2B* (units 31–40. 1970. Complete set. £44.95 + VAT) include sets of questions geared to more complex structures and increasing active vocabulary, for oral classroom work, language laboratory and individual consolidation; aural comprehension is introduced, mainly to encourage natural speech; stories in readers, for individual work, are short enough to be understood in one lesson. *Stage 3* (1972. Complete set. £33.84 + VAT) allows for different rates of progress; grammar is clearly explained in English, with attractive illustrations. Tapes are an integral part. The vocabulary covered in all 3 stages is *c.* 1,600 items. *Stage 4* (1973. Complete set. £28.05 + VAT) again allows for different rates of progress of all abilities. The many sub-divisions of materials facilitate revision and consolidation and stimulate wider reading and fluency, from reference-grammar pages, answer keys and 398 exercises to the jokes, puzzles and advertisements of the magazine.

Deutsch für Ausländer, by Hermann Kessler (Königswinter, Verlag für Sprach. Methoedik; London, European Schoolbooks, 1975) has 3 main parts: *Grundstufe* (Teil 1, 1a, 1b, 1c; wall-charts, wall pictures, flashcards, $5\frac{3}{4}''$ and $5''$ reels; textbooks, workbooks. £102.20, in all); *Mittelstufe* (Teil 2, 2a, 2b, 2c; flashcards, $5\frac{3}{4}''$ and $5''$ reels; textbook; workbook. *c.* £82, in all); *Oberstufe* (Teil, 3 3b, 3d. $5\frac{3}{4}''$ reels, textbook, readers. £25.95 in all). A 20-page brochure (and also a free copy of the very useful Lehrerheft) is available and indeed necessary, to chart the 20-odd items of this well-established and modernised comprehensive audio-lingual course with visual aids that can be used in schools and adult classes. The *Grundstufe* gives a firm, manifold and leisurely grounding in the language and, with its encouraging subtitle 'Leichter Anfang', can be used with all abilities. The 'Schneller Fortgang' of the *Mittelstufe* can be used selectively and includes topics of interest to adults. The *Oberstufe* concentrates on immediately pre-war and contemporary German writing and, together with its 12 picture-maps, gives a useful introduction to the complexities of modern German and Germany which would bridge the gap between 'O' and 'A' level work.

Deutsch als Fremdsprache, by Korbinian Braun, and others (Stuttgart, Klett; London, Harrap, 1968–72) has 2 parts 1 *Grundkurs* (Leherheft. 31 pp. £0.20; Textbook. 157 pp. £1.45; Dialogische Übungen. 159 pp. £1.45; Strukturübungen und Tests. 127 pp. £1.20; 96 b/w slides. £34 + VAT; 4-7″ discs (dialogue only). £5.60 + VAT; 4-5″ tapes (dialogue and drills). £13 + VAT); 2 *Aufbaukurs* (Lehrerheft. 78 pp. £0.25; Textbook. 156 pp. £1.70; Dialogische Übungen. 191 p. £1.80; Strukturübungen und Tests. 128 pp. £1.80; 96 Slides. £34 + VAT; 3-7″ discs £5.50; 3-5″ tapes. £11). It is a thorough and fairly traditional course, suitable for 'O'-level pupils and beyond, using contemporary topics and authors, with plenty of written as well as oral practice, with opportunities for self-help.

Deutsch durch die audiovisuelle Methode. Harrap-Didier audio-visual course (London, Harrap, 1966–67) has 2 parts: *Part 1* (Teaching guide. 216 pp. £3.65; Student's book. 115 pp. £2.50; Tapescript of drills. 110 pp. £1.05; 25 filmstrips, colour and b/w. £44 + VAT; 15-7″ discs. £10.25; 10-5″ discs. £32 + VAT; 50-5″ tapes (language laboratory version). £110 + VAT); *Part 2* (Student's book. 140 pp. £2.50; Tapescripts of drills. 128 pp. £1.05; 25 filmstrips, colour and b/w. £36 + VAT; 21-7″ discs. £36 + VAT; 50-5″ tapes (language laboratory version). £116.50 + VAT).

For 'O'-level and CSE pupils, there is C. V. Russell's *Audio visual German* (Oxford, Pergamon, 1968) in 3 parts: *Part 1* (Teacher's manual. 114 pp. £0.75; Student's book. 1966 32 pp. £0.25; 10 colour filmstrips and 5-5″ tapes. £55.55 + VAT); *Part 2* (Teacher's book. £0.75; Student's book. 1970. 54 pp. £0.25; 10 colour filmstrips and 5-5¾ tapes. £55.55 + VAT); *Part 3* (teacher's manual. £0.75; Student's book. £0.25; 10 colour filmstrips and 5-5¾ tapes. £55.55 + VAT). It is a visually attractive school-course on fairly traditional lines, as a training in oral skills, by means of oral/aural passages and exercises, backed later in the course by questions on the text and exercises based on the many illustrations for reading and writing practice.

German: a structural approach, by K. J. H. Creese and P. S.

Green (Edinburgh, Oliver & Boyd, 1967–68) has 3 levels: *Level 1* (Teacher's manual. 118 pp. £1.05; Pre-reading book. 48 pp. £0.40; Book 1. 224 pp. £0.95. 2-5″ tapes for pre-reading book. £6 + VAT; 18-5″ tapes for Book 1. £70 + VAT); *Level 2* (Teacher's manual. 140 pp. £1.20; Book 2. 224 pp. £1.10; 17-5″ tapes. £65 + VAT); *Level 3* (Teacher's manual. 104 pp. £1.20; Book 3. 267 pp. £1.20; 8-5″ tapes. £35 + VAT). It goes up to 'O' level but is also suitable for CSE pupils, with lively, stimulating illustrations in the books usable independently; Part 3 has a full grammar summary and 3,800 German–English vocabulary items.

Ich spreche Deutsch: ein audiovisueller Lehrgang, by Heinz Griesbach and Dora Schulz (Munich, Hueber; London, Interbook, 1966. Teacher's guide. Gratis; Textbook. 1973. 83 pp. DM.13.40; Glossar, Englisch. 12 pp. DM.80; 24 filmstrips. DM.296; 457 slides. DM.420; 2-4″ tapes (texts). DM.96; 4-6″ tapes (drills). DM220).

The Schulz-Griesbach-Lund course, *Auf Deutsch, bitte!* (Munich, Hueber; London, European Schoolbooks, 1974—) is to be in 4 parts. *Part 1* includes A/V introduction, new structures, grammar summaries and short illustrative texts, pictures and reading passages (Pupil's book. 80 pp. £1.45; Teacher's book. 48 pp. £0.85; Language structure drills. 5-5″ tapes, $3\frac{1}{4}$ hours. £16.25; Workbook. 96 pp. £1.35; 2-5″ tapes, 67 minutes. £5.60; Filmstrips. 18 at 24 mm, with 325 frames. £49.50; Flashcards, box of 88 at 8″ × $6\frac{1}{2}$″. £5.50; Language structure drills textbook. 88 pp. £1; German–English glossary. 20 pp. £0.44). *Part 2* includes A/V picture/dialogues, general scenes with lively illustrations to facilitate verbal expression; practice and reading texts, with communicative exercises (Pupil's book. 124 pp. £1.75; Teacher's book. Workbook. 80 pp. £1.30; Teacher's key. 22 pp. £0.44; 7″ tapes of some texts. 107 minutes. £8.90; 20 coloured slides. 36 mm. £7.95; flashcards, box of 39, 8″ × $6\frac{1}{2}$″. Language structure drills textbook; German–English glossary. 39 pp. £0.70. *Part 3* will be published in 1976.

The existing 2 parts of this course cover the language needed for 'O' level and CSE, and it is suitable for all abilities as well as adults. Spoken German is encouraged in every form, and grammar is introduced virtually subliminally as a tool for expression; written consolidation is contained in the exercises in the Übungshefte by means of varied drills, free composition as well as puzzles and nonsense passages for correction. Lavishly and attractively illustrated, clearly set out, with amusing and stimulating captions and instructions, the subject matter is pleasingly varied and easily assimilated, assuring progress with pleasure.

Der arme Millionär is a radio course in everyday German, based on Erich Kästner's 'Drei Männer im Schnee' (London, BBC, 1967. Textbook, including key to exercises and puzzles, reference section and glossary paper. 111 pp. £0.30; 2-12″ discs, each £0.90 + VAT). It is for students with some command of German, in class or at home. The book contains the texts of the broadcasts, simple grammar notes, exercises and puzzles; the disc has recordings of the broadcast scenes. Another BBC radio course in German is Stephen Kanocz's *Halb gewonnen* (London, BBC, for the School Broadcasting Council for the UK, 1971. Teacher's notes, 1. 169 pp. £2.50; Teacher's notes, 2. 173 pp. £2.50; Pupil's books, Band 1 and 2 each 144 pp. £0.12; 'Wir sind durch Deutschland gefahren': Notes to teacher. 16 pp., with 2 filmstrips. £4.90 + VAT; 'M‥nster und Münsterland': Notes for teacher. 16 pp., with 2 filmstrips. £4.90 + VAT). This course follows on *Frisch begonnen* (q.v.), but can be used independently. The first 10 programmes complete the course to CSE level, all 20 to 'O' level. The two pupil's books give the spoken texts without the Hörspiele, notes and exercises. Originally broadcast in 1971–72 as 20 programmes made in a West German radio studio. The 2 radiovision programmes. 'Wir sind durch Deutschland gefahren' and 'Münster und Münsterland' give much useful and attractive general information.

Self-tutors; courses for adults
   Deutsche AAC language system: an audio-visual self-study course for beginners of any mother tongue, by I. A. Richards, and others (Zürich, Philips; Bristol, ESL. Textbooks, parts 1 and 2. 254 pp and 12 cassettes. £75 + VAT; Course + 'mini-lab'. £154 + VAT; textbook, parts 3 and 6 cassettes. £37 + VAT) is a development of I. A. Richards' Harvard course, *Ger-*

man through pictures, for self-study by beginners.

For business men, two A/V courses are offered. The *Berlitz self-teaching record course: German* (London, Berlitz Schools of Languages, International Educational Services. Complete course: 5 booklets, 'rotary verb finder' and 5-12″ discs. £10 + VAT) is linked to grammatical and structural features, and a cultural background.

German for businessmen (London, Interlang. 1965–69. Level 1, by M. A. Tatham, and others. Lehrerhandbuch. 74 pp. £2.25. Textbook. 122 pp. £2.25; 30-5″ tapes. £102 + VAT; Level 2, by L. Penney, and others. Textbook. 252 pp. £2.75; 30-5″ tapes. £120 + VAT) is for adults needing a basic knowledge of German in a short time, aiming at oral-aural efficiency and covering a vocabulary of *c.* 1,000 items. *An intensive German course for travel and business*, by C. A. Wrings (London, Heinemann, 1972) consists of Student's manual, with teacher's introduction (151 pp. £0.90), complete with 8-5″ tapes (£40 + VAT).

German economic extracts: a selection from the financial pages of 'Die Welt', with vocabularies and exercises, by K. C. Horton (London, European Schoolbooks, 1970) consists of Textbook (96 pp. £0.75), 5-5″ tapes or cassettes (£16) or 10-5″ tapes (£33.60) or 10 cassettes (£28 + VAT).

Advanced courses

Advanced conversational German, by Otto Z. Eisner and W. G. Cunliffe (Edinburgh, Oliver & Boyd, 1966. Textbook. 160 pp. £1.10; 16-5″ tapes. £65 + VAT) is a practical course in 26 lessons, with basic dialogue on adult topics, followed by structural drills and vocabulary exercises.

Deutsch fürs Studium, by Hans-Peter Apelt and Hermann Siefert (Munich, Hueber, 1974. Tonbänder, in preparation; Testheft zum Tonbandprogramm. 120 pp. DM.8.50; Übungs- und Arbeitsbuch zum Tonband program (Drillübungen, Lösungsschlussel, Glossar Deutsch/Englisch/Französisch/ Spanisch). 126 pp. DM.15) is for advanced students at university or technical college or in business, with relevant vocabulary and learning approaches geared to all abilities.

Fortbildung in der deutschen Sprache, by Robin T. Hammond (London, Oxford University Press, 1969. Tapes from

Tutor Tape (Teacher's book. 21 pp. £0.25; Student's book. 196 pp. £1.75; Text of recordings. 32 pp. £0.25; 8-5″ tapes twin-track or 16-5″ tapes single-track. £27.60 or £23 + VAT) is a useful course for any advanced student or further education examination. It is based on 15 spontaneous dialogues with Germans from all walks of life and speech regions, leading to prepared and unprepared questions; later oral/aural exercises could include transcribing or interpreting. The textbook also contains intensive language drills on usage, vocabulary building and word formation, with ample scope for discussion, free or guided composition and even translation.

DICTIONARIES

Dictionaries: General, bilingual

Of the larger bilingual dictionaries, *Harrap's Standard German and English dictionary,* edited by Trevor Jones (Part 1: German–English. V. 1–3: A–R. 1963–74. £6 + £6 + £15) is a welcome and important work of reference, even if publication is so protracted. It includes both general and specialised terms, many idioms, proverbs, colloquialisms (Swiss and Austrian, as well). There are also adaptations for North American users, grammar notes and a pronunciation guide to loan words (Fremdwörter). Proper names and abbreviations appear in the main sequence. Harrap's German–English dictionary is outstanding for clear typography and fullness of context quotations. Part 1 is to be in 4 v.; part 2, English–German, is to follow.

Langenscheidt's Encyclopaedic dictionary of the English and German languages, by E. Muret and D. Sanders; edited by O. Springer. (Berlin, Langenscheidt; London, Methuen, 1962–75. 4 v.) is the largest completed German and English dictionary. The German–English part, with *c.* 200,000 headwords, is particularly valuable pending the completion of the Harrap, part 1. It is more encyclopaedic than the Harrap and better for specialised vocabulary, but less legible. Both, however, are of excellent value.

The *English-German and German–English dictionary*, by K. Wildhagen and W. Héraucourt (London, Allen & Unwin, 1963, 1972. 2 v. £12; £17.50) is still highly regarded for its many sentence examples. But the German–English part (xxx, (1), 1,524 pp. is virtually unaltered since the 1953 edition. The main sequence includes abbreviations, forenames, etc., but is less easy to refer to than are Harrap and Springer because of the solid appearance of the average page.

Langenscheidt's Comprehensive English–German dictionary (London, Hodder & Stoughton, 1972. 1,104 pp. £13.75) has much to recommend it, considering both quality and price. It is valuable for advanced work, aiming 'to steer a middle course between the encyclopaedic new Muret–Sanders and the [Langenscheidt] 'Concise English–German dictionary' (*see below*)' (Preface). About 120,000 headwords, including current and technical vocabulary. There is an appendix of English abbreviations, names and places. Work on the German–English dictionary continues.

Of the medium and smaller-sized dictionaries, *Langenscheidt's Concise dictionary*, by M. Messinger and W. Rüdenberg (new ed. London, Hodder & Stoughton, 1973. 656, 744 pp. £3.60) has distinct merits as a reliable desk dictionary, being cheap, easy to use and backed by the usual Langenscheidt appendices.

The *New Schöffler-Weis compact German and English dictionary*, by Erich and Erwin Weiss (London, Harrap, 1969. [xii], 562 pp.; [viii], 495 pp. £4.50) is a fairly up-to-date work for advanced students, at a moderate price – perhaps at the cost of clarity in lay-out.

From the German Democratic Republic comes the *Wörterbuch Englisch–Deutsch* (10. Aufl. Leipzig, VEB Verlag Enzyklopädie, 1966. xii, 624 pp. £1.20), first published in 1955, and its companion, the *Deutsch–Englisches Wörterbuch* (1958. xix, 786 pp.), each with *c.* 40,000 headwords and aimed halfway between school and reference use, with a slant towards science and technology. Good use is made of bold type. A list of abbreviations and bibliography are appended.

Cassell's German & English dictionary, based on the editions by Karl Breul, completely revised and re-edited by H. T.

Betteridge, with annual 'editions' (12th ed. London, Cassell, 1969. xx, 619 pp.), first published in 1957), is considered adequate for school purposes.

Pocket dictionaries include *The pocket Oxford dictionary (German–English*, by M. I. Barker and H. Homeyer; *English–German*, by C. T. Carr. Oxford, Clarendon Press, 1959–65. 448 pp.; 222 pp. £1.40) – reprints of the 1951 and 1962 editions, in 1. v. or separate (£1.25 + £0.85) – for classroom use, with a German grammar synopsis. Another is *An English–German and German–English dictionary*, by W. E. Collinson and H. Connell (Harmondsworth, Middlesex, Penguin, 1962. 576 pp. £0.80), first published 1954, and a handy dictionary, with idioms and expressions clearly set out. A third, *Langenscheidt's pocket dictionary of the German and English languages* (Berlin, Langenscheidt; London, Hodder, 1970–71. 2 v. (1,267 pp.) each £1, or £1.40 in 1 v.), is certainly worth its price, being a reliable guide to all aspects of vocabulary and usage for any level of student. *Collins' Contemporary German dictionary, German–English*, by J. M. Clark, revised by Rotraut Riddell (London, Collins, 1971, xviii, 526 pp. £0.60), a reprint of the 1969 edition, is cheap, but treatment is superficial, and equivalents are not differentiated.

Dictionaries: General, monolingual

Das grosse deutsche Wörterbuch, by Gerhard Wahrig and others (Gütersloh, Bertelsmann, 1967. 1,440 pp. DM.64) has *c.* 200,000 entries and gives definitions, correct spelling, hyphenation, pronunciation and etymology, with numerous examples, plus a preliminary 50-page 'Lexikon der deutschen Sprachlehre'. Its nearest English equivalents are probably the *Concise Oxford dictionary* and the *Advanced learner's dictionary*.

There are a number of monolingual German dictionaries that have distinct value as visual aids. One of these is *Der Sprachbrockhaus. Deutsches Bildwörterbuch für jedermann* (8. völlig. neubearb. Aufl. Wiesbaden, Brockhaus, 1972. 835 pp. illus. DM.25), originally an illustrated abridgement of *Der kleine Brockhaus* (1950. 2 v.). It has more than 62,000 headwords. A feature is the lavish use of over 5,000 carefully drawn line-drawings, with keyed parts at head and foot of pages. Entries give brief definitions, plus grammatical information. The *Brockhaus illustrated dictionary, German–English, English–German* (London, Pitman, 1961. 2 v. (xviii, 766 pp.; xii, 728 pp. £3.50), based on *Der Sprachbrockhaus*, has *c.* 3,000 clear illustrations in all and gives examples of usage.

The *Duden Bildwörterbuch der deutschen Sprache* (2., vollständig neu bearb. Aufl. Mannheim, Bibliographisches Institut; London, Harrap, 1958. 672, 114 pp.), first published in 1936, has a vocabulary of 25,000 words, with 368 pages of illustrations grouped by subjects (*e.g.*, swimming; paper-making; agricultural machinery). There are several bilingual companions to the *Duden Bildwörterbuch der deutschen Sprache* – English, French, Italian, Polish, Russian, Spanish, Czech and Hungarian, with German as the base language. The *Kinderduden: mein erster Duden* (2. völlig. neu bearb. Aufl. Mannheim; London, Harrap, 1970. 160 pp. illus.) is intended for German primary-school pupils but, because it is a handy visual aid and gives plurals of nouns, plus usage, it can be used for 'O' level, for reference purposes.

Dictionaries: Commercial

Wirtschaftswörterbuch, by R. von Eichborn (4. Aufl. Düsseldorf, Econ-Verlag GmbH., 1974. 2 v. (xxiv, 1,118 pp.; xxiv, 1,133 pp.). each £30.80), first published 1947–61, has *c.* 30,000 headwords in each volume, with numerous compounds and technical idioms. It distinguishes between British and US usage and gives idiomatic translation where English terms have no German equivalents. A reliable and extensive business dictionary.

Gunston & Corner's German–English glossary of financial and economic terms (6th ed., greatly compressed, but in content much amplified, by C. A. Gunston. Frankfurt am Main, Knapp, 1972. xxiii, 1,203 pp. £15.20); was first published in 1953. C. A. Gunston worked for 30 years in the Bank of England, and the dictionary 'contains only words which the present author has encountered in the course of his activity ... It is a book written by translators for translators'. It has *c.* 25,000 headwords, with many compounds and good use of bold type.

German–English economic terminology, by R. Renner and others (Munich, Hueber, 1965; London, Macmillan, 1966. 556 pp. £4.20) is arranged into 25 sections, each section having English and German exercises. It carries 7,000 headwords. C.-E. Dietl's *Wörterbuch der Wirtschafts-, Recht- und Handelssprache, einschliessich des Europarechts* (3. völlig. neu bearb. Aufl. Schloss Bleckede bei Hamburg. Meissner, 1970–71. 2 v.) has the advantage of covering legal terminology as well as commercial and economic. V. 1, *Anglo-amerikanisch–Deutsch*, has *c.* 9,000 headwords.

Bilingual guide to business and professional correspondence, by J. Harvard (Oxford, Pergamon, 1965) is in 2 vols. – English–German (x, 140 pp.) and German–English ([ix], 140 pp.). It is a practical guide, sectionalised by subject, and has no vocabulary index. There are various polyglot business correspondence dictionaries to repair this deficiency, such as – G. Duttweiler's *Les 20,000 phrases et expressions de la correspondence commercial et privé* (Geneva, Editions Générales, 1960. 432 pp.), covering French, German and English; and *Rhodes Handbuch der Handelskorrespondenz in deutscher., englischer, französischer und spanischer Sprache* (16. Aufl. Bad Heilbrunn, Klinkhardt, 1955. [ii], 1,164 pp.).

Deutsche Wirtschaftssprache für Ausländer, by Franz Bäumchen, is dealt with on pp. 97; K. C. Horton's *German economic extracts*, on p. 105.

Dictionaries: Scientific & technical

The need for up-to-dateness is particularly important here. L. de Vries and T. M. Herrmann's *German–English technical and engineering dictionary* (3rd ed. New York, Toronto & London, McGraw-Hill, 1972. ix, 1,178 pp. £14.60) and *English–German technical and engineering dictionary* (3rd ed. 1970. [xv], 1,154 pp. £14.60) each have more than 200,000 headwords, including compounds: they are reprints of the 2nd editions of 1965 and 1968. L. de Vries's *German–English science dictionary for students in chemistry, physics, biology, agriculture and related science* had its 3rd edition (xlii, 592 pp. £4.50) in 1959.

R. Ernst's *Wörterbuch der industriellen Technik* (Wiesbaden, Brandstetter) is in its 3rd edition (v. 1: Deutsch–Englisch. 1974. 1,061 pp. £22.50; v. 2: Englisch–Deutsch. 1971. [viii], 1,403 p. £17.35), with *c.* 30,000 headwords in each volume. It differentiates between British and US usage. Also reasonably up-to-date is A. Oppermann's *Wörterbuch der modernen Technik* (Munich, Oppermann), now in its 3rd edition. (Englisch–Deutsch. 1972. 912 pp. £18; Deutsch–Englisch. 1974. 952 pp. £18).

Dictionary of science and technology, English–German, by A. F. Dorian, with L. Herzbruch (Amsterdam, London, New York, Elsevier, 1967 (reprinted 1969). xii, 1,238 pp. £23.25) and *Dictionary of science and technology, German–English*, by A. F. Dorian, with L. da C. Monsanto (1970. [xii], 879 pp. £17.35) each have 120,000 headwords. The English–German volume is well thought of, whereas the smaller German–English part has been criticised for the shortcomings of the English equivalents.

A. A. Webel's *A German–English dictionary, scientific and general terms* ... (3rd ed. London, Routledge & Kegan Paul, 1952. xii, 939 pp.), with *c.* 60,000 headwords, and first published in 1930, is well known to translators and is still in print, at £4.50.

There are numerous German and English dictionaries, as well as polyglot dictionaries in specialised fields of science and technology. *Bailey's Technical dictionaries catalogue, 1974*, compiled by H. Lennox-Kay (Folkestone, Bailey Bros. & Swinfern, Ltd., 1974. [ii], 79 pp. £0.70) is a handy guide, being arranged alphabetically under more than a hundred subject headings, sub-divided by languages.

7

DUTCH

by P. K. KING, M.A.

INTRODUCTION

Resistance to hardware, whether in computing aids to literary or linguistic research or in laboratory teaching systems is gradually waning, though the debate on the efficacy of the personal versus the impersonal approach continues. Dutch learning abroad is likely to be confined to university students or adult groups in 'evening classes' and to individuals, an increasing number of whom will at least be familiar with direct-method teaching from their schooldays. It seems likely, therefore, that the obvious advantages of a laboratory course prepared by one or more specialists, available to teachers and learners of very mixed competence, will appeal more and more as the complaint, 'I must *see* the script and *read* the explanations' is heard less and less. Nevertheless, those who are learning a 'minor' language because they have a linguistic flair or interest, will probably have some knowledge of a second language and will at any rate have a sufficient grasp of language structure to benefit from an earlier confrontation with textual paradigms and analyses, if only for comparison with other grammar(s) known to them. Equally, pace is an essential component of stimulus, and it is unwise to err on the side of caution to the extent of insisting that the whole convoy move at the speed of the slowest ship. For this reason, some kind of systematic and controlled grading is very desirable in any course, whether in a traditional textbook or using audio (-visual) techniques, that may be used by untutored learners or only partly qualified teachers.

It is an obvious fact, apparent in the following selection of dictionaries as well as courses, that publications in a 'minor' language have to conform to commercial restraints by appealing to the largest possible market. This means that the ideal is never attainable, since the requirements of all potential users (of grammars, dictionaries and courses) will vary so greatly in age, competence, experience and aims, that one product can never satisfy them all. And yet only the product which seeks to do just that has much chance of publication.

TEXTBOOK COURSES & GRAMMARS

General courses, for use in school, university, and self-study

There is understandably no course book designed for school use, though the nearest approach to this is published in Australia where the large Dutch immigrant population accounts for the demand for A-level teaching. It is J. Smit & R. P. Meijer, *Dutch grammar and reader* (2nd ed. Melbourne, University Press, [1966]. 207 pp. £1.15. The grammar, exercises and reading texts are printed in different sections. The more elementary grammatical descriptions and exercises are distinguished from the more advanced, since the book is intended for school and university use. But the reference to 'advanced students' in the preface is misleading, since the general scope here is obviously far too limited for them. The book is intended only for use under instruction, which is as well since the unreliable phonetic description and the inaccuracies, omissions and untidy formulations in the grammar require the vigilant eye of a teacher. This can, however, be recommended as an exercise book and reader. These two later sections are carefully graded, but the choice of the English and Dutch prose passages for translation suggests that the book is intended for Dutch-born students of Dutch in an English environment, since the English prose style is considerably more advanced than the Dutch.

Since, however, Dutch is not normally a school-subject outside Holland, the grammar courses for foreigners will generally have university students and self-taught adults in mind. The best of these is W. Z. Shetter, *Introduction to Dutch. A practical grammar* (4th ed. The Hague, Nijhoff, 1974. 209 pp. £3.35).

This is the most reliable conventional grammar for general purposes, giving 'a concise presentation of the essentials of the Dutch language which could be used both for independent home study and in groups or classes under formal instruction.' The chapter on pronunciation is its weakest point since it is quite inadequate for anyone with a knowledge of phonetics and misleading for the untutored learner. The basic structure of the grammar is dealt with fairly thoroughly, including word formation and derivation. Individual chapters deal with more than one category only when these are closely related, and apart from occasional revision sections consisting of reading passages, each chapter contains an accumulative vocabulary, idiomatic phrases and exercises based on the preceding grammar. They are arranged so as to be adaptable for class-work, and keys are given for the self-tutored student. The limited scope has allowed only scant attention to negation and the modal particles. In this revised edition the chapter on the inflexion of adjectives has been rewritten, more attention has been paid to the Belgian part of the Dutch language area, and illustrations have been added.

R. B. Bird and W. Z. Shetter. *Een goed begin ... : a contemporary Dutch reader* (2nd ed. The Hague, Nijhoff, 1971. viii, 101 pp. *f*15.00) is intended as a companion to Shetter's grammar, so that the grammatical summary, included with the notes and vocabulary, is restricted to a tabular presentation of the basic paradigms. Despite some inaccuracies, the price of such compression, it provides a clear, at-a-glance reference for revision. The other half of the book is devoted to a selection of Dutch literary passages for translation. It differs considerably from the 'reader' in Smit and Meijer, in that there are Dutch passages only, all taken from twentieth-century prose and poetry, and reaching a somewhat more advanced standard.

The most readily available, but by no means equally reliable, English-language grammar is H. Koolhoven, *Teach yourself Dutch* (London, Teach yourself books, 1974. 222 pp., £0.50). The work is divided into chapters dealing summarily with grammatical points and providing short vocabularies, followed by exercises. There is a fairly sound phonetic introduction, a list of strong verbs, a Dutch–English vocabulary and a key to the exercises. In order presumably to develop interesting phrase structures as early as possible, the presentation of the grammar is entirely unsystematic so that, *e.g.*, the plural of nouns is partly dealt with in six different chapters. Orderly learning and revision and easy reference suffer from this muddled arrangement, though the least talented student will be least handicapped by this. Though this is based on a revised edition of 1961, the revision was essentially confined to the spelling, and the latest impression is substantially the same as the original of 1941. This means that the grammatical descriptions are no longer reliable and some of the idioms have a cracked ring.

Also frequently available is F. G. Renier, *Learn Dutch!* (London, Routledge & Kegan Paul, [1970]. 192 pp., £1). This substantially unrevised work written in 1941 has been replaced by audio-visual courses which provide a much more effective and more accurate direct-method approach. It cannot therefore be recommended. Finally, C. Lambregtse, *Fundamentals of practical Dutch grammar* (Grand Rapids, Eerdmans, 1965. 100 pp. $3.95), is described as 'simplified and practical studies and rules for class instruction. Equally useful for self-study.' No review copy has been received.

Reference grammars

The most detailed and methodical descriptions of Dutch as a foreign language are contained in two Scandinavian publications. The most recent is J. de Rooij and I. Wiken-Donde. *Nederlandsk grammatik* (Stockholm, Läromedelforlaget, 1972. 242 pp. Kr.55). Though written in Swedish, this is included because it is a model of its kind which has no English-language counterpart. It provides a scholarly arrangement and description of the grammar and deals with advanced points of syntax and idiom, dealt with in no other book for the foreign student. A. Holch Justesen. *Hollandsk grammatik* (Copenhagen, Jespersen, 1952. 158 pp. ƒ16), is also excellent, and the fact that it is written in Danish is less of a disadvantage in the phonetic description (pp. 13–50) by Eli Fischer-Jørgensen. In addition to a scholarly phonetic and morphemic analysis (including loan-words), there are sections on assimilation, stress, intonation and orthography.

The range of reliable reference grammars for Dutch speakers is of course considerable. The phonetic system is well covered by A. Cohen, C. L. Ebeling, K. Fokkema and A. G. F. van Holk in *Fonologie van het Nederlands en het Fries, Inleiding tot de moderne klankleer* (2nd imp. The Hague, Nijhoff, 1961, xv, 155 pp. *f*12.50), and, in more experimental terms, by B. van den Berg in *Foniek van het Nederlands* (6th imp. The Hague, van Goor, 1972. 127 pp. *f*18.90).

The grammar is clearly and extensively dealt with in E. Rijpma and F. G. Schuringa. *Nederlandse spraakkunst* (23rd imp. Groningen, Wolters-Noordhoff, 1971. 355 pp. *f*17.90). This standard traditional grammar was completely revised by J. van Bakel according to structural principles in the 21st impression. It now provides a systematic and detailed description under the headings phonetics and accentuation, morphology and grammar, syntax, semantics, gender and spelling. There is an introduction reviewing current synchronic and diachronic linguistic theory, a very useful bibliography and a reference index. As a ready reference work it will be particularly useful to teachers and advanced students. C. H. den Hertog, *Nederlandse Spraakkunst*, ingeleid en bewerkt door H. Hulshof (3rd imp. Amsterdam, Versluys, 1972–73. 3 vols., (xxix, 168 pp., xxiv, 269 pp., xiv, 153 pp.). *f*15, *f*25, *f*15), is an even more comprehensive standard work revised in the light of wide experience of use in schools and universities, but its very detailed treatment makes retrieval more difficult.

For a transformational-generative account of the syntax, an earlier work, A. Kraak and W. G. Klooster. *Syntaxis* (Culemborg, Stam-Kemperman, 1968. 298 pp. *f*24.75), can be consulted in conjunction with W. G. Klooster, H. J. Verkuyl and J. H. Luif, *Inleiding tot de syntaxis, praktische zinsleer van het Nederlands* (6th imp. Culemborg, Stam-Robijns, 1971. 152 pp. *f*8.25).

RECORDED & AUDIO-VISUAL AIDS

Of the audio-visual courses the most elementary is G. C. Berlijn and H. de Boer, *Nou jij! Audio-visuele taalmethode voor kinderen die geen of weinig Nederlands spreken* (2nd rev. imp. Purmerend, Muusses, 1974. 3 Learner's books, *f*7.50, *f*8.20, *f*7; 3 Teacher's books, *f*3.90, *f*3.90, *f*4.90; 3 tapes, *f*70 each; 3 sets of colour slides, *f*130, *f*165, *f*55). Designed to establish simple phrase structures and a vocabulary of 1,000 words (selected from frequency lists) for small children, this is obviously too elementary for examination courses, but it may have an application where, *e.g.*, younger parents have to move to Holland.

For secondary school use, there is the first part (all that has been published) of F. van Passel, *Actief Nederlands* (Antwerp, Sikkel, 1972. 3 v. Text (4th imp.), 202 pp. Fr.136; Illustrations. 176 pp., Fr.136; and Teacher's handbook (2nd imp. 1971). 212 pp. Fr.128). It is, however, intended for immigrant children in secondary and technical education in Holland and Belgium.

The first-level course with the widest application, with and without instruction, has been compiled by the Department of Linguistics, Cambridge University and the Afdeling Toegepaste Taalwetenschap at the Free University of Amsterdam. It is *Levend Nederlands. Een audio-visuele cursus Nederlands voor buitenlanders* (Cambridge University Press, 1975. Textbook. 279 pp. £3.40, 7-5" tapes, £35 + VAT, 29 film strips, £100 + VAT). The course is designed for older children and adult learners with and without instruction. Apart from introductory notes for the guidance of self-instructed students, in four languages (English, French, German and Indonesian), the course and the grammatical commentary are entirely in Dutch, and the first unit covering the phonetic system contrastively, shows that no assumptions were made about phonemic affinities with native speech. After the first unit on sounds and spelling, the course provides 23 dialogues in widespread social and professional situations, drills preceded by schematic analysis of the transformations involved, verb lists, grammatical and phonetic descriptions or transformational-generative principles, indexes and keys to 'homework'. The textbook contains halftone reproductions of the colour frames, and the drills are graded to assist the student to edit his exercises according to his own level of competence. The tapes are unexploded, and will need copying with pauses for laboratory use. This first-level course covers the basic structures including, *e.g.*, modal verbs, double infinitives, recorded speech and indirect questions.

The other first-level audio-visual courses are addressed specifically to speakers of one particular language. *Linguaphone Dutch* (London, Linguaphone Institute (International Catalogues Ltd., Linguaphone House, 207/9 Regent Street, WIR 8AU), 1957, textbooks and 4 cassettes, £49.50), provides an English commentary and vocabularies. It is attractively produced and packed in a handy wallet. The technical quality of the tapes is good but there are two significant weaknesses. The mixture of texts and illustrations makes it difficult to avoid following the text while listening (indeed the student is recommended to do so) and the choice of eminent academics to read the dialogues is little short of disastrous. Ordinary people just don't articulate like that (any more), and professors do not necessarily make the best actors.

There are two courses prepared for Francophone Belgian schoolchildren. M. J. Vriendt-de Man, S. de Vriendt, J. Eggermont, M. Wambach, C. Wuilmart and H. Schutte, *Audiovisuele methode Nederlands* (Amsterdam, Didier, 1967–70. Tapes, filmstrips and textbook 1, 139 pp. Illustrations. 71 pp.; Textbook 2. 93 pp. Illustrations. 73 pp. (prices not available). This course in 33 units, using the Guberina-Rivenc method, is intended for use under tuition. Short dialogues are followed by question-and-answer dialogues using illustrations as stimuli. There are also dictation passages. The other course is similarly inspired by the CREDIF method and is similarly structured. It is R. Maréchal and G. van Straelen- van Rintel, *Nederlands in Beeld an Klank* (Brussels, Didier, 1971. Teacher's book. 215 pp. Fr.160. Textbook. 83 pp. Fr.60. Illustrations. 63 pp., filmstrips and tapes). It is more open-mesh than the above course, since its 25 units cover much the same grammar. It does not use illustrations in its exploitation, and there is more emphasis on pronunciation exercises here. Both courses give very detailed and explicit instructions on how the course is to be used.

Of the audio-lingual first-level courses, the most widely tested and revised is W. Lagerwey. *Speak Dutch. An audio-lingual course* (4th imp. Amsterdam, Meulenhoff, 1973. x, 633 pp. *f*33.50 and tapes). This is a very close-mesh course, covering about the same grammar as *Levend Nederlands* in 30 units, of which the last three contain reading selections instead of drills, and there is no editing scheme to assist the more competent learner. Although the English language has largely been removed from the revised recordings, the English commentary and translations throughout the course scarcely accord with the author's prefaced comment 'the student who desires to master a foreign tongue must learn to think in the language which he is learning'. The first 40 pages of the text and much of the following three units are concerned with the phonetic explanation and drilling, and many of these drills are discouragingly repetitive. The structures are instanced rather than explained and the general method is clearly inspired by the CREDIF courses. The course is less suitable for the English than for the American learner (especially in the phonetic descriptions) for whom it is specifically intended.

Another, simpler, course for North Americans is L. Bloomfield, *Spoken Dutch* (New York, Holt, Rinehart & Winston, 1973 (unrev. reprint of 1964 ed.). 554 pp. Text of units 1–30. $12.00; key to exercises $1.50; 5 12″ LP (33⅓ rpm) records, $47.00; complete package with records, $55.00 or with cassettes (4 C-60 dual-track) $65.00). This course is designed for American children under class-room teaching conditions and will have somewhat limited value outside the US.

With primarily German-speaking students in mind, J. Wilmots has prepared *Voor wie Nederlands wil leren* (Diepenbeek, Economische Hogeschool, Limburg, 2nd rev. imp., 1974. Textbook, 188 pp.; Drill book, 107 pp.). Except for a Dutch–German vocabulary, Dutch is the only language of the course which consists of ten units, each with a prose passage featuring the grammatical points to be dealt with, a very simple and clear paradigmatic representation of the grammar, drills, dictation and conversation questions and topics. The course is progressive, assembling a vocabulary of 1,500 words derived from frequency lists. It really requires the guidance (and additional explanation) of a tutor. The standard of the prose passages and of the imaginative and varied drills further suggests that it would be well received by any students with a fairly advanced knowledge of German.

An unpublished Dutch laboratory course for foreign learners

which may still be available is A. Pescher- ter Meer and A. M. Fontein for the Stichting Bijstand Buitenlandse Studerenden (F. C. Donderstraat 16, Utrecht) with the title *Kursus Nederlandse Taal* (1968. Textbook 90 pp.; Drills 58 pp.; English translations and commentary 162 pp., with 23 tapes). The progressive grammar in each of the 23 units is based on a section of a serial narrative and a passage of dialogue introducing over 1,400 words based on De la Court's frequency count. It provides a first-level course whose scope is comparable to those already mentioned, but with considerably less density, presumably because the course was originally intended for teaching situations in a Dutch-language environment.

Finally, mention should be made of the courses regularly rewritten for the 'Wereldomroep' Radio Nederland, under the title *Dutch by Radio*. These courses are only published during the transmission of the course and are not available through the trade. The textbooks issued from Hilversum contain grammatical summaries with an English commentary, and questions based on the broadcast episodes, together with a gramophone record for practising pronunciation.

The only technical course is W. H. J. Kuipers. *Bandcursus. Collegetaal Nederlands voor buitenlandse eerstejaars aan de Technische Hogeschool* (3rd imp. Eindhoven, Technische Hogeschool, 24 pp.). The textbook, giving the symbolic representations of Dutch terms and formulae, is available gratis on application from teaching institutions who will also receive the two accompanying single-track $5\frac{1}{2}''$ tapes in return for two blank tapes.

The more advanced audio-lingual course is J. Wilmots, A. Wethlij, X. Staelens, J. Cajot, J. de Rooij. *Voor wie wat Nederlands kent* (Diepenbeek, Wetenschappelijk Onderwijs Limburg. 299 pp. (stencilled; not published through the trade)). This is a learning programme in 35 parts, consisting of anecdotes and reports from newspapers with lexical and grammatical explanation, exercises and keys. The principal aim is to enlarge the available vocabulary of the student by stimulating discussion in the target language. Tapes for this programme are in course of preparation.

Another, as yet unpublished, second-level programme is being prepared by H. Maureau of the Civic University of Amsterdam under the auspices of the Department of Linguistics at Cambridge University. It is likely to be published in 1977 and will consist of ten units on topics of current social, political and cultural interest, with a spoken commentary, extracts from 'live' radio discussions or talks, a detailed analysis of advanced points of grammar, idiom and style, comprehension tests and grammatical drills.

Finally, the Department of Applied Linguistics at Groningen University is publishing triennially dossiers of 'current affairs'. The compiler is J. P. Menting, director of the Department, and the annual subscription rate is *f*30. Each dossier contains a commentary introducing the topic, a cassette of specially recorded and dubbed interviews, comments, discussions, music etc., a transcript of the recordings and an explanation of the meaning of words and phrases. Sometimes newspaper articles are also included. So far the following dossiers have been issued: *Groningen*, a 'scrapbook' of impressions of life in the city and province undergoing rapid changes, with examples of the dialects; *De Vijftigers*, a presentation of popular entertainment in the fifties (with a transcript) as a background to examples of the poetry of that generation; *De auto – het openbaar vervoer in het politieke bestel*, with an introductory commentary on the Dutch party system, press comments on the traffic problem and recorded discussions, interviews, etc., on the same topic. The second issue of 1976 will have the title *Nederland en het water*.

DICTIONARIES

Dictionaries: General, bilingual

Unfortunately all the best, or at any rate most up-to-date dictionaries, whatever their size and scope, are likely to be compiled for Dutch users, since the demand, and hence reprint frequency, is much greater there. Nevertheless, the English user must bear in mind that the weighting, not to mention accuracy, of Dutch–English dictionaries compiled by Dutchmen places them at a disadvantage, quite apart from the normal omission of useful information about the pronunciation and gender of Dutch words, while similar information, which is not needed by the English user, is given against English words.

The most comprehensive bilingual work is undoubtedly H. Jansonius. *Nieuw Groot Nederlands–Engels woordenboek voor studie en praktijk*, (2nd ed. Leiden, Nederlandse UM, 1972–73. 3 vols. (1,270 pp.). *f*325). It claims to contain two-and-a-half times as much material as any other Dutch–English dictionary. It certainly contains a very great deal of contextual translation as well as a remarkably broad spectrum of technical vocabulary. Genders and pronunciation are not shown.

Of the 'standard' size bilingual dictionaries, F. P. H. Prick van Wely, *Cassell's English–Dutch, Dutch–English dictionary* (London, Cassell, 1967. 1,424 pp. £3.25), gains by being compiled (and hence including rudimentary information on pronunciation and gender) for English and Dutch use. But though it is fairly dependable, it is also rather conservative and dull. Also, being unrevised since 1971 it is now out of date, and the publishers are unable to announce the date of the next printing. This means that a choice has to be made from the dictionaries intended for Dutch users, and the joint Anglo–Dutch authorship of one of these makes it the most reliable and comprehensive. It is K. ten Bruggencate and A. Broers, *Engels woordenboek* (Groningen, Tjeenk Willink, English–Dutch. 18th ed. 1975. 896 pp. £4.75; Dutch–English. 17th ed., 1975. 1,023 pp. £5). The regular revisions to this standard dictionary are done by R. W. Zandvoort, J. Gerritsen and N. E. Osselton. The inclusion of 'taboo'-words in recent revisions is particularly welcome, and artificial 'dictionary' renderings are increasingly rare. It is very good for idiom, which obviously claims some of the space that might have gone to a larger lexis. Similar in scope to Ten Bruggencate-Broers (and also compiled for the Dutch user) is B. J. W e v e r s and P. J. V e r h o e ff. *Standaard groot Engels–Nederlands woordenboek* (Antwerp, Standaard, 1974. 921 pp. *f*42.50), but its selection of words is strangely erratic. While including a welcome number of slang and taboo words, it fails to rectify some of the established omissions and many non-ephemeral additions to usage are not included. Headwords are clearly printed, but the regular type-face is niggardly. Rather smaller in scope but, unlike the foregoing, containing a two-way dictionary in one volume, is E. Th. Verhoeff-Schot and J. R. S. Canberghe, *Nieuw Standaard Engels–Nederlands, Nederlands–Engels woordenboek* (2nd imp. Antwerp, Standaard, 1974. 1,437 pp.). It suffers from the fact that apparently no English native was consulted, so that some of the English renderings are inaccurate, and obviously there is far less room for phrases.

Kramers' Engels Woordenboek (The Hague, Van Goor, 1975. 736 pp. £5.75) is a two-way dictionary compiled by P. H. Prick-van Wely, of smaller scope but more standing (it has run through several impressions) than the foregoing. It is, however, due for revision and a two-volume revised edition is announced for 1977.

In a pocket format, there is A. Ryckaert's *Standaard Nederlands–Engels, Engels–Nederlands zakwoordenboek* (Antwerp, Standaard, 1973. 578 pp. *f*8.90), which is based on the *Nieuw Standaard woordenboek* referred to above but, since phrases are not normally given, it does not show the weakness of its bigger brother. It is a nicely printed, clearly set out, reasonably comprehensive dictionary in a strong flexible cover, and it even gains on its larger namesake in providing the genders and parts of speech of the Dutch words. Also at an attractive price (though less attractively produced) there is a two-volume *Prisma Handwoordenboek* (Antwerp, Het Spectrum, 1971). The English–Dutch volume is compiled by F. J. J. Baars and J. G. J. A. van der Schoot, 336 pp. *f*4.95, and the Dutch–English is by G. J. Visser. 325 pp. *f*4.95. A considerable amount of generally reliable information is packed into the small type of these two (bound) volumes. A single-volume alternative, attractive because it is compiled for the Englishman, is F. G. Renier, *Dutch–English and English–Dutch dictionary* (5th imp. London, Routledge & Kegan Paul, 1972, 571 pp. £1.50). Unfortunately, however, only the spelling has been revised since the first imp. of 1949 so that this is now seriously dated. Another pocket, two-way (and this time inexpensive) dictionary which was prepared for the English user, but is now out of date (unrevised since 1958), is P. and M. King, *Dutch Dictionary* (6th imp. London, Teach Yourself Books, 397 pp. £0.60). Its synopsis of the grammar, however, adds something to its usefulness.

Dictionaries: General, monolingual

Of the competitive variety of monolingual dictionaries special mention should be made of J. H. van Dale, *Groot woordenboek der Nederlandse taal met een uitvoerig supplement* (9th ed. The Hague, Nijhoff, 1970. 2 vols, xxix + 2,802 pp. ƒ94). This has so long been a household name as the most comprehensive and complete dictionary (the 'great' dictionary, *Woordenboek der Nederlandse taal* (1882–), with 24 vols. is still incomplete after 93 years) that the compiler for some years, C. Kruyskamp, is given less credit than he deserves. The large supplement (of 12,000 lemmata) is necessitated by the uncertainty about spelling reforms which were in the air when this edition was in preparation. This also gives some idea of the additional material that had to be incorporated during the ten-year period between the publishing of subsequent editions. Apart from its comprehensiveness, this dictionary is also valuable for the distinctions it makes (however rapidly these may change) between stylistic and dialectal usage and forms. M. J. Koenen and J. Endepols, *Verklarend handwoordenboek der Nederlandse taal vooral ten dienste van het onderwijs* (27th imp. Groningen, Tjeenk Willink, [c. 1970]. xii, 1696 pp. ƒ31.25) is compiled by J. B. Drewes and regularly revised to provide a better shorter version of Van Dale than the abridged Van Dale itself which is less frequently revised. Finally, *Woordenlijst van de Nederlandse taal* (The Hague, Nijhoff, 1954. lxx. 635 pp. ƒ6), is an extensive list showing the spelling and genders (but not the meaning) of 75,000 words, as authorised by the Dutch and Belgian Spelling Act of 1954. The introduction summarises the orthographic changes affected by that legislation, and this will remain the authoritative guide until the next official spelling reform.

Dictionaries: Special[1]

Since there is no catalogue of Dutch books in print, two words of warning are necessary here: the prices are often those

---

[1] My thanks are due to Miss C. Picken for her generous hospitality at the Shell Centre where all the listed special dictionaries were sighted in the library of the translation division.

prevailing at the time of publication, and there is no certainty that the titles are still in print.

There are five general dictionaries of technology and commerce. The most recent, but not the most comprehensive, is H. J. W. Peek *Standaard Nederlands–Engels technisch woordenboek* (Antwerp, Standaard, 1974. 388 pp. *f*35). Though, inevitably, a certain amount of the material here will also occur in a general dictionary, a wide range of technology and commerce is represented and the balance is good. H. Jansonius, *Technisch Engels woordenboek, Nederlands–Engels en Engels–Nederlands* (Leiden, Nederlandse UM, 1965. 555 pp. *f*78.50), is more confined to strictly technical terms and despite its emphasis on the metal industry, is very reliable and, for a two-way dictionary, reasonably comprehensive. E. L. Oberg, *Ten Bosch' Engels–Nederlands Technisch woordenboek* (4th rev. imp. Deventer, Kluwer, 1964. 436 pp. *f*22.50), is similar in scope to Peek above, and provides its complement, though it is not so up to date. J. V. Servotte. *Standaard viertalig woordenboek voor handel en financiën*, 3rd imp. (Brussels, Brepols, 1964. 960 pp. Fr.395) (French, English, Dutch, German). The scope here is similar to Oberg and Peek, with an emphasis on commerce, but, as a four-language dictionary it is less easy to handle. The most extensive, though less recent, commercial dictionary is A. Bons, *Engels handelswoordenboek*. (2nd imp. Deventer, Kluwer, 1957. 1,170 pp. *f*45), a comprehensive and useful supplement to more general Dutch–English dictionaries.

The remaining, specialised dictionaries are listed alphabetically according to the commercial or technical subject matter.

Advertising: Dictionary of Advertising and Distribution in German, Spanish, French, Italian, Dutch, Portuguese and Swedish (Basel, Verlag für Recht und Gesellschaft, 1954. 330 pp. S.Fr.80, DM.80).

Aeronautics: G. H. Frenot and A. H. Holloway, *AGARD Aeronautical multilingual dictionary*, London, Pergamon, 1960. 1,072 pp. £30. (English, French, German, Spanish, Italian, Dutch, Turkish, Russian).

Agriculture: T. J. Bezemer. *Land-, tuin- en boschbouwkundig woordenboek* (Arnhem, Van Loghum Slaterus, 1934. 295 pp.

*f*10.50). A Dutch–French–English–German agricultural and horticultural dictionary that is now seriously out of date. *See* Huitenga below.

T. Huitenga. *Nederlands–Engels woordenboek voor landbouwwetenschappen*, (Leiden, Nederlandse UM, 1976. *c*. 600 pp. *f*90). This will presumably supersede Bezemer above.

Chemistry: A. F. Dorian. *Elsevier's Dictionary of industrial chemistry in six languages* (English, French, Spanish, Italian, Dutch, German). 2 v. Amsterdam, Elsevier, 1964. *f*115.

Criminology: J. A. Adler. *Elsevier's Dictionary of criminal science in eight languages* (English, French, Italian, Spanish, Portuguese, Dutch, Swedish, German) (Amsterdam, Elsevier, 1,460 pp., *f*165).

EEC: M. H. List, and others. *Concordance in French, German, English, Italian, Dutch and Danish of the treaties establishing the European Communities* (Basel, Commission of the European Communities, Terminology Office, 1974. 414 pp. + indexes).

Electronics: W. E. Clason. *Elsevier's Dictionary of electronics and waveguides* (Amsterdam, Elsevier, 1957. 628 pp. *f*10) (English, French, Spanish, Italian, Dutch, German).

Gas: L'Union internationale de l'industrie du gaz, *Elsevier Dictionaire de l'industrie du gaz en sept langues* (French, English, Spanish, Italian, Portuguese, Dutch, German). (Amsterdam, Elsevier, 1961. 628 pp. *f*60; Supplement. 1973. 203 pp. *f*31.20).

Metallurgy: W. E. Clason, *Elsevier's Dictionary of metallurgy in six languages* (English, French, Spanish, Italian, Dutch, German). (Amsterdam, Elsevier, 1967. 634 pp. *f*72.50).

Paper: E. J. Labarre. *Dictionary and encyclopaedia of paper and paper-making with equivalents of technical terms in French, German, Dutch, Italian, Spanish and Swedish* (Oxford, University Press, 1952. 488 pp. £3.50).

Physics: W. E. Clason, *Elsevier's Dictionary of general physics in six languages* (English, French, Spanish, Italian, Dutch, German). (Amsterdam, Elsevier, 1962. 859 pp. *f*60).

Plastics: A. F. Dorian. *Six-language dictionary of plastics and rubber technology* (English, French, Spanish, Italian, Dutch, German). (London, Iliffe books, 1965. 808 pp. £25).

Rubber: Rubber-stichting (Delft). *Elsevier's Rubber dictionary in ten languages* (English, France, Spanish, Italian, Portuguese, German, Dutch, Swedish, Indonesian, Japanese). (Amsterdam, Elsevier, 1959. 1,537 pp. *f*165).

Shipping: J. Oderwald, *Technisch woordenboek voor de scheepsdienst in vier talen* (Rotterdam, Kweekschool voor de zeevaart, 1931. 298, 52 pp. *f*5.90). (Dutch, English, French, German).

Telecommunications. A. Visser. *Zestalig technisch woordenboek in hoofdzaak betreffende de verreberichtgeving* (The Hague, PTT, 1955. 778 pp. *f*17.50) (Dutch, French, English, German, Italian, Spanish).

W. E. Clason, Elsevier's Dictionary of television, radar and antennas in six languages (English, French, Spanish, Italian, Dutch, German). (Amsterdam, Elsevier, 1955. 760 pp. *f*62.50).

8

SCANDINAVIAN LANGUAGES

by M. P. BARNES, M.A.

INTRODUCTION

Although the Scandinavian languages are not normally taught in British schools, they can be read as a main or subsidiary subject in a number of universities, and are widely studied in evening classes. Many textbooks and dictionaries and much recorded material have been produced, particularly in the last few years, to help all kinds of student including those working on their own.

Once a student has mastered properly one of the continental Scandinavian languages (Danish, Norwegian, Swedish), he will have little difficulty in understanding the others. The gulf between Danish and Swedish is the widest; Norwegian and Swedish share many features of pronunciation, while the written language used by most Norwegians (*riksmål* or *bokmål*) is Danish in origin, although no Dane would now recognise it as his own. The two island Scandinavian languages, Faroese and Icelandic, have to be studied separately. Icelanders can make themselves understood in the Faroes with difficulty and vice versa, but native speakers of Danish, Norwegian and Swedish cannot understand either language without tuition. (Stories to the contrary, which enjoy wide circulation in Scandinavia, have their origin in false optimism and in too liberal a definition of 'understand'.)

Almost as many people speak Swedish as all the other Scandinavian languages together. This, combined with the comparative industrial and cultural importance of Sweden, has led many people wanting to learn a Scandinavian language to select Swedish, although recently there has been a growing interest in Norwegian. Linguistically there is not much to choose between

Danish, Norwegian and Swedish. All three have a grammatical structure very similar to that of English, but contain special difficulties of pronunciation for the English-speaking learner. The morphology and syntax of Norwegian (*riksmål*) is marginally the simplest, but for some people this advantage is outweighed by the lack of any true written or spoken standard, which can be confusing for the beginner. The grammatical structure and vocabulary of Icelandic have remained remarkably static over a period of a thousand years. While this enables those who know Icelandic well to read the medieval sagas without great difficulty, it means that the learner is faced with formal grammar almost of the complexity of Latin, and that knowledge of other languages and of 'international' terms is of less help than usual in mastering vocabulary. Icelandic pronunciation seems to cause the English-speaking learner fewer difficulties than that of Danish, Norwegian or Swedish. Faroese has a less complex formal grammar than Icelandic, but in all respects except pronunciation is closer to Icelandic than to the other Scandinavian languages. Faroese pronunciation is unlike that of Danish, Norwegian, Swedish or Icelandic, and is probably the most difficult for the English-speaking learner to master. This is partly because the written norm, modelled as it is on Icelandic orthography, bears no clear relationship to the pronunciation, and partly because Faroese contains so many sounds and combinations of sounds not found in English.

Textbooks, grammars and dictionaries. A large number of new Danish, Norwegian and especially Swedish language textbooks have appeared in recent years. Most of these have been produced in Scandinavia in response to the needs of immigrant workers; they are entirely in the language to be learnt and employ audio-visual techniques; some are accompanied by Scandinavian–English vocabularies. These courses are often very similar, and only those which address themselves specifically to the English-speaking learner or are in some way better than average are included here. Many of the older and poorer quality textbooks and grammars included in previous editions of this *Guide* have likewise been omitted even though many are still in print. What remains is a selection of items representing both traditional and more modern approaches to language learning which can reasonably be recommended to libraries and to the individual student.

Many new dictionaries and new editions of existing dictionaries have also recently been published (all of them in Scandinavia). Unhappily there is still a tendency to ignore the English-speaking user and in most he will look in vain for help with the pronunciation or inflexion of Scandinavian words. As in the case of the textbooks and grammars, only a selection of the available dictionaries appears here: abbreviated versions of longer dictionaries, technical dictionaries restricted to one branch of technology (often little more than pamphlets), pocket dictionaries (mainly for tourists) and phrase-books have for the most part been omitted.

Under **Icelandic** some inferior items have been included (with a note to this effect) because of the scarcity of material.

Editions and Impressions. The distinction between edition and impression is not as clear cut in Scandinavia as it is in Britain. Basically *utgave* (*utgåva* etc.) means edition, but it is occasionally used about books which to all intents and purposes are new impressions. *Opplag* (*upplaga* etc.) usually means impression, but it is not infrequently used about revised, even radically revised, editions. Sometimes the word *trykning* (*tryckning*) appears, particularly in Swedish books. This normally means what it says: (new) printing or reprint. In this chapter an attempt is made to distinguish between editions and impressions or reprintings according to British practice, irrespective of what Scandinavian term is used to describe a particular book.

Prices. Throughout this chapter the latest prices in Scandinavian or other currencies have been quoted for books published outside Britain, in as far as they are known. Where there is a British publisher, as opposed to an importing bookseller, the price is given in £ p. Prices are generally 1975–76, though some are earlier. Inflation in Iceland is currently running at about 50% a year, but in other Scandinavian countries it is well below 20%. Prices quoted in national bibliographies, publishers' and booksellers' lists may well differ among themselves and from those given here, depending on whether VAT or sales tax (applicable in Denmark, Iceland and Sweden) has been included or not, and at what rate. In Sweden, in addition, there is no fixed price for books. Danish and Swedish prices quoted are mostly minus VAT, Icelandic prices include the newly introduced sales tax. For various reasons it has been impossible to adopt a consistent policy in this matter. The advantage of using Scandinavian booksellers should be stressed. This is usually quicker and cheaper than going through an English bookseller. VAT is not charged on books exported, and this may balance the cost of postage.

National Bibliographies. In the classified indices of *Dansk bogfortegnelse* and *Svensk bokförteckning* there are special sections for Danish for foreigners (89.699) and Swedish for foreigners (Fct.). Here and (for bilingual dictionaries) under English language (*Dansk bogfortegnelse* 89.33 [*Engelske ordbøger*], *Svensk bokförteckning* Fe.) can be found virtually all the aids for the student of Danish or Swedish that have appeared in recent years, including many small technical dictionaries not included in this chapter (cf. above). *Norsk bokfortegnelse* has no special section for Norwegian for foreigners, but most of the relevant material can be found under 420 (English) and 439 (Norwegian school books). In *Landsbókasafn Íslands. Árbók* everything to do with the study of languages is listed under 400: *Málfræði*.

DANISH

Current Danish orthography dates from the spelling reform of 1948. This was very minor and books published before 1948 will cause the learner no problems. The introduction of the Swedish–Norwegian *å* in place of *aa* led to a change in the Danish alphabet. Whereas *aa* used to be treated as *a* + *a*, *å* was placed at the end. Danish practice now corresponds with Norwegian, both alphabets ending *x y z æ ø å*, while Swedish has the order *x y z å ä ö*.

TEXTBOOK COURSES & GRAMMARS

General Courses (all are for beginners unless otherwise stated).
It is difficult to recommend one Danish-language textbook in
particular. E. Norlev and H. A. Koefoed, *The way to Danish*
(3rd ed. Copenhagen, Munksgaard, 1968, reprinted 1973. 306
pp. D.kr.69) is probably the best all-round work, but the English
learner should note that it is written specifically for American
college instruction. It consists first of an introduction dealing
with grammatical terminology, pronunciation and the
relationship between spelling and pronunciation (pp. 11–27);
then comes the main part of the book, thirty chapters (giving a
total vocabulary of some 1,500 of the most commonly used
words in Danish) each subdivided into (1) text (telling one continuous story which is often quite entertaining), (2) explanations
of difficult terms in the text, (3) vocabulary with phonetic
transcriptions in the International Phonetic Alphabet, (4) words
and usage, (5) grammar and (6) exercises (pp. 28–261); finally
there is a cumulative Danish–English vocabulary giving pronunciation and full grammatical details (pp. 262–302), a grammatical index, and indices of special terms and practical information (pp. 303–6). Very clear explanations of Danish pronunciation, grammar and idiom; typographically excellent; suitable
for self-tuition, but it is unfortunate that there are no recordings
to accompany the book. H. A. Koefoed, *Teach yourself Danish*
(London, English Universities Press, 1958, reprinted 1975. xvi,
232 pp. £0.50) has a slightly different format from many of the
Teach yourself books: texts (untranslated anywhere in the book)
are followed by vocabularies, questions, grammatical notes and
exercises (there is a key to the questions and exercises in the normal way). This approach necessitates the inclusion of a
systematically arranged reference grammar 54 pp. long, which,
while useful to those with some knowledge of Danish, seems out
of place in a *Teach yourself* volume for beginners. There is a
clear and full introduction to Danish pronunciation using the
International Phonetic Alphabet, and the Linguaphone Institute
has issued a set of recordings (45 rpm records or cassettes. £12.;
£10.20 to schools, colleges or libraries) to accompany the book

as a whole. There is *no* cumulative glossary, only an index of Danish words, E. Bredsdorff, *Danish: An elementary grammar and reader* (Cambridge, Cambridge University Press, 1956. 2nd rev. impression 1958, reprinted 1973. xii, 301 pp. £2.80) is designed principally to take university students with no previous knowledge of the language up to first degree standard. It is reliable and good, but is hardly for the ordinary beginner unless he has the aid of a very sympathetic teacher. Excellent as a reference work for the more advanced learner who will also find the 88 pp. of reading matter with vocabulary notes and the 20 texts for translation into Danish useful material. Totally different in approach is B. Bangsgaard Laursen and P. Budtz-Jørgensen, *Lær dansk* (Copenhagen, Gjellerup, 1970, various parts subsequently reprinted in different years. Textbook. 69 pp. illus. D.kr.15.50; exercises. 97 pp. illus. D.kr.19; teachers' handbook. 21 pp. free; Danish–English word list. 56 pp. D.kr.18; 13 transparencies. D.kr.392. (D.kr.30.50 each if purchased separately); 38 picture cards. D.kr.43; 6 tapes or cassettes with 60 exercises and 5 listening tests. D.kr.770. (D.kr.133.50 each if purchased separately); textbook of the tape/cassette exercises compiled by M. Biørn. 84 pp. D.kr.20). This is a Danish version of Hildeman and Hedbäck's *Lär er svenska* (which see under Swedish). Like that course it is intended for every type of foreign learner from the immigrant worker to the university student of Danish. It is firmly based on audio-visual and direct methods and deals exclusively with the colloquial language. It is entirely in Danish except for the Danish–English word list and neither pronunciation nor grammar is properly explained or described. Transparencies, picture cards and tapes are not essential, but highly desirable if the course is to achieve maximum effect. While it seems to me to progress too quickly for those untrained in language learning, the fuss and bother of so much audiovisual hardware coupled with the lack of any serious analysis of pronunciation or grammar is likely to alienate the university student. This is a pity because the course is carefully structured and well thought out. It would be ideal for many evening classes. Less good than the above, but not to be ignored are: Ingeborg Stemann, *Danish: a practical reader* (5th ed. Copenhagen, Hagerup, 1969. viii, 287 pp. D.kr.29.75), which is a very thorough and reliable textbook, although to modern eyes it may look somewhat formal and typographically congested (first published 1938); S.-M. Hill, L. Høg and L. Kayerød, *Dansk for fremmedsprogede elever* (3rd ed. Copenhagen, Lærer-foreningernes materialeudvalg, 1975. Textbook. 103 pp. illus. D.kr.20; exercises. 109 pp. illus. D.kr.20; teachers' handbook. 52 pp. D.kr.18), which is intended primarily for school children in Denmark who are not native speakers of Danish, and makes slow but sure progress without analysing, describing or explaining anything; Aa. Salling, *Lær at tale dansk* (2nd ed. Copenhagen, Grafisk forlag, 1966, reprinted 1971. 241 pp. illus. Temporarily unavailable, to be reprinted photographically spring 1976. Previous price D.kr.30.50; 24.50), which is a lively and informal textbook for learning Danish by the direct method, but which, although intended for self-tuition as well as class work, provides only the briefest of grammatical explanations (in Danish) and gives no help with pronunciation. (According to *Books in print* a new edition of J. Dearden and K. Stig-Nielsen: *Spoken Danish*, accompanied by records or cassettes, was published by Spoken Language Services, Ithaca, N.Y., in 1973, but I have been unable to see a copy of this. The old 1946 Holt, Rinehart and Winston edition is out of print.)

For the more advanced student of Danish there are three volumes (all entirely in Danish). M. Biørn and H. Hesseldahl, *Huset i mellemgade* (2nd ed. Copenhagen, Akademisk forlag, 1969, reprinted 1973. 63 pp. illus. D.kr.16.30) is a textbook with reading passages, exercises etc. for those who have just passed the beginners' level, but who still find it difficult to read undoctored prose texts. M. Biørn and H. Hesseldahl, *Øvebog i dansk for udlændinge* (Copenhagen, Akademisk forlag, 1970, reprinted 1976. 178 pp. D.kr.43) is a book of exercises for students who are beyond the beginners' level. The exercises are arranged by part of speech or other feature and according to difficulty, and are based on structures known to cause problems to the foreign learner. I. Stemann and M. Nissen, *Moderne dansk for udlændinge* (3rd ed. Copenhagen, Gyldendal, 1969 [i.e. 1971], reprinted 1974. 207 pp. D.kr.40) together with M. Nissen, *Ordforklaringer og grammatiske øvelser* (Copenhagen, Gyldendal, 1969, reprinted 1974. 34 pp. D.kr.8.25) provides a very wide selection of reading material, an outline of grammar and exercises.

Reference Grammars. There is only one true reference grammar of Danish in English, although certain of the textbooks mentioned above could be used as such. P. Diderichsen, *Essentials of Danish grammar* (Copenhagen, Akademisk forlag, 1964, reprinted 1972. 80 pp. D.kr.22. Also available: 45 rpm record, *Danish pronunciation*, read by Diderichsen and containing spoken extracts from the book, including the Danish sound system, D.kr.9) is an extremely clearly written, comprehensive and thoroughly reliable handbook, indispensable for all who take their Danish seriously. For more advanced students P. Diderichsen. *Elementær dansk grammatik* (3rd ed. Copenhagen, Gyldendal, 1962, reprinted 1974. xv, 305 pp. D.kr.42.15), a by no means elementary grammar for Danes, can be recommended.

RECORDED MATERIAL

At the present time there is no Danish course where the main emphasis is on the spoken rather than the written word. However, by the autumn of 1976 the Linguaphone Institute hope to have issued *The Linguaphone Danish course* which will be entirely new, but based on the standard Linguaphone pattern.

DICTIONARIES

Standard Orthography. Dansk Sprognævn's *Retskrivningsord-bog* (4th ed. Copenhagen, Gyldendal, 1955, reprinted 1974. xxx, 299 pp. D.kr.20.15) lists, without definitions, the vocabulary of current Danish, using the post-1948 orthography. It gives full grammatical details (genders, inflexions, irregular forms etc.) and there is a helpful introduction dealing among other things with the use of capital letters, word division and punctuation in general.

General Translating Dictionaries. Students of Danish are lucky to have at their disposal (if anyone can afford them) two of the finest bilingual dictionaries ever compiled. H. Vinterberg and C. A. Bodelsen, *Dansk–engelsk ordbog* (2nd ed. Copenhagen, Gyldendal, 1966. 2nd impression with a supplement, 1973. 2 v. (xvi, 918; viii, 928 pp. including supplement.) D.kr.369.55) and B. Kjærulff Nielsen, *Engelsk–dansk ordbog* (Copenhagen, Gyldendal, 1964. 3rd impression with expanded supplement, 1974. xii, 1,471 pp. including supplement. D.kr.343.45) are first class by any standards. Apart from the fact that the pronunciation of the Danish entry words in the Vinterberg-Bodelsen work is not indicated, no serious criticism can be made of either. Both are extremely comprehensive and include specialised vocabulary from all walks of life. Full grammatical details of the entry words are given in the Danish–English volumes (Kjærulff Nielsen gives both grammatical details *and* pronunciation of the English entry words). There are many examples of usage in both dictionaries and different meanings are clearly defined and separated. Exemplary typography and very clear printing combined with a rigid systematisation of the material under each entry word facilitate use. In the Danish–English dictionary the range of English equivalents of the Danish entry words is an outstanding feature. Virtually all the shades of meaning in which a Danish word can be used are included, normally with examples. This work is so superior to any other Scandinavian–English dictionary that it can seriously be recommended to advanced students of Norwegian in preference to existing Norwegian–English dictionaries, and even students of Swedish can derive benefit from it. Unfortunately the prices of both dictionaries are speculative (a common feature of the Danish book trade), which puts them beyond the reach of most individuals, and, one would think, many libraries. For such people and institutions the excellent but much smaller H. Vinterberg and J. Axelsen, *Dansk–engelsk ordbog* ([*Gyldendals røde ordbøger*]. 7th rev. and enlarged ed. Copenhagen, Gyldendal. 1967, reprinted 1974. 8, 484 pp. D.kr.36.50) and H. Vinterberg and J. Axelsen, *Engelsk–dansk ordbog*) [*Gyldendals røde ordbøger*].

8th rev. ed. Copenhagen, Gyldendal, 1964, reprinted 1974. 8, 496 pp. D.kr.34.35) can be recommended. Danish–English gives full grammatical details of Danish words, but no pronunciation; English–Danish suffers from a lack of sufficient examples of usage where several Danish words are listed as equivalents of an English entry. In spite of any drawbacks these are probably the best medium-size Danish–English and English–Danish dictionaries available. Also good and reliable are A. Bolbjerg, *Dansk–engelsk ordbog* (4th ed. Copenhagen, Berlingske forlag, 1963, reprinted 1975. 558 pp. D.kr.27.40) and N. Haislund and Aa. Salling, *Engelsk–dansk ordbog* (3rd greatly enlarged ed. Copenhagen, Berlingske forlag, 1964. 564 pp. D.kr.19.50), although both will soon need bringing up to date and the Danish–English dictionary gives no help with the pronunciation, gender or inflexions of Danish words. Both volumes contain about 50,000 entry words. For those who want something smaller D. Hohnen (ed.), *Høsts engelsk–danske og dansk–engelske lommeordbog* (3rd ed. Copenhagen, Høst, 1966, reprinted 1975. 512 pp. D.kr.13.04) is a good buy. Although a pocket dictionary, it is more than large enough to meet the needs of the beginner. Gives no help with the pronunciation, gender or inflexions of Danish words, but has 6 pp. describing 'some elements of Danish grammar'.

Dictionaries of Synonyms. There are two dictionaries of Danish synonyms, and although intended for Danes either would be useful for the more advanced student. A. Karker (ed.), *Synonymordbogen* 5th ed. (Copenhagen, Politiken, 1973. 372 pp. D.kr.26.95) is probably slightly more comprehensive than U. Albeck, M. Rode and E. Timmermann, *Dansk synonymordbog* (5th rev. and enlarged ed. Copenhagen, Schultz, reprinted 1974. 301 pp. D.kr.40).

Technical Dictionaries. The only general works available are A. Warrern, *Dansk–engelsk teknisk ordbog* (4th ed. Copenhagen, J. Fr. Clausen, 1970. 368 pp. D.kr.111.60) and A. Warrern, *Engelsk–dansk teknisk ordbog* (6th ed. Copenhagen, J. Fr. Clausen, 1974. 383 pp. D.kr.118.25). Both are good, though not outstanding, and up to date. The Danish–English volume gives no help with the pronunciation, gender or inflexions of Danish words.

FAROESE

There is only one Faroese language textbook for English-speaking students. There are no Faroese–English or English–Faroese dictionaries, so a note is made below of the only translating dictionaries out of and into Faroese which exist. The order of the Faroese alphabet does not differ from the English except that between *d* and *e* comes *đ* and after *z* come *æ* *ø*.

TEXTBOOK COURSES & GRAMMARS

General Courses. W. B. Lockwood. *An introduction to modern Faroese* (Copenhagen, Munksgaard, 1955, reprinted 1964. Temporarily out of print. xii, 244 pp.) gives, as far as it goes, an excellent description of the language. It covers pronunciation (in great detail and including intonation, pp. 5–27), inflexions (pp. 28–101) and syntax (pp. 102–57), and has a small number of prose and verse texts for reading practice (pp. 158–200); there is also a Faroese–English glossary giving full grammatical details (pp. 201–44). Texts apart, this is a purely descriptive grammar and contains no exercises. It is in any case mainly for those who seek a reading knowledge of Faroese. No real attempt is made to deal with the colloquial language, which is often far removed in vocabulary, idiom and style from written or official usage.

DICTIONARIES

General Translating Dictionaries. M. A. Jacobsen and C. Matras, *Føroysk–donsk orđabók* (2nd ed. Tórshavn, Føroya Fróđskaparfelag, 1961. xxxvi, 521 pp. D.kr.50), with a supplement edited by J. H. W. Poulsen (Tórshavn, Føroya Fróđskaparfelag, 1974. viii, 252 pp. D.kr.60) is a very comprehensive Faroese–Danish dictionary, but is intended to be normative as well as informative and therefore does not include many words and phrases of Danish or international origin which are in common use in the spoken language. The companion volume is Jóhannes av Skarði. *Donsk–føroysk ordabók* (Tórshavn, Føroya Fródskaparfelag, 1967. xiv, 518 pp. Temporarily out of print, but shortly to be reissued in a revised edition). Essential for all non-native speakers who wish to write or speak Faroese, it nevertheless needs to be used with circumspection. It too is a normative dictionary, and many of the Faroese words and phrases are artificial and hardly recognised by native speakers; on the other hand, large parts of the ordinary, everyday language have been omitted.

ICELANDIC

There is little either in the way of textbooks or dictionaries that can be recommended wholeheartedly to students of Icelandic. What follows is therefore a list of such aids as are available. Most are dated and none deal properly with the modern colloquial language. Icelandic orthography is reasonably stable, and even the oldest works mentioned here hardly deviate from the modern norm (see, however, Snæbjörn Jónsson's *Primer*). The order of the Icelandic alphabet does not differ from the English except that between *d* and *e* comes *ð* and after *z* come *þ* *æ ö*.

TEXTBOOK COURSES & GRAMMARS

General Courses (all are for beginners). Stefán Einarsson, *Icelandic: grammar, texts, glossary* (2nd ed. Baltimore and London, Johns Hopkins Press, 1949, reprinted 1972. xxxviii, 502 pp. illus. £8.25) is by far the most detailed grammar for English-speaking students, but the very wealth of the detail makes it a difficult book for the beginner. As a reference work and especially a reference grammar for the more advanced student it is excellent. It contains substantial descriptions of Icelandic pronunciation (pp. 1–31), inflexions (pp. 32–104) and syntax (pp. 105–80), translation exercises based on specific sections of the grammar and with individual vocabularies (pp. 181–246), texts of various kinds for reading practice (pp. 247–93) and an Icelandic–English glossary (pp. 297–501) giving full grammatical details and a narrow phonetic transcription of the Icelandic words. Although a good introduction to rural Icelandic of thirty years ago, Stefán's book is a poor guide to the colloquial language of present-day Reykjavík where half the population now lives. (See also Recorded Material below.) P. J. T. Glendening, *Teach yourself Icelandic* (London, English Universities Press, 1961. Rev. 2nd impression 1966, reprinted 1973. xviii, 190 pp. £0.50) follows the normal *Teach yourself* pattern of grammatical explanation, vocabulary list and exercises, but has in addition several annotated translations, a list of proverbs and idiomatic expressions and 9 pp. of paradigms. The Icelandic–English vocabulary at the end is substantial (c. 1,750 entry words), but the section on pronunciation at the beginning is too brief and contains a large number of errors and ambiguities. The International Phonetic Alphabet, which might have made some things clearer, is not used. There are many errors elsewhere in the book too, which reach their climax in a completely nonsensical chapter on the differences between the medieval and modern language. *Teach yourself Icelandic* can perhaps most profitably be used together with Stefán Einarsson's grammar. More reliable than Glendening but dated both in method and content (and in the use of *je* for *é*) is Snæbjörn Jónsson, *A primer of modern Icelandic* (London, Oxford University Press, 1927, reprinted 1966. 8, 284 pp. £2). A new textbook of Icelandic which I have not seen is Einar Pálsson. *Icelandic in easy stages with notes in English* 1 (Reykjavík, Mímir, 1975. 131 pp. illus. I.kr.2,570). This contains graded lessons for practice in colloquial Icelandic designed for the foreigner living in Iceland.

RECORDED MATERIAL

The Linguaphone Icelandic course (London, Linguaphone Institute, [n.d.]. £49.50; £42.07 to schools, colleges or libraries) was compiled by Stefán Einarsson at about the same time as *Icelandic* (1942–45, see above), and follows the standard Linguaphone pattern (see under Norwegian or Swedish). First recorded (badly) in about 1947, the course has now (1975) been reissued with completely new and far more satisfactory recordings made by four Icelandic actors. None of the books for the course has been revised and the factual information is often very dated. The texts too would benefit from some revision if they are to continue to represent 'easy-flowing and perfectly natural idiomatic language'. A copy of Stefán's *Icelandic* comes with the Linguaphone set and many references are made to it throughout the course. Four of the folk-tales in *Icelandic* have been recorded as part of the course, and according to a note in the latest impression of *Icelandic* this recording, together with one illustrating the sounds of the language, can be bought separately from Linguaphone by owners of the book.

DICTIONARIES

General Translating Dictionaries. There are only two of any size and except for the relatively large number of entry words neither is good. Arngrímur Sigurdsson, *Íslenzk-ensk ordabók* (2nd enlarged ed. Reykjavík, Leiftur, 1975. 942 pp. I.kr.4,800) gives no help with Icelandic pronunciation, gender or inflexions, adds numerous archaic, slang and dialect words, with little or no indication of their connotations, to the standard English translations of the Icelandic entries, and provides few examples of usage in either Icelandic or English. A number of common words are wanting, yet the book is full of obscure Icelandic aeronautical and aviation terms, many of which hardly exist outside dictionaries and word lists. Sigurdr Örn Bogason, *Ensk-íslenzk ordabók* (2nd ed. Reykjavík, Ísafold, 1966, reprinted 1972 or 1973 [different dates on the English and Icelandic title pages]. 8, 862 pp. I.kr.4,200) far too often gives undue prominence to the literal or archaic meaning of an English entry word, sometimes to the total exclusion of the sense in which it is most commonly used. Many everyday English words are not to be found and there are a number of errors. Not recommended to the English-speaking student unless he knows both languages well enough to spot the traps. A. Taylor, *English–Icelandic, Icelandic–English pocket dictionary* (Reykjavík, Orðabókaútgáfan, 1956 [as two separate volumes], reprinted in one volume without date [1972]. 208; 176 pp. I.kr.792) is more for the tourist than the serious student (*c.* 5,500 and 4,500 entry words respectively), but both parts give the genders of Icelandic nouns, and the Icelandic–English dictionary has one or two notes on pronunciation and grammar. For the complete beginner this might be a better buy than the two larger works; it is certainly a lot cheaper. Those interested in older Icelandic are better catered for. R. Cleasby and Gudbrand Vigfusson, *An Icelandic–English dictionary* (2nd ed. Oxford, Clarendon Press, 1957, reprinted 1975. xlvi, 834 pp. £15) is an excellent and comprehensive work covering Icelandic writings from the earliest manuscripts down to *c.* 1850, though with a heavy bias on the medieval period.

Icelandic Monolingual Dictionary. Since the quality of the modern Icelandic bilingual dictionaries is generally poor, mention should be made of Árni Böðvarsson: *Íslenzk orðabók* (Reykjavík, Menningarsjómur, 1963. 12, 852 pp. Temporarily out of print, but shortly to be reissued in a revised edition). For the more advanced learner this dictionary is indispensable; fuller, more reliable and safer to use than the big Icelandic–English and English–Icelandic dictionaries.

Technical Dictionaries. What functions as the principal Icelandic technical dictionary is Sigurður Guðmundsson. *Tækniorðasafn* (Reykjavík, Menntamálaráðuneyti, 1959. 222 pp. I.kr.480), although in fact its main task is to provide a list of native Icelandic words to replace foreign or international technical terms. Icelandic entry words with (where necessary) detailed English translations (pp. 7–120), English entry words with (mostly) one-word Icelandic translations (pp. 121–222).

NORWEGIAN

Prior to 1907 written Norwegian *riksmål* was virtually indistinguishable from Danish. The language has since undergone three major alterations, in 1907, 1917 and 1938, and a minor revision in 1959. These have affected orthography, morphology, syntax and vocabulary, and their ultimate aim has been to amalgamate *riksmål* (*bokmål*) with *nynorsk* (*landsmål*). While beginners may use textbooks published before 1959 with reasonable confidence (as to the type of Norwegian therein), they should avoid any published before 1938. (This also applies to textbooks of *nynorsk* in Norwegian – none are available in English.) A comprehensive and very fair account of Norwegian language politics is E. Haugen, *Language conflict and language planning: the case of modern Norwegian* (Cambridge Mass., Harvard University Press, 1966. xvi, 373 pp. illus. $11).

TEXTBOOK COURSES & GRAMMARS

General Courses (all are for beginners unless otherwise stated). The best all-round Norwegian language textbook is undoubtedly E. Haugen and K. Chapman, *Spoken Norwegian* (2nd rev. ed. New York, Holt, Rinehart and Winston, 1964. xviii, 416, xli pp. illus. $9.95; manual $3; tapes $7\frac{1}{2}$ ips $140; $3\frac{3}{4}$ ips $70), with its companion reader, K. Chapman. *Basic Norwegian reader* (New York, Holt, Rinehart and Winston, 1966. iv, 90, 34 pp. illus. $5.45). *Spoken Norwegian* consists of 25 chapters, each divided into two halves. Most chapters contain dramatised conversation, drill based on sentence patterns in the conversation, questions on the conversation, suggestions in English for conversation in Norwegian, grammar (rules and notes in English followed by exercises), further dramatised conversation, and references to passages in the companion reader (this last in chs. 11–25 only). There is a Norwegian–English vocabulary at the end (pp. iii–xxxv) giving pronunciation and full grammatical details. The book is very clearly printed, well set out, well illustrated and properly indexed. The Norwegian is modern and colloquial and the everyday situations dealt with give the student an excellent introduction to Norway and the Norwegians. (According to *Books in print*, a new edition of *Spoken Norwegian*, under Haugen's name alone and accompanied by records or cassettes, was published by Spoken Language Services, Ithaca, N.Y., in

1973, but I have been unable to see a copy of this.) *Basic Norwegian reader* consists of well-annotated passages taken chiefly from nineteenth- and twentieth-century authors. The subject matter and vocabulary are closely coordinated with the relevant chapter in *Spoken Norwegian*. There are questions on the extracts for answer in Norwegian, and a full vocabulary at the end of the book (*c.* 1,300 entries) giving unexpected pronunciations, grammatical details and reference to *Spoken Norwegian*. A. Sommerfelt and I. Marm, *Teach yourself Norwegian* (2nd rev. ed. London, English Universities Press, 1967, reprinted 1975. xiv, 282 pp. £0.50) follows the normal *Teach yourself* pattern of grammatical explanation, vocabulary list and exercises, but is notable for its very thorough and authoritative section on pronunciation (completely revised for the new edition by T. Støverud whose contribution goes unacknowledged in the book) and the clarity of its explanations of the more difficult parts of Norwegian grammar. Even for those who are not teaching themselves, it is an indispensable reference book which all can afford. Despite a number of inaccuracies and obscurities, Bjarne Berulfsen and Philip Boardman, *Elementary Norwegian* (Oslo, University of Oslo International Summer School, 1968. vii, 120, xviii pp. illus. N.kr.30; recordings of all the texts and exercises on 18 tapes N.kr.700, or cassettes N.kr.400) is good for class or language laboratory work. Basic Norwegian grammar and vocabulary are taught in 18 chapters, each of which contains a dramatised conversation and a related reading passage, a grammar section and, most notably, extensive pronunciation and grammar drills. Not recommended for self-tuition. Totally different in approach is I. H. Arnestad and A. Hvenekilde, *Snakker du norsk?* (Oslo, Studentersamfundets Fri Undervisnings forlag, 1972, reprinted 1974. 4, 283 pp illus. N.Kr.44; teachers' handbook. 1974. 4, 76 pp. N.kr.30; recordings of exercises and dialogues on 36 tapes N.Kr.1,410, or 18 cassettes N.kr.525; 68 transparencies for overhead projector N.kr.442). This book is firmly based on audio-visual and direct methods and deals exclusively with the colloquial language. It is entirely in Norwegian except for Norwegian–English–French–German vocabularies, and no explanations, grammatical or otherwise, are offered. It is best used with the tapes and transparencies, and is clearly unsuitable for self-tuition. Given all the hardware and an enthusiastic teacher, however, *Snakker du norsk?* provides a sound, carefully structured course which has been used to good effect in teaching Norwegian to foreigners in Norway. A traditional textbook with comprehensive sections on pronunciation and grammar is E. Haugen, *Beginning Norwegian* (3rd rev. ed. London, Harrap, 1957, reprinted 1974. xii, 226 pp. £1.90). Each chapter contains readings, questions on the readings, vocabulary, grammar with examples and rules, and a large number of exercises. It can be used either in class or for private study (though there is no key to the exercises). It suffers from a number of foggy grammatical rules and from having readings which consist almost entirely of fairy or children's stories. Even the publishers claim no more than that 'it presents those elements of the language which are indispensable to reading knowledge of Norwegian.' R. and A. Maaso. *Så snakker vi norsk: Norwegian level one* (Oslo, Cappelen, 1970 reprinted in smaller format 1975. 4, 188 pp. illus. N.kr.48; recordings of dialogues, exercises etc. on 9 tapes N.kr.860, or cassettes N.kr.775 from A/S Lydbåndservice, Waldemar Thranes gate 73, Oslo 1; the remainder of the material advertised in the introduction to the 1970 printing will not now appear) is similar to *Snakker du norsk?* in that it relies more on the power of example than on explanation. However, some grammatical generalisations are included, and there are appendices containing among other things grammatical summaries and a description of Norwegian pronunciation using the International Phonetic Alphabet. Intended primarily for schools in the USA the book is lively and very clearly printed, but it progresses far too slowly, and only about half of basic Norwegian grammar is covered. Could be used for self-tuition as far as it goes.

For the more advanced student of Norwegian there is little that can be recommended. I. H. Arnestad and A. Hvenekilde, *På'n igjen* (Oslo, Studentersamfundets Fri Undervisnings forlag, 1975. 6, 137 pp. illus. N.kr.25) consists of 60 extracts from Norwegian newspapers (photographically reproduced) followed by questions, suggested exercises and passages for dictation based on the extracts. Because of the ephemeral nature of many newspaper stories some of the texts are difficult to follow in every detail. S. Klouman and Aa. K. Smidt, *Moderne norsk litteratur* (Oslo, Universitetsforlaget, 1968, reprinted with minor alterations 1972. 175 pp. N.kr.26) consists of 35 passages, some verse, from the works of Norwegian authors. On pp. 127–75 there are brief notes on the authors and explanations (in Norwegian) of difficult words and phrases.

Reference Grammars. There is only one reference grammar of Norwegian in English: B. Berulfsen, *Norwegian grammar* (3rd ed. Oslo, Aschehoug, 1971. 6, 82 pp. N.kr.30) is an indispensable supplementary work covering virtually all the essential points. For advanced learners there is O. Næs, *Norsk grammatikk* (3rd ed. Oslo, Fabritius, 1972. 464 pp. N.kr.85), a comprehensive practical and theoretical grammar of modern *riksmål* and *nynorsk*.

Special Aspects of Grammar. Pronunciation. R. G. Popperwell, *The pronunciation of Norwegian* (Cambridge, Cambridge University Press, 1963. xii, 229 pp. £4.75) is an advanced work following the methods of Daniel Jones, and is probably of more value to the phonetician than the learner of Norwegian. It is accompanied by a 45 rpm record spoken by T. Støverud.

RECORDED MATERIAL

There are only two courses in Norwegian where the main emphasis is on recordings rather than the printed word. *The Linguaphone Norwegian course* (London, Linguaphone Institute, no date, but both textbooks and recordings are from 1961–62. £49.50; £42.07 to schools, colleges or libraries) follows the standard Linguaphone pattern and includes textbook, alphabetical and collateral vocabulary with notes on pronunciation, a booklet of explanatory notes on grammar and idiom and students' instructions. The recordings are available on either 45 rpm records or cassettes. They are of a high quality, and the course as a whole can be strongly recommended. For the advanced student there is T. Støverud and R. Popperwell, *Norsk litteraturantologi,* (London, Modern Humanities Research Association, 1976. 2 v. (xx, 630; xx, 662 pp.). £12,

£7.50 each if purchased separately; 28 cassettes. £84, £36 and £48 if purchased in two sets of 12 and 16, £3.50 each if purchased separately). This monumental work aims to provide a full and representative anthology of Norwegian literature *c.* 1700–1972. The recordings, which are mostly taken from the archives of the Norwegian Broadcasting Corporation, are by Norwegian actors and authors. They have great artistic merit and are of a very high technical quality. They also cover the main varieties of spoken Norwegian. The printed texts represent exactly what is heard on the cassettes, and there are extensive textual and phonetic commentaries. The course is entirely in Norwegian and there is no vocabulary of any kind.

DICTIONARIES

Standard Orthography. The most comprehensive dictionary or word list (of *riksmål/bokmål*) giving current spellings, parts of speech, genders, inflexions etc. is J. Sverdrup, M. Sandvei and B. Fossestøl, *Tanums store rettskrivningsordbok* (4th ed. Oslo, Tanum, 1974. xxvi, 525 pp. N.kr.66). Although it adheres to the latest rules of orthography and grammar, this work is not officially sponsored. There are very few definitions, and only pronunciations which might cause difficulty for Norwegians are given. There is a helpful introduction dealing among other things with the use of capital letters, word division and punctuation in general. Contains *c.* 300,000 words. Dag Gundersen, *Norsk ordbok: bokmål og nynorsk* (Oslo, Universitetsforlaget, 1966, reprinted 1974. 247 pp. N.kr.40; 29) includes both forms of Norwegian. Gundersen gives the words with their inflexions, and distinguishes those words or forms which are only used in *riksmål/bokmål* or in *nynorsk*, but provides no definitions.
General Translating Dictionaries (see also under Danish dictionaries). The best Norwegian–English dictionary is undoubtedly E. Haugen and others, *Norwegian–English dictionary* (Oslo, Universitetsforlaget, and Madison, University of Wisconsin Press, 1965, reprinted 1974. 500 pp. $17.50; $6.95 or N.kr.29). This is the only Scandinavian dictionary of any size (over 60,000 entries) intended primarily for English-speaking

users. It covers both *bokmål* and *nynorsk* (which can make it a bit complicated to use for the beginner), gives genders, inflexions and help with pronunciation (including the tone of every word listed), and has cross references from many of the variant spellings which can occur in Norwegian. There is also a lengthy introduction (pp. 13–42) giving instructions to the user, notes on the historical background of present-day Norwegian, a guide to pronunciation and a reference bibliography. The only serious criticism of the dictionary is that the range of English equivalents of the Norwegian entry words is small. While this will not hamper the beginner, more advanced students and translators may prefer Vinterberg and Bodelsen's Danish–English dictionary (which see), even when working with Norwegian. Far and away the best English–Norwegian volume is B. Berulfsen and H. Svenkerud, *Cappelens store engelsk–norsk ordbok* (Oslo, Cappelen, 1968. 1,376 pp. N.kr.229). Based on Kjærulff Nielsen's monumental English–Danish dictionary (which see), it contains *c*. 140,000 entries and another 100,000 expressions and figures of speech. It has a very comprehensive vocabulary, including many specialised trade, professional and technical terms; under each entry combinations of the entry word with others are systematically arranged; clear printing coupled with carefully thought-out typography facilitate use. Although a dictionary of the highest standard, it is intended for Norwegian users, and no help is given with the pronunciation, gender or inflexions of Norwegian words. The same drawback applies to the following six dictionaries which are otherwise sound. W. Kirkeby, *Norsk–engelsk ordbok* (Oslo, Gyldendal, 1970, reprinted with minor alterations 1974. 480 pp. N.kr.39.50) is in some respects more detailed than Haugen's work, and should not be overlooked since the items included in the two dictionaries differ considerably. B. and T. K. Berulfsen, *Engelsk–norsk ordbok* (Oslo, Gyldendal, 1974. 427 pp. N.kr.39.50) is a completely revised version of a dictionary which was first published in 1933 and appeared subsequently in several editions and numerous impressions. The main drawback for the English-speaking user was the practice of giving several Norwegian equivalents for each English entry word, but few examples of usage to indicate the precise meaning or function of the Norwegian words. Little attempt has been made to remedy this in the new edition, but for those who cannot afford *Cappelens store*, or who want a handier volume, there is no fuller English–Norwegian dictionary available. Søren Seland, *Norsk–engelsk* (Oslo, Cappelen, 1975. xii, 304 pp. N.kr.37) is typographically much clearer than Kirkeby's dictionary (see above), but only about half the size, the number of examples of usage in particular being considerably less. The companion Cappelen volume, H. Svenkerud. *Engelsk–norsk* (Oslo, Cappelen, 1975. xvi, 304 pp. N.kr.37) is likewise typographically clearer though much smaller than the Berulfsens' dictionary (see above), but for the beginner at least the absence of large numbers of unexemplified Norwegian words, which is what accounts for the difference in size, can be a positive advantage. In addition, Svenkerud's dictionary gives synonyms of the English entry words where necessary to indicate differences in meaning, and this makes it much easier for the English–speaking user to choose among the Norwegian equivalents. The commonest as well as low-frequency English words have mostly been omitted from this work. J. H. B. Bjørge, *Engelsk amerikansk norsk ordbok* (Oslo, Fabritius, 1959. 398 pp. N.kr.31.50), as the title suggests, is notable for the place it gives to American English. With its *c*. 25,000 entry words plus compounds, derivations, phrases etc., it is about the same size as Svenkerud's dictionary, but typographically not as clear, and certainly not as up to date. W. Guy, *Norsk–engelsk ordbok for det praktiske liv* (Oslo, Gyldendal, 1952, reprinted 1974. 292 pp. N.kr.39.50) is primarily intended for shops, firms and commercial colleges in Norway, but because of the wide range of items included can be used with advantage by anyone. It ought now to be revised and brought up to date.

Dictionaries of Idiom. S. Follestad, *Engelske idiomer* (2nd ed. Oslo, Fabritius, 1972. 574 pp. N.kr.78) is an alphabetical list of 16,000 or more idiomatic expressions in Norwegian with their English equivalents and sentences illustrating usage. There is a Norwegian catchword index but no English index.

Dictionaries of Synonyms. D. Gundersen, *Norsk synonymordbok* (Oslo, Gyldendal, 1964, reprinted 1974. 223 pp. N.kr.38.50) contains over 21,000 entry words, *c*. 17,500 of

which refer to the *c*. 3,500 main articles. Although intended for Norwegians, it can be a useful book for the advanced learner.
Pronunciation Dictionaries. B. Berulfsen, *Norsk uttaleordbok* (Oslo, Aschehoug, 1969. 368 pp. N.kr.70) lists *c*. 28,000 words, including personal and place-names. The pronunciation of each word is given in the International Phonetic Alphabet, but apart from parts of speech, no other information is included. Intended for Norwegians, *Norsk uttaleordbok* is also a splendid aid for the learner, although it is a pity that the introduction contains much less information than that in I. Alnæs, *Norsk uttaleordbok* (1925), particularly since it is upon this older work that Berulfsen's is largely based.
Technical Dictionaries. The only general works available are J. Ansteinsson, *Norsk–engelsk teknisk ordbok* (Trondheim, F. Brun, 1954, reprinted 1963. 8, 327 pp. N.kr.60) and J. Ansteinsson. *Engelsk–norsk teknisk ordbok* (3rd rev. ed. by A. T. Andreassen. Trondheim, F. Brun, 1966, reprinted 1973. 8, 511 pp. N.kr.89). The Norwegian–English volume is notable for giving the genders of Norwegian nouns and parts of speech, but is now seriously in need of up-dating. The English–Norwegian dictionary is more recent and comprehensive, and contains much useful additional information for scientific and technical translators.

SWEDISH

Swedish orthography has remained stable since the spelling reform of 1906.

There have previously been a large number of textbooks, grammars and dictionaries available for English-speaking learners of Swedish (see the bibliography in B. Holmbäck and others, 'About Sweden', *Sweden illustrated* XV, 1968, reprinted and issued separately without date by the Swedish Institute), but the quantity and diversity of the material being published today is truly astonishing, and somewhat alarming for the bibliographer. For the library and the student too it presents problems. Without guidance it is impossible to weigh up the merits of all that is offered, and buying Swedish language material can be a wild gamble. Part of the difficulty is that many textbooks, recordings etc. primarily intended for immigrants in Sweden are issued as 'all purpose' courses and described as suitable for teaching Swedish in most or all other contexts. In some cases this may be true, but in others it is not. An English-speaking learner will normally make better and faster progress using a textbook which takes account of the differences between Swedish and English; a person with linguistic training, say a university student, will usually demand a more analytical approach and advance more rapidly than an immigrant worker or his child; a beginner teaching himself is not much helped by text-books entirely in Swedish. With such points in mind a careful and rigorous choice has been made here, so as to include what seem to me the best examples of each type of course that I have seen. Because of the sheer volume of the material as much has probably been omitted as included. The majority of courses omitted, however, are immigrant worker orientated and almost identical in approach to similar items described in this chapter. (Up to date, but crude bibliographical details of most of what is available can be obtained from The Swedish Institute, Postbox 7072, 103 82 Stockholm 7.)

Bibliographical note: Book prices in Sweden are not fixed and varying prices are given in lists and brochures for many of the volumes included here. The exact year of publication of, and number of pages in, certain of the items that make up the large audio-visual courses cannot always be guaranteed, since sometimes the publishers' brochures, the Swedish Institute lists and the actual books are in disagreement, and I have not always been able to see every item included in such courses.

TEXTBOOK COURSES & GRAMMARS

General Courses for Beginners. There are two very good audio-visual/direct method courses for beginners. Both are entirely in Swedish except for Swedish–English word lists. S. Higelin, B. Svensson, K. Peterson and B. Hammarberg, *Svenska för er* (2nd rev. ed. Stockholm, Sveriges Radios förlag, 1972 [in progress].

Part 1: textbook. 93 pp. S.kr.24.40 (revised); exercises. 92 pp. S.kr.23.40 (revised); teachers' handbook. 80 pp. S.kr.14.65 (revised); Swedish–English word list. 50 pp. S.kr.13.65 (revised); Part 2: textbook. 61 pp. S.kr.24.40 (revised); exercises. 62 pp. S.kr.23.40 (revised); teachers' handbook. 63 pp. S.kr.14.65; Swedish–English word list. 46 pp. S.kr.13.65. All illus. except word lists. 8 tapes to go with Part 1 S.kr.230.25, or 4 cassettes. S.kr.157.45; 4 tapes to go with Part 2 S.kr.185.30, or 3 cassettes. S.kr.119.10) is a very carefully planned and structured course in colloquial Swedish for two terms of concentrated study, one part per term. There are no explanations, generalisations or rules, which makes it difficult to use the books without a teacher. The aim of the course is to teach Swedish pronunciation and basic morphology and syntax using a vocabulary of 1,600 of the most common words. The emphasis is entirely on practical everyday situations the learner is likely to meet in Sweden. In addition to the textbooks, recordings etc. noted above, a comprehensive set of audio-visual aids and further tapes are available in connection with this course, as well as a wide selection of more general audio-visual material (details from Sveriges Radios förlag, 105 10 Stockholm). The course *can* be taught without tapes, pictures, cards etc., but it is desirable to have at least the basic tapes/cassettes for which prices are given above. *Svenska för er* is widely used both in Sweden and abroad. An additional textbook which can be studied in conjunction with *Svenska för er* (or other beginners' courses) is S. Higelin and others, *Samtal på svenska* (Stockholm, Sveriges Radios förlag, 1973. 64 pp. illus. S.kr.16.60. Libraries can obtain recordings of the texts by special order to the publishers, no price given), 20 conversational pieces reflecting everyday situations (with monolingual word lists), accompanied by examples of prepositional usage and instructions for students and teachers (Swedish only). N.-G. Hildeman and A.-M. Hedbäck, *Lär er svenska* (Stockholm, Almqvist och Wiksell, 1968, mostly reprinted 1972–73. Textbook. 69 pp. illus. S.kr.20; exercises. 99 pp. illus. S.kr.20; key to exercises. 28 pp. S.kr.3; teachers' handbook. 24 pp. S.kr.9; Swedish–English word list. 68 pp. S.kr.15. Recordings of the texts on 7 45 rpm records S.kr.90, 3 tapes S.kr. 200 or 3

cassettes S.kr.200. Recordings of some of the exercises for use
in language laboratories together with a booklet S.kr.510, the
booklet alone S.kr.7) is very similar to the previous course. It is
shorter, and there is therefore not as much detail or repetition of
structures, nor is quite the same emphasis placed on giving the
learner practical information about everyday life in Sweden. Virtually no explanations, generalisations or rules are given, but
since there is a key to the exercises, this is a slightly better
course for self-instruction than *Svenska för er*. It too is used
widely in Sweden and abroad. An earlier English version still
available is N.-G. Hildeman, A.-M. Beite and S. Higelin, *Learn
Swedish* (4th ed. Stockholm, Almqvist och Wiksell, 1973,
reprinted 1974. 189 pp. illus. S.kr.22. Recordings of the texts on
5 45 rpm records S.kr.85, 2 tapes S.kr.170 or 2 cassettes
S.kr.110). In many ways this is preferable to the monolingual
course, partly because it has the English-speaking learner in
view and partly because grammatical rules and explanations are
given, but it is much briefer than *Lär er svenska* in the early
stages and additional practice would seem necessary. A book
designed to supplement *Learn Swedish* is N.-G. Hildeman and
others, *Practise Swedish* (2nd ed. Stockholm, Almqvist och
Wiksell, 1963, reprinted 1975. 103 pp. S.kr.16) which consists
of numerous grammatical and English-Swedish translation exercises. Although the vocabulary and grammatical content of the
2nd edition are closely adjusted to *Learn Swedish* (beware of
the 1st edition [1957] where they are not), the book can easily be
used in conjunction with other readers or textbooks since it contains a Swedish–English vocabulary listing all the words which
occur in the exercises. A key is also available: N.-G. Hildeman
and I. Olsen, *Key to Practise Swedish* (Stockholm, Almqvist och
Wiksell, 1963, reprinted 1965. 56 pp. S.kr.15). M. Holm and M.
Mathlein. *Svensk, svenska* (Stockholm, Skriptor, 1974, reprinted
1975 [teachers' handbook and Swedish–English word list give
no date of publication, handbook printed 1975]. Textbook. 155
pp. illus. S.kr.55; teachers' handbook. 32 pp. illus. S.kr.10;
Swedish–English word list. 46 pp. S.kr.14. 10 tapes S.kr.880 or
5 cassettes S.kr.500. Transparencies also available, price unknown) is an audio-visual/direct method course whose authors
have clearly begun to suspect that language learning may con-

sist of more than imitation. The textbook comprises 40 lessons (entirely in Swedish), each of which has a text illustrating a point of grammar, a grammatical generalisation based on this (seldom a rule, usually a table of examples from which the student must draw his own conclusions) and a small number of exercises. There is a strong emphasis on teaching correct pronunciation and intonation, and a monolingual word list and index at the end gives the word tone, gender and inflexional endings of each word entered. This course cannot be wholly recommended for self-tuition; it is, however, probably the best choice for those who want the advantages of audio-visual and direct method teaching combined with enough phonetic and grammatical systematisation to enable the student to understand something of what he is learning. This is especially so if it is used in conjunction with E. Nylund-Brodda and B. Holm (ed.), *Enspråkiga övningar i svenska* 1–2 (Stockholm, Skriptor, Book 1 1967, 10th *upplaga* 1974 [this *upplaga* is in fact a new edition as may some or all of the other *upplagor* have been]; Book 2 1968, 8th *upplaga* 1975. Book 1: xii, 189 pp. illus. S.kr.40; Book 2: viii, 211 pp. S.kr.40. Also available: teachers' handbook for Book 1. 1974. 29 pp. S.kr.10; key to Book 1. 1974. 21 pp. S.kr.14; teachers' handbook for Book 2. 1975. 24 pp. S.kr.10. A key to Book 2 can also be expected. Tapes are available to accompany both Books, price unknown), which provides the best, most comprehensive and largest collection of grammatical exercises for students of Swedish I have seen. The two Books follow the arrangement of Swedish grammar in *Deskriptiv svensk grammatik* (which see below) and for each point dealt with in the exercises the student is referred to the relevant paragraph(s) in the grammar. *Enspråkiga övningar i svenska* is part of the same series as *Svensk, svenska* (both go under the title *Svenskkursen*) and provides an excellent supplement to this, but it is meant for use with any Swedish language textbook. It can be thoroughly recommended for class work and self-tuition. Much more traditional but good and reliable textbooks are: (1) R. J. McClean, *Swedish: a grammar of the modern language* (i.e. *Teach yourself Swedish*. 3rd rev. ed. London, English Universities Press, 1969, reprinted 1975. xiv, 322 pp. £0.60) which follows the normal *Teach yourself* pattern of grammatical explanation, vocabulary list and exercises, but is more thorough than many books in this series and takes the student up to University of London General Degree level (note also in the *Teach yourself* series: J. S. Oswald, *Swedish phrase book*. 1958, reprinted 1974. 156 pp. £0.40); (2) H. H. Borland. *Swedish for students* (London, Harrap, and Heidelberg, Julius Groos, 1970. 4, 288 pp. £2.10; DM.16) which is an excellent introduction to Swedish on much the same lines as the *Teach yourself* book, but with slightly greater emphasis on the colloquial language (intended mainly for students at universities or evening classes, but also suitable for self-tuition, particularly if the key to the exercises is obtained, published only by Julius Groos [n.d.]. 54 pp. DM.5); (3) I. Björkhagen. *First Swedish book* (9th rev. ed. Stockholm, Svenska Bokförlaget, Norstedt, 1964 [1st ed. 1923], reprinted 1967. 174 pp. S.kr.16) which consists mainly of reading passages, exercises and proses illustrating the rules given in the author's *Modern Swedish grammar* (see below), to which reference is continually made. This book, even in its revised form, is not as up to date as *Teach yourself Swedish* or *Swedish for students* and much of the reading matter is far removed from the situations a foreigner is likely to encounter in Sweden today. In addition to these three, Cambridge University Press is shortly to publish a textbook firmly in the traditional mould: G. Hird, *Swedish: an elementary grammar-reader for university students.* 'Grammar-reader' are the operative words here, for the emphasis is very much on grammatical rules and on written and literary Swedish. The book also contains exercises, including Swedish composition (without key), copious vocabularies with full grammatical details, and grammatical tables. Good for university students, but a bit daunting for others.

General Courses for Intermediate Students. There are a large number of courses, readers etc. available for students just past the beginner's stage or at a more advanced level. A well-structured direct method course with all the audio-visual trappings is L. Bruzæus and U. Wallin, *Svenska, Mera svenska, Ännu mera svenska* (Lund, Kursverksamheten vid Lunds Universitet. *Svenska*: 1972. 239 pp. illus. S.kr.35; *Mera svenska*: 1971. 184 pp. illus. S.kr.32; *Ännu mera svenska*: 1971. 177 pp. illus. S.kr.32. In addition there are the following aids: for

Svenska: teachers' handbook. 1974. 73 pp. S.kr.15; key to exercises. 1973. 37 pp. S.kr.3; 4 tapes (or cassettes, number and price unspecified) S.kr. 175; for *Mera svenska:* teachers' handbook. 1972. 77 pp. S.kr. 18; 6 tapes (or cassettes, number and price unspecified) S.kr.195; teachers' handbook for audio material. 1972. 38 pp. S.kr.15; students' handbook for audio material. 1971. 57 pp. S.kr.12; for *Ännu mera svenska:* teachers' handbook. 1974. 67 pp. S.kr.12; 4 tapes (or cassettes, number and price unspecified) S.kr.145. In addition a key to the exercises in *Mera svenska* and a teachers' and a students' handbook for the audio material in *Ännu mera svenska* are shortly to be published). This takes the student who has had *c.* 240 hours teaching to a very advanced level. A wide range of authentic Swedish texts (simplified in *Svenska*, unabridged in the other two textbooks) form the basis of many and varied oral and written exercises, topics for discussion, songs etc. The course is entirely in Swedish, but it could be used for self-tuition by a student with some background in the language. Strongly recommended except for certain of the texts which seem to be crude attempts at indoctrination: anti-Americanism and po-faced self-praise are both in evidence. A slightly less ambitious course that aims to bridge the gap between textbooks for beginners and ordinary Swedish prose and verse is S. Kristiansen, D. Lundh and G. Manne, *Svenssons* (Uppsala, Kursverksamhetens studieförlag, 1973. Swedish–English word list, 1975; textbook and exercises reprinted 1976. Textbook. 120 pp. illus. S.kr.18.50; exercises, 122 pp. illus. S.kr.20.50; Swedish–English word list. 60 pp. S.kr.14.50; teachers' handbook. 110 pp. illus. S.kr.37; tapes with recordings of the textbook material. S.kr.225; grammatical exercises for language laboratory work. 72 pp. S.kr.36; tapes of these exercises. S.kr.400 and 'elevblad'. illus. S.kr.93; transparencies with additional textual material. 26 pp. illus. S.kr.225; 'rättningsmallar'. 4 pp. S.kr.17. No one, including the publishers, could tell me exactly what the 'elevblad' or 'rättningsmallar' are. The former presumably contain additional tasks or help for the student doing language laboratory work, the latter seem to be some kind of aid for correcting written exercises.) Through 22 texts we follow the daily life of an ordinary Swedish family. Entirely in

Swedish, but with notes on the content of each text, explanations of difficult words and grammatical rules and examples. Recommended. G. Manne and A. Hjorth, *Leva bland människor* (Stockholm, Sveriges Radios förlag. Textbook. 1972, reprinted 1975. 8, 146 pp. S.kr.29; exercises. 1973, reprinted 1975. 208 pp. illus. S.kr.29; stencilled Swedish–English vocabulary available free from The Swedish Institute) is an anthology of relatively simple prose and verse texts from the works of various Swedish authors and writers, followed by suggested topics for discussion based on the texts. The textbook is entirely in Swedish as is the book of exercises which contains questions on the texts, grammar and vocabulary exercises, essay subjects etc. Eminently suitable for those who have been through *Svenska för er* or a comparable beginners' course. A small and inexpensive exercise book with particular emphasis on prepositional usage is S. Boström, *Från av till över: övningsbok i svenska språket för utlänningar* (Stockholm, Folkuniversitetets förlag, 1959, reprinted 1974. 61 pp. illus. S.kr.7).

General Courses for Advanced Students. There are a number of readers of varying degrees of difficulty. All place greater emphasis on literary than on colloquial Swedish. S. Higelin, *Om Sverige och svenskarna* (Stockholm, Almqvist och Wiksell, 1964, reprinted 1970. 241 pp. illus. S.kr.31.25) aims to introduce the student to Sweden, Swedish society and history, and also to provide examples of various literary styles. Well annotated and with a Swedish–English vocabulary giving full grammatical details of the Swedish entry words. S. Higelin, *Från Fakiren till Jolo* (Stockholm, Folkuniversitetets förlag, 1963, reprinted 1971. 79 pp. illus. S.kr.10; exercises compiled by E. Hansel. 1968. 79 pp. illus. S.kr.19; Swedish–English vocabulary. 1964, reprinted 1971. 32 pp. S.kr.5. Recordings of all the texts on 5 two-track tapes. S.kr.270, or 5 one-track tapes S.kr.300) contains 23 short pieces written during the last 80–90 years by various authors and journalists. There are brief notes on the contributors, and some of their more important publications are listed. Words are entered in the vocabulary in order of appearance in the texts; full grammatical details are given, but the 1,000 most common Swedish words, as well as others easily understood, are omitted. More difficult texts are to be found in L. O'Callaghan (ed.). *An intermediate reader in Swedish* (Stockholm, Swedish Institute, [n.d.]. 160 pp. Free to schools, libraries and universities), although the student is greatly helped by the inclusion of several English translations. Where a piece is not translated, a Swedish–English vocabulary is provided. In addition to the reading matter the book contains brief notes in Swedish (and in some cases also in English) on the contributors, notes on the language, extensive grammatical exercises, and essay topics. Especially recommended for students working on their own. P. Brandberg and R. J. McClean. *A Swedish reader* (London, Athlone Press, 1953, reprinted 1963. 174 pp. £1.50) is a literary anthology containing pieces by 15 authors, mostly twentieth-century but also earlier. There are introductory notes on the authors and footnotes explaining difficult words and phrases, but no vocabulary. A companion volume is R. J. McClean. *A book of Swedish verse* (London, Athlone Press, 1968. 187 pp. £1.50). In addition to an introduction and footnotes, this anthology contains information on metrical features and on unusual linguistic forms that may be encountered in Swedish poetry. Only for very advanced students is M. G. and G. Lokrantz, *Litterära texter* (Stockholm, Swedish Institute, 1972. 198 pp. S.kr.5), an anthology of Swedish literature from the Viking Age to the present day. The early texts are for the most part in modern Swedish translation. Entirely in Swedish, with occasional footnotes on difficult words and phrases and brief notes on the pieces and/or authors included in the selection.

Specialist Courses. In connection with *Svenska för er* (see above) two additional courses are available. For those with a special interest in the language of industry and commerce there is R. Horneij and M. Wibring, *Svenska för er inom industrin* (Stockholm, Sveriges Radios förlag, 1973. 80 pp. illus. S.kr. 24.40), while for nurses, doctors etc. there is G. Ekroth, S. Higelin and A. Hjorth, *Svenska för er inom sjukvården* (Stockholm, Sveriges Radios förlag, 1971. 6, 138 pp. illus. S.kr.71.30). Each course is accompanied by a number of additional aids published separately (details from Sveriges Radios förlag).

Reference Grammars. There are three Swedish grammars in

English. The most comprehensive is still I. Björkhagen, *Modern Swedish grammar* (9th ed. Stockholm, Svenska Bokförlaget, Norstedt, 1962, reprinted 1966. xii, 200 pp. S.kr.12.50) which has a particularly full section on pronunciation. Slightly less detailed is A.-M. Beite and others, *Basic Swedish grammar* (3rd ed. Stockholm, Almqvist och Wiksell, 1966, reprinted 1975. 168 pp. S.kr.27), but this is a better book for students since it deals very clearly with precisely those points of Swedish grammar which cause an English-speaking learner difficulty, and has more modern, colloquial examples than Björkhagen. G. Rosén, *A short Swedish grammar* (Stockholm, Folkuniversitetets förlag, 1970. 25 pp. S.kr.5) covers only the very basic points of pronunciation, morphology and word order. It is useful for quick reference, but not a proper grammar. Entirely in Swedish, but comprehensive, clear and reliable are E. Nylund-Brodda, B. Holm and others, *Deskriptiv svensk grammatik* (Stockholm, Skriptor, 1972, reprinted 1975. 211 pp. S.kr.40) and H. Lindholm, *Svensk grammatik* (Lund, Kursverksamheten vid Lunds universitet, 1974. 192 pp. S.kr.26). Lindholm's book has a particularly good description of Swedish pronunciation, but otherwise *Deskriptiv svensk grammatik* is clearer and easier to use, and typographically infinitely superior. For those who want an even more comprehensive grammar than these, there is O. Thorell, *Svensk grammatik* (Stockholm, Esselte studium, 1973. x, 302 pp. S.kr.69), a Swedish grammar for Swedes.

Special Aspects of Grammar. Pronunciation. S. Higelin and others, *Svenskt uttal* (Stockholm, Sveriges Radios förlag, 1972. 136 pp. S.kr.27.35; recordings of all the exercises on 14 tapes. S.kr.1,250.05) contains varied pronunciation exercises. Particular emphasis is placed on phonemic contrasts and on special difficulties experienced by speakers of English and certain other languages. I. Cronlind, *Uttalsövningar* (Göteborg, Kursverksamheten vid Göteborgs Universitet, [n.d.]. 2, 28 pp. S.kr.11) is a similar but much briefer set of pronunciation exercises. Since as far as can be seen there are no recordings to accompany the book, it can clearly only be used where a teacher is available.

RECORDED MATERIAL

Most of the courses in Swedish for foreigners now available place a strong emphasis on recorded aids, but there are only two where the recordings seem to be the central feature of the course. E. Hansel and S. Higelin, *Svenska på svenska* 1–2 (2nd ed.Stockholm, Skriptor, 1970, part 1 reprinted 1971. 2, 162 and 4, 157 pp. S.kr.30 each; recordings of part 1 on 14 tapes S.kr.1,010, of part 2 on 13 tapes S.kr.960) consists of respectively 40 and 45 carefully graded exercises for language laboratory work which take the student from the rudiments of Swedish pronunciation to moderately complicated grammatical structures. The course can be studied on its own, but is best used in conjunction with other textbooks or grammars. Suitable for self-tuition. *The Linguaphone Swedish course* (London, Linguaphone Institute, no date, but revised and reissued about 1962. £49.50; £42.07 to schools, colleges or libraries) follows the standard Linguaphone pattern and includes textbook, alphabetical and collateral vocabulary with notes on pronunciation, a booklet of explanatory notes on grammar and idiom, and students' instructions. The recordings are available on either 45 rpm records, cassettes or tapes. With so many other excellent, fully recorded courses available, Linguaphone now seems a little outdated in method, content and idiom. It is, however, compiled specifically for self-tuition, unlike any of the courses emanating from Sweden, and is *considerably* cheaper than most of these if they are purchased in their entirety. For these reasons it can still be recommended.

DICTIONARIES

Standard Orthography. *Svenska Akademiens ordlista över svenska språket* (10th ed. Stockholm, Norstedt, 1973. xvi, 616 pp. S.kr.40) is a comprehensive work giving full orthographical and grammatical details of most words found in standard modern Swedish. There are few definitions, however, and pronunciation and stress are only indicated when they might cause problems for a Swede. A much smaller word list of the same type (*c.* 22,000 words) is A. S. Gustafsson (editors A. Almhult and N. Ivan), *Svensk ordlista* (10th rev. ed. Stockholm, A. V. Carlson, 1965, reprinted 1970. 108 pp. S.kr.5.40).

General Translating Dictionaries. Good, reliable and comprehensive dictionaries are the pair: R. Santesson and others, *Svensk–engelsk ordbok* (Stockholm, Esselte studium, 1968, reprinted 1975. xvi, 979 pp. S.kr.69) and K. Kärre and others, *Engelsk–svensk ordbok* (3rd ed. Stockholm, Esselte studium, 1953, reprinted 1974. xvi, 973 pp. S.kr.61), although the latter is now in need of up-dating. The Swedish–English volume gives grammatical details of the Swedish entry words, but no guide to pronunciation. Typographically it is excellent. (An abbreviated version of this dictionary is *Svensk–engelsk pocket ordbok*, Stockholm, Esselte studium, 1973. xvi, 480 pp. S.kr.35). Also good, although typographically the Swedish–English volume leaves something to be desired, are E. Gomer and others, *Modern svensk–engelsk ordbok* (2nd ed. Stockholm, Prisma, 1972, reprinted 1975. xvi, 566 pp. S.kr.38) and H. B. Danielsson (ed.). *Modern engelsksvensk ordbok* (3rd ed. Stockholm, Prisma, 1974, reprinted 1975. xii, 394 pp. S.kr.32). The Swedish–English volume contains brief notes on Swedish pronunciation and grammar, and gives help with the pronunciation and tone of individual entry words where there is likely to be any doubt. Grammatical details of the entry words are also supplied, but mostly by means of a complicated system of symbols whose significance must be memorised if the user is to avoid having to look up the gender and/or inflexions of a word separately. The English–Swedish volume is more up to date than the one published by Esselte studium, but considerably smaller; it lacks the larger dictionary's copious examples of usage, and determining the precise meaning of the Swedish translations can sometimes be difficult for the learner. A. Tornberg and M. Ångström, *Svensk–engelsk ordbok* (Stockholm, Esselte studium, 1940, reprinted 1975. iv, 220 pp.) and R. Nöjd, *Engelsk–svensk ordbok* (Stockholm, Esselte studium, 1939, reprinted 1974. viii, 248 pp. The two bound together S.kr.32; *Engelsk–svensk ordbok* available separately. S.kr.16) are considerably smaller (*c.* 25,000 words each) and older than either of the other two pairs, and give no help with Swedish pronunciation or inflexions, but they are a lot cheaper and would suit the beginner using a course where detailed explanation of the pronunciation and grammar is given. O. Lindén, V. Petti and others, *Niloés engelsk–svenska och svensk–engelska lexikon* (Stockholm, Niloé, 1960. 2nd rev. ed. of Swedish–English, 1962–63, both recently reprinted without date. 190; 192 pp. S.kr.8) contains only the 7,000 most common Swedish and English words (with the addition of a number of terms useful to tourists), gives the briefest of definitions and no grammatical details whatsoever. It is notable, however, for giving the pronunciation of every entry word in the International Phonetic Alphabet.

Dictionaries of Synonyms. A. F. Dalin, *Svenska språkets synonymer* (7th rev. ed. Stockholm, Liber förlag, 1971, reprinted 1975. 432 pp. S.kr.33.15) is more a small thesaurus than a dictionary. Synonyms or near synonyms are grouped under a number, and individual words must be sought in an index. The work is particularly useful for the advanced learner because, unlike *Roget's Thesaurus*, it explains (in Swedish) the differences in meaning, connotation and style between the words listed in each group.

Pronunciation Dictionaries. E. Wessén, *Våra ord: deras uttal och ursprung* (Stockholm, Esselte studium, 1961, reprinted 1973. x, 502 pp. S.kr.55), although principally an etymological dictionary, gives the pronunciation (though *not* in the International Phonetic Alphabet) of a limited number of Swedish words, mostly of foreign origin.

Technical Dictionaries. I. E. Gullberg, *A Swedish–English dictionary of technical terms used in business, industry, administration, education and research* (Stockholm, Norstedt, 1964. Temporarily out of print. xvi, 1,246 pp.) is the best Scandinavian–English technical dictionary and an excellent work by any standards. Even excluding common non-technical words there are some 130,000 entries. Subject fields are specified, and a clear distinction is made between British and American usage. Translations of the names of many organisations in all the Scandinavian countries are given. The only defect is the absence of any details of the gender or inflexions of the Swedish entry words. Also very good are the two volumes by E. Engström: *Svensk–engelsk teknisk ordbok* (9th ed. Stockholm, Svensk

Trävaru-tidning, 1974. 851 pp. S.kr.75) and *Engelsk–svensk teknisk ordbok* (12th ed. Stockholm, Svensk Trävaru-tidning, 1971. 858 pp. S.kr.75). More narrowly 'technical' than Gullberg's dictionary, they are at least as comprehensive in the scientific and industrial fields, containing *c.* 110,000 and *c.* 100,000 words and expressions respectively. Both volumes lack any kind of grammatical information about the entry words. A much smaller work but useful because it is easier to carry around, is H. G. Freeman, *Engelsk–svensk teknisk ordbok* (Stockholm, Läromedelsförlagen, 1972. 16, 143 pp. S.kr.31), compiled on the basis of an English–German work. For those concerned with the law there is a small, but useful dictionary: T. Backe, A. Bruzelius and E. Wångstedt. *Concise Swedish–English glossary of legal terms* (Lund, Gleerup, and South Hackensack N.J., Rothman, 1973/74. 164 pp. S.kr.51.95; $13.50).

RUSSIAN COURSES

by NICHOLAS J. BROWN, B.A.

INTRODUCTION

Although the number of students of Russian in the United Kingdom has not expanded to the extent predicted in the middle of the sixties, the production of teaching materials has not been allowed to stagnate. It may indeed be true that the total number of different courses currently in print is no larger than at the end of the sixties and that in some fields (*e.g.* specialist courses for scientists) the number is actually smaller, but there is no doubt that quality has improved. Two heartening developments are the appearance of good audio-visual aids and the increasing flow of well-produced materials prepared in the USSR itself.

The principal faults that one still meets in Russian course materials can be listed as follows, in order of seriousness:

1. Incorrect Russian – though this is increasingly rare since courses are now normally produced with the active participation of native Russian speakers, often Soviet citizens.
2. Unstressed texts – stressing is a major problem for beginners and advanced students alike, yet the USSR continues to produce unstressed material for foreigners.
3. Self-tutors without keys to the exercises.
4. Reference works without indexes – a common Soviet failing.
5. Dull textbook presentation – an attractive layout is particularly desirable in schoolbooks.
6. Recorded courses that do not take full advantage of their medium – lack of voice variety, unimaginative drills, shortage of lively dialogue, music, sound effects.

The range of choice in Russian courses remains reasonably wide. The author of this section was able to inspect over one hundred works that can be regarded as teaching materials for foreigners learning Russian (excluding readers, song-books, phrase-books, vocabularies and academic studies). Those one hundred works, all currently available in Britain (December 1975), can be classified as follows:

1. *Grammar Courses for Non-Specialist Beginners:* 40 titles
1.a. School courses for younger pupils (11–14 years): 7 titles (including 4 with recordings)
1.b. Courses for older pupils, students, adults, to be used with a teacher: 21 titles (including 10 with recordings)
1.c. Self-tutors: 12 titles (including 6 with recordings)
2. *Intermediate and Advanced Courses* (non-beginners): 27 titles
2.a. Up to around 'O' level: 8 titles (including 2 with recordings)
2.b. Post 'O' level: 19 titles (including 8 with recordings)
3. *Courses for Specialist Beginners:* 12 titles
3.a. For Specialists requiring a general reading knowledge: 5 titles
3.b. For Chemists: 2 titles
3.c. For Social Scientists: 2 titles (including 1 with recordings)
3.d. For Librarians: 2 titles
3.e. For Businessmen: 1 title (with recordings)
4. *Advanced Courses for Specialists:* 6 titles
4.a. General: 1 title
4.b. On Commercial Correspondence: 1 title
4.c. For Scientists: 4 titles
5. *Reference Works on Grammar and Usage:* 13+ titles
5.a. Up to 'O' level: 3 titles
5.b. Advanced: 8+ titles (depending on the availability of certain Soviet reference grammars)
5.c. Background: 2 titles
6. *Phonetics Courses:* 8 titles (including 5 with recordings)

A number of recommendable works have recently gone out of print and it is possible that publishers will continue to cut their lists and decline to reprint for the relatively small Russian market. Availability has been an important criterion in making recommendations and, with the exception of one Phonetics course (Bryzgunova), no out of print works have been included.

Prices are those applicable in December 1975, except where otherwise stated.

Those interested in examining currently available Russian teaching materials for themselves are advised to consult the well-qualified staff and the rich stocks of the Library of the Centre for Information on Language Teaching (CILT) at 20 Carlton House Terrace, London SW1. Their assistance in the preparation of this chapter is gratefully acknowledged, though the responsibility for all statements is mine alone.

COURSES & AUDIO-VISUAL MATERIAL

1. Grammar Courses for Non-Specialist Beginners

1.a. *For younger pupils.* M. Vyatyutnev, and others, *Russkii yazyk* (Moscow, Pedagogika, 1971–72. UK distributor Collet's) consists of six attractively produced books (including 3 for the teacher) and 17 6″ flexible plastic discs with about 5 minutes playing time per side. At £7.70, or £6.20 without the teacher's books, this course is excellent value for money: there is plenty of colour and visual material in the books and the recordings are lively, with children's voices and songs. This course requires a very competent teacher (the books are unstressed) but he is likely to find it interesting to work with. For an enthusiastic review of Vyatyutnev see *Journal of Russian studies*, no. 24 (1972).

For the teacher with more money to spend and 4 or 5 years for the 'O' level course the Nuffield Foundation/Schools Council: *Vperyod!* is excellent, with strong emphasis on the audio-visual approach. Stages 1, 2 and 3 were published by Macmillan Education (London, 1967–69), and stages 4 and 5 by E. J. Arnold (London, 1971–72). The 16 pupil's books, 5 teacher's books, 28 tapes, 39 film strips, 88 flashcards, 5 packs of playing cards, 2 sheets of cardboard money and 2 wallcharts cost around £200 + VAT on the tapes, but the parts can be purchased separately. The whole course, particularly levels 4 and 5, is of very high quality and is noteworthy for its lively tapes, wealth of background information on the USSR, and quantity of graded reading texts. It is perhaps regrettable that so much effort was put into a set of materials that have turned out to progress too slowly for the realities of Russian timetabling in most of our schools, but for any teacher who can take pupils to 'O' level from the age of 11 the Nuffield/Schools Council course, the UK's largest Russian project so far, can be highly recommended.

1.b. *Courses for older pupils, students, adults.* There is a good range of choice in this area and most needs and preferences seem to be catered for. For school beginners of around 13 to 15 the best of the *traditional* courses is still A. A. Haywood, *A first Russian book* (3rd ed. London, Harrap, 1970. 194 pp. £0.90) and *A second Russian book* (2nd ed. rev. London, Harrap, 1975. 271 pp. £1.80). Two tapes at £7.20 + VAT each, or two cassettes at £6 + VAT each, are available from the Tutor Tape Company but they carry only the texts from the books and are entirely optional. Haywood's two volumes have been in use since the beginning of the sixties (though the first edition, un-corrected, should not be used) and seem likely to remain in print. They provide excellent preparation for 'O' level.

For teachers who prefer the audio-lingual and audio-visual methods of language teaching, the most elaborate, most expensive, most thorough and most reliable integrated course (designed to last at least four years to 'A' level standard) is Maria Lapunova and others, *A-LM Russian*, from the US publishing house Harcourt Brace Jovanovich (New York and London, 1963–71). This is in four separate levels and second editions of levels 1 and 2 have been available since 1970–71. The complete set of teacher's books, pupil's books, posters, cue cards, student practice records and 129 7″ language laboratory tapes costs well over £500, and is thus only suitable for large school departments or universities; it would suit the less confident teacher but hardly the teacher who likes to use his own materials and do all the grammatical explanation etc. himself.

Smaller and cheaper (at around £228 net in mid-1975 for the 62-tape language laboratory version), but equally recommendable for schools, is the two-part A. Menac and Z. Volos, *Harrap-Didier audio-visual Russian course* (London, Harrap, 1963–67). This is aimed more at oral-aural competence than *A-LM*, contains £60 worth of colour and black-and-white film strips as an integral component, and requires a highly competent, methodologically informed teacher prepared to avoid translating into English and able to adjust to the American angle of the course. There are three positive assessments in *Journal of*

Russian studies, nos. 9 (1963) and 12 (1965).

The teacher who desires an audio-visual approach but wants to keep costs down and use more of his own material could be well advised to use the lively introductory course by L. M. O'Toole and P. T. Culhane: *Passport to Moscow* (London, Oxford University Press, 1972). This consists of a student's book (200 pp. £2), a teacher's book (24 pp. £0.65), a workbook (24 pp £0.30) and 70 black-and-white flashcards (£3.80) plus 9 5″ tapes of the lessons (£44 + VAT) and 6 5″ exercise tapes, *i.e.* drills (£32.50). Though the tapes seem a little overpriced, *Passport to Moscow* with its illustrations, music, cartoons is very suitable as a first year course for older school children and upwards, as suggested in a positive review in *Modern languages*, no. 3 for 1973.

Sixth form and adult beginners in general have a wide choice. The 'best buy' among the courses combining a sound and thorough intellectual approach with plenty of recorded material is V. Kostomarov, *Russkii yazyk dlya vsekh*, consisting of six conveniently separate volumes (textbook, oral speech manual, exercise book, reader, 3,000-word dictionary, printed text of the recordings) and 10 LP records, all for £14.50 + VAT. It is published by Progress (Moscow, 1972. Distributed in the UK by Collet's) and as a Soviet production lacks the gloss of its Western equivalents – line drawings instead of photographs, rough paper, no sound effects on the records. However, the Russian and the grammatical explanations are thoroughly reliable, and the material is fully up to date. If a competent teacher is available to cope with the course's rough edges, caused particularly by the fact that the materials are aimed at the international market and not specifically English speakers, *Russkii yazyk dlya vsekh* is excellent value for money. It has been much praised in print: see particularly *Journal of Russian studies*, nos. 25 (1973) (two positive assessments), 26 (1973), and 28 (1974).

At time of going to press, *Russkii yazyk dlya vsekh* has appeared in an improved 3rd ed. (1976) with an additional 112 pp. booklet of grammar notes in English. Including 21 7″ records, the price is a bargain £8.50 (1977).

Ealing Technical College, *Ealing course in Russian* (Madrid, Editorial Mangold, 1972. Distributed in UK by European

Schoolbooks) can be proposed as Kostomarov's main audio-visual/lingual competitor in the adult intensive course market. The Ealing course is specifically intended for English speakers as a one-year intensive course and is more expensively produced with transparencies and tapes, at a correspondingly much higher price: the 286 pp. textbook, 30 overhead projector transparencies (or slides or filmstrips), and 30 5″ tapes (or 15 twin half-track tapes) cost from £85 to £135 (estimated prices), depending on the alternative components chosen. The textbook course is more traditional than Kostomarov with more grammatical explanation and English sentences for translation; it could be used on its own (£2.50 approx.), without the A/V materials, as an 'old-fashioned' grammar. It is also duller than Kostomarov.

Another useful recorded course for adults is the American G. H. Fairbanks and R. L. Leed, *Basic conversational Russian* (London, Holt Rinehart, 1964–67). Fairbanks and Leed aim at a lower level of proficiency than Kostomarov or Ealing, providing a vocabulary of only a thousand words and emphasising oral skills. There is a teacher's manual, a well produced glossy 350 pp. textbook, a laboratory manual and a workbook (£9 approx. for the four) plus two records (£6 approx.) or six tapes, twin half-track (£24 approx.). These materials make a fairly economical half-year semi-intensive course for sixth formers or university students, allowing for about 120 hours of instruction.

Among the textbook courses without recordings, intended for intensive use by serious adult students, the principal recommendation is W. Harrison, Y. Clarkson and S. Le Fleming, *Colloquial Russian* (London, Routledge and Kegan Paul, 1973. xii, 428 pp. £3.95; £1.75). This is a solid, demanding 'A' level standard grammar with lively reading material and a good variety of types of exercise. There is a high proportion of text to grammatical explanation and a good mixture of colloquial and literary passages (despite the title). Its oddities are minor ones, such as the occurrence of the word *zubilo* in lesson 7, and the book should appeal to able students.

A similarly intensive 'A' level grammar course for able students, but with the disadvantage of being a much older publication, is R. Hingley and T. J. Binyon, *Russian: a*

beginner's course (London, Allen and Unwin, 1962. 330 pp.
£1.40 in late 1975). This textbook is rather more concentrated
than *Colloquial Russian* and has less reading material. It is likely to become unavailable soon.

Finally in this section one can recommend three bargain buys,
suitable for motivated but impecunious or part-time students
(*e.g.* in evening classes). The first and most readily available of
these is J. L. I. Fennell (comp.): *Penguin Russian course: a complete course for beginners* (Harmondsworth, Penguin Books, 7th
reprint 1974. xxiv, 348 pp. £0.50; 8th reprint 1975. £0.90). This
concentrated course is an adaptation of a Soviet work and is
reliable but unexciting. 3 tapes (£12.60 + VAT) or 3 cassettes
(£10.50 + VAT) or a language laboratory version of 16 tapes
(£33.60 + VAT) or 16 cassettes (£28 + VAT) carrying recordings of the basic texts and the exercises are available from the
Tutor Tape Company as an expensive optional extra.

A second cheap but less readily available concise and steeply
graded textbook is N. Potapova, *Fifty lessons in Russian*
(Moscow, Progress, 1972. 232 pp. Distributed in UK by
Collet's. £0.60). Rather sketchy and somewhat dull, this bargain
introduction might suit a teacher who planned to use his own
materials in class and required the students to purchase only the
most basic kind of reference work.

Also a bargain, but containing a lot more material than the
above two recommendations, is the four-volume Soviet course
also by N. Potapova: *Learning Russian* (edited and translated
by N. Kadisheva), (Moscow, Progress, latest reprint. 1972. 4 v.
208; 144; 158; 150 pp. distributed in UK by Collet's. £3 for the
set). The grammar goes beyond 'O' level, and the vocabulary to
'A' level; the first three books contain the lessons and plenty of
reading material, while the fourth is a reference volume with
grammatical tables and vocabularies. Like the above two titles
this is a functional introduction to Russian with few frills. Of the
three, the *Penguin Russian course* is easily the most convenient
to obtain, and the availability of tapes gives it a further
advantage.

1.c. *Self-tutors.* The best and not surprisingly the most expensive of the courses designed for home use without a teacher is
I. G. Miloslavskii, *Linguaphone Russian course* (London,

Linguaphone Institute, 1971). The two well-produced hardback volumes – a textbook and a grammar/vocabulary handbook and a paperback exercise book form a set with 16 7″ records (or 2 tapes or 2 cassettes) at a total cost of approximately £40; extra optional practice material is available. The set is pleasant to use and the Russian is good, up to date and idiomatic. There is a key to the exercises, and the course could be used for 'O' level preparation.

A cheaper but less professional production than the Linguaphone course is A. Pressman, *Basic conversational Russian* (not to be confused with the identically named course by Fairbanks and Leed included in 1.b above). This consists of a 216 pp. hardback quarto volume with 4 LP records, published by Oldbourne, London (1960 reprinted 1967), quite good value at an estimated price of around £8.50. It shows a slightly unexpected scientific bias in the later lessons (*e.g.* Pythagoras' theorem is given in Russian on p. 89), there are very few exercises, and it is hardly a course in *conversational* Russian, but for anyone desiring a fairly concentrated self-tutor of written Russian, with recordings to add variety to the task, *Basic conversational Russian* is an economical introduction.

An even cheaper introduction, for casual learners, is the 1973 BBC production by M. Frewin and A. Braithwaite: *Ochen priyatno: a BBC Radio course for beginners in Russian* (London, BBC Publications, 1973). The 136 pp. illustrated paperback and 2 accompanying LPs cost £3.02 + VAT (Sept. 1975); a 7″ pronunciation disc with explanatory leaflet is also available at £0.90 (Sept. 1975). *Ochen priyatno* is not for determined students or professional linguists, but the recordings are animated and the approach popular. It could be used as a supplement to a more demanding traditional textbook such as Harrison (see 1.b above).

Of the self-tutors without a recorded component E. Jackson and E. B. Gordon: *Russian made simple* (London, W. H. Allen, 1967. 299 pp. £1.25) can be recommended. As *Journal of Russian studies* no. 21 (1971) commented, the assiduous student could tackle 'O' level with this book. Though unexciting in its presentation (rather pedestrian texts, old-fashioned grammar exposition), it is value for money, readily available, reliable, and certainly not over-subtle (cf. its title).

Those simply in need of a low-cost no-frills introduction to Russian could use as self-tutors any of the three bargain titles (Fennell and the two Potapova works), described at the end of section 1.b, since all have keys to the exercises.

Lastly, mention should be made of T. Karlovna: *Kratkii put: A short cut to Russian* ([N.p.], Quick Results Centre, 1971. Distributed by Collet's). The rough and ready paper textbook, 86 pp. (£1) and the 4 tapes (£7 + VAT) contain '14 intimate lessons' (title page), constituting the only published self-tutor that tries to create the effect of a teacher's presence. The grammatical explanation is actually on the tape (in English), in the rich aristocratic tones of a very human Russian lady with a liking for mnemonic verses and encouraging asides to the student. The Russian is occasionally old-fashioned but the course is attractive; imitation of Tamara Karlovna's English accent will help the student's Russian. *Kratkii put* is not long enough to reach a high level but some people would find its chattiness stimulating.

2. Intermediate and Advanced Courses

2.a. *Up to around 'O' level.* Which work, if any, a teacher would find most appropriate in this category will depend largely on what is being used, or has been used, as the student's basic course. In schools, teachers not using an elaborate audio-visual course and wishing to supplement a basic grammar such as Haywood (1.b) with some recorded material for aural/oral practice could try C. E. Kany and A. Kaun, *Elementary Russian conversation* (London, Harrap (with Heath), 1946 reprinted 1966). The small soft-covered 73 pp. textbook (£0.30) contains the texts of dialogues of varying length recorded onto a single tape (£3.60 + VAT) or cassette (£3 + VAT) or onto 8 'exploded' (*i.e.* with gaps for student repetition) language laboratory tapes (£33.60 + VAT) or cassettes (£28 + VAT). There is also a 6-tape/cassette version (£21.60 + VAT/£18 + VAT respectively), suitable for home study. The book contains some basic grammar and notes that translate tricky points in the dialogues. The recordings are interesting, with bits of humour;

the discrepancies between the printed and the recorded texts are minor. The single tape/cassette version would make a very useful self-tutor in addition to a grammar course.

M. Frewin and A. Braithwaite: *Svidanie v Moskve* (London, BBC Publications, 1974) (a continuation of the same authors' *Ochen priyatno* – see 1.c above) is a recorded course which could follow any basic introduction to Russian; however, it would have to be supplemented by the teacher in order to provide a full grammatical grounding for 'O' level. The 151 pp. book (£1.40) and the two LP records (£2.60 + VAT) or cassette (£3.40 + VAT) would suit evening classes or students wishing to refresh their basic Russian.

If the need is primarily for printed materials to develop the pupil's active skills, S. Moore and D. Rix *Let's speak Russian* (London, University Tutorial Press, 1968. 43 pp. £0.50) can be used in the early stages of learning Russian (it employs the present tense only). The material is largely in the form of short texts (with accompanying pictures) based on Soviet reality, with questions to be answered by the pupils orally.

At a slightly more advanced level than Moore and Rix there is N. Harley, *Start Russian by talking* (2nd rev. ed. Wellingborough, Collet's, 1972. 81 pp. £0.55). This consists of short passages, including proverbs and rhymes (no illustrations), with questions. The most difficult texts (the last 7 of the 40) have translations. There are also grammatical tables (8 pp.) and a Russian–English vocabulary.

For extra grammatical practice there is a useful work which can also serve as a self-tutor: S. Khavronina and A. Shirochenskaya, *Russian in exercises* (Moscow, Progress, 1973. Distributed in UK by Collet's. £0.95). The 351 pp. of this hard-backed book contain no fewer than 797 graded exercises arranged according to grammatical theme, *e.g.* cases, verbs, syntax, participles, a useful section on aspect. There is a key (45 pp.) to those exercises that need one. There are also occasional short texts for retelling (*pereskaz*). This book provides excellent, if somewhat dry, revision material right up to 'O' level.

Worth mention as a *visual* aid for near-beginners is I. K. Gerkan, *Russkii yazyk v kartinkakh* (Moscow, Progress, 1970. 240 pp. Distributed in UK by Collet's. £0.75). This is a set of

very simple exercises based on neat drawings of which a few are in colour. There is a key to the exercises but no grammar notes.
2.b. *Post 'O' level.* There are eleven works which can be recommended as useful aids for students who are already well grounded in the basics of Russian grammar and vocabulary. Three of those are textbook courses (two with optional tapes), one is a work on verbs, four are recorded courses mainly for *aural* practice, two are books of texts with notes and exercises designed to increase active vocabulary and fluency in idiomatic colloquial Russian, and there is one visual aid. Not included is the wide range of good annotated and stressed *readers* that fall outside the scope of this guide.

One of the best known and most useful post 'O' level text-books is S. A. Khavronina, *Russian as we speak it* (2nd rev. ed. Moscow, Progress, 1968 reprinted 1973. 268 pp. Distributed by Collet's. £0.90). This is a continuation course with illustrated texts, dialogues, grammar notes, exercises and a 2,500-word Russian–English vocabulary. It is recommended for its useful, idiomatic, contemporary Russian; the preface's claim that 'the material ... is contemporary and frankly utilitarian' is a fair description. 3 tapes (£12.60 + VAT) or 3 cassettes (£10.50 + VAT) of the texts, phrases and dialogues are available through Collet's; there is an 'exploded' language laboratory version on tapes (£33.60 + VAT) or cassettes (£28 + VAT). The course has a key and would make a worthwhile self-tutor.

At a more advanced level than Khavronina, nearer 'A' level, and intended primarily for university students there is C. E. Townsend, *Continuing with Russian* (New York, McGraw-Hill, 1970. xxii, 426 pp. £4.80 in 1974). (There is also an instructor's manual including a key to the exercises which is available from the USA at $1.95; the 13 tapes, quoted in 1974 at $195, would seem to be a dispensable accompaniment to what is basically a classroom course in written Russian). The book is a well produced American hardback with academic pretensions, *e.g.* a root list with the necessary accompanying morphological explanations, and bookish translation exercises involving technical vocabulary and sentences in *Pravda* style ('Lenin defined law as an expression of the will of the people.' p. 233). The lessons contain grammar revision, Russian texts both literary and conversational, a large amount of vocabulary, quantities of sentences for translation into Russian or English, and plenty of grammar notes. The book is aimed at students planning to take a degree involving Russian.

As a third post 'O' level course book it is possible to include the new, very attractively produced Soviet work from the Moscow University Nauchno-metodicheskii tsentr: V. G. Kostomarov, V. I. Polovnikova and L. N. Shvedova, *Russkii yazyk dlya inostrannykh studentov* (Moscow, Russkii yazyk Publishing House, 1974. 440 pp. Distributed by Collet's. £2). The volume is well illustrated, including photographs in colour. The course is in 25 lessons, with each fourth lesson devoted to revision; the whole book is in Russian, which makes a teacher almost essential. There are plenty of texts, consisting mainly of up to date information on the USSR. Some of these are heavy going, but the main fault of this book is the inexplicable fact that it is *not stressed*: not even obscure personal and geographical names (of which there is no shortage) have stress marks, and the teacher will have to do a fair amount of research if he wants to be sure that his pronunciation is correct. He will also have to watch out for misprints and mistakes (*e.g.* 2 on p. 65). This book cannot be unreservedly recommended, but it might suit a confident teacher wishing to give his 'A' level students something fairly demanding that is also genuinely Soviet and attractive to look at.

For extra post-elementary study of the trickiest subject in Russian grammar i.e. the verb, one can recommend L. S. Muravyova: *Verbs of motion in Russian* (Moscow, Russian Language Publishing House, 1975. 272 pp.). This is the almost unaltered 2nd ed. of the same title published by Progress, Moscow in 1973; it is available from Collet's at £1.50. This attractive, illustrated hardback, fully stressed and with explanations in English, is full of helpful information on tense, prefixes, meaning, stress and aspect in the use of verbs of motion; there are 580 exercises, with a key, 17 pages of tables, 9 reading texts, and 5½ close-print pages of methodological advice for the teacher.

Aural aids are expensive and tend to be regarded as something of a extravagance, since the student is required simply to listen and comprehend rather than participate actively. Nevertheless, listening comprehension is an important skill, and it can be actively tested with repetition exercises or question-and-answer drills. N. Gottlieb, *Improve your Russian comprehension* (London, Dent, 1972). is a fairly demanding set of texts and exercises for the student with a very sound basic knowledge of Russian. The 6 tapes plus accompanying (completely unstressed) 94 pp. paperback text of the ten taped lessons cost over £30. + VAT and contain ten bookish passages (history, education, a lot of Tolstoy, science) with exercises on the contents of the texts, on synonyms, antonyms and syntax.

Rather less demanding than *Improve your Russian comprehension*, a lot lighter in tone, but without any exercises is C. E. Kany and A. Kaun, *Advanced Russian conversation* (London, Harrap (with Heath), 1950). This old publication consists of a single tape (£4.80 + VAT) or cassette (£4. + VAT), playing time 1½ hours, and a 128 pp. booklet (£0.45) with the texts of the 25 taped dialogues plus grammar notes and translations of difficult words and phrases; there is a long errata slip noting most of the discrepancies between the book and the tape. The recording is slow and clear and the material is by no means dull; a student studying on his own would find *Advanced Russian conversation* useful practice.

Similar to Kany and Kaun but newer is A. Blum, *Russian dialogues* (Oxford, Pergamon, 1968). The single tape costs £4.95 + VAT and carries 16 dialogue-playlets adapted from stories by Il'f and Petrov (7), Chekhov (5), and Zoshchenko (4). The speakers are clear though evidently not actors and the dialogues are full of humour. The accompanying textbook (£2.20; £1.40) has the tape texts, translations of difficult words and phrases (no grammar) and a vocabulary (with many omissions). Like Kany and Kaun this would make a good course for home use.

The most interesting of the post-beginner's taped aids but also the most demanding and the poorest value for money is A. Blum, *Russkie perezvony: albom sovetskikh magnitnykh zapisei* (Oxford, Pergamon, 1972). The hardback book (xviii, 138 pp.) is overpriced at £3.80 and the 2 tapes cost £7 each. The book is an unstressed transcript of the tapes plus some generally not very helpful notes. The tapes are interesting, being unedited Soviet recordings complete with music, footsteps on Red Square, children, Lenin's voice, background hiss, natural (often very fast) speech; some recordings, *e.g.*, the collective farm chairman's rambling reminiscences, could only be followed by the best post 'A' level students. There is too little guidance in the textbook for this set of recordings to be of much use to any but university-level students.

As a post-elementary *visual aid* there is B. P. Pockney and L. N. Saharova, *Longman loops: Russian* (London, Longman, 1968). 12 cineloops (in colour) portray a fairly engaging little Martian's adventures in Moscow and 12 very short tapes carry a suggested Russian commentary to the loops (the text is printed on accompanying leaflets). The total cost £90 + VAT (£72 for the loops, £18 for the tapes) is high and the tapes are of little value, but the loops can be used with effect to develop pupils' active Russian.

Lastly in this section brief mention can be made of two cheap Soviet printed aids to improved Russian: M. Fridman and others, *Russkii yazyk: teksty, kommentarii, uprazhneniya* (Moscow, Progress, 1972. 256 pp. Available from Collet's. £0.45), and N. I. Formanovskaya (ed.), *Tak uchatsya i zhivut studenty* (2nd ed. Moscow University, 1970. 107 pp. illus. Available from Collet's. £0.35). Both of these are basically texts in idiomatic, colloquial Russian with notes (Formanovskaya is all in Russian), phrases, and exercises (questions, blanks to be filled in) without keys. Both works are stressed. Both works require good post 'O' level Russian.

3. Courses for Specialist Beginners

A 'specialist' is here someone who wants to learn Russian for a restricted purpose rather than to use it for conversation or reading on 'everyday' topics. Nearly all publications for such 'special purposes' are designed to provide a *reading* knowedge in a particular discipline: there are only two courses on the open market intended to provide *oral* skills as well, viz. the course for social scientists under 3.c. below and the one for businessmen under 3.e. Scientists and other specialists can of course use any normal 'non-specialist' introductory course (1.c. above) and then proceed to tackle texts in their own field with a good dictionary. The advantage of a 'specialist' course ought to be a saving of time and effort, in that all pronunciation, grammatical and lexical points irrelevant to the specialist's purpose should be excluded; however, few of the specialists' courses currently available are as efficient in this respect as they could be: most of those recommended below go into inappropriate detail, have poor indexes, and require unnecessary active learning of grammatical forms.

3.a. *For specialists requiring a general reading knowledge.* As a purely functional minimum recognition grammar it is possible to use J. Mullen, *Companion reference grammar* (1972. 144 typescript pp.) which is one of the components of the *Birmingham University Language Laboratory course in Russian for social scientists* (see 3.c. below for further publication details). The *Companion reference grammar* can be purchased separately for £1 and used along with a dictionary by any linguistically competent reader with at least prior knowledge of the Russian alphabet.

Among works which are more genuinely *courses* than the above, the best and most readily available is probably M. Beresford, *Complete Russian course for scientists* (Oxford, Clarendon Press, 1965, reprinted 1971. xviii, 227 pp. £2.50). Despite the title, the texts in this book are sufficiently general to make it suitable for scientists or non-scientists (from sixth form upwards) wishing to acquire a reading knowledge of Russian. It has a useful 3½ pp. endings table, a rootlist with cross-references to other forms of the same root, a rather rough 2½ pp. grammatical index, 2 pp. of useful Russian abbreviations, but no key to the small number of exercises or to the Russian texts. For positive reviews see *Journal of Russian studies* nos. 14 (1966) and, particularly, 29 (1975).

G. E. Condoyannis, *Scientific Russian: A concise description of the structural elements of scientific and technical Russian* (London, Wiley, 1959 reprinted 1966. xii, 225 pp. illus. £3.35 in 1974) aims to be more of a reference work than Beresford. It gives first a 'bird's eye view' of Russian grammar and then

becomes a reference guide in the form of tables. However there
is no index to the various tables. There is an alphabetical list of
noun and adjective endings and instructions on the use of a Russian dictionary. The reading passages are more technical than
Beresford's and the book's method is more functional.
3.b. *For Chemists.* Although Beresford (3.a.) is probably better
as an introduction to Scientific Russian, and also cheaper, scientists specialising in chemistry may prefer J. W. Perry, *Scientific
Russian* (New York and London, Interscience (Wiley), 1950,
reprinted 1967. xxviii, 565 pp. estimated price £5) because of
Perry's heavy emphasis on chemical texts as illustrative
material. This book expects the learner to acquire much more
active knowledge of Russian than Beresford and sets a lot of
exercises for translation into Russian (no key provided). There is
no endings list, but the index and reference systems are a little
better than Beresford's. Perry has an odd penchant for phrases
of marginal use to the scientist *e.g.*, 'Grandfather takes the cow
to the water trough' on p. 451.
3.c. *For Social Scientists. The Birmingham University
Language Laboratory Course in Russian for social scientists.*
(Birmingham University, Department of Russian Language and
Literature, 1972–74) consists of 5 quarto paper-covered
volumes reproduced from typescript and an expensive unimaginative audio section (25 tapes of the basic grammar course
for £75.80 and 7 tapes of texts from the readers for £21.94). The
Basic course (1972. 2, vi, 324 pp. £2.) (the first of the five quarto
volumes) contains grammar and could be used as a self-tutor
with the tapes, but would be little use without them. The *Companion reference grammar* (1972. 144 pp. £1) is a very useful
minimum recognition grammar with a full alphabetical endings
table though no index. The three readers *Sociology reader*
(1974. 113, xxxviii pp. £1.25), *Economics reader* (1974. 113,
xxxviii pp. £1.25), and *Politics reader* (1974. 125, xxxviii pp.
£1.25) are linked to the grammar volumes but could be used on
their own; they all contain the same xxxviii pp. supplement of
grammar notes and translation aids, to which the user is referred
by superscript marks in the texts. Each text is preceded by very
helpful vocabulary notes explaining the use of Soviet specialist
terms in the given social science field. Stress is not marked and

there is no Russian–English vocabulary other than the technical terms discussed in the lessons.

3.d. *For Librarians.* G. P. M. Walker, *Russian for librarians* (London, Clive Bingley, 1973. 126 pp. £3) is poor as a language course and contains 15 confusing elementary errors in the grammar section; however, apart from the suitably functional sketch of basic grammar, it contains a great deal of information on the abbreviations, special terminology and transliteration systems used in Russian bibliographies and book annotations. It also includes a section on distinguishing other Cyrillic languages (such as Ukrainian and Moldavian) from Russian. Despite the grammar mistakes and the large amount of space wasted on lists of rather random vocabulary items (as if librarians couldn't use Russian–English dictionaries!), this book is useful. Rosalind Kent, *Reading the Russian language: a guide for librarians and other professionals* (New York, Marcel Dekker Inc., 1974. xii, 229 pp. Distributed in UK by Chandos Books. £8.50) is inferior to Walker's book and contains over three times as many elementary language mistakes; however, it contains a more elaborate sketch of Russian grammar than Walker, and fulfils its basic task fairly adequately.

3.e. *Russian for Businessmen.* There is a perhaps surprising dearth of published Business Russian courses in this age of *détente.* The one available is an audio-lingual course, designed for use with a teacher only: M. A. A. Tatham and F. C. English, *Russian for the businessman* (London, Interlang, 1965). This expensive work consists of a 74 pp. teacher's manual and a xviii, 108 pp. student's book both in paper covers and cheaply reproduced from typescript at £2 each, plus 30 shortish tapes costing over £100. The books have nothing on pronunciation, no grammatical explanation, no stresses and no translation of the texts – the course would be unusable without a teacher. The tapes consist of dialogues, reasonably lively, telling the story of the signing of an Anglo–Soviet business contract (including travel situations and social occasions) together with 'exploded' dialogues for student repetition and large numbers of thorough but very dull structure drills; the language is close to everyday Russian and only about 4% of the vocabulary is at all technical. The course can only be recommended to a teacher conducting a language laboratory course and using the 'direct method' (i.e. no translation into English).

4. Advanced Courses for Specialists

4.a. *General.* V. N. Vagner and Yu. G. Ovsienko: *Russian: uchebnik russkogo yazyka dlya lits, govoryashchikh na angliiskom yazyke* (Moscow, Vysshaya shkola, 1967, reprinted 1975. 656 pp. Distributed in UK by Collet's. £2.50 approx.) is a course produced for English speakers studying in the USSR and actually starts from scratch with the alphabet and pronunciation; the first 40 of the 62 lessons have instructions in English. In the UK it could well be used as a follow-up course, after an introduction to Russian, by those who plan to read specialised texts.

4.b. *On Commercial Correspondence.* There is one well produced textbook viz. S. Kohls, *Business Russian* (London, Pitman, 1971. 230 pp. £1.50 in 1974–75). This was originally published in the GDR as a course for those engaged in commercial correspondence with the USSR. 'A' level standard is assumed and nearly all the explanation is in Russian; all the translator has done for the English edition is put the German vocabularies, texts for translation and footnotes into (good) English. The work contains a wealth of information on Comecon procedures and technical terms, model letters and forms, some vocabulary for business meetings and travel. There is a key to some of the exercises, but no index. Only the vocabularies (including phrases) are stressed.

4.c. *For Scientists.* The following three courses are all intended for students already possessing a good knowledge of Russian who want practice (including writing in Russian) and information in technical fields. All are unstressed and entirely in Russian. N. G. Listopad and others, *Posobie po russkomu yazyku dlya studentov-inostrantsev, obuchayushchikhsya v tekhnicheskikh vuzakh* (Moscow, Vysshaya shkola, 1971. 224 pp. Distributed by Collet's. £0.45), includes an introduction to scientific and technical terms, how to read formulae in Russian and has a 23 pp. list of common scientific phrases listed alphabetically under the main verb. G. I. Makarova, *Pervyi raz po-russki* (L'vov, Izdatel'stvo L'vovskogo universiteta, 1966. Available from Collet's.), consists of three separate booklets: no. 1 is on arithmetic, algebra and technical drawing (124 pp. illus., with key. £0.20); no. 2 covers anatomy, botany and zoology (124 pp. illus., with key. £0.20); no. 3 deals with geography and history (236 pp. maps, with key. £0.60); all three have multilingual vocabularies including English. L. S. Badrieva and others, *Posobie po russkomu yazyku dlya studentov-inostrantsev tekhnicheskikh vuzov* (Moscow, Vysshaya shkola, 1972. 376 pp. Collet's. £0.75), is attractively bound in green boards with silver and green titling and is the most advanced of these three works; it contains texts from chemistry and materials science, and information on the grammar of Russian scientific style (with a bias towards chemistry).

5. Reference Works on Grammar and Usage

5.a. *Up to 'O' level.* Specifically for this purpose there is A. A. Haywood, *'O' level Russian* Volume 2 (London, Harrap, 1965. 282 pp. £1.15). This is a junior reference work with a 13 pp. index; linked to the grammar sections there are 38 pp. of translation and grammar exercises and 17 pp. of English–Russian vocabulary. P. Henry, *Manual of modern Russian prose composition (modern Russian usage)* (2nd ed. London, University of London Press, 1966. 176 pp. £0.80), like Haywood, offers a convenient way of checking on elementary grammar points (though there is no grammar index); Henry is more detailed and could also be used after 'O' level. A reprint of Henry is due shortly at £1.80.

5.b. *Advanced.* The best of the reference works as far as the subtler points of Russian usage are concerned is F. M. Borras and R. F. Christian, *Russian syntax. Aspects of modern Russian syntax and vocabulary* (2nd ed. Oxford, Clarendon Press, 1971. 456 pp. £5; £3.25). This work is designed to help English speakers acquire idiomatic Russian: it discusses the use of aspect, cases, numerals, the translation of English prepositions, difficult nouns, verbs, adjectives and so on. The book is in eight chapters: seven deal with the parts of speech and the eighth tackles word order; inside each chapter there are further sub-divisions and each separate point is numbered. A 22½ pp. index provides a partially effective reference system. Borras and Christian is not a replacement for a grammar book, but it is an excellent additional tool, particularly for undergraduate prose composition work.

In a similar category, but usable as an advanced revision course with more morphology and less semantics than Borras and Christian, there is I. Pulkina and E. Zakhava-Nekrasova, *Russian (a practical grammar with exercises)* (2nd ed. Moscow, Izdatel'stvo Russkii yazyk, 1974. 608 pp. Distributed by Collet's. £1.50). This is a full and up-to-date post 'O'-level reference work in English, marred by the absence of both an index and a key to the 847 exercises. Students would find it very useful on the standard difficult topics *e.g.*, aspect, verbs of motion, participles, and it could well serve as a class and home revision manual for 'A' level students and first year undergraduates.

I. M. Pul'kina: *A short Russian reference grammar* (2nd ed. Moscow, Progress, currently reprinting, 1975. 351 pp. To be available from Collet's. £1.25), is a more basic reference grammar than the preceding, with a great deal of material on stress and morphology and a rather obscure chapter on pronunciation. It is quite good on aspect. Again there is unfortunately no index and the student would probably find it essential to make his own. Unlike Pulkina and Zakhava-Nekrasova, this volume has no exercises and is intended purely as a home reference tool covering all the fundamentals of Russian grammar.

Two other rather older but recommendable reference grammars are N. Forbes, *Russian grammar* (3rd ed. rev. and enlarged by J. C. Dumbreck. Oxford, Clarendon Press, 1964. xii, 438 pp. £1.25), and B. O. Unbegaun, *Russian grammar* (Oxford, Clarendon Press, 1957 reprinted 1962. xxx, 319 pp. £1.90). Forbes is suitable for intermediate students preparing for 'A' level and has a short grammatical index (2½ pp.) as well as a long index (28 pp.) of words and phrases. The explanations are not as full or as up to date as in the previously mentioned Soviet works. Unbegaun is a scholarly work concerned particularly with morphology (including word formation); it contains useful information for teachers of Russian and linguistically inclined undergraduates.

For advanced university students conversant with Russian linguistic terminology a detailed reference grammar in Russian is the Academy of Sciences, *Grammatika sovremennogo russkogo yazyka* (Moscow, Izdatel'stvo Nauka, 1970. 768 pp.). This solid tome is the largest Soviet grammar available outside libraries (where the three-volume Academy Grammar, Izdatel'stvo AN SSSR, 1952–54 reprinted 1960, can be consulted); it is notable for its 14 pp. alphabetical index. Also available, with some effort, is the new edition of the key work of the grandfather of all current Soviet work on Russian: V. V. Vinogradov, *Russkii yazyk (grammaticheskoe uchenie o slove)* (2nd ed. Moscow, Vysshaya shkola, 1972.) a detailed and scholarly examination of the grammatical categories of Russian.

5.c. *Background.* A recent work that can be recommended in a category of its own is G. Gerhart, *The Russian's world. Life and language* (New York, Harcourt Brace Jovanovich, 1974. xiv, 258 pp. Distributed in U.K. by Chandos Books £6.35 (1977)). This work is particularly useful when students want to know not only how *izba, lapti,* or *pech'* translate but also what they look life and how they fit into the Russian's environment. The thematic chapters include such useful but scarce information as how to read mathematical formulae in Russian, how the inside of a peasant's hut is arranged, how peasants dress, how a Russian ties his shoes ... The book is in soft covers and is well printed in two columns with clear bold headings and plenty of illustrations; the text is in English with extracts in Russian from Russian publications (translated in a separate section placed before the 12 pp. index.).

6. Phonetics Courses.

Since most beginners' courses include a phonetic introduction there is presumably little demand for separate phonetics practice in addition to actual use of the language. Thus theoretical and practical study of Russian sounds and intonation tends to be neglected. Perhaps neglect explains the disappearance in the UK of a useful course, well known and popular among teachers of Russian to foreigners in the USSR: E. A. Bryzgunova, *Zvuki i intonatsiya russkoi rechi* (Moscow, Progress, 1969). Copies of the 252 pp. hardback textbook (reprinted 1972), in Russian, are available from Collet's at £0.50 but the 10 records (which sold for £13.75) seem to be temporarily(?) unavailable. This course goes from simple sounds through the intonation constructions of Russian to the intonation patterns of complete texts; the wealth of material can also be used for aural comprehension exercises.

R. I. Avanesov, *Russkoe literaturnoe proiznoshenie* (Moscow, Prosveshchenie, 1972) is an authoritative work, all in Russian, consisting of a 414 pp. hardback book, 12 7" flexible plastic records, and a 48 pp. paper transcript. Six of the records carry the sounds of Russian, while the other six are interesting texts (Chekhov, Prishvin, Gor'kii, prose and poetry) transcribed in Russian and the Cyrillic phonetic notation in the book and in the paper transcript. Avanesov's materials are much less of a practical course for foreigners than Bryzgunova, and there is nothing on intonation. They are available from Collet's as a boxed set at £3.50 (1977).

In English there is a theoretical study (i.e. no recordings) of Russian phonetics employing the International Phonetic Alphabet transcription system: D. Jones and D. Ward, *The phonetics of Russian* (Cambridge, Cambridge University Press, 1969. 307 pp. £6.30). Reviews have been mixed, but this is still the fullest work of its kind in the United Kingdom. D. Ward, *Russian pronunciation illustrated* (Cambridge, Cambridge University Press, 1966. 101 pp. £0.95), is an amusing paperback for non-beginners familiar with the IPA; unlikely Russian phrases concocted to illustrate the various pronunciations of Russian letters in different positions in the word or phrase are accompanied by an IPA transcription and a suitably unlikely drawing.

RUSSIAN: DICTIONARIES

by W. F. RYAN, M.A., D.Phil.

The range of Russian dictionaries and Russian and English dictionaries is now fairly large. Most are published in the Soviet Union[1] but an increasing number is now being published in England and America. When consulting or buying dictionaries the following points should be borne in mind: Soviet dictionaries are designed for Russian users and frequently do not contain much grammatical information; two-language dictionaries are normally designed for use in the country of publication and are not necessarily very helpful to users speaking the other language; constraints on the choice and acceability of vocabulary varies from country to country; Soviet dictionaries are usually much cheaper than British or American dictionaries but are printed on poor paper which soon yellows and are very poorly bound.

Russian–English Dictionaries (including two-way dictionaries). The standard Soviet dictionary which has gone through many editions is A. I. Smirnitskiĭ. *Russko-angliĭskiĭ slovar'* (8th stereotype ed. Moscow, Sovetskaya entsiklopediya, 1969. 766 pp. £3.). with 50,000 entries and in large format. Although good it is very selective in its coverage and has some oddities of English. The best dictionary designed for anglophone users is M. Wheeler, *The Oxford Russian–English Dictionary* (Oxford, Clarendon Press, 1972. 918 pp. £8.75) with 70,000 entries. This gives a wide coverage and includes vulgarisms and is not subject to political constraints. It gives grammatical and phraseological usage and expanded definitions of some purely Russian or Soviet concepts. L. Segal's *English–Russian, Russian–English dictionary* (London, Lund Humphries, 1953. 2,160 pp.) is

---

[1] The distributor of Soviet dictionaries in the United Kingdom is Collet's of London and Wellingborough.

typographically excellent but is arbitrary, unsystematic, often very inaccurate and not to be recommended. M. A. O'Brien, *New English–Russian and Russian–English dictionary* (London, Allen and Unwin, 1958. 363,344 pp. £3.50) is the first properly designed dictionary for English users but its often inappropriate equivalents and its small smudgy type (it was first printed in 1930) do not recommend it. The best pre-Revolutionary dictionary is that of A. Alexandrov: *Polnyĭ russko-angliĭskiĭ slovar'*. Although it is still available in reprints it must be considered completely outdated except for specialist historical purposes. Rather smaller than Smirnitskiĭ but a good reader's bookshelf dictionary is A. M. Taube and others (editor R. Daglish), *Russko-angliĭskiĭ slovar'* (Moscow, Sovetskaya entsiklopediya, 1965, reprinted (3rd stereotype ed.) 1970. 1,052 pp. £1.50); 34,000 entries.

The following smaller dictionaries are worth consideration: Jessie Coulson, *The pocket Oxford Russian–English dictionary* (Oxford, Clarendon Press, 1975. 397 pp. £2.50) has 30,000 entries and is based on Wheeler's *Oxford Russian–English dictionary* (see above). W. Harrison and Svetlana Le Fleming, *Russian–English and English–Russian dictionary* (London, Routledge and Kegan Paul, 1973. xii, 568 pp. £1.95), with 25,000 entries each way, is good, modern and very useful for its size. B. A. Lapidus and S. V. Shevtsova, *A Russian–English dictionary for the foreign student* (Moscow, Gos. izd. inostrannykh i natsional'nykh slovareĭ, 1962. 563 pp.) has 11,000 entries and grammatical appendices. It is a very useful student's dictionary which explains the main uses of the commoner Russian words and has also been published in the USA at a much increased price as *The Learner's Russian–English dictionary* (Cambridge, Mass., M.I.T. Press, 1963. xxii, 688 pp. $10; $3.95). *Langenscheidt's Russian–English, English–Russian dictionary*, by E. Wedel and A. Romanov (Berlin and Munich; London, Methuen, 1964. 505 pp.) is a large pocket dictionary very good for its size, with 35,000 entries overall. J. Grosberg's *The EUP concise Russian and English dictionary* (London, English Universities Press, 1957. xix, 271 pp. £0.75) has 18,000 entries. The US War Department *Dictionary of spoken Russian: Russian–English, English–Russian* (New York, Dover; Lon-

don, Constable, 1958. 573 pp. £5.50) is a dictionary of
colloquial usage of some use but with a small and arbitrary
choice of headwords. A useful dictionary at school level is P.
Waddington's *A basic Russian–English vocabulary* (London,
Methuen, 1962. xvi, 355 pp.) which has 3,300 words with an
English–Russian index.
English-Russian Dictionaries. The standard Soviet dictionary
has long been V. K. Myuller, *Anglo-russkiĭ slovar'* (16th
stereotype ed. Moscow, Gos. izd. inostrannykh i natsional'nykh
slovareĭ, 1971. 912 pp. £3); 70,000 words. While still the best
one-volume dictionary it suffers from occasionally odd English
and is designed for use by Russians. The same drawbacks also
apply to the dictionary which has largely superseded it: I. R.
Gal'perin, *Bol'shoĭ anglo-russkiĭ slovar'* (Moscow, Sovetskaya
entsiklopediya, 1972. 2 v. (822; 863 pp.) £8.50 the set); 150,000
words. This must nevertheless be considered the most outstanding English–Russian dictionary at present. An excellent
student's dictionary is S. Folomkina and H. Weiser, *A Learner's
English–Russian dictionary for English-speaking students*
(Moscow, Gos. izd. inostrannykh i natsional'nykh slovareĭ,
1962 reprinted 1970. 655 pp. £1) with 3,500 entries and grammatical appendices. Although having few entries, the commonest words are included with a clear separation of meanings
and many examples of the commonest word combinations and
idioms. It has been expensively reprinted in the USA (Cambridge, Mass., M.I.T. Press, 1963. 744 pp. $14.95; $3.95).
Russian–Russian Dictionaries. There is no really good descriptive dictionary of Russian; almost all are normative, didactic
and prudish. The only dictionary to escape this is V. I. Dal',
Tolkovyĭ slovar' zhivago velikorusskago yazyka (Moscow,
1863–66. 4 v.). This was extensively revised and amplified by
Baudouin de Courtenay in the 3rd edition (St. Petersburg and
Moscow, 1903–09, reissued 1912–14 and in a reduced offset
edition in Tokyo, 1934). This edition is the best for reference.
The Soviet reissue of 1935 is of the 2nd edition and is less useful.
Dal''s dictionary is excellent on both standard literary and
dialect Russian. The standard modern dictionary of literary
Russian is the *Slovar' sovremennogo russkogo literaturnogo
yazyka* (Moscow and Leningrad, 1948–65, 17 v.) published by

the Academy of Sciences. Examples of words are given in
literary contexts, usually from the 18th century onwards. The
shorter Academy dictionary is the *Slovar' russkogo yazyka*
(Moscow, Gos. izd. inostrannykh i natsional'nykh slovareĭ,
1957–61. 4 v.). This also gives contexts but has been criticised
for both its coverage and its principles of presentation. The best
medium-length dictionary is D. N. Ushakov, *Tolkovyĭ slovar'
russkogo yazyka* (Moscow, Sovetskaya entsiklopediya,
1935–40. 4 v. Reprinted in Moscow and Ann Arbor, 1948). It
gives contexts and stylistic levels and has a good coverage
(85,289 entries). A regularly reprinted one-volume dictionary is
S. I. Ozhegov, *Slovar' russkogo yazyka* (10th ed. Moscow,
Sovetskaya entsiklopediya, 1973. 846 pp. £3.50). This is useful
and fairly up to date. It has 57,000 entries, indicates
phraseological usage and some grammatical points but does not
give contextual illustrations. All the above-mentioned dictionaries are in large format.

Specialised Dictionaries. *Antonyms*: L. A. Vvedenskaya. *Slovar'
antonimov russkogo yazyka* (Rostov on Don, Rostovskiĭ universitet, 1971. 168 pp.); N. P. Kolesnikov. *Slovar' antonimov
russkogo yazyka* (Tbilisi, Tbiliskiĭ universitet, 1971. 314 pp.).

Dialect: F. P. Filin. *Slovar' russkikh narodnykh govorov*
(Moscow and Leningrad, Nauka, 1965– v. 1–10 to date).

Encyclopedic: Entsiklopedicheskiĭ slovar' (Moscow,
Sovetskaya entsiklopediya, 1963–64. 2 v. illust.) is useful for
historical and present-day personages and places, Soviet institutions, etc.

Etymological: The standard modern work is M. Fasmer,
Etimologicheskiĭ slovar' russkogo yazyka (Moscow, Progress,
1964–74. 4 v.). This is a translated and expended version of
Max Vasmer, *Russisches etimologisches Wörterbuch*
(Heidelberg, Winter, 1953–58. 3 v.) which, being in German,
may be convenient for some users. A new work in progress is
N. M. Shanskiĭ, *Etimologicheskiĭ slovar' russkogo yazyka*
(Moscow, Moskovskiĭ universitet, 1963– v. 1–5 to date). One-
volume etymological dictionaries are: N. M. Shanskiĭ and
others, *Kratkiĭ etimologicheskiĭ slovar' russkogo yazyka* (2nd
ed. Moscow, Prosveschenie, 1971. 541 pp. £1) and G. P.
Tsyganenko, *Etimologicheskiĭ slovar' russkogo yazyka* (Kiev,

Radyans'ka shkola, 1970. 598 pp.).

Historical: The standard dictionary of Old Russian (11th–17th century) is I. I. Sreznevskiĭ, *Materialy dlya slovarya drevnerusskogo yazyka* (St. Petersburg, 1893. 3 v. Reprinted in facsimile Moscow, Gos. izd. inostrannykh i natsional'nykh slovareĭ, 1958). There is a reverse-alphabetic index: *Indeks a tergo do Materialow do słownika jezyka staroruskiego I. I. Srezniewskiego* (Warsaw, Państwowe wydawnictwo naukowe, 1968. 386 pp.). A condensed version of Sreznevskiĭ in a single small volume is H. Lunt, *Concise dictionary of old Russian* (Munich, Fink Verlag, 1970. [x], 85 pp.). A new dictionary is in progress: S. G. Barkhudarov (ed.), *Slovar' russkogo yazyka XI–XVII vv.* (Moscow, Nauka, 1975– v. 1–2 (A–V) have appeared to date.

Homonyms: O. S. Akhmanova, *Slovar' omonimov russkogo yazyka* (Moscow, Sovetskaya entsiklopediya, 1974. 448 pp.) has English, French and German translations.

Orthography and Stress: The standard work is S. G. Barkhudarov and others, *Orfograficheskiĭ slovar' russkogo yazyka* (13th ed. Moscow, Russkiĭ yazyk, 1974, 450 pp. £1.50); 106,000 entries. D. E. Rozental', *Slovar' udareniĭ dlya rabotnikov radio i televideniya* (3rd ed. Moscow, Sovetskaya entsiklopediya, 1970. 688 pp.) has 63,000 entries and includes names of people, places, journals, titles of works, etc., for use in the news media. For the treatment of compound words see V. Z. Buchkina and others, *Slitno ili razdel'no?* (Moscow, Sovetskaya entsiklopediya, 1972. 479 pp.); 43,000 entries.

Phraseological: A. I. Molotkov. *Frazeologicheskiĭ slovar' russkogo yazyka* (2nd ed. Moscow, Sovetskaya entsiklopediya, 1968. 543 pp.); 4,000 entries; P. Borkowski. *The great Russian–English dictionary of idioms and set expressions* (London, the author, 1973. xvi, 384 pp. £6); 8,600 entries; A. V. Kunin. *Anglo-russkiĭ frazeologicheskiĭ slovar'* (3rd ed. Moscow, Sovetskaya entsiklopediya, 1967. 2 v. (738;[2], 739–1,264 pp.); 25,000 entries.

Reverse: Obratnyĭ slovar' russkogo yazyka (Moscow, Sovetskaya entsiklopediya, 1974. 944 pp.); 125,000 entries; H. H. Bielfeldt. *Rückläufiges Wörterbuch der russischen Sprache der Gegenwart* (Berlin, Akademie-Verlag, 1965. 392

pp.); 80,000 entries.

Synonyms: A. P. Evgen'eva, *Slovar' sinonimov russkogo yazyka* (Moscow, Nauka, 1970–71. 2 v. (680; 856 pp.). £9.35) is large but with a very arbitrary selection of headwords—it is essential to use the cross-reference index. It contains illustrative material from literature and is careful to distinguish stylistic levels. Z. E. Aleksandrova, *Slovar' sinonimov russkogo yazyka* (Moscow, Sovetskaya entsiklopediya, 1968. 600 pp. £1.10) has 9,000 main entries. It is arranged on different principles from Evgen'eva and has no illustrative material but is useful for quick reference.

Technical Dictionaries. There is now a considerable number of technical dictionaries published in the USSR Most are, of course, English–Russian dictionaries but it should be remembered that even the Russian–English dictionaries are designed for Russians and do not therefore contain grammatical information or stress markings. The following list contains dictionaries published in England or the USA, Russian–English dictionaries published in the USSR and English–Russian dictionaries which contain Russian–English indexes. Most Soviet technical dictionaries are sold out very soon after publication and reissues are not very common.

General: A. E. Chernukhin, *Anglo–russkiĭ politekhnicheskiĭ slovar'* (2nd ed. Moscow, Sovetskaya entsiklopediya, 1971. 671 pp.) has 80,000 entries in large format. A. E. Chernukhin, *Russko-angliĭskiĭ tekhnicheskiĭ slovar'* (Moscow, Ministerstvo oborony, 1971. 1,027 pp.) has 80,000 entries and a very wide coverage, especially in military technology. It is best used in conjunction with the previous entry. L. I. Callaham's *Russian–English chemical and polytechnic dictionary* (3rd ed. New York and London, Wiley, 1975. xxviii, 852 pp. £19.85) is the standard Western reference work. It is good and well-produced but limited in scope and expensive. M. H. T. and V. L. Alford, *Russian–English science and technology dictionary* (Oxford and New York, Pergamon Press, 1970. 2 v. (1,423 pp.) £15.50 the set) has over 100,000 entries and gives stresses, grammatical information and separation of word elements; it includes abbreviations in the main text. *Soviet Russian scientific and technical terms: a selective list* (Washington, D.C., Library

of Congress, Reference Department, Aerospace Information
Division, 1963. 668 pp.) has 26,000 entries.
Aerospace: M. M. Konarski, *A Russian–English dictionary of
modern terms on aeronautics and rocketry* (Oxford, Pergamon
Press, 1962. 515 pp.) has 14,500 entries. A. M. Murashkevich,
Anglo-russkiĭ raketno-kosmicheskiĭ slovar' (Moscow,
Ministerstvo oborony, 1966. 920 pp.) is a very full dictionary
with 50,000 entries but English–Russian only. I. F. Borisov,
Anglo-russkiĭ slovar' po aviatsionno-kosmicheskim materialam
(Moscow, Ministerstvo oborony, 1972. 485 pp.) covers all
materials, techniques, materials characteristics, fuels, and
lubricants used in aerospace technology and associated fields,
with 19,000 terms and a Russian–English index.
Agriculture: A. N. Rozenbaum and others, *Anglo-russkiĭ
slovar' po sel'skokhozyaĭstvennoĭ tekhnike* (Moscow,
Sovetskaya entsiklopediya, 1972. 379 pp.); Russian–English index and illustrated indexes; P. A. Adamenko. *Anglo-russkiĭ
slovar' po zhivotnovodstvu* (Moscow, Sovetskaya entsiklopediya,
1972. 452 pp.); 25,000 entries; Russian–English index; A. V.
Peterburgskiĭ. *Anglo-russkiĭ pochvenno-agrokhimicheskiĭ
slovar'* (Moscow, Sovetskaya entsikopediya, 1967. 432 pp.);
20,000 entries; Russian–English index; B. N. Usovskiĭ and
others, *Russko-angliĭskiĭ sel'skokhozyaĭstvennyi slovar'*
(Moscow, Fizmatgiz, 1960. 504 pp.) covers agriculture and
related subjects and gives the Latin of botanical names; 30,000
entries.
Astronomy: O. A. Mel'nikov. *Anglo-russkiĭ astronomicheskiĭ
slovar'* (Moscow, Sovetskaya entsiklopediya, 1971. 504 pp.);
20,000 entries; Russian–English index.
Botany: N. N. Davydov. *Botanicheskiĭ slovar'; russko-
angliĭsko-nemetsko-frantsuzsko-latinskiĭ* (2nd ed. Moscow, Fizmatgiz, 1962. 355 pp.); 6,000 entries in Russian, English, German, French and Latin with cross-reference indexes; O. S.
Grebenshchikov. *Geobotanicheskiĭ slovar'* (Moscow, Nauka,
1965. 226 pp.); 2,660 entries in Russian, English, German and
French with cross-reference indexes.
Cartography: G. L. Galperin, *Anglo-russkiĭ slovar' po kar-
tografii, geodezii i aerofototopografii* (Moscow, Gos. izd. fizikomatematicheskoĭ literatury, 1958. 546 pp.) covers all aspects of

maps, their preparation and publication, surveying, aerial photography and military applications and has a Russian–English index.

Chemistry: see *General*.

Computers, Cybernetics: V. K. Zeĭdenberg. *Anglo-russkiĭ slovar' po vychislitel'noĭ tekhnike* (2nd ed. Moscow, Russkiĭ yazyk, 1974. 535 pp.); 24,000 entries; Russian–English index; L. K. Ptashnyĭ, *Anglo-russkiĭ slovar' po avtomatike, kibernetike i kontrol'noizmeritel'nym priboram* (2nd ed. Moscow, Sovetskaya entsiklopediya, 1971. 428 pp.) is mainly concerned with automation applications; 20,000 entries; Russian–English index.

Electronics: English–Russian, Russian–English electronics dictionary (New York, McGraw-Hill, 1958. 943 pp.) gives 22,000 Russian terms. It covers a very wide range of subjects but is outdated in some areas, e.g. computers. I. K. Kalugin and others, *Anglo-russkiĭ slovar' po sovremennoĭ radioelektronike* (2nd ed. Moscow, Sovetskaya entsiklopediya, 1972. 448 pp.) has 20,000 entries; Russian–English index.

Engineering: (see also *General*). L. D. Bel'kind, *Anglo-russkiĭ slovar' po detalyam mashin* (Moscow, Gos. izd. fizikomatematicheskoĭ literatury, 1959. 309 pp.) comprises 10,000 entries, with a Russian–English index, on machine components. V. T. Zolotykh, *Anglo-russkiĭ slovar' po svarochnomu delu* (2nd ed. Moscow, Sovetskaya entsiklopediya, 1967. 376 pp.) is on welding and has 12,000 entries, a Russian–English index and an illustrated appendix.

Geology: T. A. Sofiano, *Russko-angliĭskiĭ geologicheskiĭ slovar'* (Moscow, Fizmatgiz, 1960. 559 pp.) covers geology and allied sciences; 30,000 entries.

Law: N. P. Prischepenko. *Russian–English law dictionary* (New York, Praeger, 1969. 146 pp.); S. N. Andrianov and A. S. Nikiforov. *Anglo-russkiĭ yuridicheskiĭ slovar'* (Moscow, Mezhdunarodnye otnosheniya, 1964. 340 pp.); A. S. Berson and others, *Anglo-russkiĭ patentnyĭ slovar'* (Moscow, Sovetskaya entsiklopediya, 1973. 232 pp.) is on patents; 7,500 entries; Russian–English index.

Library science: G. S. Zhdanov and others. *Slovar' terminov po informatike* (Moscow, Nauka, 1971. 359 pp.); 3,035 entries,

Russian–English and English–Russian.

Linguistics: O. S. Akhmanova. *Slovar' lingvisticheskikh ter-minov* (Moscow, Sovetskaya entsiklopediya, 1966. 606 pp.); 7,000 entries, with English, French, German and Spanish translations and an English–Russian cross-reference index; J. Paternost. *Russian–English glossary of linguistic terms* (University Park, Pa., Pennsylvania State University, 1965. v. 230 pp.); reproduced from typescript.

Medicine: Yu. B. Eliseenkov and others, *Russko-angliĭskiĭ meditsinskiĭ slovar'* (Moscow, Russkii yazyk, 1975. 647 pp.) comprises 50,000 entries on all aspects of medical science, genetics and biochemistry. It gives many Latin equivalents. S. Jablonski, *Russian–English medical dictionary* (New York and London, Academic Press, 1958. xi, 423 pp.) has 29,000 entries and E. A. Carpovich, *Russian–English biological and medical dictionary* (New York, Technical Dictionaries, 1958. 398 pp.) has 32,650 entries.

Physics: I. Emin. *Russian–English physics dictionary* (New York and London, Wiley, 1963. 554 pp.); 25,000 entries.

Photography and Cinematography: A. A. Sakharov, *Anglo-russkiĭ slovar' po fotografii i kinematografii* (Moscow, Fizmatgiz, 1960. 395 pp.) covers all aspects of photography, cinematography and professional slang and has 10,000 entries and a Russian–English index.

Plastics: M. G. Gurariĭ and S. S. Iofe, *Anglo-russkiĭ slovar' po plastmassam* (Moscow, Fizmatgiz, 1963. 144 pp.) covers the chemistry and production of plastics. Some terms are now out-moded. There is a Russian–English index.

Social Sciences: R. E. F. Smith's *A Russian–English dictionary of social science terms* (London, Butterworths, 1962. 495 pp.), with 35,000 entries, covers a very wide range of subjects in the general field of politics, economics, sociology, administration, education, etc., with explanations and translation equivalents; it is invaluable.

Soviet Institutions: Barry Crowe's *Concise dictionary of Soviet terminology, institutions and abbreviations* (Oxford, Pergamon Press, 1969. 182 pp. £2.60) is a considerable but by no means complete list of specifically Soviet terms, mainly in the field of adminstration, politics and economics, and including abbreviations and acronyms. There is an English–Russian index.

Statistics: S. Kotz. *Russian–English dictionary of statistical terms and expressions* (Chapel Hill, N.C., University of North Carolina Press, 1964. xviii, 115 pp.).

10

UKRAINIAN

by VICTOR SWOBODA, B.A., M.A.

INTRODUCTION

Ukrainian is an East Slavonic language, and it is the language of some 50 million Ukrainians living in the Ukrainian Soviet Socialist Republic (where they comprise three quarters of the Republic's total population of 49 million), as well as in other republics of the USSR, in Poland, Czechoslovakia, Rumania, Canada, the USA, Great Britain, Australia, and some West European and Latin American countries. The number of the speakers of Ukrainian exceeds that of any other Slavonic language except Russian. It may be also noted that nearly half of the population of the USSR are non-Russians, among whom the Ukrainians are as numerous as all the others put together. Ukrainian is more closely related to Byelorussian and Russian than to the other Slavonic languages; the relationship between Russian and Ukrainian is reminiscent of that between Spanish and Portuguese, or Spanish and Catalan, and the fate of Ukrainian over its history, both older and more recent, is rather reminiscent of that of Catalan.

The Ukrainian alphabet is Cyrillic, differing from the Russian one by the absence of four letters and the presence of three specifically Ukrainian letters, but some letters common to both languages are pronounced differently. On the whole, the pronunciation of literary Ukrainian follows its spelling more closely than is the case with Russian. The stress is free, as in Russian, and is unfortunately left unmarked in ordinary print; it is, however, normally marked in textbook courses, grammars and readers for non-natives, and in all dictionaries (the rare exception is noted below). Ukrainian is a richly inflected language, like

Russian or Latin.

In this country, Ukrainian is studied mostly by British-born children of Ukrainian extraction, some 50–80 of whom have been taking GCE 'O' level examinations in this subject each year over the past decade or so. There is provision for the study of Ukrainian as a subsidiary subject in the faculty of arts of the University of London (at the School of Slavonic and East European Studies, also under intercollegiate arrangements); postgraduate research in Ukrainian subjects is also pursued in the same university.

Information on all aspects of Ukrainian life, including language, literature, culture, geography, history, institutions, etc., can be found in two English-language encyclopaedic works: *Soviet Ukraine* (Kiev, Editorial Office of the Ukrainian Soviet Encyclopedia, Academy of Sciences of the Ukrainian SSR, [1969]. 572 pp. Rbl.4.80) and *Ukraine: a concise encyclopaedia* (Toronto, University of Toronto Press, 1963–71. 2 v. (lxxxi, 2,579 pp.) $97.50).

TEXTBOOK COURSES & GRAMMARS

Only textbooks published in Kiev can be relied upon to offer spelling and vocabulary currently used in the Ukrainian SSR; such is Yu. O. Zhluktenko and others, *Ukrainian: a text-book for beginners* (Kiev, 'Vyshcha shkola', 1973. 351 pp. Rbl.1.12), comprising 54 lessons, each with a text, dialogues, vocabulary, grammar, and exercises: translating the text into English (no key), translating into Ukrainian (a key at the end of the book), and grammar exercises of the 'objective' or 'multiple choice' type. This is followed by 28 pp. of profusely illustrated additional reading material about Kiev, and five pp. of poetry by prominent authors; a reference chapter with declension and conjugation paradigms; and Ukrainian–English (about 2,000 words) and English–Ukrainian vocabularies. Another textbook, similar but more elementary is H. I. Makarova, *Learn Ukrainian* (Kiev, 'Vyshcha shkola', 1975. 255 pp. Rbl.0.68).

Among textbooks published in the West, those written by Yar Slavutych, of the University of Alberta (Canada), most closely reproduce the current literary language of the Ukrainian SSR. The series begins with his *Ukrainian in pictures* (Edmonton, Alta, Gateway, 1965. 90 pp.), suitable for younger schoolchildren, which introduces some 400 words and simple grammar. For older children and adults, there is a preparatory course, *An introduction to Ukrainian* (Edmonton, Slavuta, 1962. 22 pp.), to be followed by *Ukrainian for beginners* (4th rev. ed. Slavuta, 1968. 60 pp.) which consists of ten lessons, and ultimately by his *Conversational Ukrainian* (4th ed. Gateway, 1973. [xxxii], 608 pp. £4.50) 19 of whose preliminary unnumbered pp. are identical with *An introduction to Ukrainian*, but they are absent in the first two editions of *Conversational Ukrainian*. This final stage comprises 75 lessons, each consisting of a bilingual dialogue, a reading passage, phraseology, grammar, exercises: translation into Ukrainian and answering in Ukrainian questions asked in Ukrainian on the reading passage; and a vocabulary. The volume is concluded by collected paradigms and an index of over 4,000 Ukrainian words used, with references to lesson vocabularies instead of translation. There are no English–Ukrainian glossaries or keys to exercises in any of Slavutych's courses, nor does he claim that they can be used for self-study. In common with the great majority of present-day Ukrainian print in the West, Slavutych uses the old orthography which originated in the second half of the nineteenth century and was abolished in the Ukrainian SSR in 1933, at the time of the purges. The most noticeable differences between the old and the post-1933 orthography are found in the spelling of some types of loan words, while the vast majority of native Ukrainian words are spelt identically according to either orthography. An additional deviation from the standard language is caused by the intrusion of West Ukrainian dialectal vocabulary, which affects, though relatively slightly, G. Luckyj and J. B. Rudnyćkyj: *A modern Ukrainian grammar* (Winnipeg, Ukrainian Free Academy of Sciences, 1958. iv, 186 pp.; two earlier editions, Minneapolis, University of Minnesota Press, 1949, 1950), which comprises 39 lessons, each consisting of a short text, grammar, vocabulary, and exercises: a translation into Ukrainian and grammatical ones; at the end there are paradigms and a Ukrainian–English vocabulary of over 2,000 words; no keys. A further deviation towards West Ukrainian and Canadian Ukrainian vocabulary is found in the thorough course by J. W. Stechishin: *Ukrainian grammar* (Winnipeg, Trident Press, 1966. xxxiv, 502 pp. £2.40), of 74 lessons, each having grammar, a vocabulary and exercises: Ukrainian and English sentences for translation, the volume being concluded by a Ukrainian–English vocabulary of nearly 2,000 words, an English–Ukrainian one, and a subject (including grammar) index. Finally, a textbook in German ought to be mentioned, J. B. Rudnyćkyj. *Lehrbuch der ukrainischen Sprache* (4th rev. ed. Wiesbaden, Harrassowitz, 1964. 204 pp.), of which Luckyj and Rudnyćkyj's grammar referred to above is in fact an abridgement. The 38 lessons are followed by a 17 pp. reader of additional literary texts; grammatical tables offer more than mere collected paradigms but include also very welcome lists of 70 common nominal suffixes and 46 adjectival ones with explanation of their meaning and use; individual glossaries to each lesson are, unusually, gathered at the end of the book, with each word being supplied with phonetic transcription; there are also a general Ukrainian–German vocabulary of some 2,500 words and a short (about 120 words) German–Ukrainian one.

Among reference grammars, one has been published in English: A. Medushevsky and R. Zyatkovska, *Ukrainian grammar* (Kiev, 'Radyans'ka shkola', 1963. 212 pp. Rbl.0.44); it has also exercises following each section, but they are of the type usually found in textbooks of Ukrainian for native learners, and include no texts for translation; there is a glossary of over 2,000 words. Two major parts of grammar are dealt with in two works: Charles E. Bidwell, *Outline of Ukrainian morphology* (Rev. ed. Pittsburgh, Pa., University of Pittsburgh, 1971. iii, 69 pp. $1.25), a concise summary, 'structural' in approach, for advanced students; and an excellent detailed presentation of the chief part of syntax by the renowned Slavist of Columbia University, George Y. Shevelov: *The syntax of modern literary Ukrainian: the simple sentence* (The Hague, Mouton, 1963. 319 pp.). Both works use Latin-character transcriptions of Ukrainian, the second one without stresses. Though in French, the concise 43 pp. reference grammar forming the first part of Élie Borščak: *Lectures ukrainiennes avec grammaire, commentaire et lexique* (Lectures annotées de l'Institut d'Études slaves. Paris, Droz, 1946. vi, 156 pp. FFr.15.85), is to be recommended. Its second part consists of literary prose and verse texts, annotated and with a 2,500-word glossary.

The most detailed Ukrainian grammar in Ukrainian is the standard five-volume work *Suchasna ukrayins'ka literaturna mova* (Kiev, 'Naukova dumka', 1969–73. (2,561 pp.) Rbl.12.26), the volumes being subtitled: I *Vstup*. *Fonetyka*; II *Morfolohiya*; III *Syntaksys*; IV *Leksyka i frazeolohiya*; and V *Stylistyka*. More compact ones are: Shevelov's work which appeared under his pseudonym, Yuriĭ Sherekh, *Narys suchasnoyi ukrayins'koyi literaturnoyi movy* (second title-page: Jury Šerech, *An outline of modern literary Ukrainian*) (Munich, 'Molode zhyttya', 1951. 402 pp.), and two Kiev-published grammars, M. P. Ivchenko, *Suchasna ukrayins'ka literaturna mova* (Kiev, Vyd. Kyyivs'koho universytetu, 1965. 504 pp. Rbl.0.73), and the two-volume work, M. A. Zhovtobryukh and B. M. Kulyk, *Kurs suchasnoyi ukrayins'koyi literaturnoyi movy*, vol. I (4th ed. Kiev, 'Vyshcha shkola', 1972. 402 pp. Rbl.0.98), with vol. II, subtitled *Syntaksys*, by Kulyk alone (2nd rev. augmented ed. Kiev, 'Radyans'ka shkola', 1965. 283 pp. Rbl.0.69). The latest orthography and punctuation rules are set out in A. Buryachok and others, *Dovidnyk z ukrayins'koho pravopysu* (Kiev, 'Radyans'ka shkola', 1973. 280 pp. Rbl.1.07), which includes an 11,000-word orthographic dictionary with partly indicated pronunciation.

Two comparative grammars, both in Ukrainian, can be very useful to the advanced student: Yu. O. Zhluktenko, *Porivnyal'na hramatyka anhliĭs'koyi ta ukrayins'koyi mov* (second title-page: *A comparative grammar of English and Ukrainian*) (Kiev, 'Radyans'ka shkola', 1960. 160 pp. Rbl.0.50), and T. V. Baĭmut and others, *Porivnyal'na hramatyka ukrayins'koyi i rosiĭs'koyi mov* (2nd rev. augmented ed. Kiev, 'Radyans'ka shkola', 1961. 268 pp. Rbl.0.46); this one compares Ukrainian with Russian as well as with Byelorussian.

Two prose and poetry readers may be noted: C. H. Andrusyshen (ed.), *Readings in Ukrainian authors* (Winnipeg, Ukrainian Canadian Committee, 1949. vi, 240 pp.), which has notes on difficult idioms and on the authors, and a 5,500-word glossary; and V. O. Buyniak (ed.). *Readings in Ukrainian authors* 2 parts, part 2 subtitled *Notes and vocabulary* (Saskatoon, University of Saskatchewan, 1962–64, 50; 104 pp.), whose texts are unstressed, but the 4,500-word vocabulary is stressed.

DICTIONARIES

M. L. Podvez'ko's standard *Ukrayins'ko-anhliĭs'kyĭ slovnyk* (Podvesko, *Ukrainian–English dictionary*) (2nd rev. augmented ed. Kiev, 'Radyans'ka shkola', 1957. 1,019 pp. Rbl.1.96) has about 60,000 words (NB: the Western [n.p.] facsimile 1962 reprint is of its *first* 1952 ed., 1,011 pp.); it includes modern Ukrainian vocabulary, but does not include less frequently used Ukrainian words for which the native user is expected to know their more usual synonyms and look them up instead. The non-native user is left at a disadvantage here, and the larger volume, C. H. Andrusyshen and J. N. Krett, *Ukrayins'ko-anhliĭs'kyĭ slovnyk – Ukrainian–English dictionary* (Toronto, University of Toronto Press, 1957. xxx, 1,163 pp. £4.80), may come to the rescue with its 95,000 words, though it is weak on modern vocabulary (the relatively few words whose spelling differs between the pre- and post-1933 orthographies are mostly given in this dictionary in both forms). Anything not found in either source may be discovered in the Ukrainian–Russian dictionaries, the largest one being the 121,700-word I. M. Kyrychenko (editor-in-chief), *Ukrayins'ko-rosiĭs'kyĭ slovnyk* (Kiev, Vyd, Akademiyi nauk Ukrayins'koyi RSR, 1953–63. 6 v. (civ, 3,580 pp.) Rbl.12.), with B. D. Hrinchenko, *Slovar' ukrayins'koyi movy* (Kiev, Vyd. Akad. nauk Ukr. SSR, 1958–59. 4 v. (lvi, 2,136 pp.) Rbl.4.40; a facsimile reprint of the original Kiev 1907–9 ed.), though dated, still very important as a stand-by for any older, rare and folk-lore vocabulary excluded from the former, or, ultimately, in the eleven-volume monolingual dictionary, now in progress of publication, *Slovnyk ukrayins'koyi movy* (Kiev, 'Naukova dumka', 1970–74. v. I–V (3,773 pp.) Rbl.17.87), having nearly reached the half-way house with 70,000 words. Difficulties with the formation of irregular or anomalous declensional and conjugational forms and with their accentuation can be resolved, when the above dictionaries do not help, with the aid of special dictionaries which supply such forms, with stress, but carry no translations or definitions of meanings; these are: the 'orthographic dictionary', S.I. Holovashchuk and others, *Orfohrafichnyĭ slovnyk ukrayins'koyi movy* (Kiev, 'Naukova dumka', 1975. 856 pp. Rbl.1.96), listing some 114,000 words, the 52,000-word 'accentuation dictionary', M. I. Pohribnyĭ *Slovnyk naholosiv ukrayins'koyi literaturnoyi movy* (2nd rev. augmented ed. Kiev, 'Radyans'ka shkola', 1964. 639 pp. Rbl.0.78), and the 50,000-word I. R. Vykhovanets' and others, *Ukrayins'ka literaturna vymova i naholos: slovnyk-dovidnyk* (Kiev, 'Naukova dumka', 1973. 724 pp. Rbl.1.79), which additionally indicates pronunciation. The pre-1933 orthography is represented in the orthographic dictionary of H. Holoskevych: *Pravopysnyĭ slovnyk* (second title-page: G. Holoskevych, *Ukrainian language dictionary*) (London, Association of Ukrainians in Great Britain, 1961. 451 pp. £1.25; a facsimile reprint of 7th ed. Kiev, 1930.). Ukrainian phraseology is listed in two dictionaries, one Ukrainian–Russian and vice versa: I. S. Oliĭnyk and M. M. Sydorenko. *Ukrayins'ko-rosiĭs'kyĭ i rosiĭs'ko-ukrayins'kyĭ frazeolohichnyĭ slovnyk* (Kiev, 'Radyans'ka shkola', 1971, 351 pp. Rbl.1.26) with some 7,000 Ukrainian phrases, and the other monolingual, H. M. Udovychenko, *Slovnyk ukrayins'kykh idiom* (Kiev, 'Radyans'kyĭ pys'mennyk', 1968. 463 pp. Rbl.0.92) with over 2,200 idiomatic phrases explained and words fully indexed.

For translating into Ukrainian, the standard dictionary is M. L. Podvez'ko and M. I. Balla, *Anhlo-ukrayins'kyĭ slovnyk – English–Ukrainian Dictionary* (Kiev, 'Radyans'ka shkola', 1974. 663 pp. Rbl.3.90) with some 65,000 words. Any gaps left in it may be filled from K. T. Barantsev: *Anhlo-ukrayins'kyĭ frazeolohichnyĭ slovnyk – English–Ukrainian phrase-book* (Kiev, 'Radyans'ka shkola', 1969. 1,052 pp. Rbl.2.52), which has some 30,000 phrases, or through the intermediary of Russian with the aid of the larger Russian–Ukrainian dictionary, *Russko-ukrainskiĭ slovar'* (Kiev, 'Naukova dumka', 1968. 3 v. (xl, 2,183 pp.) Rbl.5.52) with its 120,000 words.

The uses of *a tergo* dictionaries are not yet widely realised; they can be of definite value to the serious student of grammar. One that has so far appeared, V. Nin'ovs'kyĭ, *Ukrayins'kyĭ zvorotnyĭ slovnyk* (second title-page: Niniovs'kyj, *Ukrainian reverse dictionary*) (Edmonton, Ukrainian Book Store, 1969. 482 pp.), is a list of some 60,000 words (without the interpretation of meaning) alphabetised starting from the last, not the first, letter of the word (the words themselves are, however, spelt in the conventional way).

In the absence of Ukrainian–English and English–Ukrainian technical dictionaries, the large Russian–Ukrainian one, M. M. Matiĭko and others, *Rosiĭs'ko-ukrayins'kyĭ tekhnichnyĭ slovnyk* (Kiev, Derzhavne vydavnytstvo tekhnichnoyi literatury URSR, 1961. 648 pp. Rbl.2.81), with its 80,000 words, may be of some use.

11

BYELORUSSIAN

by A. B. McMILLIN, Ph.D.

Byelorussian is not a new language, being formed in the 14th and 15th centuries, but its development has been many times interrupted and hindered, with the result that only in 1933 was the orthography finalised. A member of the East Slavonic linguistic group, it is morphologically close to Russian and Ukrainian, whilst sharing a considerable part of its lexical resources with Polish. The interest of Byelorussian for most foreigners lies in its various unusual philological features and in the rich and varied literature which has been written in it, particularly during the last seventy years.

TEXTBOOK COURSES & GRAMMARS

The Byelorussian section (pp. 129–91) of R. G. A. de Bray's pioneering *Guide to the Slavonic languages*, revised and greatly improved in its second edition (London, Dent, 1969. £9.75), has for many years been the English-speaker's only introduction to Byelorussian, but recently two separate guides have become available, of which the first, V. Pashkievich, *Fundamental Byelorussian*, Book 1 (Toronto, The Byelorussian–Canadian Coordinating Committee, 1974. 332 pp. $14; $10), is specifically designed as a textbook for beginners, but cannot be recommended owing to its many errors, naïve style and inconsistent use of an archaic orthography. Far more valuable as an introduction is Peter Mayo's admirably lucid and accurate *A grammar of Byelorussian* (Sheffield, The Anglo-Byelorussian Society in association with the Department of Russian and Slavonic Studies, University of Sheffield, 1976. 66 pp. £1) which, using Russian as a convenient but not essential point of comparison, supercedes de Bray as a source of information on pronunciation, spelling and morphology, and is likely to remain a standard work of reference for many years.

For those who approach Byelorussian through Russian another recent publication may be recommended: A. A. Krivitskiĭ, A. E. Mikhnevich and A. I. Podluzhnyĭ, *Belorusskiĭ yazyk dlya nebelorussov* (Minsk, 'Vyšejšaja škoła', 1973. 272 pp.), as may the second edition of M. Hurski's *Paraŭnalnaja hramatyka ruskaj i biełaruskaj moŭ. Fanietyka i marfałohija* (Minsk, 'Vyšejšaja škoła', 1972. 264 pp.). The standard reference grammar of literary Byelorussian remains the two-volume *Hramatyka biełaruskaj movy* published by the Byelorussian Academy of Sciences in Minsk (1962–66), whilst among reliable but more concise sources of information is L. I. Burak's *Sučasnaja biełaruskaja mova* (Minsk, 'Vyšejšaja škoła', 1974. 352 pp.). Finally, M. Cikocki's two-volume *Praktyčnaja stylistyka biełaruskaj movy* (Minsk, 'Narodnaja aśvieta', 1962–65) is a useful guide for advanced students. For detailed studies of other particular aspects of the language readers are referred to the excellent bibliography in Mayo's publication (*supra*) and to the annual bibliography published since 1973 by Alexander Nadson in the *Journal of Byelorussian Studies* (London).

RECORDED MATERIAL

Two guides to Byelorussian pronunciation have been prepared by A. Kalada: *Vyraznaje čytańnie* (Minsk, 'Vyšejšaja škoła', 1970. 184 pp. with 3 7″ records), and, more varied and useful, *Vyraznaje čytańnie satyryčnych vieršaŭ, bajek i dramatyčnych tvoraŭ* (Minsk, 'Vyšejšaja škoła', 1973. 248 pp. with 5 10″ records).

DICTIONARIES

The largest bilingual dictionaries of the modern literary language available in 1975 are those produced by the Foreign Languages Publishing House in Moscow: the heavily russified

Russko-belorusskiĭ slovar' (*c.* 86,000 words, 1953. 787 pp.) and the somewhat more reliable *Belorussko-russkiĭ slovar'* (*c.* 90,000 words, 1962. 1,048 pp.). More recent, and to some extent more accurate, are the second editions of two concise school dictionaries by S. M. Grabchikov: *Russko-belorusskiĭ slovar'* (Minsk, 'Narodnaja aśvieta', 1969. 280 pp.) which lists *c.* 15,300 words, and *Belorussko-russkiĭ slovar'* (Minsk, 'Narodnaja aśvieta', 1975. 240 pp.), listing *c.* 14,000 words. Comprehensive monolingual dictionaries are nearing completion at the Byelorussian Academy of Sciences, but in the meantime the second edition of another useful school dictionary listing *c.*70,000 words may be recommended: A. Ja. Bachańkoŭ, I. M. Hajdukievič and P. P. Šuba, *Tłumačalny słoŭnik biełaruskaj movy* (Minsk, 'Narodnaja aśvieta', 1972. 376 pp.).

A number of valuable specialised dictionaries are available. M. P. Łoban and M. R. Sudnik's *Arfahrafičny słoŭnik* (3rd ed. Minsk, 'Narodnaja aśvieta', 1971. 304 pp.) is a reliable guide to the spelling of *c.* 15,000 words; on phraseology the standard work is N. V. Haŭroš, I. Ja. Lepiešaŭ and F. M. Jankoŭski's *Fraziealahičny słoŭnik* (Minsk, 'Narodnaja aśvieta', 1973. 352 pp.) listing *c.* 1,500 literary phrases, whilst H. M. Małažaj's *Biełaruskaja pieryfraza: karotki słoŭnik* (Minsk, 'Vyšejšaja škoła', 1974. 160 pp.) lists *c.* 800 examples of periphrasis clearly and concisely. Amongst thematically organised dictionaries may be mentioned A. L. Jurevič's *Słoŭnik linhvistyčnych terminaŭ* (Minsk, MVSS i PA BSSR, 1962. 246 pp.) which includes a short glossary of Byelorussian translations of Russian terms, and A. A. Makarevič's *Karotki litaraturaznaŭčy słoŭnik* (2nd ed. Minsk, 'Vyšejšaja škoła', 1969. 224 pp.) incorporating articles on over 600 words and phrases. A major dictionary for social scientists is N. V. Birillo and M. R. Sudnik's *Russko-belorusskiĭ slovar' obshchestvenno-politicheskoĭ terminologii* (Minsk, 'Nauka i tekhnika', 1970. 452 pp.) listing *c.* 17,000 terms. Finally, I. Ja. Jaškin's *Biełaruskija hieahrafičnyja nazvy* (Minsk, 'Navuka i technika', 1971. 256 pp.) lists *c.* 3,000 words and will undoubtedly prove a useful tool for librarians and geographers[1].

[1] All the books and materials mentioned in this survey are available at the Francis Skaryna Byelorussian Library, 37, Holden Road, London N12 8HS.

12

BULGARIAN

by V. PINTO, M.A., Ph.D.

INTRODUCTION

'The earliest recorded form of Slavonic is Old Bulgarian, into which two Byzantine missionaries, Kyrillos and Methodos, both from Salonica, translated the Gospels in the mid 9th century ... Slavonic languages carry on a case system as complicated as that of Latin and Greek, Bulgarian alone having freed itself from this incubus[1].'

With features of such special interest, Bulgarian, spoken today by under ten million persons principally resident in Europe's most south-easterly valleys and mountains between the Danube and the Aegean, has hitherto attracted remarkably little study in the English-speaking world. In secondary education it has hardly ever acquired even minority recognition as an extra-curricular subject. In higher education Bulgarian language and literature are offerable as a single subject, major or subsidiary, at London University (School of Slavonic and East European Studies) for B.A. Honours degrees (internal and external), likewise for higher degrees. It is a minor subject at Leeds University and offerable at London 'A' and Cambridge 'O' levels for the General Certificate of Education.

Bulgarian belongs to the South (or Balkan) Slavonic group of languages in that rather close-knit branch of the Indo-European family. Written exclusively in the Cyrillic script of the Slav Christian Orthodox tradition, it is distinguished by several Balkan linguistic features typical also of non-Slavonic south-east European languages, *e.g.* its definite article, its shedding of the infinitive form, and most spectacular of all, its evolution into a modern analytic language. It is thus the only Slavonic language

[1] F. Bodmer, *The loom of language* (London, 1943), p. 414.

207

comparable to English in having since medieval times almost entirely cast off its case endings and in relying here instead very largely on prepositions.

For learners of modern Bulgarian the challenge lies in the peculiarly rich verbal system. This combines with a (by Slavonic standards) rather full and sensitive range of tenses and moods the characteristic Slavonic verbal aspects, which mandatorily and with morphological diversity mark all verbal forms as to the completion or incompletion envisaged in their meaning, their perfectiveness or imperfectiveness.

A succession of orthographical reforms culminating in the still current and annually reissued regulations of 1945 have kept the educated written and spoken standard languages closely aligned. The present day 'literary' language thus reflects speech as spoken in the educational system and the media with a generally reliable and consistent regularity of phonetic spelling. For students of the Bulgarian language of today these reforms have of course reduced somewhat the value of most earlier grammars and dictionaries, whatever their historical interest.

For the place of Bulgarian among the Slavonic languages are recommended W. J. Entwistle and W. A. Morison, *Russian and the Slavonic languages* (2nd ed. London, Faber, 1965. 407 pp. £5) and R. G. A. De Bray, *Guide to the Slavonic languages* (Rev. ed. London, Dent, 1970. xxvi, 798 pp. £9.75) – see its sections 1: Old Slavonic (Old Bulgarian) and 6: Macedonian, as well as 5: Bulgarian.

TEXTBOOK COURSES & GRAMMARS

Since the position of the syllabic stress in Bulgarian is as variable as in Russian (or, for that matter, English), works marking this receive priority here. For self-study the following grammar manuals and courses with their graded exercises are recommended. A. B. Lord, *Beginning Bulgarian* (The Hague, Mouton, 1962. 165 pp. £4) has 16 lessons of grammar followed by texts for translation from and into Bulgarian and a vocabulary concluding each lesson. It is accented (except for translation texts) and suitable for beginners' self-study once its numerous errata have been corrected. S. Ghinina and others, *A*

Bulgarian textbook for foreigners (Sofia, Nauka i Izkustvo, 1965. xi, 409 pp. £2.50) is the English version of the official Bulgarian manual for teaching (and self-study) of the Bulgarian language for foreign students, issued repeatedly, also concurrently in French, German and Russian. Part 1 in 51 lessons covers pronunciation, spelling and 'main points of morphology and syntax'; part 2 in 30 lessons offers fuller detail on 'grammatical categories'. Each lesson begins with a Bulgarian text, followed by grammar and exercises. Reasonably comprehensive, the course is presented from the native Bulgarian rather than from the English learner's point of view. There is no index but contents are listed in English also. The texts of the 81 lessons were recorded on 3 tapes in 1968 (but not commercially distributed) under the auspices of the now defunct Committee for Cultural Relations, Sofia.

There is a comprehensive manual not without errata but of interest to students with a knowledge of Russian: E. I. Bezikovich and T. P. Gordova-Rybal'chenko, *Bolgarsky yazyk* (Leningrad, Leningrad University, 1957. 536 pp. Rbl.9.10). A textbook of Bulgarian for Russian higher educational (economics and law) institutions, commissioned by the USSR State Universities' General Board, it has 61 lessons each with a Bulgarian reading text, grammar and exercises. Except in the texts, it marks stress.

The pair of complementary pocket *razgovorniks* (conversation/phrase books), M. Alexieva and E. Paunova, *Conversation English–Bulgarian* (Sofia, Nauka i Izkustvo, 1966. 233 pp. £0.35) and M. Filipova and V. Filipov, *Bulgarian–English phrasebook* (Sofia, Nauka i Izkustvo, 1972. 223 pp. £0.35), have been repeatedly reissued in inexpensive paperback for travellers. Beginning with brief phonetic and grammatical introductions, they list under thematic headings in three collateral columns (Bulgarian, English, transliteration) the more common vocabulary and phrases of everyday life. Stress is marked only on transliterations instead of on the Bulgarian of the Bulgarian–English one.

For advanced self-study or use with a teacher, there are two manuals entirely in Bulgarian. D. Ilieva and others, *Bulgarski ezik za chuzhdestranni studenti* (2nd ed. Sofia, Nauka i Izkustvo, 1972. 268 pp. Lv.1.36) is the official textbook of the preparatory Bulgarian course at the Foreign Students Institute, Sofia. Part 1 has 38 lessons with Bulgarian reading text, grammar and exercises, cartoon-like illustrations and a lively conversational approach; part 2 contains further reading material, exercises and photo illustrations. Omission of stress marking throughout calls for teacher's guidance. The second manual, by R. Nitsolova and others: *Uchebnik po bulgarski ezik* (Sofia, Sofia University, 1975. 289 pp. (offset).), was prepared specially for and is issued exclusively to participants in the annual Sofia University Summer Seminar for Foreign Bulgarianists and Slavists. Designed for the teaching of Bulgarian in Bulgarian to foreign students of mixed nationality, it has texts and exercises but no grammar nor marking of stress.

A pair of paperbacks written specially 'for foreign students' in Bulgarian, accented and published by Nauka i Izkustvo, Sofia, 1962, deserve mention: L. Savova and M. Marinova, *Kratka bulgarska gramatika* (138 pp. Lv.0.39) and D. Tilkov, *Kratka prakticheska fonetika na bulgarskiya ezik* (90 pp. Lv.0.29).

As further companions to Bulgarian language self-study, two readers are recommended. V. Pinto, *Bulgarian prose and verse. A selection with an introductory essay* (London, Athlone Press, 1957. xli, 211 pp. £1.25), stress-marked throughout, is a representative anthology of modern Bulgarian life and letters in chronological order, 1850–1942. The variety of content and of language styles makes possible the grading from easier to more difficult passages by teacher's guidance. In A. B. Lord and D. E. Bynum, *A Bulgarian literary reader* (The Hague, Mouton, 1968. 200 pp.) stresses are marked only in the glossary. Its mere 96 pp. of texts include a short life of each author in English.

Reference Grammars. For a comprehensive up-to-date survey of the grammar of contemporary standard Bulgarian with valuable brief historical references to account for the evolution of its present forms, see S. Stoyanov, *Gramatika na bulgarskiya knizhoven ezik* (Sofia, Nauka i Izkustvo, 1964. 452 pp. Lv.1.68). N. Kostov and E. Nikolov, *Bulgarski ezik* (Sofia, Narodna prosveta, 1974. 426 pp. Lv.1.25) is a standard textbook in Bulgaria's primary teachers' training colleges, being an updated version of L. D. Andreychin: *Osnovna bulgarska gramatika* (Sofia, Hemus, 1942. 559 pp.). Outstanding among Bulgarian reference grammars by foreign scholars are L. Beaulieux (with the collaboration of S. Mladenov), *Grammaire de la langue bulgare* (Paris, Librairie ancienne Honoré Champion, 1933. xii, 409 pp.), reprinted in today's Bulgarian orthography (2e éd. Paris, Institut d'Études slaves, 1950. xvi, 409 pp. FFr.25.70), which contains one of the best analyses of the categories of the Bulgarian verb, and Y. S. Maslov, *Ocherk bolgarskoy grammatiki* (Moscow, Foreign Languages Publishing House, 1956. 292 pp. Rbl.5.25) with its accompanying analysis of the verb *Morfologiya glagol'nogo vida* (Moscow, Academy of Sciences of the USSR, 1963. 183 pp. Rbl.0.82).

RECORDED MATERIAL

In addition to the tapes for the textbook of S. Ghinina and others (see above), a 3-disc course (Ein Kursus mit drei Platten) at 45 rpm was issued in 1962 by Eterna, VEB Deutsche Schallplatten, Berlin W.8: *Wir lernen bulgarisch sprechen* in the series Sprachen für jedermann, disc no. 5 70 026 A. Language laboratory exercise-texts for use at the Foreign Students Institute, Sofia (see above D. Ilieva and others) in 45 lessons have been transcribed by Y. Antonova: *Uprazhneniya po bulgarski ezik za rabota v ezikovite kabineti* (Sofia, 1970. 203 pp. (duplicated and stapled)).

DICTIONARIES

Small pocket dictionaries, each approximately 10,000 entries, both by I. Harlakova and E. Stankova, published by Nauka i Izkustvo, Sofia, are *English–Bulgarian dictionary* (1967. 487 pp.) and *Bulgarian–English dictionary* (1970. 420 pp.). Large pocket-size dictionaries by T. Atanasova and others are *Bulgaro-angliyski rechnik* (Sofia, Narodna prosveta, 1958. 700 pp.) and *Anglo-bulgarski rechnik* (Sofia, Narodna prosveta, 1965. 495 pp.). Of portmanteau-size here sadly no bilingual dictionary yet exists. At heavy-weight desk-size there are by T. Atanasova and others: *English–Bulgarian dictionary* (Sofia,

Bulgarian Academy of Sciences, 1973. 2 v. 1: A–I. 827 pp., appendix of newer words 38 pp.; 2: J–Z. 806 pp., appendix of newer words 56 pp.) and *Bulgarian–English dictionary* (Sofia, Nauka i Izkustvo, 1975. 1,021 pp. Lv.8.36). For the standard major reference dictionary the now rare G. Chakalov and others, *Bulgarsko–angliyski* (Sofia, Nauka i Izkustvo, 1961. 982 pp. Lv.6.62) is likely to retain its value for its range of examples and marking of the stress, something surprisingly absent from all the other above listed dictionaries except the first mentioned miniature ones. Valuable, too, for the English-speaking student are the detailed subject lists of words classified in 17 chapters under headings comprehensively displayed in English and Bulgarian initially as Contents in M. Alexieva, B. Atanasov and M. Pozharlieva, *Anglo-bulgarski tematichen rechnik* (Sofia, Narodna prosveta, 1969. xxiii, 559 pp. Lv.2.16). Unstressed.

Bilingual dictionaries linking Bulgarian with other languages (especially Balkan and Slavonic) exist in variety too considerable to list here, ranging in size from the model most miniature K. Haralampieff, *Langenscheidts Universal-Wörterbuch: Bulgarisch-Deutsch, Deutsch–Bulgarisch* (Berlin, 1967. 448 pp. Swiss Fr.7.60) to some 58,000 entries in S. B. Bernshteyn, *Bolgarsko-russky slovar'* (Moscow, 1967. 768 pp. Rbl.3.15) and its complementary volume. Of special interest to Russian-speaking users are the comparative Russian–Bulgarian analyses of K. Babov and A. Virgulev: *Tematichen rusko-bulgarski rechnik* (Sofia, Narodna prosveta, 1961. 887 pp.), which has an index of Russian words (pp. 680–887) and accents Russian only, and K. Panchev: *Diferentsialen rusko-bulgarski rechnik* (Sofia, Nauka i Izkustvo, 1963. 222 pp. Lv.1.22). Linking Bulgarian to its closest linguistic relative, Macedonian, is M. Mladenov and others, *Bulgarsko-makedonski rechnik* (Skopje, Prosvetno Delo, 1968. 674 pp.).

For monolingual Bulgarian dictionaries, until the projected 12-volume Academy lexicon appears, the major work is *Rechnik na suvremenniya bulgarski knizhoven ezik* (Sofia, Bulgarian Academy of Sciences, 1955–59. 3 v.). In one volume is L. Andreychin and others, *Bulgarski tulkoven rechnik* (Rev. 3rd ed. Sofia, Nauka i Izkustvo, 1973. 1,133 pp. Lv.9.30). Stress is marked in both.

Ancillary to them in various special areas are:

Etymology: V. Georgiev and others. *Bulgarski etimologichen rechnik* (Sofia, Bulgarian Academy of Sciences, 1974. 2 v.); stressed.

Phraseology: K. Nicheva and others. *Frazeologichen rechnik* (Sofia, Bulgarian Academy of Sciences, 1974. 2 v.).

Rarer words: S. Ilchev and others. *Rechnik na redki, ostareli i dialektni dumi* (Sofia, Bulgarian Academy of Sciences, 1974. 606 pp.).

Foreign words: A. Milev and others. *Rechnik na chuzhdite dumi* (Sofia, Nauka i Izkustvo, 1958. 743 pp.).

Synonyms: L. Nanov. *Bulgarski sinonimen rechnik* (5th ed. Sofia, Nauka i Izkustvo, 1968.)

Specialised Dictionaries. *Agriculture*: S. Botev and I. Kovachev. *Zemedelska entsiklopedia* (Sofia, Staykov, [n.d.]. 2 v.).

Automobile: N. Nitsov and others. *Avtomobilen rechnik* (Sofia, Tehnika, 1969. 682 pp.); in 3 sections, followed by index lists of Russian, English, German, French and Italian terms, pp. 457–682.

Literature and literary criticism: L. Georgiev and others. *Rechnik na literaturnite termini* (Sofia, Nauka i Izkustvo, 1971. 1,1?1 pp. bibliog. index. Lv.4.28).

Medicine: G. D. Arnaudov and others. *Meditsinsko-farmatsevski naruchnik* (2nd rev. ed. Sofia, Nauka i Izkustvo, 1951. 3 v. 1: Latin–Bulgarian; 2: Bulgarian–Latin; 3: Russian–Latin.).

Technical: Concise English–Bulgarian Technical Dictionary (Sofia, Tehnika, 1971. 400 pp.); I. Zhelyazkov and others. *Ilyustroven technicheski rechnik za vsichki* (Sofia, Tehnika, [n.d.]. 315 pp.).

13

MACEDONIAN

by H. LEEMING, B.A., Ph.D.

Macedonian is the official language of the Socialist Republic of Macedonia, one of the federal republics of Yugoslavia. It is spoken by about one million people, and became established as a literary language after the Second World War. Macedonian is a South Slavonic language whose grammar is closely related to that of Bulgarian. The alphabet is identical with Serbian Cyrillic, with the exception of *S* (*dz*) and the letters *Ќ* and *Ѓ*, which replace Serbian *ħ* and *ѓ*.

TEXTBOOK COURSES & GRAMMARS

There is a grammar for speakers of English written by an American Slavist who applies the structuralist approach and has a tendency to replace traditional grammatical terminology with his own. None the less this grammar states the facts clearly and gives copious examples drawn from contemporary books, journals and newspapers studied on the spot. This is H. G. Lunt's *A grammar of the Macedonian literary language* (Skopje, 1952. xv, 288 pp.) a scholarly work with an informative introduction and a full account of the grammar.

A text-book designed primarily for the children of Macedonian emigrants is by Krum Tošev and Dragi Stefanija: *A textbook of the Macedonian language* (Skopje, 1965. 186,[32] pp.). This consists of three parts, the first (pp. 1–89) containing 36 lessons each with a text, vocabulary and notes on the grammar, the second (pp. 99–186) a series of short readings with vocabulary and biographical notes; the third part ([32] pp.) is a short dictionary of words used in the book. The book is marred by numerous misprints; tenses are introduced piecemeal and no full tables of conjugation are given; no stresses are marked after lesson four – Macedonian has a regular pattern of initial stress in words of two and three syllables, and antepenultimate stress in longer words. Typography is clear, although unimaginative; numerous photographs of Macedonian scenes illustrate the book.

The standard reference grammar for speakers of Macedonian is by Blaže Koneski: *Gramatika na makedonskiot literaturen jazik* (2nd ed. Skopje, 1957. 2 v.). A shorter grammar for secondary school pupils is by Krume Kepeski: *Makedonska gramatika* (Skopje, 1950. 155 pp.).

A concise account of the Macedonian Language, with information on the phonology, morphology, dialects and the relationship of Macedonian to the other Slavonic languages is given in R. G. A. De Bray, *Guide to the Slavonic languages* (Rev. ed. London, Dent, 1969. £9.75) Section 6, pp. 243–312.

DICTIONARIES

A two-language dictionary for speakers of English is Dušan Crkvenkovski and Branislav Gruiḱ. *Anglisko-makedonski rečnik* (Skopje, Prosvetno Delo, 1971. 422 pp.). Meanings are numbered, derivatives are usually grouped under head-words, numerous phrases illustrate usage; since Macedonian has no infinitive the verbal form given is the third person singular, present tense. There are two pocket-size dictionaries compiled by the same authors, *Mal makedonsko-angliski rečnik* (Skopje, Provetno Delo, 1965. 390 pp.), which includes more than 30,000 words and phrases; and *Mal anglisko-makedonski rečnik* (Skopje, Prosvetno Delo, 1965. 307, 3 pp.), containing more than 30,000 words and phrases; equivalents are numbered where words have more than one meaning; there is a short glossary of cardinal and ordinal numerals and expressions of quantity.

A full dictionary of the Macedonian literary language with meanings given in Serbo-Croat is edited by Blaže Koneski: *Rečnik na makedonskiot jazik* (Skopje, 1961–66. 3 v.).

Specialised Dictionaries. A comprehensive orthographic dictionary with commentary is Krume Tošev, *Pravopis na makedonskiot literaturen jazik so pravopisen rečnik* (Skopje, Prosvetno Delo, 1970. 610 pp.). A very useful tool for the Slavist and philologist is the reverse dictionary compiled by Vladimir Miličiḱ: *Obraten rečnik na makedonskiot jazik* (Skopje, 1967. [12], 388, [2] pp.). This includes all the headwords from the three-volume dictionary mentioned above (pp. 1–318), a separate list of geographical and other proper names (pp. 319–25), an index of words with irregular stress (pp. 329–54) and a table showing the relative frequency of suffixes (pp. 355–87).

14

SERBO-CROAT

by E. C. HAWKESWORTH, B.A., M.Phil.

INTRODUCTION

Serbo-Croat (or Croato-Serb) belongs, with Bulgarian, Macedonian and Slovene, to the southern branch of the Slavonic language group. Macedonian and Slovene are spoken respectively in the southern and northernmost republics of the Yugoslav Federal Republic, while Serbo-Croat is spoken by the great majority of Yugoslavs – Serbs, Croats, Montenegrins, and the inhabitants of Bosnia and Hercegovina. Serbo-Croat has three basic dialects, known as *štokavian, kajkavian* and *čakavian*, according to the interrogative pronoun what? (*što, kaj* and *ča?*). Of these, *štokavian* is established as the standard literary language.

Within the *štokavian* dialect there are three sub-dialects, depending on the pronunciation of the Old Slavonic *jat* (*e, je or ije*, and *i*) and known, according to these variations, as *ekavian, jekavian* (or *ijekavian*) and *ikavian*. Of these, *ekavian* and *jekavian* have equal status within the literary language, and can loosely be described as the variants spoken respectively by Serbs and Croats. Both the Latin and Cyrillic scripts can be used: for historical reasons the Latin alphabet is used in the western regions, while Cyrillic predominates in the east and south.

TEXTBOOK COURSES & GRAMMARS

Not surprisingly, there are no courses especially designed for 'O' and 'A' level work, but there are several general courses for adults, suitable for study, with or without tuition. *Teach yourself*

Serbo-Croat, by Vera Javarek and Miroslava Sudjić (2nd ed. London, Teach yourself books, 1972 reprinted 1973. xii, 237 pp. £0.50) remains particularly useful for students with no previous knowledge of any Slavonic language. It contains 25 lessons, introducing grammatical points gradually and providing exercises for translation from and into Serbo-Croat, with a key for self-correction and a short general vocabulary. The series also includes a *Serbo-Croatian reader*, by Vera Javarek (London, Teach yourself books 1974. x, 192 pp. £0.60). One of the inevitable short-comings of the *Teach yourself* series, conditioned by lack of space, is the lack of grammatical reference sections in the books themselves. This is in part compensated by Thomas Magner's *Introduction to the Croatian and Serbian language* (State College, Pa., Singidunum Press, 1972, vii, 351 pp.; an improved version of the *Introduction to the Serbo-Croatian language*, 1956 and 1962). This work has several advantages: the revised title reflects the parity between the two main variants of the literary language, and the thirty lesson dialogues have been separated into 'Croatian' and 'Serbian' versions so that the similarities as well as the differences are immediately apparent. As well as the lessons themselves, which cover a considerable amount of material quite rapidly, the book contains a short 'reader', providing illustrations of various aspects and usages of the language in both alphabets, and a grammar. The book does not include a glossary, although a separate dictionary has been published intended for use in conjunction with the textbook. A third course which, like the *Teach yourself* edition, combines an introduction to the basic grammar and a volume of reading passages is that of Slavna Babić: *Serbo-Croat for foreigners* (2nd ed. Belgrade, Kolarčev narodni univerzitet, 1969 reprinted 1973. xii, 231 pp. £1.95), for which there is also a set of records available; and *Serbo-Croatian reading passages* (Belgrade, Kolarčev narodni univerzitet 1968. xvi, 208 pp. £1.60). The volume of reading passages is particularly useful, once the basic grammar of the language has been mastered. The textbook itself covers the most essential aspects of the language at quite a leisurely pace, and is certainly useful for the less ambitious student.

Grammars. Two works, which are mainly grammars, contain

some of the elements of textbooks as well: Monica Partridge's *Serbo-Croatian practical grammar and reader* (London, New York, Toronto, McGraw-Hill, 1964. 220 pp. £2), a full and detailed account of the language, with very useful grammatical explanations. This work is particularly useful for students with some prior knowledge of a Slavonic language, and for reference, and has the great advantage of having full accent marks throughout. The other work is Oton Grozdić, *Serbo-Croatian grammar and reader* (New York and London, Hafner, 1969. v, 133 pp. $7.75), which contains all the most essential information, preceded by imaginative introductions, but is not presented sufficiently clearly either for use by a complete beginner, or as a reference grammar.

The main grammar in Serbo-Croat is T. Maretić, *Gramatika hrvatskoga ili srpskoga književnog jezika* (3rd ed. Zagreb, Matica Hrvatska, 1963. 668, [3] pp.), a very substantial and detailed work, although not very clearly laid out. Two shorter works are also useful for quick reference, although they are obviously not as comprehensive as Maretić: *Gramatika hrvatskosrpskoga jezika*, by I. Brabec, M. Hraste and S. Živković (9th ed. Zagreb, Školska knjiga, 1970. 280 pp.) and *Kratka gramatika hrvatskosrpskog književnog jezika za strance*, by J. Hamm (Zagreb, Školska knjiga, 1967. 124 pp.), which was designed specifically for the use of foreign learners. Both these works are on the whole well laid out for easy reference.

AUDIO-VISUAL MATERIAL

The most important recorded course is that produced by Linguaphone (1974). The texts have all been recorded in Belgrade and are consequently in the Serbian, or *ekavian* variant of the language. Produced as it is by a very experienced organisation, the course is on the whole excellent, covering a great deal of material in thirty lessons, with translations of all the texts, a vocabulary and detailed grammatical explanations for reference. The course includes a set of correspondence exercises. There is also an audio-visual course, produced in Zagreb, for students wishing to learn the *jekavian* variant, but the lessons are more elementary and the general standard of production not comparable with the Linguaphone course: *Hrvatskosrpski Audio-vizuelna metoda*, main editor: Ljudevit Jonke, produced by Jugoton, Zagreb.

DICTIONARIES

The most important bilingual dictionaries are: *Englesko-hrvatski Rječnik*, main editor Rudolf Filipović (6th ed. Zagreb, Zora, 1971. xxi, 1,467 pp.), this dictionary is still based on the original 1955 edition, although it has been extended with each publication, but a new edition is in preparation; the *Enciklopediski englesko-srpskohrvatski rečnik*, in two volumes, edited by S. Ristić, Ž. Simić and V. Popović (Belgrade, Prosveta and Cambridge, Cambridge University Press, 1956.) provides an equivalent for the *ekavian* variant. The best *Serbo-Croatian–English dictionary* is that of Morton Benson (Philadelphia, University of Pennsylvania Press and Belgrade, Prosveta, 1971. iv, 807 pp. $27.50). There are two compact bilingual dictionaries, both with considerable inadequacies, but more convenient than the larger ones: F. Bogadek, *New English–Croatian and Croatian–English dictionary* (3rd ed., corrected. New York, Hafner, 1947. vii, 531, 497, 46, 7 pp.) and M. Drvodelić, *Englesko–hrvatskosrpski rječnik, Hrvatskosrpsko–engleski rječnik* (3rd ed. Zagreb, Školska knjiga, 1970. 2 v.); a new improved version of this dictionary is in preparation.

The most important monolingual dictionaries are the comprehensive *Rječnik hrvatskog ili srpskog jezika*, produced in 21 volumes by the Yugoslav Academy of Science and Art, originally edited by D. Daničić, 1880–1974. Another dictionary, *Rečnik srpskohrvatskog književnog i narodnog jezika*, was begun by the Serbian Academy of Sciences in Belgrade in 1959, and had reached v. 8 (intonirati-jurve) in 1973. A more compact dictionary is *Rečnik srpskohrvatskog književnog jezika*, produced jointly by the publishing houses Matica Srpska and Matica Hrvatska, in Novi Sad and Zagreb, 1967–73 (v. 1–5: A–S).

Specialised dictionaries. The most important is the excellent etymological dictionary, edited by Peter Skok, in 4 volumes: *Etimologijski rječnik hrvatskog ili srpskog jezika* (Zagreb, JAZU, 1971–74.). There is also a *Russian–English–Serbo-Croatian maritime dictionary,* edited by S. Vekarić and N. Safonov (Belgrade, Rad, 1966. xii, 496 pp.) and an English–Serbian dictionary of contemporary administrative terms: A. Jovanović, *Englesko–srpski rečnik privrednih, komercionalnih, finansiskih, političkih i pravnih izraza* (Belgrade, Savremena administracija, 1957.).

15

SLOVENE

by H. LEEMING, B.A., Ph.D.

Slovene (Slovenian) is the official language of Slovenia, the northernmost of the Socialist Republics of Yugoslavia. It is a South Slavonic language spoken by over one and a half million people in Slovenia, and also in neighbouring territories in Italy and Austrian Carinthia and Styria. There are a number of strongly differentiated dialects; the literary language is based on the central dialects of Lower Carniola with an admixture of Highland features.

Compared with English the Slovene alphabet lacks *q*, *w*, *x*, *y*, but has three additional letters: *č*, *š*, *ž*. The consonantal characters, with the exception of *l* and *v*, have a constant phonetic value, although the orthography does not indicate regressive assimilation or devoicing of final consonants. The richness of the vocalic system is not reflected in the orthography: *e.g.*, the letter *e* represents four possible phonetic values in stressed syllables. For this reason it is best to have the help of a native speaker, or access to recorded material.

COURSES, GRAMMARS & RECORDED MATERIAL

There is an excellent course for speakers of English, with an amusing and lively text of 49 methodically graded lessons, illustrated by clearly spoken and professionally recorded gramophone records: Jože Toporišič. *Zakaj ne po slovensko. Slovene by direct method. With 6 gramophone records with texts spoken by theatre actors, radio and TV announcers* (Ljubljana, Slovenska Izseljenska Matica, [n.d.]. 272 pp.). The first sixteen lessons are accompanied by a phonetic transcription in the International Phonetic Alphabet. There is a key to the exercises, a summary of grammar in tabular form and an accentuated glossary of all words used in the text. A slim booklet of convenient size for the tourist containing 24 lessons with accentuated texts, essential grammatical information, exercises without key and accentuated glossary is Franc Jakopin, *Slovene for you* (Ljubljana, Slovenska Izseljenska Matica, 1962. 114 pp.). Anyone who approaches Slovene with a knowledge of Serbo-Croat may find special interest in a grammar designed for speakers of Serbo-Croat, Janko Jurančič, *Slovenački jezik* (Ljubljana, Državna Založba Slovenije, 1971. 290 pp.).

The standard grammar for readers of Slovene is by Anton Bajec, Rudolf Kolarič and Mirko Rupel: *Slovenska slovnica* (Ljubljana, Državna Založba Slovenije, 1968. 349, [2] pp.). This surveys phonology, orthography, morphology and syntax. A concise account of the Slovene language, together with 6 texts, a grammar containing information on the phonology, morphology, dialects and characteristic features of Slovene compared with other Slavonic languages is given in R. G. A. De Bray, *Guide to the Slavonic languages* (Rev. ed. London, Dent, 1969. £9.75), Section 8, pp. 363–434. A compendious reference grammar is available in the French language: Claude Vincenot, *Essai de grammaire slovène* (Ljubljana, Mladinska Knjiga, 1975. [8], xxiv, 345 pp. £25). This very thorough and scholarly work covers phonetics (pp. 1–42), morphology (pp. 45–138), 'static syntax' (pp. 131–240), 'dynamic syntax' (pp. 243–345), and provides a bibliography of books and articles on the Slovene language (pp. 347–53).

As a reader, there is a parallel text: Matej Bor, *A wanderer in the atom age*, translated by Janko Lavrin (Ljubljana, Država Založba Slovenije, 1970. 69 pp.).

DICTIONARIES

Perfectly adequate for most purposes is the Slovene–English dictionary by Janko Kotnik, *Slovenski-angleški slovar* (Rev. ed. Ljubljana, Državna Založba Slovenije, 1967. 831 pp.). Slovene accents are given in headwords; there are copious examples of

English synonyms and phrases; lists of Christian and
geographical names are given without accentuation (pp. 815–8;
818–24); a short list of Slovene proverbs is appended (pp.
830–1). An English–Slovene dictionary designed primarily for
the Slovene reader is by Anton Grad, Ružena Škerlj and Nada
Vitorovič: *Angleško-slovenski slovar* (Ljubljana, Državna
Založba Slovenije, 1967. 1,120 pp.). This gives the pronunciation of English words; Slovene accentuation is not marked; there
is a glossary of proper names, a list of English abbreviations, a
table of English irregular verbs, tables of weights and measures.
Exhaustive definitions are given and copious examples of
English phraseology supplied. Convenient pocket-size dictionaries are the paperbacks: Anton Grad, *Slovensko-angleški
slovar* (Maribor, Obzorja, 1965. 441 pp.); and, by the same
author and publisher, *Angleško-slovenski slovar* (Maribor, Obzorja, 1971. 598 pp.).

A one-language dictionary of the Slovene literary language is
in course of publication by the Slovene Academy of Arts and
Sciences, *Slovar slovenskega knjižnega jezika*, v. 1–2, (A–H;
I–Na), (Ljubljana, Državna Založba Slovenije, 1970–75.
xcii,844; 1,030,[1] pp.). The most complete dictionary which
covers sources from the 16th century and includes dialect words
and forms is M. Pleteršnik, *Slovensko–nemški slovar*
(Ljubljana, Katoliška Tiskarna, 1894–95. 2 v. (xvi,883; 978, ix
pp.).

Specialised Dictionaries. Joseph Paternost, *Slovene–English
glossary of linguistic terms* (University Park, Pa., Pennsylvania
State University, 1966. 339 pp.) is by no means as limited as the
title would suggest and provides short indexes in English and
Slovene. *Orthographical dictionaries*: Over 27,500 entries with
more than 100,000 words are given in *Slovenski pravopis*, edited
by A. Bajec and others (Ljubljana, Državna Založba Slovenije,
1962. 1,054 pp.). A shorter one, with introduction (pp. 11–52),
dictionary (pp. 53–421), 20,000 entries and 50,000 words and
phrases, and appendix of abbreviations (pp. 422–31) is S. Bunc,
Mali slovenski pravopis (Maribor, Založba Obzorja, 1966. 433
pp.).

16

CZECH

by David Short, b.a.

Czech is a West Slavonic language spoken in Bohemia, Moravia and parts of Silesia by something over nine million people. With Slovak it is a recognised official language in Czechoslovakia. There are also islands of Czech speakers in Austria, Rumania and Jugoslavia, as well as less close-knit Czech communities in North America.

As a product of the changing fortunes of the Czechs through history the conservative modern literary language is at considerable variance with the everyday speech of the majority, the so-called Common Czech, which is based largely on the dialect of Central Bohemia. The frontiers between the literary language, its spoken version (colloquial Czech), Common Czech and the dialects are still not firmly established and continue to be a matter of debate among Czech linguists.

The language retains most of the typical Slav features of structure, but its vocabulary betrays the consequences of centuries of contact between the Czechs and the neighbouring German-speaking peoples. Czech has a Latin script because Irish monks reached the Czech Lands before Cyril and Methodius. The orthography has long been simplified by the use of diacritics (´ and ˇ) and is generally phonematic.

TEXTBOOK COURSES & GRAMMARS

The two commonly available grammars produced in the West are those by W. R. and Z. Lee, *Teach yourself Czech* (2nd ed. London, English Universities Press, 1964, reprinted 1974. xxiii,242 pp. £0.60), and W. E. Harkins, *A modern Czech grammar* (New York, Columbia University Press, 1953. 338 pp.

$13.50). While neither is perfect, both can be used as class course-books with proper teacher guidance. In spite of slight alterations since the first edition *Teach yourself Czech* still calls for some revision while remaining a useful skeleton course. Another course, K. Brusak's *Introduction to Czech*, is in use in manuscript form in some institutions in London and Cambridge; it is hoped that it will be published before long. In organisation and the ultimate level of attainment to which it leads, it will be the best grammar of Czech available in English. Much of the material in it will also be available on tapes (see below).

The textbooks emanating from Czechoslovakia suffer the disadvantage of having been prepared for anglophone students from the developing countries, rather than for the British or American learner, whose aim in studying Czech probably goes beyond the practicalities of everyday life in the Czech environment. The exception is Miloš Sova's *A practical Czech course for English-speaking students* (Prague, Státní pedagogické nakladatelství, 1962. 528 pp.), which is useful as a self-teacher and as a classbook. The author has been involved in writing Czech courses in English since the war, when he published the forerunner of the present book as *A modern Czech grammar* (London, Čechoslovák, 1944. xxxix,402 pp.). The layout of both versions is similar: a fairly extensive outline of pronunciation, stress and patterns of sound change (in the more recent version reworked as *Phonetic lessons* 1–10); a progressive course (26 lessons in the London version, 48 in the Prague version); and an outline reference grammar. Both versions contain a selection of reading passages and literary extracts, although the choice leaves something to be desired.

Another course-book from Prague is M. Šára, J. Šárová and A. Bytel, *Čeština pro cizince – Czech for English speaking students* (Prague, Státní pedagogické nakladatelství, 1970. 556 pp. index). The foreword states explicitly that it is for use by foreign students coming to Czechoslovakia, which is also why it is framed to meet initially the everyday requirements of such students: the authors deliberately aim at colloquial Czech rather than the standard literary language, since the forms involved in the former provide a system of greater simplicity and regularity than those of the latter. The transfer to the literary standard is made gradually in the course of the second half of the book, which is aimed more at comprehension than learning. The whole book is presented as an attempt at teaching Basic Czech, as codified by Professor Poldauf in 1962. Another such attempt is that by I. Poldauf and K. Šprunk: *Čeština jazyk cizí* (Prague, Státní pedagogické nakladatelství, 1968. 418 pp.). In the quadrilingual explanation of the book's purpose, the authors explain that it is intended for advanced learners of a non-philological bias, as a tool to approaching specialist works written in Czech. It is possibly useful to only such people, since it uses Czech itself as the medium of explanation, and it is conspicuously and deliberately untraditional in the presentation of linguistic data at all levels of analysis.

The current standard reference grammar of Czech in Czech is B. Havránek and A. Jedlička, *Česká mluvnice* (Prague, Státní pedagogické nakladatelství, 1960. 487 pp. and later editions.), which has largely superseded that of F. Trávníček: *Mluvnice spisovné češtiny* (Prague, Slovanské nakladatelství, 1951. v. 1–2. (1,498 pp.)). A useful concise prescriptive grammar, including syntax, word-formation, etc., is V. Šmilauer's *Nauka o českém jazyce* (Prague, Státní pedagogické nakladatelství, 1972. 334 pp.), which is an adaptation of the author's *Novočeská skladba* (Prague, Státní pedagogické nakladatelství, 1966. 574 pp.) and *Novočeské tvoření slov* (Prague, Státní pedagogické nakladatelství, 1971. 218 pp.). The standard descriptive grammar in the West is A. Mazon's *Grammaire de la langue tchèque* (3e éd. Paris, Institut d'Études Slaves, 1952. 292 pp. FFr.17.10), in addition to which there is the appropriate section in R. G. A. de Bray's *Guide to the Slavonic languages* (Rev. ed. London, Dent, 1969. £9.75. pp. 435–511.).

RECORDED MATERIAL

The Linguaphone Institute has produced records of sections of the *Teach yourself Czech* course mentioned above, and the texts and exercises of Brusak's forthcoming grammar will also be available on tape. Master tapes are currently held at Cambridge University, from where they may be borrowed.

DICTIONARIES

The situation with bilingual Czech and English dictionaries leaves much to be desired. There are two English–Czech dictionaries that can be commonly obtained, the larger is by A. Osička and I. Poldauf: *Velký anglicko-český slovník* (Prague, Academia, 1970. 636 pp. index and maps.), and the smaller, but more practical, *Anglicko–český slovník* (3rd ed. Prague, Státní pedagogické nakladatelství, 1968. 877 pp.), by J. Caha and J. Krámský. The former is the fourth revised edition of a post-war dictionary, the revisions being predominantly in the shape of additions (a 98-page appendix of new entries) rather than corrections or deletions. The common Czech–English dictionary is that by I. Poldauf: *Česko–anglický slovník* (3rd ed. Prague, Státní pedagogické nakladatelství, 1968. 1,237 pp.), a medium-size dictionary marred by excessive and sometimes misleading cross-referencing. Except for certain pre-war dictionaries, often very reliable but now unavoidably outdated (notably V. Cheshire, V. Jung and L. Klozner: *Česko–anglický slovník*, v. 1. Prague, J. Otto, 1933. 881 pp., and V. Cheshire, V. Jung and A. Šrámek: *Česko–anglický slovník*, v. 2. Prague, J. Otto, 1935. 1,022 pp.) and bilingual dictionaries involving other languages than English, Poldauf's medium dictionary is all the English learner of Czech has available until Poldauf publishes (1978) his entirely new and larger Czech–English dictionary. The great merit of this will be that it will be the first post-war dictionary to have been produced with the full and consistent collaboration of a British scholar, R. B. Pynsent.

The Czech language is also poorly covered by monolingual dictionaries, of which the only one that can be recommended is the large *Slovník spisovného jazyka českého*, edited by B. Havránek, J. Bělič and others, which appeared in fascicles between 1958 and 1970, to be published bound in four volumes in 1971 (Prague, Academia. v. 1: A–M. xxviii,1,311 pp.; v. 2: N–Q. 1,192 pp.; v. 3: R–U. 1,079 pp.; v. 4: V–Ž. 1,011,xx pp.). For those requiring a smaller dictionary, mention should be made of that by F. Trávníček: *Slovník jazyka českého* (Prague, Slovanské nakladatelství, xv,1,801 pp.), in fact the fourth and last edition of a dictionary previously published as of co-

CZECH 229

authorship between Trávníček and P. Váša. The dictionary is marred by the authors' purism and is only to be found in libraries and occasionally in second-hand bookshops in Czechoslovakia.

Specialised Dictionaries. Among the special dictionaries the *Anglicko–český technický slovník* (Prague, Státní nakladatelství technické literatury, 1969. 1,026 pp.) and its approximate counterpart, *Česko–anglický technický slovník*, edited by J. Feigl and E. Klinger (Prague, Státní nakladatelství technické literatury, 1963. 930 pp.) are moderately comprehensive, but call for updating. Commerce is covered by D. Závada's matching *Anglicko–český obchodní slovník* (Prague, Orbis, 1955. 519 pp.) and *Česko–anglický obchodní slovník* (Prague, Orbis, 1958. 913 pp.). As with all books from Czechoslovakia that are not republished with any regularity, there is always a problem of supply with special dictionaries.

For the ordinary learner, beginner or advanced, there is one invaluable aid in the dictionary of Czech orthography, *Pravidla českého pravopisu*, which is republished, sometimes with substantial changes, quite frequently. The latest edition (1977) contains details of recent major spelling reforms and is published in Prague by Academia. Concise versions of the work are published by Státní pedagogické nakladatelství as school editions.

One other book that perhaps should be mentioned, although of use to the tourist rather than to the serious language learner, is the phrase-book *Say it in Czech* (2nd ed. Prague, State Pedagogical Publishing House, 1970. 379 pp.) by A. Krušina. Although its scope is fairly broad, it cannot, nor does it pretend to provide an answer to every need, and so suffers the weaknesses shared by all such publications.

17

SLOVAK

by DAVID SHORT, B.A.

Slovak is a West Slavonic language spoken chiefly in the Eastern part of Czechoslovakia, the Slovak Socialist Republic, but with Czech (q.v.) it shares official language status throughout Czechoslovakia. Within that country it is spoken by around 4 million people, with many thousands more in colonies particularly in N. America and the Balkans. The stabilised literary form of the language is of relatively recent date (mid 19th century); throughout most of the area's history Slovak was simply a spoken language replaced either by Latin, and later Hungarian, as the official language, or Czech, as the language of the Protestant Church. Slovak is held to be the one Slavonic language most easily comprehensible to all the Slavs, and, for native speakers, Slovak and Czech are almost completely mutually intelligible. The main potential barrier to intelligibility between Czechs and Slovaks is the proliferation of Hungarian, Turkish, Rumanian and Old Czech elements in Slovak.

The orthography is similar in principle, but not identical in detail, to that of Czech (q.v.).

It is the misfortune of Slovak that it has long been neglected by foreign-language learners. The study of Slovak is generally approached only after a knowledge of Czech has been acquired, and Czech then becomes the medium of instruction. That this remains true is evident from the textbook and other material available.

TEXTBOOK COURSES & GRAMMARS

These are few and far between. Most early material consisted of handbooks either for Slovak native speakers or for Czechs.

The exception up to the Second World War was J. J. Konuš's *Practical Slovak grammar, with an extensive English–Slovak and Slovak–English vocabulary* (Pittsburgh, the author, 1939. 117, 119 pp. map.). Since, however, most people still approach Slovak with a prior knowledge of Czech, the grammar *Slovenština, Vysokoškolská učebnice pro studující českého jazyka* (Prague, SPN, 1957. 186 pp. 3rd ed. 1964. 191 pp.) is the most useful in existence. The detailed early sections on the phonology and pronunciation, based as they are on a confrontation with Czech, tempt one to conclude that the differences between Czech and Slovak are after all more substantial than the superficial systematic differences in the morphology and the chance differences in the vocabulary suggest at first sight. Very similar to the foregoing in conception, but intended as a prescriptive grammar for Slovaks themselves, is E. Pauliny's *Krátka gramatika slovenská* (Bratislava; Slovenské pedagogické nakladateľstvo, 1960. 191 pp. 4th ed. 1971. 194 pp.). The fullest descriptive grammar is that by E. Pauliny, J. Ružička and J. Štolc: *Slovenská gramatika* (5th ed. Bratislava, Slovenské pedagogické nakladateľstvo, 1968. 583 pp. map.). The work includes an outline history of the language, a description of the dialects, and an extensive section on style. The most important reference grammar available outside Czechoslovakia is J. Bartoš and J. Gagnaire, *Grammaire de la langue slovaque* (Paris, Institut d'Études Slaves, 1972. 267 pp.); in fact this is a co-edition published simultaneously by Matica slovenská in Bratislava. In English there is also the appropriate section in R. G. A. de Bray, *Guide to the Slavonic languages* (Rev. ed. London, Dent, 1969. £9.75 pp. 513–587).

DICTIONARIES

Slovak is relatively better placed where dictionaries are concerned than the general position of the language would suggest. There are two good Slovak–English dictionaries, namely: J. J. Konuš, *Slovak–English phraseological dictionary* (Passaic, N. J., Slovak Catholic Sokol, 1969. 1,664 pp.), which has a slightly misleading title, since it is a standard bilingual dictionary based on single-word entries under which are given such idiomatic phrases as include those words; and the slightly smaller work by J. Vilikovská, P. Vilikovský and J. Šimko: *Slovak–English dictionary* (Bratislava, Slovak Pedagogical Publishing House, 1964. 522 pp.). There are also two main English–Slovak dictionaries. The larger and better as regards modern usage is J. Šimko. *English–Slovak dictionary* (Bratislava; Slovak Pedagogical Publishing House, 1967. 1,443 pp.). The other, which is more instantly obtainable in view of the country of publication, cannot be recommended unreservedly, since it contains many translations that the modern Slovak speaker in Slovakia rejects as non-existent or at best fanciful. *Hrobak's English–Slovak dictionary*, by P. S. Hrobak (Middleton, Penn., Jednota, 1944. xxx,702 pp. 2nd ed. New York, Robert Speller, 1965. $12.50) is included here on the grounds of the insight it may provide into the Slovak of North America.

The standard Slovak lexicon is *Slovník slovenského jazyka* (Bratislava, Slovenská akadémia vied, 1959–68. 6 v. (815; 647; 909; 759; 847; 333 pp.), published under the general editorship of Štefan Peciar.

The learner of Slovak is well advised to keep abreast of the changing orthographic norm: the language and language-teaching journals of Slovakia contain a constant stream of articles on matters of orthographic principle and detail, and many of the suggestions made and conclusions reached are incorporated in successive editions of the *Pravidlá slovenského pravopisu* (11th ed. Bratislava, Vydavateľstvo Slovenskej akadémie vied, 1971. 422 pp.).

18

POLISH

by B. W. MAZUR, B.A.

INTRODUCTION

Polish is a West Slavonic language. Like Russian, but unlike any of the other Slavonic literary languages, it has enjoyed an uninterrupted development from its medieval beginnings to the present day. It is spoken by a population of over thirty-three million people and has several regional varieties or dialects. The educated speech of Warsaw and Cracow is accepted as the literary standard. There are very large communities of Polish emigrants, and their descendents, in North and South America, Western Europe, Australia – an estimated 10–12 million people.

Polish has many of the characteristics common to the Slavonic languages as a whole. These contrast with some purely Polish features (the preservation of nasal vowels). It uses the Latin script and though the agglomeration of consonantal clusters can seem, at first sight, forbidding the orthography is consistent, the relation of letter to sound is stable and words have a regular stress on the penultimate syllable. An inflected language, it has a very mobile word order and is particularly rich in verbal meanings. While there have been periodic attempts to remove foreign elements from its vocabulary Polish has not been victim of the thorough-going purism witnessed in other countries; it retains a great number of completely assimilated and accepted loanwords ranging from early Czech and German, Latin, Italian, French through to modern English.

The principles of modern Polish orthography and punctuation were codified in 1956. Students should beware of old spellings in dictionaries and texts published before that date.

Polish is not taught in British schools. Most Polish com-

233

munities run their own local part-time Saturday schools and classes, varying in quality and size. In 1973 there were some 700 entries for the GCE 'O' and 'A' level examinations in Polish. As a subsidiary or optional subject Polish can be studied at several universities in the UK; only London offers a full B.A. Honours degree in Polish Language and Literature, and a combined honours degree in Polish and Russian. Part-time and evening courses are available up and down the country from year to year according to demand.

There is an indispensable handbook of reference aids and primary sources (also of libraries and museums) for students of Polish language and literature: J. Czachowska and R. Loth, *Przewodnik polonisty* (Wrocław, Ossolineum, 1974. 620 pp. £6.15). It includes a bibliography of the most important dictionaries (pp. 23–48). P. Grzegorczyk, *Index lexicorum Poloniae* (Warsaw, PWN, 1967. 286 pp.) is a bibliography of monolingual, bilingual and specialised dictionaries. Richard C. Lewanski's *A bibliography of Slavic dictionaries* (2nd rev. and enlarged ed. Bologna, Instituto Informatico Italiano, 1973. 4 v.), a comprehensive and well-produced reference manual, devotes volume 1 to Polish.

The two main Polish bookshops in London are Earlscourt Publications, 129/130, Shepherd's Bush Centre, London W12, and Orbis Books, 66, Kenway Road, London SW5 ORD.

TEXTBOOK COURSES & GRAMMARS

The choice of available textbook courses for English students is small, standards are modest and presentation is generally poor. One drawback is that the language and subject matter tend too often to be somewhat unimaginative and sometimes more than a little dated. The social situations and atmosphere portrayed commonly suffer from the same defects. The most urgent need is for an integrated series of textbooks comparable in content, style and pace to some of those currently available for the teaching and learning of French, Spanish or German.

There are several introductory courses for beginners. None are designed specifically for 'O' and 'A' level students, and few are sufficiently flexible to cater for the needs of students at different levels.

The most modern and self-sufficient textbook currently available in English is Alexander M. Schenker's *Beginning Polish* (Rev. ed. Vol. I: Lessons; Polish–English Glossary; Vol. II: Drills; Survey of Grammar; Index. Yale Linguistic Series. New Haven and London, Yale University Press, 1973. (xviii,491; xi, 452 pp. £4.25; £2.95 per vol.). Sound and reliable, with an extensive descriptive apparatus which can serve as a useful rudimentary reference grammar of the language, it is well produced and has the major advantage of employing good modern colloquial Polish. 'The book', in the words of the author, 'is planned for an intensive year course'. Volume I can be used as a classroom text or for self-teaching. It consists of 25 lessons; each lesson is divided into sentences, introducing the student to spoken, conversational Polish, followed by notes on pronunciation, grammar and a vocabulary. Volume II contains the accompaning drills and is specifically designed for the classroom. As a self-teacher the book may be too long and detailed for some students, and teachers. It is nonetheless the best such handbook in English. The Survey of Grammar and the Index are two major omissions from the first edition published in 1966–67. A set of tapes to both volumes can be obtained from the Yale Language Laboratories, 111 Grove Street, New Haven, CT 06510, USA Volume I consists of 36 7″ reels at $129; Volume II consists of 49 7″ reels at $179.

Two textbooks published and most commonly available in this country are of much earlier origin and out of necessity have had to withstand long usage. First published in 1948, revised and enlarged in 1964, M. Corbridge–Patkaniowska's *Teach yourself Polish* (London, English Universities Press, 1973. 299 pp. £0.60) is a useful and reliable simplified course for beginners. Clearer explanations of some points of grammar aided by a more visual lay-out of the material and a grammatical reference section would overcome its most obvious shortcomings. Chronologically earlier (first published in 1941), J. A. Teslar's *A new Polish grammar* (8th ed. Edinburgh and London, Oliver and Boyd, 1962 reprinted 1967. 469 pp.) may still appeal to some students, particularly those who like to approach a language through a conscientious assimilation of the basic rules of grammar. Essentially it contains 60 lessons with notes and exercises, a section on grammar, a Polish–English/English–Polish vocabulary, and a key for self-correction. Aiming to give the student a thorough grounding in the structure and main features of the language, its general arrangement is to begin with the distinction of the three genders of nouns, then lesson by lesson to discuss the use of the cases, their meanings and variations, and finally to deal with the Polish verb. For teaching and learning the language it remains a serviceable tool suitable for classwork or as a self-teacher. The short grammatical reference section is particularly useful. Not surprisingly, however, the content and style of its texts is dated and the language, as in *Teach yourself Polish*, does not reflect modern spoken Polish.

Two more recent courses for beginners published in Poland, and easily obtained here, are disappointing and on closer familiarity frustratingly tedious: W. Bisko and others, *Mówimy po polsku. A beginner's course in Polish* (2nd ed. Warsaw, Wiedza Powszechna, 1973. 327 pp. £1), available with a set of 4 LP records, and Z. Bastgen, *Let's learn Polish* (3rd ed. Warsaw, Wiedza Powszechna, 1974. 277 pp. £1). Intended as teach-yourself textbooks their general lay-out is similar; an introduction to pronunciation and spelling, lessons, key to the exercises and short outlines of grammar. On all accounts they leave much to be desired. The most frequent everyday situations which both attempt to portray will neither familiarise the student with contemporary Polish life nor introduce him to vocabulary which will be of most use. Some, no doubt, might find them to be not entirely objectionable. A number of recent comparative studies in Poland of Polish and English gives grounds for hope that this in turn will lead to a greater awareness of the needs of the English student learning Polish and of the textbooks required. Promisingly titled, E. Maliszewska's *Polish grammar exercises for foreign students* (Lublin, 1975. 136 pp.) is a short, modest book of drills intended for classroom use. The material it is claimed has been graded and selected from the point of view of the English–Polish contrastive analysis. As an addition to the standard works of grammar some might find it a useful aid in teaching the language at lower levels.

There is a conspicuous lack of textbooks for the more advanced student. Alexander M. Schenker's *Fifteen modern Polish short stories. An annotated reader and glossary* (Yale Linguistic Series. New Haven and London, Yale University Press, 1970. 186 pp. $10; $5) may be used, as the author suggests in the introduction, as a companion volume to his *Beginning Polish* and is intended for the use of first and second year students of the language. The stories selected vary in style and length and have been graded in order of increasing difficulty. The volume serves also as a useful introduction to some representative modern post-war Polish writers. *Communicating in Polish* by Bernard Penny and Krystyna Malinowska (Washington, D.C., Department of State, Foreign Service Institute, 1974. 260 pp. £3.75) is a particularly valuable new addition. Designed to teach students to speak Polish and to live and work in Poland it is a combination of photographs and texts; each of these is followed by questions directly relating to it and leading on to associated topics of conversation. A short glossary of less familiar words is provided but there are no grammatical explanations. Well conceived and well produced it is a very flexible classroom text. Its panorama of contemporary life in Poland, its choice of practical situations, and its language are knowledgeable, accurate and fully up to date. Adaptable to suit all levels it is ideally suited for students who are already familiar with the basic structure of the language.

Grammars. Two works mentioned above: Alexander M. Schenker, *Beginning Polish* and J. A. Teslar, *A new Polish grammar*, though primarily intended as textbooks for teaching and learning the language may properly be used as basic reference grammars. The exposition of grammatical material is often fairly extensive and both contain summaries of grammar at the end – very convenient for purposes of revision or quick reference, particularly for students with little or no prior knowledge of the language.

The standard descriptive grammar of Polish is S. Szober, *Gramatyka języka polskiego* (12th ed., edited by W. Doroszewski. Warsaw, Państwowe Wydawnictwo Naukowe, 1971. 390 pp.) a comprehensive and detailed university manual which, with revisions, has survived unfailingly for over half a century. H. Grappin, *Grammaire de la langue polonaise* (Paris Institut des Études Slaves, 1942. 2nd ed., 1949. 3rd ed., 1963. 324 pp. FFr.28.), its old and equally solid companion, is still a useful work but clearly needs some revising. It has been largely superseded by Etienne Decaux: *Petite grammaire polonaise* (Paris, Centre de Documentation Universitaire et S.E.D.E.S. 1966–67. 4 fasc. (81; 45; 99; 100 pp.) FFr.10.25; 7; 11.75; 12.50). Intended for advanced students of the language who are to use it as a complement to both class work and the traditional manuals of grammar it is recommended as a concise work of ready reference. The imposing array of facts and information on phonetics, modern Polish orthography, morphology, noun declensions and verb conjugations is set out clearly and systematically with an appealing economy of explanation. A very practical and accessible descriptive grammar in two volumes with exercises is by B. Bartnicka-Dąbrowska and others: *Gramatyka opisowa języka polskiego z ćwiczeniami* (Warsaw, Państwowe Zakłady Wydawnictw Szkolnych, 1964. 284; 404 pp.). Students might like to use it as a partial alternative to Szober's more imposing manual, and its material is readily adaptable for classroom use.

Philologists, particularly those interested in comparative Slavonic philology, will find a concise description of Polish phonology and morphology in R. G. A. de Bray's *Guide to the Slavonic languages* (Rev. ed. London, Dent, 1969. £9.75) pp. 589–671.

RECORDED MATERIAL

The tapes to the two volumes of Schenker's *Beginning Polish* have been mentioned above. Polish Radio have produced a basic course of Polish consisting of 76 lessons with explanations of vocabulary and sentence structures in English. Judging by the sample tape the course would seem to suffer from the same weaknesses as the textbooks published in Poland, two of which have also been mentioned above. The musical content, if it is at all representative, will take some people back many years. The price of one set of cassettes plus the textbook is U.S. $113. Tape recordings, speed 7½ ips or 3¾ ips, cost $150 and $100 respectively. Polish Radio also produces recordings of poetry, prose and drama some of which are extremely good. Tapes and further information are available from Polish Radio – Wifon, ul. Woronicza 17, Warsaw 02-625, Poland.

DICTIONARIES

The range of dictionaries of the Polish language is both comprehensive and well produced. While some of the major projects, first begun in the early fifties, are still in the process of completion there is now almost a full record of Polish lexis from earliest times up to the present day. Most major scholarly ventures are undertaken under the auspices of the Polish Academy of Sciences (PAN)[1] and generally published by Ossolineum; the two other largest publishers of dictionaries and reference works are Państwowe Wydawnictwo Naukowe (PWN) and Wiedza Powszechna (WP).

Historically important as the first dictionary of the Polish language, S. B. Linde's *Słownik języka polskiego* (Warsaw, 1807–14. 6 v. 2nd rev. and enlarged ed. Lwów, Ossolineum, 1854–60) remains a valuable source of information for students and scholars. A photo-offset edition of the second edition was published by the Państwowy Instytut Wydawniczy, Warsaw, 1951. Comparable in status to the *OED* the dictionary of contemporary Polish containing 120,000 entries in eleven volumes is *Słownik języka polskiego*, general editor W. Doroszewski (Warsaw, PAN, 1958–69). The concise version: *Mały słownik języka polskiego*, editors, S. Skorupka and others (Warsaw, PWN, 1974. 1,034 pp. £6.75) contains some 35,000 entries. Another, four-volume, dictionary of the Polish language is in preparation.

There is an equally good selection of bilingual dictionaries

---

[1] In standard English usage the term 'science' has a restricted application to the natural and physical sciences. Polish 'nauka', plural 'nauki', as in 'Polska Akademia Nauk', also includes those disciplines which in English are referred to as the humanities.

and despite periodic difficulties all can be obtained here. The two large standard ones are: *The Kościuszko Foundation dictionary*. Vol. I: English–Polish by K. Bulas and F. J. Whitfield; Vol. II: Polish–English by K. Bulas, L. L. Thomas and F. J. Whitfield, (The Hague, Mouton, 1959–61 reprinted 1964. 1,037; 772 pp; published by photo-offset, Warsaw, 1961–62 reprinted 1967. £8,20 per vol.), and J. Stanisławski, *The great English–Polish dictionary. Wielki słownik angielsko–polski* (Warsaw, WP, 1964. 1,175 pp. £4.50) with its companion *The great Polish–English dictionary. Wielki słownik polsko–angielski,* (4th ed., Warsaw, WP, 1975. 2 v. 572; 607 pp.). Of the two, Stanisławski's larger selection of words, phrases and expressions gives better value and greater help to the user. The Kościuszko dictionary has sometimes the advantage of being a bit more confident of its English, albeit American English.

The following is a selection of smaller, shorter dictionaries all of which are reliable and good value for money: *A practical English–Polish dictionary. Podręczny słownik angielsko–polski* (4th ed. Warsaw, WP, 1975. 913 pp. £2.25) and its companion *A practical Polish–English dictionary. Podręczny słownik polsko–angielski* (Warsaw, WP, 1973. 1,032 pp. £2.25) both by J. Stanisławski and others; T. Grzebieniowski, *A concise English–Polish and Polish–English dictionary. Mały słownik angielsko–polski i polsko–angielski* (8th printing. Warsaw, WP, 1974. 307 pp. £2.25); J. Jasłoń and J. Stanisławski, *English–Polish and Polish–English pocket dictionary* (Warsaw, WP, 1972. 421 pp. £1.80).

Specialised dictionaries. As a supplement to the standard dictionaries of the language there are several important and valuable aids. *Słownik poprawnej polszczyzny*, editor W. Doroszewski (Warsaw, PWN, 1974. 1,056 pp. £8.15) is an extremely practical dictionary guide to the correct usage of words, their spelling, accentuation, punctuation and inflexion. No student should dispense with its services. S. Skorupka's *Słownik frazeologiczny języka polskiego* (2nd ed. Warsaw, WP, 1974. 2 v. (788; 906 pp.) £7.) is an extensive dictionary of phrases and expressions. A dictionary of synonyms, *Słownik wyrazów bliskoznacznych*, editor S. Skorupka (7th ed. Warsaw, WP, 1972. 448 pp.), serves a readily identifiable purpose. *Słow-*

nik wyrazów obcych, editor J. Tokarski (Warsaw, PWN, 1974. 825 pp.) with some 35,000 entries is particularly useful for a language in which every fourth word is on average of foreign origin; there is also W. Kopaliński's *Słownik wyrazów obcych i zwrotów obcojęzycznych* (9th enlarged ed. Warsaw, WP, 1975. 1,108 pp. £3.75).

The comprehensive and authoritative dictionary of modern Polish orthography and spelling is the *Słownik ortograficzny i prawidła pisowni polskiej* by S. Jodłowski and W. Taszycki (8th enlarged ed., conforming to the resolutions of the Polish Academy of Sciences' Committee on Language in 1956. Wrocław, Ossolineum, 1973. 814 pp. £1.12).

A venture of major scholarly importance, half-completed to date, is Franciszek Sławski's *Słownik etymologiczny języka polskiego* (Warsaw, Tow. Miłośników Języka Pol., 1952–73. v. 1–4. A–Ł.). Meanwhile, the first dictionary of the Polish language, originally published in 1927, Aleksander Brückner's *Słownik etymologiczny języka polskiego* (Warsaw, WP, 1974. 805 pp. £5.10) remains an interesting and valuable, though by no means infallible work. An eminent and untiring scholar, possessed of a great intuitive sense, Brückner's bold, often stimulating interpretations, unsubjected to the rigours of any 'academic' method, are a testimony to his wish to produce a dictionary which would be accessible to and understood by the layman. Despite the errors, the omissions, and one's own suspicions it retains a charm all its own.

Several additional items might conveniently be listed here. *Słownik terminologii językoznawczej*, editors Z. Gołąb and others (2nd ed. Warsaw, PWN, 1972. 847 pp. £4.33) is a practical dictionary-guide for students of language and linguistics and includes indices of English, French, German and Russian terms with their Polish equivalents. M. Kniagininowa and W. Pisarek's *Poradnik językowy* (2nd rev. and enlarged ed. Warsaw, 1969. 474 pp.), is equally practical as a handbook of language for the Press, Radio and T.V. It is worth noting that an encyclopaedic guide to the Polish language covering contemporary Polish, its history and historical grammar, lexicography, dialects, onomastics etc., is in preparation under the editorship of S. Urbańczyk. A more 'esoteric' but scholarly work is B.

Wieczorkiewicz's dictionary of Warsaw dialect past and present, *Gwara warszawska dawniej i dziś* (3rd rev. and enlarged ed. Warsaw, Państwowy Instytut Wydawniczy, 1974. 625 pp. £3.05). A dictionary of student slang, *Słownik gwary studenckiej* by L. Kaczmarek and others (Wrocław, Ossolineum, 1974. 477 pp.), is not without its own peculiar interest.

Piotr Borkowski's *An English–Polish dictionary of idioms and phrases* (2nd ed. London, Odnowa, 1970. 204 pp. £1.50) is the first, though modest attempt of its kind. The alphabetic arrangement based on key words is sometimes confusing but it is undoubtedly a useful aid.

At the other end of the scale *Polish for travellers* (Lausanne, Editions Berlitz, 1973. 192 pp. £0.40) offers a good selection of general information for the tourist and a generous pocketful of phrases covering most situations. Magdalena Hall and Jillian Norman's *Polish phrase book* (London, Penguin Books, 1973. 217 pp. £0.40) is a more modest alternative.

Technical dictionaries. The choice of monolingual, bilingual and polyglot dictionaries published in Poland or under the auspices of international organisations is quite extensive and varied ranging from science and technology through medicine, law, international affairs to tourism, detergents and bee-keeping.

The best general Polish–English technical dictionary is S. Czerni and M. Skrzyńska's *Polish–English technical dictionary. Słownik techniczny polsko–angielski* (2nd rev. and enlarged ed. Warsaw, Wydawnictwa Naukowo-Techniczne, 1970. 666 pp.) and its counterpart *English–Polish Technical Dictionary. Słownik techniczny angielsko–polski* (2nd rev. and enlarged ed. Warsaw, WNT, 1968. 807 pp.) published also by Pergamon Press, Oxford, 1962. A concise edition of both parts was published Warsaw, 1962–63. (244; 174 pp. 2nd ed. 1966.). A third revised and enlarged edition of the *Polish–English Technical dictionary* was due to be published in 1976 under the amended title *Polish–English dictionary of science and technology. Słownik naukowo-techniczny polsko–angielski*; it is to be updated to include the most recent technical and scientific terminology and to contain some 75,000 entries – a 25% increase. Similarly, the *English–Polish dictionary of science and technology* (Warsaw,

WNT, 1973. 892 pp.) is a 3rd revised and enlarged edition of the earlier technical dictionary. The 4th edition was published in 1975 (£7.50).

In specialised fields the following are a representative sample of bilingual and polyglot manuals. Chemistry is covered by D. Kryt's *English–Polish chemical dictionary. Słownik chemiczny angielsko–polski* (2nd rev. and enlarged ed. Warsaw, WNT, 1964. 365 pp.), and her *Polish–English chemical dictionary. Słownik chemiczny polsko–angielski* (Warsaw, WNT, 1967. 400 pp.); physics by W. Skibicki's *A glossary of physics. Polish–English–French–German–Russian. Słownik terminów fizycznych* (Warsaw, WNT, 1961. 776 pp.). Medical terminology is dealt with by S. Jędraszko's *English–Polish and Polish–English medical dictionary. Słownik lekarski angielsko–polski i polsko–angielski* (3rd ed. Warsaw, Państwowy Zakład Wydawnictw Lekarskich, 1969. 683 pp.); electrical engineering by H. Zimnicki's *English–Polish and Polish–English dictionary of electrical engineering* (Warsaw, WNT, 1961–62. 2 v. (639; 372 pp.)); Z. Pentlakowa's *Słownik petrograficzny* (Warsaw, 1962. 344 pp.) and R. Żyłka's *Geological dictionary* (Warsaw, 1970. 1,439 pp.) are both published by the Wydawnictwa Geologiczne, and give equivalents in English, Polish, Russian, French and German. A short dictionary by J. Matera and others *Energia jądrowa i słownik terminów technicznych* (Warsaw, PWN, 1963. 215 pp.) is a compilation of nuclear terms in English with French, Russian and Polish equivalents. The field of trade and economy is well-catered for by W. Swieżewska's *Słownik handlowo-ekonomiczny polsko–angielski* (Warsaw, Państwowe Wydawnictwo Ekonomiczne, 1970. 995 pp.).

Two other dictionaries deserve mention: J. W. Nixon's *Słownik terminów statystycznych* (Warsaw, Główny Urząd Statystyczny, 1968. 116 pp.), a dictionary of statistical terms providing entries in English with French and Polish equivalents, and J. Paruch's *Słownik skrótów* (Warsaw, WP, 1970. 389 pp.) – a very useful pocket-size reference book of 800 abbreviations.

19

RUMANIAN

by D. J. DELETANT, B.A., Ph.D.

INTRODUCTION

Rumanian is a Romance language descended from the Latin spoken in the province of Dacia two thousand years ago. The Roman Emperor Trajan conquered Dacia in a campaign lasting from A.D. 105–107 and colonised it with settlers from all parts of the Empire who inter-married with the local population and romanised it. Dacia was abandoned by the Romans in A.D. 271 and the province became a gateway to the south for numerous invaders, including the Slavs who, in the 6th and 7th centuries finally cut off Dacia from the rest of the Romance-speaking world.

Rumanian is divided into four dialectal groups, separated from each other by Slavonic and Greek-speaking areas: (1) Daco-Rumanian or Rumanian proper, spoken in Rumania, Soviet Moldavia (Bessarabia), and parts of Yugoslavia and Hungary bordering on Rumania; (2) Arumanian or Macedo-Rumanian, spoken in some communities in Greece, Albania, Yugoslavia and Bulgaria; (3) Megleno-Rumanian, spoken in the Greek–Yugoslav border region; (4) Istro-Rumanian, spoken in a small number of villages in the peninsula of Istria on the Adriatic.

Isolated from the other Romance languages, Rumanian has developed several morphological features that distinguish it from the rest of the Romance family e.g. the postpositioning of the definite article, a three-case system with forms for the nominative/accusative, vocative and genitive/dative. The vocabulary is basically of Latin origin but it has, at different periods, been heavily influenced by Slavonic, Hungarian, Greek and Turkish, influences that are still reflected today. Until the end of the 18th century, when a Latinist movement in Transylvania encouraged the use of the Latin alphabet, Rumanian was written in the Cyrillic alphabet.

TEXTBOOK COURSES & GRAMMARS

As is is no longer possible to take 'O' and 'A' level in Rumanian, it is not surprising that there are no textbooks designed for this work. There are, however, several good general courses suitable for study with or without tuition. *Teach yourself Romanian* by M. Murrell and V. Ştefănescu-Drăgăneşti (London, English University Press, 1970 reprinted 1974. vi, 428 pp. £0.75) is the easiest to obtain for British students. It contains thirty-two lessons, two grammatical appendices, a key to the exercises, as well as a Rumanian word list and English–Rumanian vocabulary. Equally thorough, but less suitable for study without a tutor and designed for American students, is J. E. Augerot and F. D. Popescu, *Modern Romanian* (Seattle and London, University of Washington Press, 1971. xiii, 329 pp. $12.) More difficult to obtain are *A course in modern Rumanian* by A. Cartianu and others (Bucharest, Publishing House for Scientific Books, 1958. 360 pp.) and its companion *An advanced course in modern Rumanian* (2nd ed. Bucharest, Publishing House for Scientific Books, 1964. 365 pp.). Both are characterised in places by stilted English and by the fact that they do not indicate the stress of Rumanian words, but the lessons and exercises are well-graded. B. Cazacu and others, *A course in contemporary Romanian* (Bucharest, Editura didactică, 1969. 563 pp. (with two records)), intended for use with a tutor, is a detailed course of thirty lessons with full grammatical reference sections that will take the student to approximately the equivalent of 'A' level standard, as indeed all the aforementioned courses do. Equally satisfactory is O. Delarăscruci and I Popescu, *Curs de limba română* (Bucharest, Editura didactică, 1971. 2 v. (with records)), although the reference sections are less detailed. Useful, but rather dated, is G. Nandriş, *Colloquial*

Rumanian (2nd ed., rev. London, Routledge and Kegan Paul, 1966 reprinted 1969. xx, 352 pp. £2.95).

The only reader readily obtainable in this country is E. D. Tappe, *Rumanian prose and verse* (London, Athlone Press, 1956. xxvii, 195 pp. £1.85), which presents chronologically selections from the major Rumanian authors and poets of the 19th and 20th centuries. It is not a graded reader but each passage has explanatory footnotes and the book is prefaced by a short essay on Rumanian literature.

Grammars. The standard grammar of Rumanian is that of the Rumanian Academy: *Gramatica limbi române* (2nd ed. Bucharest, 1963. 2 v.) A major criticism of this work is that it does not always give the Rumanian stress. This is also a fault in Şt. Popescu, *Gramatica practică a limbii române cu o culegere de exerciţii* (Bucharest, Editura didactică, 1971. 598 pp.) which is shorter and intended for less advanced students. An excellent guide to Rumanian grammar, including stress, is A. Lombard, *La langue roumaine. Une presentation* (Paris, Klincksieck, 1974. xv, 396 pp. FFr. 96.) which, although shorter than the Academy grammar, is in many respects more informative about popular as well as literary usage. It is simple to use for reference and very clearly presented.

RECORDED MATERIAL

There are no recorded courses in Rumanian that go much beyond the elementary stage. The only recorded material available to the general public is provided by the records that accompany B. Cazacu and others, *A course in contemporary Romanian* (Bucharest, 1969. 2 records) and O. Delarăscruci (vol. I) and I. Popescu (vol. II), *Curs de limba română* (Bucharest, 1971. 4 EP records). Both take the student to approximately the same level. The former, a course of thirty lessons, has, in its two accompanying discs, recordings of all the texts in the book as well as of exercises specially designated. The latter has fifty-three lessons but the recorded material is less extensive.

DICTIONARIES

Of English–Rumanian dictionaries the most comprehensive is that compiled by the Institute of Linguistics in Bucharest *Dicţionar englez-român* (Bucharest, Institutal de Lingvistică, 1974. xxxii, 855 pp.). More compact is *Dicţionar englez-român* (Bucharest, Editura ştiinţifică, 1971. 1,068 pp.) edited by L. Leviţchi and A. Bantaş. Even more convenient, but with fewer English–Romanian entries, is the English–Rumanian/Rumanian–English *Dicţionar de Buzunar* (Pocket dictionary) (2nd ed. Bucharest, Editura ştiinţifică, 1973. 1,131 pp.) edited by A. Bantaş. Its title, however, belies its format. By far the best Rumanian–English dictionary is that of L. Leviţchi: *Dicţionar român–englez* (3rd ed., revised by the author and by A. Bantaş. Bucharest, Editura ştiinţifică, 1973. 1,085 pp.)

Still the most exhaustive dictionary of Rumanian is *Dicţionarul enciclopedic ilustrat* (Bucharest, Cartea românească, [1931]. xxiv, 1,948 pp.), edited by I. A. Candrea and Gh. Adamescu. This includes both dialectal variants and words found in the earliest Rumanian texts of the 16th century. When complete, the authoritative dictionary will be that published by the Rumanian Academy: *Dicţionarul limbii române* (Bucharest, Academia română, 1913–48 A–LO; continued as *DLR*, serie nouă, with letter M appearing in 1965). At present letter R has been reached (1975). Useful, but with several lacunae, is *Dicţionarul limbii române moderne* (Bucharest, Editura Academiei, 1958. [vi], 961 pp.) The more recent neologisms adopted by Rumanian are only to be found in *Mic dicţionar enciclopedic* (Bucharest, Editura enciclopedică română, 1972. [xiv], 1,730, xxxii pp.) which is modelled on Larousse and is an excellent work of reference. Although bilingual, H. Tiktin, *Dicţionar român–german* (Bucharest, Imprimeria statuluĭ, 1903–25. 3 v.) deserves mention here as an outstanding dictionary of Rumanian that ranks alongside that of Candrea and Adamescu.

Specialised Dictionaries. The only etymological dictionary of note is that of A. Cioranescu: *Diccionario etimológico rumano* (La Laguna, Biblioteca Filológica, 1958. [iv], 918 pp.) which is far from exhaustive. There is an excellent technical dictionary in two volumes: *Dicţionar tehnic englez-român* (Bucharest, Editura tehnică, 1967. xi, 1,301, [i] pp.); *român-englez* (1970. xi, 1,118 pp.). Its only defect is that it does not give the stress of Rumanian words. *Lexicon maritim englez-român* (Bucharest, Editura ştiinţifică, 1971. 852 pp.) is a detailed dictionary of nautical terms. The last five years have seen the appearance of dictionaries of antonyms and synonyms: *Dicţionar de sinonime*, (Bucharest, Editura Albatros, 1972. 488 pp.); M. Bucă and O. Vinţeler, *Dicţionar de antonime* (Bucharest, Editura enciclopedică română, 1974. 260 pp.), both of which are useful but fragmentary.

Of the major dialects only Macedo-Rumanian (Arumanian) has a reasonably accessible dictionary: T. Papahagi, *Dicţionarul dialectului aromân* (2nd ed., enlarged. Bucharest, Editura Academiei, 1974. 1,437 pp.).

20

MODERN GREEK

by PETER MACKRIDGE, M.A., D.Phil.

INTRODUCTION

Modern Greek is not taught in schools in the United Kingdom, and is available at only a few universities. The paucity of teachers of the language outside Greece has resulted in a dearth of good teaching materials for the foreign student. This situation is exacerbated by the fact that demotic Greek has traditionally been relegated to third place in Greek schools, after ancient and purist Greek.

Modern Greek is directly descended from ancient Greek, both in vocabulary and morphology, but for complex reasons the language exists in two forms: the purist (*katharévousa*), a written language made up of a mixture of ancient and colloquial elements, is used in almost all official and scientific writing, and until 1974 in many newspapers, while the demotic (*dimotikí*) is the colloquial form of the language and is used in creative literature. Nevertheless, it is possible today, for the first time, to speak of standard modern Greek, a term which covers the spoken language of the urban centres and much of the countryside, and the language of newspapers and of other prose in which the writer is not aiming to write in purist Greek; this term excludes words and forms belonging to the extreme varieties of both demotic and purist. But the concept of standard modern Greek will take some time to become universally accepted, and in the meantime the situation will remain confused.

One result of this confusion is that the language used in dictionaries is mainly purist, while that employed in course-books is always demotic. The 'demotic' of different course-books, however, varies considerably between the extreme 'rural' variety and a 'bureaucratic' variety that borders on the purist.

We still await a good grammar and syntax of standard modern Greek *in Greek*: there is certainly nothing very good in English.

Books are available from Hellenic Bookservice, 122 Charing Cross Road, London, WC2H 0JR.

TEXTBOOK COURSES & GRAMMARS

There are naturally no secondary school materials available. All course books are for beginners, and none goes beyond an elementary level.

Demotic Greek, by P. Bien and others (3rd ed. Hanover, N. H., University Press of New England, 1972. 286 pp. £3), is a course book accompanying reel-to-reel tapes. Each lesson contains reading passages, vocabulary, grammatical rules, substitution and transformation drills. At the end of the book are a 'general grammatical survey' and a glossary.

The best self-tuition course without audio aids is Ann Arpajolu's *Modern spoken Greek for English–speaking Students* (New York, Hadrian Press, 1964. 433 pp. £5.25). Each lesson in this comprehensive course contains a reading passage, followed by vocabulary, grammar and exercises. Another self-instruction course is *Introduction au grec moderne*, by André Mirambel (3rd ed. Paris, Maisonneuve, 1973. 318 pp. £5), in which each lesson consists of sentences and vocabulary lists, with translations of the sentences at the end of the book.

Sappho Mavroulia's *Ta nea ellinika gia xenoglossous* (2nd ed. Athens, 1967. 281 pp. £3) is a direct-method course. The lessons consist of reading passages, dialogues, grammar, exercises and vocabulary. There are annotated passages from Greek authors at the end, followed by inflection tables.

Grammars. Because of the complexity of the flexional system, grammars of modern Greek tend to be confusing. There is no satisfactory exposition of morphology which can be easily used for reference, and syntax and usage are hardly touched on in any book.

J. T. Pring's *A grammar of modern Greek on a phonetic basis*

(London, University of London Press, 1973. 127 pp. £0.80) deals briefly with pronunciation and grammar, including some syntax. The author often uses the International Phonetic Alphabet instead of the Greek alphabet, which means that the book is more suitable for students of spoken rather than of written Greek. By contrast, *Reference grammar of literary Dhimotiki* (Bloomington, Indiana University, 1964. 188 pp. $5), by F. W. Householder and others, intended for advanced students, is based on the usage of selected Greek authors. André Mirambel's *Grammaire du grec moderne* (3rd ed. Paris, Kliencksieck, 1969. xxiv, 246 pp. £2.60) contains a little information on syntax and usage, but tends to be over-demotic, disregarding purist forms in common use.

In Greek, the standard demotic grammar is M. A. Triandaphyllidis' *Mikri neoelliniki grammatiki* (Rev. ed. Thessaloniki, 1975. 203 pp. £1.25), which includes many historical notes and is too comprehensive for any but advanced students. *Synchroniki grammatiki tis koinis neoellinikis*, by G. Babiniotis and P. Kontos (Athens, 1967. 262 pp.), is a synchronic descriptive grammar based on Athenian spoken Greek and the language of newspapers. Each section contains exercises, in which the language tends to be 'bureaucratic'; the book is intended for advanced students.

The only syntax of demotic Greek is A. A. Tzartzanos' *Neoelliniki syntaxis* (Athens, 1946–63. 2 v. (352; 326 pp.) £3). A pioneering work, but insufficient indexing makes it difficult for the reader to find his way around. A syntax of purist Greek is *Syntaktikon tis neas ellinikis glossis*, by D. N. Monoyos and others (Athens College, 1969. 188 pp.). This is intended for Greek secondary school students, and the whole text is in purist Greek.

Descriptions of the language. George Thomson's *A manual of modern Greek* (London, Collet's, 1967. xiv, 112 pp. £1.20) is a short introduction to modern Greek, not divided into lessons, with reading passages from Greek authors and vocabulary. The emphasis is on literary demotic rather than spoken Greek. André Mirambel's *La Langue grecque moderne* (Paris, Kliencksieck, 1959. 473 pp. FFr. 64.) is a more comprehensive description of the language.

Reader. The only modern Greek reader intended for English-speakers is J. T. Pring's *Modern Greek reader for beginners* (London, University of London Press, 1964. 77 pp. £0.85), which assumes a mastery of the essentials of the grammar, although each text is followed by grammatical notes referring to the author's *Grammar of modern Greek*.

Greek–English translation. L. G. Ftyaras' *Modern Greek translation* (Rev. ed. London, Longman, 1974. xlvi, 103 pp. £0.65), although primarily intended for Greek-speakers working on the L.C.E. and C.P.E., is most useful for English-speakers too. 'A few hints on translation' are followed by 40 annotated and 20 unannotated passages from Greek authors. *Notes on translating idiomatic modern Greek*, by G. A. Trypanis (Athens, Cacoulides, 1954. 168 pp. £2), consists of notes on difficulties encountered in translating from Greek into English, a list of Greek idioms with English equivalents, and graded translation passages from Greek authors, some with English translation, some with notes only, and others without either.

DICTIONARIES

Bilingual. *The Oxford dictionary of modern Greek (Greek–English)*, by J. T. Pring (Oxford, Clarendon Press, 1975. xvi, 219 pp. £3), though small (under 20,000 words), is the most accurate modern Greek–English dictionary in existence. It contains most of the words likely to be met in conversation and in reading newspapers, with a few examples and idioms.

The Penguin-Hellenews *Anglo-ellinikon lexikon* (Athens, Hellenews, 1975. xiv, 926 pp. £7) is an English–Greek dictionary with all explanatory material in Greek. Greek translations tend to be more purist than demotic, which contrasts with the modernity of the English entries. About 40,000 words. *Mega angloellinikon lexikon* (Athens, Odysseus, [n.d.]. 4 v. (xii, 960; 930; 940; 1,067 pp.) £50) is a comprehensive English–Greek dictionary. Greek interpretations usually have the purist word first, then the demotic, but there are many illustrations of usage and idioms.

I. Kykkotis' *Modern English–Greek and Greek–English dictionary* (Rev. ed. London, Lund Humphries, 1969. 644 pp. £2.20) is a handy dictionary, although both vocabulary and grammar tend more towards purist than demotic, and many of the Greek words are in fact Cypriot without their being indicated as such. Charis Patsis' *Lexiko anglo–elliniko* (Athens, 1967. 718 pp. £6.50) and *Lexiko ellino–angliko* (Athens, 1967. 559 pp. £6.50) are both intended for Greek-speakers. All the Greek is demotic.

Greek only. *Lexikon tis neas ellinikis glossis (Proïas)* (3rd ed. Athens; Dimitrakos, [n.d.]. 2 v. (2,664; 555 pp. addenda. £25) is the most easily usable of the monolingual dictionaries of modern Greek. Comprehensive and accurate, it contains many examples and idioms, both colloquial, literary and official. Over 75,000 words. *Synchronon lexikon tis ellinikis glossis* (Athens, Atlas, 1961. xxxv, 1,074 pp.) is the only dictionary to give a clear indication, after each word, of whether it exists in ancient Greek, purist and demotic. Definitions tend to be brief, without examples. About 60,000 words.

Mega lexikon tis ellinikis glossis (Athens, Dimitrakos, 1933 – [c. 1952]. 9 v. (8,056 pp.)) is a monolingual dictionary of ancient, medieval and modern Greek, with examples of usage from authors. It is especially useful for the study of semantic change.

Specialised dictionaries. Th. Vostantzoglou's *Analytikon orthographikon lexikon tis neoellinikis glossis* (Athens, [n.d.] xvi, 608 pp.) is an extremely handy spelling dictionary, indicating the syllabification of each word and referring in each entry to tables of inflexion at the end of the book; there is also an indication of whether each word belongs to the purist or the demotic.

The same author's *Antilexikon* (2nd ed. Athens, 1962. xxiv, 1,138 pp. £18) is a compendious and invaluable 'thesaurus' of purist and demotic Greek, divided into 'concept' sections. The author attempts to differentiate 'synonymous' words from each other.

The standard etymological dictionary of literary demotic and spoken modern Greek is *Etymologiko lexiko tis koinis neoellinikis*, by N. P. Andriotis (Rev. ed. Thessaloniki, 1971, xxiv, 443 pp. £5.50), which contains about 22,000 words. It is clearly set out, with etymologies kept as brief as possible: it does not go back beyond classical Greek.

Phase books. Berlitz *Greek for travellers* (London, 1973. 192 pp. £0.50 – cassette also available) is probably the handiest, but neither it nor the *Collins Greek phrase book* (London, 1974. 160 pp. £0.50) contains a glossary at the back. The *Penguin Greek phrase book* (1975. 256 pp. £0.60) has this, but is marred by many printing errors and by several literal (i.e. un-Greek) translations from English.

21

FINNISH

by J. E. O. SCREEN, M.A., Ph.D., A.L.A.

Finnish, which is spoken by approximately 4½ million people in Finland as their first language, has a reputation for peculiarity and difficulty. That it is a Finno-Ugrian language and, as such, related to Hungarian is quite widely known. Less common is the realisation that Finnish and Hungarian have been developing separately for so long that their relationship is in structure rather than in vocabulary.

Interest in Finnish has grown in Britain in recent years and some evening classes are held at an elementary level. University courses are offered only at the University of London. In view of the language's reputation it cannot be over-emphasised to the intending student that Finnish is neither more nor less difficult than other languages, given adequate facilities.

TEXTBOOK COURSES & GRAMMARS

The Finnish course most generally used in evening classes has been Maija-Hellikki Aaltio's *Essential Finnish* (London, University of London Press, 1964. 315 pp.). This is now out of print but the more recent Finnish version can be obtained from Finland[1]. Maija-Hellikki Aaltio, *Finnish for foreigners 1* (8th rev. ed. Helsinki, Otava, 1973. 253 pp. Fmk. 23.50) and *Finnish for foreigners 2* (7th rev. ed. Helsinki, Otava, 1974. 192 pp.

---

[1] In many cases it will be advantageous to order Finnish books from booksellers in Finland, *e.g.* Suomalainen Kirjakauppa, PL 105, 00101 Helsinki 10, or Akateeminen Kirjakauppa, Keskuskatu 1, 00100 Helsinki 10.

Fmk.19.50) have as their primary aim to teach the beginner spoken Finnish and the different constructions used in the written language are considered more briefly. Book 1 has 25 and Book 2 15 lessons. The practical nature of the dialogues which introduce each lesson has a ready appeal. There are exercises with a key at the end of each book and word lists and indexes are provided. The same author's *Finnish for foreigners 1. Oral drills* (2nd ed. Helsinki, Otava, 1973. 78 pp. Fmk.11.; 5 tapes or cassettes. Fmk.205) is intended to reinforce the basic declensions and conjugations and the elementary conversation and pronunciation of the first lessons. Vilho Kallioinen, *Finnish conversational exercises. Elementary level* (Helsinki, Suomalaisen Kirjallisuuden Seura, 1974. 164 pp. Fmk.15) serves a similar purpose in that it is intended for the practice of basic grammar in class.

A. H. Whitney's *Teach yourself Finnish* (London, Teach Yourself Books, 1956, reprinted 1973. 301 pp. £0.50) has an introduction on pronunciation followed by 20 lessons, each arranged in a set pattern of grammatical notes, vocabulary, exercise (Finnish into English, with key at the end of the book), and a reading. The grammar is comprehensive and detailed. The vocabularies are, however, intimidatingly long and hard-going for the beginner using the book as a self-tutor. The determined student will nevertheless find his persistence rewarded while the teacher who uses the book will find the readings, which form a connected story, a convenient series of texts. (*Finnish reader*, edited by A. H. Whitney (London, Teach Yourself Books, 1971. 191 pp. £0.50) is helpful for the same purpose.)

The serious student, especially if he is accustomed to grammatical terminology, will find John Atkinson's *A Finnish grammar* (3rd ed. Helsinki, Finnish Literature Society, 1969. 131 pp. Fmk.6) a useful means of acquiring quickly a basic knowledge of the grammar for reading the language. English teachers of Finnish will find it helpful for reference (in spite of the absence of an index) although they, and their more advanced students, will turn also to standard grammars such as Aarni Penttilä, *Suomen kielioppi* (2nd ed. Porvoo, Söderström, 1963. 692, 36 pp. Fmk.62) and E. A. Saarimaa, *Kielenopas. Oikeakielisyysohjeita* (8th ed. Porvoo, Söderström, 1971. 362 pp. Fmk.29).

RECORDED MATERIAL

The Linguaphone Finnish course (London, Linguaphone
Institute. 3 books; cassettes or records. £49.50) is a revised version of an old conversational course. There are 60 recorded
lessons, based on familiar or practical situations, and which are
reproduced in the textbook, *Suomen kielen kurssi* (© 1970. 123
pp.). Vocabulary and an outline of the grammar are produced
separately as *Vocabulary and text of sound recordings* (© 1970.
82 pp.) and *Grammar* (© 1957. 87 pp.). The provision of a
tutorial service enhances the value of the course.

The recorded element of M–H. Aaltio's *Finnish for foreigners
1. Oral drills* has been mentioned in the previous section. Practice in elementary grammar is also the aim of Vilho Kallioinen:
Suomen kielen harjoituksia ulkomaalaisille (2nd rev. ed.
Helsinki, Suomalaisen Kirjallisuuden Seura, 1972. 118 pp.
Fmk.8). The exercises are reproduced on 2 tapes with gaps for
answers. The tapes must be ordered separately.

DICTIONARIES

The linguistic isolation of Finns, which makes their learning
of foreign languages essential, is reflected in the style of linguistic
dictionaries published in Finland in which features intended to
assist the foreigner are relatively rare. Users should note that
Finnish publishers frequently describe reprints as editions and
that the date of printing is not necessarily the date of the last
revision.

The beginner is most likely to encounter the two small dictionaries by A. Wuolle: *English–Finnish dictionary. Englantilais–suomalainen koulusanakirja* (13th ed. Porvoo,
Söderström, 1973, reprinted 1975. 546 pp. Fmk.18) and *Finnish–English dictionary. Suomalais–englantilainen
koulusanakirja* (11th ed. Porvoo, Söderström, 1974. 448 pp.
Fmk.24.50). They are in many ways adequate for the beginner
who does not aim to advance very far – significantly their Finnish titles describe them as school dictionaries – but libraries

and most students will find larger dictionaries not only essential but better value in the long run.

The best large Finnish–English dictionary is V. S. Alanne's *Suomalais–englantilainen suursanakirja. Finnish–English general dictionary* (3rd ed. Porvoo, Söderström, 1968, reprinted 1972. xxxiv, [i], 1,111 pp. Fmk.88). Features especially valuable to the English user include the indication with an asterisk of words subject to consonant gradation, the citation alongside the infinitive of the present tense first person singular where this is irregular and, in some cases, references to infinitives from other verb forms. There are many examples of usage and some colloquialisms. The companion English–Finnish volume is by Raija Hurme and Maritta Pesonen: *Englantilais–suomalainen suursanakirja. English–Finnish general dictionary* (Porvoo, Söderström, 1973. xi,1,183 pp. Fmk.82). This recent work is more up to date than Alanne, though not to be compared with it in quality, and is the most extensive English–Finnish dictionary. Although it is designed for Finns (the notes on usage appear only in Finnish) the English user has been helped by the indication of phrases in Finnish where the syntax differs from that in English. The other large English–Finnish dictionary is Aune Tuomikoski and Anna Slöör, *Englantilais–suomalainen sanakirja* (6th ed. Helsinki, Suomalaisen Kirjallisuuden Seura, 1973. xiii,1,100 pp. Fmk.35), which is much older in origin. However, its broad scope ensures its continued value and the examples of usage are frequently more accurate than those in Hurme and Pesonen.

A medium-sized English–Finnish dictionary is Eeva Riikonen and Aune Tuomikoski, *Englantilais–suomalainen sanakirja* (9th ed. Helsinki, Otava, 1974. 832,[3] pp. Fmk.49). There are understandably fewer examples of usage and idiomatic expressions than in the larger works and in date of original compilation it falls between the two. There is a medium-sized Finnish–English dictionary by P. E. Halme: *Suomalais–englantilainen sanakirja* (2nd ed. Helsinki, Suomalaisen Kirjallisuuden Seura, 1973. 632 pp. Fmk.28) which effectively meets its aim to cover the practical linguistic needs of everyday life. The typography of Halme is superior to that of any of the other dictionaries mentioned.

The tourist may benefit from two books by Berlitz: *Englantilais–suomalainen suomalais–englantilainen sanakirja. English–Finnish, Finnish–English dictionary* (Lausanne, Berlitz, 1974. 332 pp. £0.50) and *Finnish for travellers* (Geneva, Berlitz, 1970, reprinted 1972. 176,[1] pp. £0.40). A free pronunciation record is advertised with the latter.

Teachers will find invaluable Tuomo Tuomi, *Suomen kielen käänteissanakirja. Reverse dictionary of modern standard Finnish* (Helsinki, Suomalaisen Kirjallisuuden Seura, 1972. xxx, 545 pp. Fmk.130) and the forthcoming frequency dictionary of literary Finnish by M. Branch, A. Niemikorpi and P. Saukkonen to be published by Söderström by mid-1978. The standard dictionary of the Finnish language is *Nykysuomen sanakirja* (4th unabridged popular ed. Porvoo, Söderström, 1973. 3 v. (xviii,735; [iv],840; [iv],806 pp.) Fmk.316).

The largest of the specialised dictionaries, the title of which is self-explanatory, deserves mention: Y. Talvitie, *English–Finnish technical and commercial dictionary with short Finnish–English index* (5th ed. Lahti, Tietoteos, 1974. 808 pp. Fmk.198).

22

HUNGARIAN

by Peter Sherwood, b.a.

INTRODUCTION

Hungarian (Magyar), the native language of over 13 million people in Central and Eastern Europe, is a Uralic language genetically unrelated to the Indo-European ones surrounding it. Perhaps for this reason it has acquired the reputation – shared by its cousin, Finnish – of being 'difficult' to learn. It is certainly true that much of the basic vocabulary cannot be related to anything the student is likely to have encountered previously, nor should he expect to be able to converse after one or two hours' study; but those willing to apply themselves steadily will be richly rewarded by a language that is not so much difficult as quite different and, indeed, arguably more logical in its grammar than many major languages. There is, for example, a consistent relationship between orthography and pronunciation; there are no 'difficult' sounds; there is no gender; stress is always on the first syllable; and new words are generally formed by the addition of one or more of a small set of suffixes, resulting in only 58,000 major entries in the largest Hungarian dictionary (compare the *OED*, with over 400,000). At a steady hour a day the student should, within six or seven months, have access to the history and literature (both going back at least seven centuries) of a hospitable and beautiful country which has already transcended its linguistic isolation to become renowned throughout the world for its cuisine and music. It has a great deal more to offer.

TEXTBOOK COURSES & GRAMMARS

The only textbook intended for both classroom and private use is *Learn Hungarian* by Z. Bánhidi, Z. Jókay and D. Szabó, in collaboration with J. Tarján (4th ed. Budapest, Tankönyvkiadó, 1975. 531 pp. 46 *ft.*). This is a traditional grammar in 30 graded lessons, with exercises, an elementary two-way dictionary and a key. It is, however, an adaptation of a textbook written in German; not every grammatical rule given should, therefore, be regarded as definitive, nor is every turn of phrase in it felicitous or even correct. The United States' Foreign Service Institute publishes a *Hungarian basic course* by A. A. Koski and I. Mihalyfy: *Units 1–12* (Washington, D.C., 1962. 266 pp. $2); *Units 13–24* (Washington, D.C., 1964. 267–606 pp. $2.50). This provides less grammatical information and in no obviously graded sequence, but there is a battery of drills and exercises which make it perhaps more suitable for classroom work with a qualified instructor than for individual use. No other grammar or course for English speakers can be recommended.

The standard reference grammar of Hungarian is J. Tompa (ed.), *A mai magyar nyelv rendszere* (Budapest, Akadémiai Kiadó, 1970. 2 v. (599; 579 pp.) 90 ft. each). A much briefer work written for the non-specialist is E. Rácz and E. Takács, *Kis magyar nyelvtan* (4th ed. Budapest; Gondolat, 1974. 313 pp. 22 ft.). In languages other than Hungarian the only widely-available work is a version of the standard reference grammar in German: J. Tompa, *Ungarische Grammatik* (The Hague, Mouton), 1968. 426 pp. £11.50); a condensed version is also available: J. Tompa, *Kleine Ungarische Grammatik* (Budapest, Akadémiai Kiadó, 1972. 247 pp. $9.40).

RECORDED MATERIAL

The preface to the fourth edition of *Learn Hungarian* (see above) includes the following note: 'Supplementary records (Record Series for *Learn Hungarian* made available by the Hungarian Recording Company "Hungaroton") can also be obtained . . . (these) contain an almost complete text of the lessons;

nevertheless, certain parts had to be omitted because of restrictions on playing time.' (p. 6). At the time of writing the records had not yet arrived in England. Tapes for the Foreign Service Institute course are said to be obtainable.

DICTIONARIES

The standard dictionary of Hungarian is G. Bárczi and L. Országh (chief editors.), *A magyar nyelv értelmező szótára* (Budapest, Akadémiai Kiadó, 1959–62. 7 v. (1,091; 1,137; 939; 1,347; 1,315; 883; 671 pp.) 1,300 *ft.*). This contains 58,000 main entries, exhaustive definitions and a wealth of literary illustrations. A more practical proposition may be J. Juhász and others (editors), *Magyar értelmező kéziszótár* (2nd ed. Budapest, Akadémiai Kiadó, 1975. XV, 1,550 pp. 260 *ft.*). This has about 70,000 head-words (including many modern terms not defined elsewhere) and 850 helpful illustrations and diagrams.

The English–Hungarian dictionaries are all produced under the editorial guidance of L. Országh and published by Akadémiai Kiadó, Budapest. The largest pair, each with over 110,000 entries, are *Angol-magyar szótár* (3rd ed. 1970. 2 v. (XIII, 2,344 pp.)), and *Magyar–angol szótár* (3rd ed. 1969. 2 v. (VIII, 2,159 pp.) 460 *ft.* each set of 2 vols.). The concise dictionaries each contain about 37,000 entries: *Angol-magyar kéziszótár* (6th ed. 1971. 1,091 pp), and *Magyar–angol kéziszótár* (5th ed. 1971. XVI, 1,179 pp. 120 *ft.* each.) The smallest pair each contain about 22,000 words: *Angol–magyar szótár* (10th ed. (an unchanged reprint of 7th ed. 1974). 1975. 608 pp.), and *Magyar–angol szótár* (9th ed. (an unchanged reprint of 7th ed. 1972). 1974. 464 pp. 26 *ft.* each). A pocket-size tourists' dictionary is also available, the English–Hungarian part bound tête-bêche with the Hungarian–English, and each containing about 10,000 words: T. Magay and others (editors), *Útiszótár: Angol–magyar/Magyar–angol* (Budapest, Terra, 1972. 314, 316 pp. 33 *ft.*). Those with some knowledge of the language will find the following phrase-book helpful: L. T. András and M. Murvai, *How to say it in Hungarian. An*

English–Hungarian phrase-book with lists of words (4th ed. Budapest, Tankönyvkiadó, 1973. 238 pp. 14 *ft.*).

Of the vast range of multilingual dictionaries published in Hungary there is room to mention only the largest English–Hungarian/Hungarian–English technical dictionaries: E. Nagy and J. Klár (editors.), *Angol–magyar műszaki szótár* (2nd ed. Budapest, Akadémial Kiadó, 1959. VIII, 792 pp.), and E. Nagy, J. Klár and L. Katona (chief editors.), *Magyar–angol műszaki szótár* (Budapest, Akadémiai Kiadó, 1957. VIII, 752 pp.); each costs 300 *ft.* and contains over 100,000 entries. Librarians may be particularly interested in Z. Pipics, *Dictionarium Bibliothecarii Practicum/ad usum internationalem in XX linguis/* (5th ed. Budapest, Akadémiai Kiadó, and München, Verlag Dokumentation, 1971. 375 pp. 150 *ft.*).

23

ARABIC

by D. Grimwood-Jones, m.a.

INTRODUCTION

Arabic is used today as an official language by about 115 million people in North Africa, Chad, Mauretania, Sudan, Arabia and the Persian Gulf, Jordan, Israel, Syria, Lebanon, Iraq and certain of the Central Asian republics. It was used in Spain until the sixteenth century, Sicily till the eighteenth, and pockets of Arabic speakers exist today in Cyprus, South America and parts of the East African coast. The language of Malta can be considered as an Arabic dialect. As a written language, it is theoretically in use by all Muslims as the language of the Qur'ān, though in countries such as Turkey it has been superseded by native-language translations.

Arabic, like Hebrew, Aramaic and some of the languages of Ethiopia is a Semitic language, based on a triliteral root system. Roots consist entirely of consonants, of which there are 28 in Arabic; there are three vowels, which have the sounds 'a' (short 'a' as in 'cat'), 'i' (as in 'bit') and 'u' (as in 'put'), but these are not normally written except in the Qur'ān, where they appear above or below the consonant vowelled. They are not considered as letters in their own right. It is the modification of the vowelling of the three basic consonants or 'radicals' with the prefixing and/or insertion of certain other letters that determine differences in words based on a common idea: thus the root K-T-B which has the idea of writing produces derivatives such as KaTaBa – he wrote/to write; KāTiB – a writer; maKTaBa – library. The system is flexible enough to admit neologisms, *e.g.* miKTāB – typewriter; muKāTiB – reporter.

Arabic grammatical rules were fixed by scholars in the

seventh and eighth centuries A.D., and the impetus for this was provided by the Qur'ān. The early Arab conquests had brought vast areas of the known world under Muslim control, and difficulties arose with the conversion of peoples whose native language was not Arabic. Mispronunciation, misspelling and variant readings of the word of God as revealed to his prophet Muḥammad and set down in the Qur'ān could be blasphemy; from the time of the third caliph 'Uthmān (644–656 A.D.) who ordered the standardisation of the text of the Qur'ān, generations of Arab grammarians took it as a linguistic and syntactic model, painstakingly noting every grammatical detail. Such was the success of their labours, that the structure of written Arabic remained virtually unchanged until the nineteenth century.

Vocabulary too changed little until the nineteenth century. Then, following upon Napoleon's expedition to Egypt in 1798, first Egypt, and then most of the rest of the Arab world, was opened up as never before to the influence of western ideas which could not be expressed adequately in Arabic. This sparked off a revival of Arab interest in their own language and literature, a revival known as the 'Nahḍa' or 'Renaissance'. Towards the end of the century a movement grew to replace foreign loan words where possible with native Arabic words derived from existing roots, and ideas of language academies were put forward. Academies were eventually set up in Damascus (1919), Cairo (1932) and Baghdad (1947) to consider language reform and suggest neologisms; their work continues today and several thousand 'new' words have been coined, though it is difficult to estimate how many of these gain popular acceptance. One instance may be given here of a failure: the 'correct' word for telephone is 'hātif', meaning 'calling out', or in the terminology of mysticism 'invisible voice'; the word in common use is 'tilifūn'. Interestingly, not just the noun has been taken over: the verb 'to telephone' has become subtly arabicised to 'talfana', and is treated as if it were a normal Arabic root.

Arabic as so far discussed refers only to the 'written' language, whether classical or modern (although modern Arabic is becoming increasingly (and more properly) described as 'standard' or 'modern standard' Arabic, as it is used not only for written communications, but also for public speeches, and even on occasion as the spoken language of the educated Arab). It is a peculiarity of Arabic that while, for example, a Moroccan and a Kuwaiti could write perfectly intelligible letters to each other, were they to meet on the street they might well not understand a word of what each was saying. As the written language became crystallised and virtually ossified by early Qur'ānic study, the spoken language of the various regions developed as all other living languages, each distinguished by its own accent, syntactic peculiarities and even vocabulary.

All this multiplies the problems of the western student, who is faced with difficulties enough as it is – in the case of the written language mastering a totally unfamiliar script, and in any case trying to come to grips with a grammatical structure which, though highly logical, is unlike any European language, and a vocabulary which is totally strange. While it is true that as a tourist or businessman learning for fun, knowledge of a dialect would be adequate – and possible, since dialect grammars are generally written in transcription – it is surely more satisfying to be able to read street signs, notices and newspaper headlines, even if one goes no further. A good grounding in the written language not only opens the door to the enormous literature of Arabic, and provides one with an instant method of communication all over the Arab world, it also gives one a starting point for a study of any of the dialects. Given time and effort, it can be a richly rewarding experience.

GRAMMARS

One point that can be noted about Arabic grammars is the difference in approach of European and American authors. Generally speaking, European writers tend to carry on the tradition of 19th century grammarians and favour a grammar/translation approach; Americans prefer audio-lingual teaching methods.

a. Classical Arabic

For many the standard grammar remains G. W. Thatcher's

Arabic grammar of the written language (London, Lund Humphries, 1942; reprinted New York, Ungar, n.d. ii, 460, 99 pp. £3.75) a well laid-out book which could be used for self-study. It contains 49 lessons with exercises, with a supplement of selections from the Qur'ān, fables, modern journals, examples of letters, etc. English–Arabic and Arabic–English vocabularies and a Key to the exercises are appended. However, probably the most widely used grammar in Britain today is J. A. Haywood and H. M. Nahmad's *A new Arabic grammar of the written language* (London, Lund Humphries, 1962. Key, 1964. ix, 687 pp. £2.50; Key. £1). This was designed to replace the 6th ed. of Thatcher by modernising content and simplifying grammatical language, and though it does not quite come up to the standard of the original, it has some extremely useful sections, such as the chapter 'How to use an Arabic dictionary'. It has a good selection of pieces from classical and modern authors, and appendices on colloquial Arabic dialects and a guide to further study.

b. Modern Arabic (*see also* Recorded and Audio-visual aids.)

An excellent grammar of the traditional type is D. Cowan's *An introduction to modern literary Arabic* (Cambridge, University Press, 1958; reprinted 1975. xi, 205 pp. £2.70 [paperback ed.]). It can be used as a self-study course, and its 25 lessons, consisting of grammatical notes, examples, exercises and translations, are designed to lay the groundwork for a study of either classical or modern written Arabic. The Middle East Centre for Arabic Studies in Shemlan, Lebanon has produced *The MECAS grammar of modern literary Arabic* (Beirut, Khayat's, 1965. xviii, 264 pp.). Written for the Centre's courses (which include students of several different nationalities) the Centre has to avoid grammatical terms which would have to be explained before they were understood. The vocabulary in the book is closely related to the Centre's *Selected word list of modern literary Arabic* (Beirut, Khayat's, n.d.) and their reader *The way prepared* (Beirut, Khayat's, 1962) and the grammar should be used in conjunction with these two. It is not suitable for self-study. One very useful little book for people working on their own who want a simple reading knowledge as a means of getting at the literature in their own subject is A. F. L. Beeston's *Written Arabic: an approach to the basic structures* (Cambridge, University Press, 1968; reprinted 1975. 116 pp. £2.25 [paperback ed.]). An all-too-rare feature is the oversized Arabic script used in the initial chapters to help the beginner, but the fact that the book has no exercises (to encourage the student to get on to his desired reading as soon as possible) means that a good deal of supplementation is required to make up a complete course. A work on a much larger scale, which was used quite extensively at one time is J. Kapliwatsky's *Arabic language and grammar* (Jerusalem, Rubin Mass. Vol. 1 (12th ed.). 1974. iv, 168 pp. £3.50; vol. 2 (7th ed.). 1975. 151 pp. £2.50; vol. 3 (4th ed.). 1963. 207 pp.; £2.75; vol. 4 (4th ed.) 1968, 224 pp. £3.50), which has useful verb tables and an extensive vocabulary.

c. **Dialects** (*See also* Recorded and Audio-visual aids.)

Chad. There is little material available apart from S. Abu Absi and A. Sinaud's *Basic Chad Arabic* (Bloomington, Indiana, The Intensive Language Training Center, 1969. 2 v.) Volume 1 (v, 49 pp.) of this is devoted to what the authors call the Pre-speech phase, in which the lessons are divided into Notes (containing brief grammatical details with illustrations) and Comprehension, which involves listening to an instructor or tape and then writing down the details asked for. Volume 2 (iv, 239 pp.), the Active phase, concentrates on dialogues and texts.

Egypt. T. F. Mitchell's *An introduction to Egyptian colloquial Arabic* (London, O.U.P., 1956. xii, 285 pp.) is best used with an instructor. Although written with oil company employees in mind, it adequately fulfils the vocabulary needs of the general reader. The work is divided into two parts, part one consisting of 35 lessons with exercises, part two of 33 texts, of which nine are directly concerned with the petroleum industry. There are appendices on Greetings and Exclamations and oaths, and Arabic–English and English–Arabic vocabularies. A work with a rather different approach is S. A. Hanna and N. Greis' *Beginning Arabic – a linguistic approach: from cultivated Cairene to formal literary Arabic* (2nd rev. ed. Leiden, E. J. Brill, 1972. x,

296 pp.) in which Cairo Arabic is taught as a first stage in learning spoken or written, literary or classical Arabic.

Gulf. Until recently a neglected area of Arabic dialect studies, becoming more prominent with the growth of outside commercial interests in the region. A new book taking advantage of the growing interest in the Gulf is Hamdi A. Qafisheh's *A basic course in Gulf Arabic* (Tucson, University of Arizona Press/Beirut, Librairie du Liban, 1975. xxii, 482 pp. £12.25). Based on the Abu Dhabi dialect as modified by the dialects of Bahrain and Qatar, it is designed for use in the United Arab Emirates, Qatar, Bahrain and Kuwait, and has 42 lessons, each consisting of text, translation, vocabulary, grammar and drills.

Iraq. R. J. McCarthy and F. Raffouli's *Spoken Arabic of Baghdad* (Publications of the Oriental Institute of Al-Hikma University, Linguistic series, 1 and 2; Beirut, Librairie Orientale, 1964–65. 2 v.) is unusual in that it includes Arabic script as well as transcription of exercises and texts, not normally found in a dialect grammar. Vol. 1 (xxxvi, 548 pp. £Leb.16) contains the grammar and exercises; vol. 2 (xxviii, 571 pp. £Leb.18) is a useful collection of texts with translations and notes.

Malta. Apart from Aquilina's *Teach yourself Maltese* (*see* Self study courses) there is E. F. Sutcliffe's *A grammar of the Maltese language with chrestomathy and vocabulary* (London, O.U.P., 1936. xvi, 282 pp.) Phonology and syntax are covered in nine chapters; the remainder of the book is devoted to a chrestomathy of selections from religious literature, proverbs, secular literature and examples of epistolatory style.

Palestine. A useful book is F. A. Rice and M. F. Sa'id's *Eastern Arabic: an introduction to the spoken Arabic of Palestine, Syria and Lebanon* (Beirut, Khayat's, 1960. xxvi, 400 pp.), first issued under the title *Jerusalem Arabic*. The 30 units in the work have sections of pattern sentences, structure sentences, alternative expressions and grammar; there is also information on greetings, telling the time, etc., drills and pronunciation practice and vocabularies.

Sudan. The available material here is rather outdated, reliance still being placed on works such as J. Spencer Trimingham's *Sudan colloquial Arabic* (2nd ed. London, O.U.P., 1946. vi, 176 pp.). Originally written for the needs of government officials and missionaries, it is based on the Omdurman dialect, with some Gezira dialectal material. It is divided into two parts: part 1 consists of 33 lessons with texts, facing-page translations and grammar (no exercises); part 2 has conversations and vocabulary and dialectal material.

Syria. An intensive course which was originally prepared for use in the US Foreign Service Institute is C. A. Ferguson and M. Ani's *Damascus Arabic* (2nd printing. Washington, D.C., Center for Applied Linguistics, 1965. viii, 313 pp.). The 29 units in the book, which include sections on pronunciation, analysis and topics for free conversation deal with such practical topics as 'In a shop', 'Renting a house' etc. *See also* Rice and Sa'id under 'Palestine'.

Tunisia. The *Tunisian Arabic basic course*, I and II, by P. L. Inglefield, K. Ben Hamza and T. Abida (Bloomington, Indiana University, 1970. 366 pp.) has dialogues, grammar notes and exercises in 71 lessons, with some reading passages.

SELF-STUDY COURSES

Apart from those works listed in the general 'Grammars' section and in 'Recorded and audio-visual aids' which can be used for self-study, there are three books in the 'Teach yourself' series which can be mentioned. A. S. Tritton's *Teach yourself Arabic* (London, English Universities Press, 1943; reimpression 1975. 296 pp. £1, paperback) is an adequate though not highly recommended course of 36 lessons, each consisting of grammatical notes, vocabulary and exercises. T. F. Mitchell's *Colloquial Arabic: the living language of Egypt* (London, English Universities Press, 1962; reimpression 1975. 240 pp. £0.50, paperback) has sections on the linguistic background and hints on pronunciation, with some useful sentences and vocabulary, though it has no exercises. J. Aquilina's *Teach yourself Maltese* (London, English Universities Press, 1965; reimpression 1973. x, 240 pp. £0.50, paperback) is divided into three parts: sounds and letters; grammar (morphology); the verb. Exercises are included.

REFERENCE GRAMMARS

i. *General*

The standard work is W. Wright's *A grammar of the Arabic language* translated from the German of Caspari and edited with numerous additions and corrections. 3rd ed. rev. by W. Robertson Smith and M. J. de Goeje (reissued with corrections by A. A. Bevan) (Cambridge, University Press, 1933, reprinted 1967, and issued as one paperback volume the same year; reprinted 1975. ix, 317, xx, 450 pp. £5, paperback). Another favoured reference grammar is M. S. Howell's *A grammar of the classical Arabic language* (4 v. in 7. Allahabad, Govt. Press, 1886–1911; reprinted Amsterdam, 1973; Beirut, 1975). Both are based on grammatical usages of classical Arab authors.

A desire to provide students with a simple comprehensive treatment of the present-day literary language, when the only available reference grammars were on medieval Arabic, has led to the production of V. Cantarino's *Syntax of modern Arabic prose* (Oriental series, 4; Bloomington, Asian Studies Research Institute, 1974–.). Of the three volumes projected, only Vol. 1 (xvi, 168 pp. £6.60) has so far appeared.[1] This deals with the simple sentence, and is divided into sections on the nominal sentence, verbal sentence, negative particles and interrogative sentences.

There are no good modern grammars in Arabic, reliance still being placed on the classical treatises of early Arab grammarians like Sībawaihi and Zamakhsharī. Good editions of the works of these two are 'Amr b. 'Uthmān Sībawaihi: *Kitāb Sī-bawaihi; Le livre de Sibawaihi, traité de grammaire arabe*. Texte arabe publié par H. Derenbourg (2 v. Paris, Imprimerie Nationale, 1881–89. Vol. 1: xliv, 460 pp.; vol. 2: ii, 497 pp.) and Maḥmūd b. 'Umar al-Zamakhsharī: *al-Mufaṣṣal, opus de re grammaticum*, ad fidem codicum manu scriptorum edidit J. P. Broch (Christianiae, 1859. iv, 230 pp.).

[1] Vols. 2 and 3 were published in 1975.

ii. *Dialects*

Most of the dialect reference grammars that have been produced have appeared as volumes in a series published by Georgetown University Press. All present an outline of the phonology, morphology and syntax of the language, and like the whole Georgetown programme, they are orientated towards the educated American who is a layman in linguistic matters. The grammars in question are M. W. Cowell's *A reference grammar of Syrian Arabic* (Washington, D.C., Georgetown University Press, 1964. 576 pp. Georgetown Arabic series, 7. $6.50), W. M. Erwin's *A short reference grammar of Iraqi Arabic* (1963. 392 pp. Georgetown Arabic series, 4. $5) and R. S. Harrell's *A short reference grammar of Moroccan Arabic* (1962. xxiii, 263 pp. Georgetown Arabic series, 1. $4.50). Tapes of the phonology sections alone of these are available from the Publication Dept., School of Languages and Linguistics, Georgetown University, Washington, D.C. 20007. Apart from these, there is T. M. Johnstone's scholarly *Eastern Arabian dialect studies* (London, O.U.P., 1967. xxxii, 268 pp. London Oriental series, 17. £6) which covers the phonology, morphology and syntax of the dialects of Kuwait, Bahrain, Qatar and the Trucial Coast, and includes texts in transcription and translation, with comments and notes.

Phonology and Script (*See also* Recorded and Audio-visual aids.) Two carefully produced books on the subject are D. A. Abdo and S. N. Hilu's *Arabic writing and sound system* (Beirut, Ras Beirut, 1968. xii, 126 pp.) and S. A. Hanna and N. Greis's *Writing Arabic – a linguistic approach; from sounds to script* (2nd rev. ed. Leiden, E. J. Brill, 1972. x, 142 pp.). The Abdo and Hilu introduces writing and sound simultaneously, with some information on the basic structures of the language, and has exercises in reading, writing and pronunciation. The Hanna and Greis (a companion volume to their *Writing Arabic – a linguistic approach: from cultivated Cairene to formal literary Arabic*, q.v.) is intended to relate Arabic writing to Arabic sounds in a graded manner, and incorporates frames and diagrams which have been used with students in a language laboratory. It also includes several samples of writing styles.

READERS & CHRESTOMATHIES

i. *Classical*

There are two standard Classical Arabic chrestomathies, both of which have been in use for some decades. R. E. Brünnow and A. Fischer's *Arabische Chrestomathie* (9th ed. (Lehrbücher für das Studium der orientalischen Sprache, 3). Leipzig, Verlag Enzyklopädie, 1966. 168, 183 pp. DM12.) has selections from the Qur'ān and other classical prose works, with a glossary and extensive notes. T. Nöldeke's *Delectus veterum carminum arabicorum*. Glossarium confecit A. Muller (3. unveränderte Auflage. Wiesbaden, Otto Harrassowitz, 1961. 254 pp. DM26) has a very similar layout to Brünnow and Fischer, except that the extracts are mainly poetical. All notes are in Latin. On a more elementary level, and for readers with no German or Latin, there is M. C. Lyons' *An elementary classical Arabic reader* (Cambridge, University Press, 1962. viii, 237 pp.) which consists of pieces of relatively straightforward narrative prose, sometimes adapted, and poems or fragments of poems. The texts, all fully vowelled, cover only pages 1–77; the remainder of the book is taken up by the glossary and notes.

ii. *Modern*

The *Contemporary Arabic readers*, edited by E. McCarus and others (Ann Arbor, University of Michigan, 1962–66) is a useful series which progresses in difficulty from one volume to the next, though each can be used independently, and all assume a basic knowledge of modern Arabic grammar. Vol. 2: *Arabic essays* (Pt. 1: Texts, vi, 78 pp.; pt. 2: Notes and glossaries, iv, 208 pp.) has 20 texts by famous modern writers, of which only 15 are glossed: here, as in the other volumes, students are expected to be familiar with J. M. Landau's *A word count of modern Arabic prose* (Washington, D.C., American Council of Learned Societies, 1959). Vol. 3. *Formal Arabic* (Pt. 1: Texts. vii, 118 pp.; pt. 2: Notes and glossaries. iv, 219 pp. $7.00) covers the language of documents and formal address. Vol. 4: *Short stories* (Pt. 1: Texts. xiii, 93 pp.; pt. 2: Notes and glossaries. iv, 274 pp. $7.50) includes ten short stories and a play, and vol. 5: *Modern Arabic poetry* (Pt. 1: Texts. xiii, 108

pp.; 2: Notes and glossaries. iv, 308 pp. $7.50) has selections
from 31 authors, with texts vocalised as in the originals. On a
smaller scale, there is C. Rabin's *Arabic reader*. 2nd ed. rev. by
H. Nahmad (London, Lund Humphries, 1962. viii, 175 pp. £1)
which has 31 modern prose passages with vocabulary and
extensive notes, and the Middle East Centre for Arabic Studies'
The way prepared (Beirut, Khayat's, 1962. ii, 82 pp.), the
vocabulary for which is based on a list of 3,000 words drawn up
for use in MECAS based on the frequency of each word in
Arabic newspapers, periodicals and books. It has ten sections of
300 words each, containing short passages on different topics.
On a more advanced level, there is F. J. Ziadeh's *A reader in
modern literary Arabic* (Princeton, N. J., Princeton University
Press, 1964. xii, 426 pp.), which has prose passages from fiction
and non-fiction, with notes and exercises, and indexes of idioms
and set phrases and grammatical points; W. M. Brinner and M.
A. Khouri's *Readings in modern Arabic literature*. Pt. 1: *The
short story and the novel* (Leiden, E. J. Brill, 1971. xii, 456 pp.
Gld. 16), designed for third year students and including selections from different generations of writers, with biographical
notes and detailed vocabulary lists; and S. A. Hanna and N.
Greis's *Arabic reading lessons: second level* (Salt Lake City,
Middle East Center, University of Utah, 1964. 195 pp.) with
texts, short stories, grammatical notes and exercises. For
newspaper Arabic, volume 1 of the *Contemporary Arabic
readers* mentioned above: *Newspaper Arabic* (1962. viii, 280 pp.
$4.50) is designed to complement a basic course, and consists of
classroom exercises. Tapes of the preparatory sentences and
texts are available on 22 reels ($7\frac{1}{2}$ ips) at $1.00 dubbing fee per
reel, obtainable from the Language Laboratory, University of
Michigan, 1401, Mason Hall, Ann Arbor, Michigan 48104.
Another reader of newspaper Arabic, but with no notes or exercises, is H. Nahmad's *From the Arabic press: a language reader
in economic and social affairs* (London, Lund Humphries, 1970.
135 pp. £1.50, paperback) which is also intended to be a guide
to Arab progress in social and economic fields during the years
1957–67. On the more technical side, there is M. Mansoor's
Legal and documentary Arabic reader (2 v. Leiden, E. J. Brill,
1965. Vol. 1: xxii, 300 pp.; vol. 2: viii, 277 pp., £4.90 per vol.)

and V. Daykin's *Technical Arabic* (London, Lund Humphries, 1972. 131 pp. £2.75, paperback), a scientific and technical reader having 55 texts with translations and vocabulary.

RECORDED & AUDIO-VISUAL AIDS

i. General

The most extensive course, covering the sounds, writing systems and basic structures of the modern language is *Elementary modern standard Arabic*, by P. F. Abboud and others (Ann Arbor, University of Michigan, 1968. 580 pp. Tapes. *Writing supplement*, 28 pp. Text and supplement $6. Tapes are available from the University of Michigan, Audio-Visual Center, Tape Duplication Service, 416 Fourth St., Ann Arbor, Michigan 48103). Lessons consist of text, vocabulary, grammar and drills, those drills recorded on tape not being written out in the book. There are also appendices of verb tables, days and months, proper nouns and a glossary. The course can be followed by P. F. Abboud and others' *Modern standard Arabic, intermediate level* (Ann Arbor, Center for Near Eastern and North African Studies, University of Michigan, 1971. Pt. 1: 280 pp.; pt. 2: 264 pp.; pt. 3: 272 pp. $9. Tapes to accompany textbook, from Director, Languages Laboratory, 1401 Mason Hall, Ann Arbor, Michigan 48108). An attempt to introduce the student to modern newspaper Arabic is provided by F. J. Ziadeh and R. B. Winder in their *An introduction to modern Arabic* (Princeton, University Press/London, O.U.P., 1957. xii, 298 pp. Records and tapes. Text: £4.35). Lessons consist of an illustrated text, grammatical analysis, practice text and exercises. Both grammar and exercises need supplementation from other sources, but the appendices are very useful, particularly 'Paradigms': tables fully conjugating the 12 types of verb in all their derived forms, and 'Verbs and their prepositions' indicating which verb takes one or more prepositions. A new work (not seen) has been produced by L. J. McLoughlin, Director of Studies of the Middle East Centre for Arabic Studies, Shemlan, Lebanon: *A course in colloquial Arabic* (Beirut, Librairie du Liban, 1974. 149 pp. and 2 tapes) and Linguaphone has a new

Literary Arabic course projected which they hope to bring out in May, 1976.

ii. Dialects

a. **Algeria**. The Linguaphone course in Algerian Arabic, recorded largely by a team of announcers in the Arabic Service of French radio aims to give a good basic vocabulary and an insight into the cultural background of the country by means of descriptive monologues and dialogues. The set consists of two textbooks with 16 records, and costs £49.50, which includes enrolment in their Advisory Correspondence Service.

b. **Egypt**. The Linguaphone course, recorded some time ago, includes a special Sounds record for mastering the sounds of Egyptian Arabic. In addition to the textbooks of transliterated and translated material, there is a third book giving the Arabic characters. The complete set comprises 16 records or two cassettes with the three textbooks, and costs £49.50, including enrolment in the Advisory Correspondence Service. A work to be used with an instructor is W. Lehn and P. F. Abboud's *Beginning Cairo Arabic* (Preliminary ed. University of Texas Middle East Center, 1965. 298 pp. Tapes. $7.50 for text) which is designed to give speech practice.

c. **Gulf**. There is available (not seen) a course on the language of Saudi Arabia and the Gulf, consisting of a textbook and four cassettes published recently by Osman Arabic Centre, London for £35.

d. **Iraq**. The most useful work is W. M. Erwin's *A basic course in Iraqi Arabic* (Georgetown Arabic series, 11; Washington, D.C., Georgetown University Press, 1969. xxii, 389 pp. Tapes. Text: $6) which is designed for use with an instructor and has a good selection of dialogues and drills. Tapes are available from Publications Department, School of Languages and Linguistics, Georgetown University, Washington, D.C. 20007. Of M. Y. Van Wagoner's *Spoken Iraqi Arabic* (2 v. New York, Henry Holt & Co., 1949–58) only vol. 1 (x, 220 pp. $7, paperback; cassette course $70, records $55) comprising 13 units with practices, guide to pronunciation, analysis and conversation, is complete: vol. 2 (unpaginated) was published with some chapters not written and others in draft only. A key to the exercises was published in 1960.

e. **Morocco**. *A basic course in Moroccan Arabic*, by R. S. Harrell and others (Georgetown Arabic series, 8; Washington, D.C., Georgetown University Press, 1965. xiv, 395 pp. Text: $6) provides a thorough introductory course in the language. Vocabulary has been restricted to 650 basic entries, which is sufficient however for the 97 simple conversations in a variety of social situations which are included in the book. Recordings to accompany the lessons and pronunciation drills are available in either a set of 37 5″ reels of magnetic tape ($100) or a set of 19 C.60 cassettes ($60) and can be ordered from the Publications Department, School of Languages and Linguistics, Georgetown University, Washington D.C. 20007. Also good, and with a wider range of vocabulary, are two books by E. T. Abdel-Massih: *An introduction to Moroccan Arabic* (Ann Arbor, Michigan University, Center for Near Eastern and North African Studies, 1973. xix, 438 pp. Tapes) and *Advanced Moroccan Arabic* (also published by the Center for Near Eastern and North African Studies, 1974. xii, 244 pp. Tapes available for pt. 2: texts).

f. **Syria**. The National Audiovisual Center of the Foreign Service Institute, Dept. of State, Washington, D.C. has produced *Levantine Arabic: introduction to pronunciation* (not seen) which includes 19 reels of tapes ($53) or ten cassettes ($32.50) with textbook ($1). Text and tapes can be ordered from Sales Branch, National Audiovisual Center, Washington, D.C. 20409.

g. **Tunisia**. A 12-week intensive course is provided by R. J. Scholes and T. Abida's *Spoken Tunisian Arabic* (Preliminary ed. Bloomington, Indiana University, Intensive Language Training Center, 1966. 2 v. and tapes). (Not seen.)

iii. **Phonology and Script**

A clearly set out book which can be used for individual self-instruction is E. N. McCarus and R. Rammuny's *A programmed course in modern literary Arabic: phonology and script* (Ann Arbor, University of Michigan, Center for Research and Language Behaviour, 1970. 202 pp. Text: $3). It is not a complete course in itself, but designed for use with an elementary textbook. Tapes for the phonology sections are available at a cost of $15 for 3¾ ips and $24 for 7½ ips and can be ordered from the Director, Language Laboratory, 1401 Mason Hall, University of Michigan, Ann Arbor, Michigan 48108. There is also *Phonology and script of literary Arabic*, by S. H. Al-Ani and J. Y. Shammas (Montreal, McGill University, Institute of Islamic Studies, 1967. vii, 118 pp. Tapes) which includes Arabic script in a variety of hands to accustom readers to differences in style, and an appendix of examples of different scripts.

DICTIONARIES

1. Dictionaries: General, bilingual

a. *Arabic–English*

The authoritative dictionary of the classical language is E. W. Lane's *Arabic–English lexicon*. Vol. 1, pts. 1–8 (all published) (London, 1863–93; reprinted New York, F. Ungar, 1955–56 and Beirut, Librairie du Liban, 1968. 3,064 pp. *in toto.* $169.95). Drawn from the classical Arab grammarians, it gives the meanings of words in the form of examples from these, together with synonyms and variant readings. On a smaller scale, and immensely useful for the study of early texts, J. G. Hava's *Arabic–English dictionary for the use of students* (Beirut, Catholic Press, 1951, reprinted 1968. vii, 915 pp. £Leb.15) is a mine of obscure terms and expressions.

For modern Arabic, the standard work is Hans Wehr's *A dictionary of modern written Arabic*, trans. and ed. by J. Milton Cowan (3rd printing. Wiesbaden, Harrassowitz, 1971. xvii, 1,110 pp. £17.50), a really excellent dictionary. For those not wishing to spend quite so much, a good, cheap substitute is Maan Z. Madina's *Arabic–English dictionary of the modern literary language* (New York, Pocket Books, 1973. 791 pp. £1.50, paperback). Another Arabic–English dictionary, which has been in use for a number of years, is *Elias' modern dictionary, Arabic–English* by E. A. Elias (9th ed. Cairo, Elias, 1962, reprinted 1972. 872 pp. £6) which is illustrated.

b. *English–Arabic*

Regrettably, there is no English–Arabic dictionary which comes up to the standard of Wehr. Another problem for westerners is posed by the fact that most English–Arabic dictionaries are aimed primarily at Arab students learning English. N. Doniach's *The Oxford English–Arabic dictionary of current usage* (Oxford, Clarendon Press, 1972. xii, 1,392 pp. £12) has tried to rectify this, but can be criticised for containing too many explanations of what the English words mean, rather than giving equivalents. A well-planned, illustrated dictionary, which contains nearly 40,000 entries of words in contemporary English and American usage, is H. S. Karmi's *Al Manar, an English–Arabic dictionary* (London, Longmans/Beirut, Librairie du Liban, 1970; reprinted 1975. xiv, 904 pp. £3). A larger work is Munir Ba'albaki's *Al-Mawrid; a modern English–Arabic dictionary* (Beirut, Dār al-'Ilm lil-Malā'yīn, 1970. 1,090 pp.) which is printed in very small type. It gives alternative English/American spellings, and includes a number of technical terms and colloquialisms. Both Karmi and Ba'albaki are designed for Arab readers, as is E. A. Elias' *Elias' modern dictionary, English–Arabic* (18th ed. Cairo, Elias, 1972. 816 pp.) and shares the common drawback that shades of meaning in the Arabic equivalents are often not sufficiently well explained, and cross-checking with a good Arabic–English dictionary is necessary. Aimed at foreign readers, and useful as a basic wordlist, is the Middle East Centre for Arab Studies' *A selected word list of modern literary Arabic* (Beirut, Khayat's, 1959. 162 pp.) which is intended to comprise the intelligent layman's vocabulary, and includes a gazetteer of Arabic names of continents, countries and towns.

c. *Languages other than English*

There are some very good dictionaries of Arabic with a language other than English. In French, a major work appearing in fascicules is the *Dictionnaire arabe–français–anglais (langue classique et moderne)* by R. Blachère and others (Paris, G. P. Maisonneuve, 1964–) which as a trilingual dictionary will be of equal value to English readers. Other important French works

are A. de Biberstein Kazimirski's *Dictionnaire arabe–français,
contenant toutes les racines de la langue arabe, leurs dérivés,
tant dans l'idiome vulgaire que dans l'idiome littéral, ainsi que
les dialectes d'Alger et de Maroc* (2v. Paris, 1860; reprinted
Beirut, Librairie du Liban, 1971. xvi, 3,032 pp. $54.55) where
each word is fully vowelled, and Jean-Baptiste Belot's *Dictionnaire français–arabe*. Nouvelle éd. entièrement refondue sous la
direction de R. P. R. Nakhla (3rd ed. Beirut, Imprimerie
Catholique, 1970. v, 745 pp.). In German, a scholarly new dictionary is the *Deutsch–arabisches Wörterbuch*, by G. Schregle
and others (Wiesbaden, Otto Harrassowitz, 1974. xii, vii, 1,472
pp. DM268), while in Russian a work constructed along the
same lines as Wehr's dictionary is K. K. Baranov's
Arabsko–russkiĭ slovar' (Moscow, Gosudarstvennoe Izd.
inostrannykh i Natsional'nykh Slovareĭ, 1958).

ii. Dictionaries: General, monolingual

Of the works produced by classical Arab authors, two in particular deserve mention. The first of these is Muḥammad b.
Mukarram Ibn Manẓūr's Monumental *Lisān al-'Arab* (New ed.
15v. Beirut, 1968) written in the 13th century, which is arranged
in rhyme order according to final radical, and discusses variant
spellings and vocalisation. A modernised and shortened version,
commissioned by the Academies in Cairo, Damascus and
Baghdad, and the universities in Syria and Rabat has been
produced the *Lisan al-'Arab al-muḥiṭ*, ed. by Yūsuf Khaiyāṭ
and Nadīm Mir'ashlī (3v. Beirut, Dār Lisān al- 'Arab, 1970).
The second work is Muḥammad Murtaḍā al-Zabīdī's *Tāj al-
'arūs min jawāhir al-qāmūs* (Al-turāth al-'arabī, 16; 14v.
Kuwait, Govt. Press, 1965–72) an 18th century commentary on
an earlier work (Fīrūzābādī's *Qāmūs*) containing about 120,000
entries.

Of 20th century monolingual works, there is the *Munjid al-
ṭullāb*, revised by Fu'ād Afrām al-Bustānī (12th ed. Beirut, Dār
al-Mashriq, 1971. 690 pp. £Leb.6) designed for students, and its
larger companion *al-Munjid fī al-lugha wal-a'lām* (11th ed.
Beirut, Dār al-Mashriq, 1973. xviii, 800 pp., plus maps. £10).
Also good is a recent illustrated dictionary produced by the

Academy of the Arabic Language in Cairo, *al-Mu'jam al-wasīt*, ed. by Ibrāhīm Anīs and others (2nd ed. 2v. Cairo, 1972–73. 1,067 pp.).

iii. Dictionaries: Special and technical

There are scores of Arabic technical dictionaries, covering everything from Agriculture to Zoology. Good multi-subject dictionaries are Ahmad al-Khatib's *A new dictionary of scientific and technical terms, English–Arabic* (Beirut, Librairie du Liban, 1971. xv, 751 pp. £11.93) an illustrated work containing over 60,000 terms from all branches of science and technology, and Jirwān Sābiq's *Majama' al-lughāt: qāmūs al-iqtiṣād, al-ḥuqūq, al-tarbīya wal-ta'līm* ... (Beirut, The author, 1971. 1,189 pp.) a trilingual dictionary (Arabic–French–English, French–English–Arabic and English–French–Arabic) which covers economics, law, sociology, statistics, political and diplomatic sciences. The Academy of the Arabic Language in Cairo's *Majmū'at al-muṣṭalaḥāt al-'ilmīya wal-fannīya allatī aqrahā al-Majma'* (4v. Cairo, 1957–62), a dictionary of technical terms collected by the Academy, covers an impressive range of subjects, but is difficult to use: some sections are French–Arabic, some French–Arabic–English, some English–Arabic and some monolingual. All notes are in Arabic.

For dictionaries of synonyms, there is Ibrāhīm al-Yāzijī's *Nuj'at al-rā'id wa shir'at al-wārid fī al-mutarādif wal-mutawārid* (Beirut, Librairie du Liban, 1970. 555 pp. $15.90) and Rufā'īl Nakhla's *al-Munjid fī al-mutarādif wal-mutajānisāt* (2nd ed. Beirut, Catholic Press, 1969. 265 pp.); for language errors, Muhammad al-'Adnānī's *Mu'jam al-akhṭā' al-shā'i'a* (Beirut, Librairie du Liban, 1973. 368 pp. $11.35) quotes classical texts as evidence of correct usage. For grammatical terms, a dictionary where the English equivalents have been taken from the grammars of Howell and Wright (q.v.) is P. Cachia's *The monitor: a dictionary of Arabic grammatical terms, Arabic–English and English–Arabic* (London, Longmans/Beirut, Librairie du Liban, 1974. 88 pp. (English) and 110 pp. (Arabic) £2.25). A further type of specialist dictionary which ought to be mentioned is dictionaries of the

Qur'ān. There is no outstanding Qur'ānic dictionary, and until one appears reliance will have to be placed on J. Penrice's *A dictionary and glossary of the Ḳor-ān* (London, Henry King, 1873, reprinted London, Curzon Press, 1971, with introduction by R. B. Serjeant. viii, 166 pp. £3.75) which is based on the Qur'ān text published by Flügel and printed at Leipzig in 1834, and F. Dieterici's *Arabisch–Deutsches Handwörterbuch zum Koran und Thier und Mensch von dem König der Genien* (2nd rev. ed. Leipzig, J. C. Hinrichs, 1894).

iv. **Dictionaries: Dialects**

a. **Algeria.** A good dictionary, but which suffers from not being printed but photographed manuscript in a variety of hands, is M. Beaussier's *Dictionnaire pratique arabe–français, contenant tous les mots employés dans l'arabe parlé en Algérie et en Tunisie.* Nouvelle éd. rev. par M. Ben Cheneb (Algiers, La Maison des Livres, 1958. viii, 1,093 pp.) with A. Lentin's *Supplément au Dictionnaire pratique arabe–français de Marcelin Beaussier* (Algiers, La Maison des Livres, 1959. vii, 312). Both were published first in the nineteenth century, like Kazimirski (see p. 280) and a good modern dictionary is urgently needed.

b. **Arabia and the Gulf.** Here too a good up-to-date dictionary is lacking, the only works available being the meticulously-researched glossaries of the Comte de Landberg: *Glossaire de la langue des bédouins 'Anazeh,* publié par K. V. Zetterstée (ppsala, Lundequist, 1940. vi, 105 pp. Uppsala Universitets Årsskrift 1940–2) and the enormous *Glossaire datînois* (3v. Leiden, E. J. Brill, 1920–42. liv, 2,976 pp. 414 Gld.), neither of which would help the student or businessman looking for a modern, all-purpose dictionary of the colloquial language. There is a fairly recent monolingual dictionary: Jalāl al-Ḥanafi's *Muʿjam al-alfāẓ al-kuwaitīya* (Baghdad, Matba at As ad, 1964. 424 pp.) on the dialect of Kuwait, containing about 2,500 words with notes as to their meanings, origins and uses.

c. **Egypt.** A well used dictionary, intended for those with only a slight knowledge of Arabic grammar, is S. Spiro's *Arabic–English dictionary of the modern Arabic of Egypt* (2nd ed. Cairo, 1923. xx, 660 pp.), in which the arrangement is purely alphabetical, not by radical. The dictionary was reprinted (Beirut, Librairie du Liban, 1973. $15.90) along with the 3rd ed. (1929) of the author's *An English–Arabic vocabulary of the modern and colloquial Arabic of Egypt*, with a new preface by P. Cachia (Beirut, Librairie du Liban, 1974. viii, 586 pp. $11.80). A monolingual dictionary on the Egyptian dialect is 'Abd al-Mun'im Saiyid 'Abd al-'Āl's *Mu'jam al-alfāẓ al-'āmmīya al-miṣrīya ḏhāt al-uṣūl al-'arabīya* (Cairo, Maktabat al-Nahḍa al-Misrīya, 1971. 276 pp.).

d. **Iraq**. The two basic dictionaries, both entirely in transliteration, are *A dictionary of Iraqi Arabic, English–Arabic*, by B. E. Clarity and others (Washington, D.C., Georgetown University Press, 1964. 202 pp. Georgetown Arabic series, 6. $5) and D. R. Woodhead and W. Beene's *A dictionary of Iraqi Arabic, Arabic–English* (Washington, D.C., Georgetown University Press, 1967. xiii, 509 pp. Georgetown Arabic series, 10. $6). As in all the Georgetown dictionaries, technical terms have been avoided where possible. Only the first two letters of the alphabet have so far been covered by Jalāl al-Ḥanafī's monolingual dictionary of the Baghdadi dialect *Mu'jam al-lugha al-āmmīya al-baghdādīya* (Baghdad, Maṭba'at al-'Ānī, 1963–66. Vol. 1: ii, 434 pp.; vol. 2: 213 pp.).

e. **Lebanon**. A dictionary designed for foreign students learning the Eastern Mediterranean dialects, Raja T. Nasr's *An English–colloquial Arabic dictionary* (Beirut, Librairie du Liban, 1972. viii, 320 pp. $11.35) is up-to-date and convenient to use. Anīs Furaiḥa's *A dictionary of non-classical vocables in the spoken Arabic of Lebanon* (Beirut, American University, 1947; reprinted 1973. Oriental series, 19.) contains about 3,000 words, with meanings and explanations of their origins. Also relevant are Barthélemy and Denizeau (*see* Syria) and Bauer (*see* Palestine).

f. **Malta**. The standard dictionary for Maltese is G. Barbera's *Dizionario maltese–arabo–italiano, con una grammatica comparata arabo–maltese* (4 v. Beirut, Imprimerie Catholique, 1939–40). The Arabic is given in script, and there are numerous cross-references from verbal nouns to roots. There is an index of foreign words included, and one of Arabic words.

g. **Morocco**. There are two Georgetown dictionaries for the area, both entirely in transliteration: *A dictionary of Moroccan Arabic, Arabic–English*, by R. S. Harrell and others (Washington, D.C., Georgetown University Press, 1966. xix, 268 pp. Georgetown Arabic series, 9. $5) and R. S. Harrell and H. Sobelman's *A dictionary of Moroccan Arabic, English–Moroccan* (Washington, D.C., Georgetown University Press, 1963, 228 pp. Georgetown Arabic series, 3. $4). Based on the speech of educated Moroccans from Fez, Rabat and Casablanca, they presuppose a familiarity with basic Moroccan grammatical structure. However, irregular derived words and numerous illustrative sentences are included. There is also the nineteenth century work by Kazimirski (see p. 280).

h. **Palestine**. Y. Elihai's *Dictionnaire de l'arabe parlé palestinien, français–arabe* (Jerusalem, Imprimerie Yanetz, 1973. 419 pp.) deals principally with the dialects of Nazareth and Jerusalem, and contains about 5,000 current words and idiomatic phrases. Also available is Leonhard Bauer's *Deutsch–Arabischer Wörterbuch der Umgangssprache in Palästina und im Libanon* (2nd rev. ed. Wiesbaden, Otto Harrassowitz, 1957. 421 pp. DM36); and Barthélemy and Denizeau (*see* Syria) includes Jerusalem Arabic.

i. **Sudan and Central Africa**. Previous work on Chad and the Sudan has been made largely obsolete by the appearance of A. Roth-Laly's *Lexique des parlers arabes tchado–soudanais; an Arabic–English–French lexicon of the dialects spoken in the Tchad–Sudan area* (Paris, C.N.R.S., 1969–72. 4 fasc. 545 pp. F 124.90), which is compiled from the combined works of four leading authorities. Words are listed according to the order of the Arabic radicals, then the translation is given in either French or English (depending on which author is quoted), with an indication of any variants recorded by the others. A nicely produced monolingual dictionary is 'Aun al-Sharīf Qāsim's *Qāmūs al-lahja al-'āmmīya fī al-Sūdān* (Khartoum, University, 1972. xvi, 858 pp.).

j. **Syria**. The most extensive work is A. Barthélemy's *Dictionnaire arabe–français (dialectes de Syrie, Alep, Damas, Liban, Jerusalem)* (6 fasc. Paris, Geuthner, 1935–59. 955, 76 pp.) with its supplement by C. Denizeau, *Dictionnaire des parlers arabes*

de Syrie, Liban et Palestine (Paris, G. P. Maisonneuve, 1960.
579 pp. Études arabes et islamiques, Études et documents, 3).
Roots are given in Arabic script, but all derived forms, etc. are
in transliteration. There is also K. Stowasser and M. Ani's *A dictionary of Syrian Arabic, English–Arabic* (Washington, D.C.,
Georgetown University Press, 1964. 281 pp. Georgetown
Arabic series, 5. $5) and previous comments on the Georgetown
dictionaries apply here. An Arabic–English companion volume
was projected, but seems not to have been published.

k. **Tunisia.** Apart from Beaussier and Lentin (*see* Algeria) there
is the *Lexique du parler arabe des Marazig (sud tunisien)* by G.
Boris (Paris, Imprimerie Nationale, 1958. 701 pp. Études arabes
et islamiques, Études et documents, 1) which has catchwords in
Arabic script.

24

JAPANESE

by CHARLES DUNN, B.A., Ph.D.

INTRODUCTION

Apart from the 100 or more millions of Japanese in the homeland, there are sizeable populations in the New World, particularly Brazil, Hawaii and the western seaboard of the USA, who use Japanese, but only in Japan does it fully preserve its independence in face of English and Portuguese. It has an outlier in the language of the Ryūkyū Islands (Okinawa), which is considered as a dialect of Japanese, and its constructions are similar to those of its near neighbour, Korean, and also to those of Mongolian and Turkish, although relations of vocabulary are proving difficult to establish. The learning of Japanese as a foreign language is thus rarely helped by any processes of association, except, for example, that a knowledge of Turkish might facilitate the study of the Japanese verb.

The first problem for the speaker of most European languages when confronting Japanese is how to cope with sentences that terminate with the verb, the form of which incorporates information about time, mood, polarity (positive/negative), and where qualifiers (adjectives, relative clauses) precede the qualified. Pronunciation does not normally cause much trouble, particularly when taught by efficient aural/oral methods, but for those who wish to go beyond the mere ability to converse, which, is after all, of very limited usefulness, since it will not help in the reading of street signs, let alone newspapers or a modern novel or a scientific article, there is the need to learn the two syllabaries (*hiragana* and *katakana*), of 48 signs each, and the 1,800 or so *tōyōkanji* ('currently used Chinese characters') which the Ministry of Information has selected from the thousands which used theoretically to be available since the adoption of the Chinese writing system over a thousand years ago. The Japanese system can confidently be described as the most inefficient in existence in the modern world, since it uses a combination of Chinese characters (*kanji*) (whose form gives a general idea of the meaning, but whose pronunciation depends upon an often arbitrary choice between one, two, or often more Sino–Japanese sounds on the one hand, and a selection of native Japanese readings on the other) with the syllabaries, one of which, *hiragana*, is commonly used to write the particles which indicate the role of a noun, etc., in a sentence, and also the inflexions of a verb, and can be used to represent phonetically whole words if the writer does not choose to use a Chinese character. The other syllabary, *katakana*, is most often used to transcribe foreign words, which is not too simple in itself seeing that the signs, with the sole exception of a final *n*, represent open syllables. It is possible to write Japanese purely phonetically, by using the syllabaries or romanisation, but unfortunately there exist, particularly among the borrowings from Chinese which constitute in Japanese a section of the vocabulary of similar importance to words of Latin and Greek derivation in English, innumerable homophones, the meanings of which can only be differentiated by the use of Chinese characters. The dual nature, Chinese and Japanese, of the vocabulary (not to mention many borrowings from English) makes it large and expressive.

Romanisation exists in two main forms, one of which, known as the Hepburn system, attempts an English representation of the pronunciation of the syllables, and the other, the so-called 'official' system, seeks to reproduce the *kana* syllables phonemically. These two systems coincide to a considerable extent and the differences between them are easily learnt. The Hepburn system is much more widely used than the other, and a slightly modified form (the modification consisting of maintaining the syllabic *n* as such, and not altering it to *m* before *b*, *m*, *p*) has been adopted by the publisher, Kenkyusha, for its dictionaries, and by the British Standards Institution.

Over the last hundred years, a form of the spoken language has become the universal medium for all writing. Before that time, and, in some official styles, until 1945, there were separate

written languages for different purposes, including the purely
literary, as in poetry and novels, and for the comprehension of
all pre-modern texts an ability to handle the appropriate
language is a necessity.

COURSES & GRAMMARS

General. Japanese is only occasionally taught in secondary
education schools outside Japanese-speaking areas, and no
suitable school textbooks are available. GCE examinations,
however, exist, and for these the recommended books are C. J.
Dunn and S. Yanada's *Teach yourself Japanese* (London,
English Universities Press, 1958. vii, 310 pp.) and P. G. O'Neill
and S. Yanada's *An Introduction to written Japanese* (London,
English Universities Press, 1969, 243 pp. £2.35). The former
uses romanised Japanese and teaches virtually all the constructions of the modern style, with a basic vocabulary chosen for its
usefulness, and the second, which presents more or less the same
vocabulary and constructions, teaches the two syllabaries and a
first selection of some 660 *kanji*. It has Japanese text, romanisation and translations, and lists all the *tōyōkanji*; it uses legible
pen-written forms as well as printed ones. A suitable follow-up
to the second of these is P. G. O'Neill's *Essential kanji* (New
York, Tokyo, Weatherhill, 1973. 325 pp. $7.95) which presents
2,000 *kanji*, including the whole of the *tōyōkanji*, in an order
suitable for learning by association, and also acts as a useful dictionary of readings, common compounds, and stroke order, the
last being necessary as a guide to how to write *kanji* and how to
analyse them. M. Pye's *The study of kanji* (Tokyo, Hokuseido,
1971. xi, 305 pp.) covers the same sort of range as *Essential
kanji*, but with more aids to learning. It has considerable
originality of method, and some students find it more attractive
than other textbooks.

It seems that university departments engaged in the teaching
of languages from scratch are rarely satisfied with courses
prepared by other universities. The result is that there has been a
minor proliferation of Japanese courses. The Yale school of
linguistics is represented by E. H. Jorden's *Beginning Japanese*

(New Haven and London, Yale University Press, 1962–63. 2 v. (409; 410 pp.) £10 (£2.20 pbk.) each, which uses romanised Japanese, and contains all the material (exercises, drills, etc.), on a basis of situation dialogues, to equip the learner with the capability of speaking and understanding a wide range of utterance. A related course in writing, H. I. Chaplin and S. E. Martin's *A Manual of Japanese writing* (New Haven and London, Yale University Press, 1967. £15 (£3.75 pbk.) the set) is in three volumes of which vol. 1 (xi, 369 pp.) has explanations and the romanised form of the text, vol. 2 (330 pp.) has the text in Japanese printed forms, and vol. 3 (vi, 378 pp.) has vocabulary and other lists. The number of *kanji* taught comprises only the 881 specified for teaching in schools by the Japanese Ministry of Education. Another course to be recommended is A. Alfonso's *Japanese Language Patterns* (Tokyo, Sophia University, 1971, 1,230 pp.). In contrast to these bulky works, there is the very practical intensive course in the spoken language, *Nihongo no kiso* (Tokyo, Association for Overseas Technical Scholarship, 1973. 188 pp. and charts), which has been prepared for the first instruction of technical trainees. Various supplementary versions of this are published to suit the learner's own language; the English one is subtitled *Foundations of Japanese* (xiv, 113 pp.).

Specialised. Three programmed self-tuition courses teach separate areas of the language. They are all by P. G. O'Neill and are entitled *Japanese kana workbook* (Tokyo and Palo Alto, Kōdansha International, 1967. 128 pp. £0.90), *A programmed course in respect language in modern Japanese* (London, English Universities Press 1966. xi, 142 pp. £1.25) and *A programmed introduction to literary style Japanese* (London School of Oriental and African Studies, 1968. 249 pp. £1.75). The first of these is designed to teach beginners the two syllabaries, the second is in effect an exhaustive study of the processes whereby one expresses levels of politeness vis-à-vis one's interlocutor and the degree of respect to the person spoken about, and the third is a conversion course from modern Japanese into the literary styles of the last thousand years.

Reference grammars. S. E. Martin's *A reference grammar of Japanese* (New Haven and London, Yale University Press, 1975. 1,198 pp., £24) is the standard work in this field. T.

Ikeda's *Classical Japanese grammar illustrated with texts* (Tokyo, The Tōhō Gakkai, 1975. viii, 356 pp.) gives a full account, in English, of the literary language, but does not take it beyond the 11th century. R. A. Miller's *The Japanese language* (Chicago and London, University of Chicago Press, 1967. xix, 428 pp. 25 plates. £7.90) is a historical study, authoritative in parts. G. Sansom's *An historical grammar of Japanese* (Oxford, Clarendon Press, 1946, 347 pp.) is still valuable if used with discretion. J. Jelinek's *Japanese–English grammar dictionary* (Sheffield, University Centre of Japanese Studies, 1974.) is a product of his work on intensive courses in Japanese reading for scientists, but to date only the first volume (A–D. xvi, 127 pp. £4.50) has appeared.

Readers. Two of these, which take the student through a considerable range of styles in the modern language, and form a useful supplement to the other courses, are H. Hibbett and G. Itasaka's *Modern Japanese, a basic reader* (2nd ed. Cambridge Mass., Harvard University Press, 1967. £4) and R. A. Miller's *A Japanese reader (graded lessons in the modern language)* (Rutland, Vt. and Tokyo, Tuttle, 1962. 250 pp. $12.95). The first of these readers is in two volumes, I (ix, 273 pp.) having vocabularies and notes, and II the Japanese texts (306, 129 pp.).

RECORDED MATERIAL

The publisher of Jorden's *Beginning Japanese* sells a full set of tapes to accompany that course and thus makes it completely self-instructive. A set of cassettes is available from the Association of Overseas Technical Scholarship to accompany their *Nihongo no kiso*. Linguaphone's *Japanese Course* offers a good set of recordings, but requires the student to progress at breakneck speed.

DICTIONARIES

The Japanese publishing business is huge, and vast numbers of dictionaries of all sorts are continually being produced. The following lists are therefore highly selective, and based on the author's preferences, which are, however, founded on use, and, he thinks, can be relied upon.

Kanji dictionaries. For the English-speaking student of Japanese wishing to discover the readings of *Kanji* and the compounds in which they are used in Japanese, A. N. Nelson's *The modern reader's Japanese–English character dictionary* (Rev. ed. Rutland, Vt. and Tokyo, Tuttle, 1966. 1,109 pp. £8) is indispensable, at least until his knowledge of Japanese enables him to use Japanese works. An intermediate dictionary, which gives explanatory material in English, and English translations for difficult words and expressions although written mainly in Japanese, is *Gaikokujin no tame no kanji jiten [Dictionary of Chinese characters for Foreigners]* (2nd ed. Tokyo, Agency for Cultural Affairs, 1973. 1,161, 102, 4 pp.).

A Japanese who wishes to look up *kanji* usually has recourse to works which are ostensibly dictionaries of classical Chinese, but which always give Japanese readings and explanations. Near perfection is reached by the mighty 13-volume T. Morohashi: *Dai kanwa jiten* (Tokyo, Daishūkan shoten, 1960.) with its 48,902 *kanji* entries, which even scholars in the Chinese field constantly consult. A handy pocket-sized dictionary, T. Ogawa and others. *Shin jigen* (Tokyo, Kadokawa, 1973. 1,279, 79 pp.), with 9,921 main *kanji* entries, is a reliable source of all the information that the normal reader of Japanese is likely to require.

Kanji are normally arranged in dictionaries in a classification based on a 'radical', i.e. a basic character such as 'wood', 'water', etc., of which there are 215 and of which one at least is to be found in each *kanji*, and the number of extra strokes needed to complete the *kanji*. In fact, some of the old radical components of *kanji* are losing their identity in the new forms now in use, and it is becoming usual to look up *kanji* in lists which are arranged in order of total number of strokes, or lists of readings. Of course, if one knows no readings at all for the *kanji* concerned, one cannot use this method of finding it, but in fact it often happens that when one has a little experience one can make an intelligent guess at a Sino-Japanese reading, seeing that the part of the *kanji* which is not its radical is often its 'phonetic', i.e. it gave the pronunciation in an early form of

Chinese, and often provides a hint at the modern Japanese pronunciation. Every *kanji* dictionary has such lists, which refer to the page on which the *kanji* occurs, or, more often, its serial number in the dictionary.

There are particular problems in reading Japanese personal and place names, which sometimes use apparently arbitrary readings of the *kanji* employed. P. G. O'Neill's *Japanese names* (New York and Tokyo, Weatherhill, 1972. 359 pp. £8.75) is particularly useful for this purpose.

Bilingual dictionaries. Japanese–English and English–Japanese dictionaries, the former using romanised Japanese entries in alphabetical order, are written for the use of Japanese speakers studying English, and so suffer from drawbacks for English users. In particular, the Japanese phrases and sentences which demonstrate the uses of the words concerned are written in the Japanese script, so that a certain standard of attainment is necessary before they can be used. The fullest are K. Masuda's *Kenkyusha's New Japanese–English dictionary* (4th ed. Tokyo, Kenkyusha, 1974. 2,110 pp.) and T. Iwasaki and J. Kawamura's *Kenkyusha's New English–Japanese dictionary* (4th ed. Tokyo, Kenkyusha, 1960. 2,204 pp.). F. J. Daniels's *Basic English writers' Japanese–English wordbook* (Tokyo, Hokuseido, 1969. viii, 699 pp.) has a rather restricted range of entries, but the examples and the many alternative translations (into Basic English) give an excellent insight into the range of meaning of the entries. The order of the romanised entries is that of the *kana* syllabaries.

Monolingual dictionaries. These are sometimes called *kana* dictionaries, because the entries are written in *kana* and arranged in *kana* order. The explanations are written in the normal mixture of *kanji* and *kana*. The new 20-volume *Nihon kokugo jiten* (Tokyo, Shōgakukan, 1975.) will probably replace the old *Daijiten* (Tokyo, Heibonsha, 1934–36. 26 v. Reprinted: 1953–54. 13 v.) which, although dated, was the most valuable of the large dictionaries. The medium format is excellently represented by I. Shinmura's *Kōjien* (2nd ed. Tokyo, Iwanami, 1972. 2,448 pp.), which covers both the old and new usage. Two smaller works, also put out by Iwanami, are, for the old form of the language, S. Ono and others, *Kogo jiten* (Tokyo, Iwanami,

1974, 1,488 pp.), and, for the modern, M. Nishio and others, *Kokugo jiten* (2nd ed. Tokyo, Iwanami, 1974. 1,170 pp.) Even more compact is T. Yamada and H. Tsukishima's *Shinchō kokugo jiten* (Tokyo, Shinchōsha, 1965. 2,170, 76 pp.), which contains both old and new words. *Gaikokujin no tame no kihongo yōrei jiten [Dictionary of basic Japanese usage for foreigners]* (Tokyo, Agency for Cultural Affairs, 1971. 1,122, 188 pp.) uses no English or romanisation and is therefore for fairly advanced students. It does, however, illustrate with simple examples and is potentially of considerable pedagogic value.

Cursive script dictionaries. The *kanji* dictionaries mentioned above require an ability to analyse the *kanji* involved at least into its strokes before it can be looked up. An added difficulty is encountered when one is trying to read documents in cursive script (*sōsho*) and in the special forms of *kana* which often accompany cursive *kanji*. This is a very difficult area for which to prepare dictionaries, and one of the most systematic attempts, which also has some assistance for English readers in that it uses some romanisation and has English explanations, is O. Daniels's *Dictionary of Japanese (sōsho) writing forms* (London, Lund Humphries, 1944. 309, xix, 48 pp.).

Technical dictionaries. The bilingual dictionaries mentioned above have a surprisingly large number of technical terms explained. Of the many specialised bilingual dictionaries which have been appearing over the years, three have been noted as of high quality, J. Fujita's *Kenkyusha's English–Japanese dictionary of trade and industry* (New ed. Tokyo, Kenkyusha, 1970. xv, 1,181 pp.), T. Nagano's *Dictionary of biological terms, English–Japanese, Japanese–English* (Tokyo, Sankyō, 1972. 573 pp.) and *The Oriental Economist's Japanese–English dictionary of economic terms* (Tokyo, Oriental Economist, 1974. 546, 81 pp.).

25

CHINESE

by A. C. Barnes, b.a.

INTRODUCTION

Standard Chinese (i.e. the Mandarin dialects as a whole) is spoken by five hundred million people and is being taught as a matter of Government policy in the non-Mandarin speaking areas of China (roughly, the area south of the Yangse and east of 110° E.).

Structurally, Chinese resembles English: the morphology has been streamlined to about the same extent, and word-order rather than morphology is used to express grammatical relationships. The lexis is almost entirely native and, unlike English, Chinese draws on its own lexical resources, ancient and modern, for the formation of new technical terms. Most words are of two or three syllables, though usually analysable into invariant monosyllabic morphemes (living or dead), hence the old misleading description of Chinese as a 'monosyllabic language'. Phonetically, it presents very few difficulties: the tonal element is far less important than the layman is given to understand and may be ignored with very little loss of intelligibility (it is ignored, for instance, in Chinese shorthand), and, as in English, there is a strong word-stress.

Modern written Chinese, based largely on the spoken language, has come into general use since the First World War, almost entirely superseding the Classical Chinese that had until then been in use for all writing except some fiction. The term 'Classical Chinese' is applied to the language of all Chinese writing of the past two and a half millennia up to the First World War, including the Confucian Classics. Though developing various widely divergent styles, this classical language remained remarkably consistent, especially over the last two millennia. It was abandoned on the pretext of being an inadequate vehicle for twentieth-century ideas, despite the fact that it had proved admirably adaptable to an immense variety of technical and artistic purposes. Though modern written Chinese is largely based on the colloquial so far as its grammar and basic vocabulary are concerned, the inevitable poverty of the existing colloquial dialects has forced modern Chinese writers to fall back on the abundant resources of the Classical language, and even to borrow from Japanese, for creating new terms and even for composing political slogans. And with the spread of literacy and education, this new written language is enriching the spoken language and providing a channel back to life for elements from the ancient written language. This means that one cannot study modern Chinese without paying some attention to the Classical language (richly rewarding in itself), though this may be deferred to a later stage of one's studies. Twentieth–century academic writing is particularly prone to mixed Classical-and-Modern styles, and it is no longer possible to draw a dividing line between the two languages.

A useful first introduction to Chinese for the layman who wishes to gain a general idea of what Chinese is like is:

NEWNHAM, R. *About Chinese*. Penguin Books, 1971 (reprinted 1973). 188 p. £0.65.

Deals with pronunciation, script, grammar. Includes an annotated bibliography of textbooks and dictionaries.

A fuller bibliography is:

YANG, W. L. Y. and YANG, T. S. *A bibliography of the Chinese language*. New York, American Association of Teachers of Chinese Language and Culture, 1966. xiv, 171 p.

Details of a bibliography of dictionaries are given below under 'DICTIONARIES'.

SCRIPT

If the language itself (apart from the completely unfamiliar vocabulary) is relatively easy, the script is a nightmare of complexity and inefficiency and constitutes the principal deterrent to the study of Chinese. It is syllabic, with no word-division, and nowadays written from left to right except for special purposes such as spine-titling. Most syllabic signs (characters) consist of a phonetic element with or without the addition of a determinative element that often gives a clue to the meaning of the syllable represented; but the script reached its present form over two thousand years ago, since when Chinese phonology has changed drastically, words have undergone extensions of meaning, and characters have been re-used as phonetic loans, with the result that phonetic and determinative clues now offer little assistance to the student, who is confronted with the learning of several thousand apparently arbitrary syllabic signs (four thousand are adequate for most purposes). This represents a considerable investment of time and effort, and unless one is prepared to go all the way with the learning of the script, the return in terms of fluent reading ability will be small.

An added complication is that the script (like the Japanese script after the Second World War) has been simplified by government decree. This means that the student has to learn both the old and the 'new' forms of characters (actually most of the 'new' printed forms are hand-written abbreviations of long standing). He will, for instance, be confronted with a word printed in simplified characters in a newspaper and be unable to find it except in a dictionary printed in traditional characters. The simplifications are of two kinds: (a) the abolition of 1,821 characters representing variant spellings of other characters, (b) the simplification of 506 individual characters (of which 132 occur as elements of more complex characters) and of 14 elements occurring only in combination. Since the latter 146 elements occur in thousands of characters and since no limit has been placed on the number of characters ancient and modern, common and rare, in which they may be replaced by the simplified forms, it is impossible to say how many characters will be affected altogether. On the average, every third character in a piece of running text will be partly or wholly simplified by the omission or replacement of constituent elements.

ROMANISATION

The principal systems of romanisation in current use in text-books and dictionaries are (1) Wade-Giles, the traditional English system, (2) the Yale University system, (3) Gwoyeu Romatzyh (G.R.), the old official Chinese system, which indicates tonal difference by differences in spelling, and (4) Pinyin Zimu, the new official Chinese system, which is gradually replacing the other three. Others encountered are the French, German and Russian systems and the old Chuyin Tzumu alphabet based on elements from the Chinese script. A detailed description of transliteration systems is *Guide to transliterated Chinese in the modern Peking dialect*; compiled and introduced by I. L. Legeza (Leiden, Brill, 1967–69). V. 1: *Conversion tables of the currently used international and European systems with comparative tables of initials and finals.* V. 2: *Conversion tables of the outdated international and European individual systems with comparative tables of initials and finals.*

ARRANGEMENT

The two main methods of arrangement of Chinese entries in dictionaries and indexes are (*a*) by the sound of the word, and (*b*) by the shape of the character. For the former purpose one of the above-mentioned romanisations is usually employed and presents no special problems. The latter may be subdivided into two types: (*a*) the traditional arrangement, and (*b*) various new systems. With the traditional arrangement, characters are classified primarily under 'radicals' and secondarily under the number of strokes in the character. The 'radicals' are 214 character-elements, largely coinciding with the determinative elements, though sometimes quite arbitrarily chosen. The new systems are based on the shapes of the strokes taken in the order in which they are written (the Russian system takes them in *reverse* order and the 'four corner' systems ignore the writing order) and/or the number of strokes. Since the new simplified characters often have no traditionally recognised radical, Chinese lexicographers and indexers are having to abandon the traditional system in favour of one of the newer systems, though of course the traditional system must be known if one is to use any but the latest works of reference.

TEXTBOOKS, GRAMMARS AND READERS OF THE MODERN LANGUAGE

In the 1967 edition details were given of the Mirror Series of textbooks and readers published by the Institute of Far Eastern Languages of Yale University. These are still being reprinted and additions have been made to the series, but they are becoming outdated by newer textbooks and details will not be given here. Nor will details be given of the teaching materials currently being compiled by the Chinese Language Project at Cambridge University, since these are not available through the normal commercial channels though they are made available to teaching departments; for further information contact the Director of the Project at the Faculty of Oriental Studies, University of Cambridge.

Apart from the Mirror Series and the Cambridge material there are two sets of integrated textbooks – the Peking series and the de Francis series – and miscellaneous textbooks from other sources.

(A) THE PEKING SERIES

From the point of view of authenticity and up-to-dateness, this series must inevitably be attractive to the student who is primarily interested in the living spoken and written language and who is prepared to accept the limitations imposed by beginning his studies entirely in the simplified script. All the titles in this series use fully simplified characters throughout and, of course, Pinyin romanisation.

Elementary Chinese (Jichu Hanyu). Peking, Commercial Press. 1971–72. 2 pts. (iv, 244 pp.; i, 387 pp.). £0.30 each part. 8 cassettes available at £12 the set.

This course is bilingual (Chinese and English) throughout to facilitate use with a native teacher; it is available also in other languages. It is a revision of *Modern Chinese reader* (Peking, 1958), which was compiled as the basic course for foreign students at Peking University and the Peking Foreign Language Institute. Part 1 contains lessons 1–36 (of which 1–12 are preliminary pronunciation and writing practice); Part 2 contains lessons 37–66 and a complete vocabulary for both parts (romanisation of first character, characters, part of speech, romanisation of whole word, English equivalent, reference to number of lesson). Each lesson consists of (1) sentences illustrating new grammar (romanisation, characters, English), (2) text (romanisation, characters), (3) new vocabulary (characters, part of speech, romanisation, English), (4) explanation of grammar (bilingual), (5) exercises, and (6) stroke-order of new characters. The total vocabulary is 916 words, written with 786 characters. Large, clear printed characters in 'brushed' style.

The main defect of this otherwise excellent course is the paucity of exercise material. This defect has been remedied by the following title.

JAMIESON, J. C. and SHIH, L. L. *Elementary Chinese companion.* Vol. 1. Berkeley, Center for Chinese Studies, University of California, 1974. x, 418 pp. (Studies in Chinese Terminology, No. 16). £4.95.

Intended to supplement the deficiencies of the preceding work with 'exercises, reviews, and structural and lexical analysis'. It consists of 22 units corresponding to lessons 13–66 of *Elementary Chinese*, a phonetic system conversion table, and an index to the grammar. At the end of each unit an English translation of all the exercise material is provided as a key. The work operates within the language framework of *Elementary Chinese* except for 83 extra vocabulary items in the later units. Handwritten characters, legible if not beautiful.

Chinese reader (Hanyu duben). Peking, Commercial Press, 1972. 2 pts. (vi, 239 pp.; iii, 295 pp.), 3 colour plates. £0.30 each part. 7 cassettes available at £11 the set.

Intended as a continuation of *Elementary Chinese*, though the format is different. Part 1 consists of 18 lessons and a general vocabulary of new items in Part 1; Part 2 contains 14 lessons (19–34), a general vocabulary of new items in Part 2, and an index to grammar notes for both parts. Each lesson consists of a text in characters, a list of new words (same format as *Elementary*

Chinese), notes (with additional examples) on selected new grammatical and lexical items, and a limited amount of exercise material. The number of new words in Parts 1 and 2 is 996 and 1,061 respectively. Same style of 'brushed' typeface as *Elementary Chinese.* Illustrated with line drawings.

Easy Chinese Readings. (Hanyi jianyi duwu). Peking, Commercial Press, 1975. vi, 110 pp. £0.20.

Intended as a companion volume to *Chinese reader*, Parts 1 and 2. It 'aims at consolidating the student's mastery of the vocabulary and syntax in *Elementary Chinese* ... and in *Chinese reader.*' Consists of 26 passages in characters (anecdotes, descriptions of famous places), each provided with list of new words (same format as *Elementary Chinese*), but no general vocabulary for the whole volume. New vocabulary totals 497 items. Large printed characters in normal printed style (unlike *Elementary Chinese* and *Chinese reader*). Illustrated with line drawings.

Chinese reader (Hanyu duben). Part 3. Peking, Commercial Press, 1975. i, 327 pp. £0.30. Cassettes awaited.

This and Part 4 (awaited, no details yet) are intended to follow Parts 1 and 2, the difference being that the texts included in these two volumes are mainly original works. Part 3 consists of 14 lessons (35–48), each consisting of a text, a vocabulary of new words, and fairly extensive notes on grammar and selected lexical items with additional examples, but no exercise material. New vocabulary totals 2,285 items. Large, legible characters in normal printed style (not 'brushed'). Illustrated with line drawings.

Chinese for beginners. Series 1. London, Guanghwa Co., 1975. iii, 130 pp. £0.50. Text and 2 cassettes, £3.90, Two 10" records, £1.10.

This title is independent of the preceding titles in this section. Reprint of a series of lessons published in the Language Corner of the magazine *China reconstructs*, July 1972–December 1973. Consists of (1) a brief introduction to pronunciation, script and grammar, (2) 24 lessons, and (3) key to exercises. Each lesson contains (1) a text in characters with interlinear romanisation and word-for-word English translation, (2) a free translation of the text, (3) notes on grammar, and (4) a limited amount of exercise material. Of limited usefulness to the serious student, but should enable the interested non-specialist to understand quickly how Chinese works and what is entailed in learning it. Can be recommended to libraries for this purpose.

(B) THE DE FRANCIS SERIES

This American series is widely used in schools and universities. It has the disadvantage of being old-fashioned (pre-1949-ish) in content as compared with the more recent material in the preceding section, but it has certain advantages that may outweigh this consideration for many users: (*a*) it uses the traditional, unsimplified script, providing a better foundation for students whose interest extends beyond strictly contemporary language, (*b*) it contains a wealth of exercise material from which teachers may select according to the needs of the class and which should provide for all the needs of the self-taught student, and (*c*) full recordings of all the material are available. The first-stage textbooks (the first three titles below) are in the process of revision and the new editions are expected in Autumn, 1976, but no details or prices are yet available. The general features of the series are: (*a*) Pinyin romanisation and traditional characters throughout, (*b*) vocabulary introduced over the series in order of frequency, (*c*) fundamental approach is through sentence patterns, (*d*) subject-matter is mainly domestic and social, but the language and the social situations are on the whole those of a generation ago and could give the student a very distorted first impression of life in China today.

The prices given below have been calculated from the dollar prices at a rate (66p to the dollar) suggested by the publishers. Prices are given for paperback editions only; hardback editions are available, but expensive (*e.g.* £15 as against £4) and are not usually stocked by retailers in the U.K. Complete tape-recordings are available as indicated.

DE FRANCIS, J. *Beginning Chinese.* Rev. ed. New Haven, Yale University Press, 1963. (New revised ed. forthcoming.) xxxi, 498 pp. £4. Tapes, £97.

Four units of six lessons each, every sixth lesson being a revision of the preceding five. 600 vocabulary items. Sentence-stress and breath-groups marked (an unusual feature in textbooks of Chinese).

Excellent, very full exercises of all kinds. Romanisation only used in this volume. A vocabulary is appended, also an introduction to the Chinese script.

DE FRANCIS, J. *Character text for beginning Chinese.* New Haven, Yale University Press, 1964. (New revised ed. forthcoming.) 436 pp. £4.

References to pagination of preceding work enabling the student to use them in conjunction. Very clearly handwritten. 494 characters are introduced at this stage. A stroke-order chart is included, as well as four indexes arranged from lesson to radical number, from stroke number to lesson, from radical to lesson, and from pronunciation to lesson.

DE FRANCIS, J. *Beginning Chinese reader.* New Haven, Yale University Press, 1966. (New revised ed. forthcoming.) 2 v. x, xxii, 432 and 572 pp. £8. the set. Tapes, £55.

48 lessons consisting of eight sets of five lessons each introducing ten characters plus one revision lesson. Each lesson contains, apart from new vocabulary, illustrative sentences (Chinese text with English translation) and Chinese texts without an English translation (these constitute the bulk of the material). A total of 400 characters and 1,250 compounds are introduced within a running text of 120,000 words. The characters are printed and are large and clear; characters in vocabularies are brushed and are larger still. A supplementary lesson gives some practice in the simplified script in current use, though not without errors. Charts of stroke-order are included, and also indexes of characters by lesson, number of strokes and radical, variant forms of characters, and finally an alphabetically arranged vocabulary with characters and references.

DE FRANCIS, J. *Intermediate Chinese.* New Haven, Yale University Press, 1964. xii, 542 pp. £4. Tapes, £120.

A continuation of *Beginning Chinese,* arranged on the same general pattern. Very full exercises of all kinds. Non-review lessons contain dialogue, illustrative sentences for new vocabulary and grammar, review sentences, monologues, questions, English translation of dialogue, English translation of illustrative sentences and review sentences, and notes. Appended is a glossary of new vocabulary only (*c.* 1,000 items), with references.

DE FRANCIS, J. *Character text for intermediate Chinese.* New Haven, Yale University Press, 1965. iv, 434 pp. £4.

DE FRANCIS, J. *Intermediate Chinese reader.* New Haven, Yale University Press, 1967. 2 v. (xvi, 1,428 pp.). £9. Tapes, £85.

Five sets each of five lessons plus one revision lesson, with final index (same format as *Beginning Chinese reader*). Continues principles of 'selection of characters on the basis of frequency' and the 'provision of large numbers of compounds and a large amount of reading matter relative to the number of characters' (specifically 400 new characters, 2,500 compounds, and about 200,000 characters of running text).

DE FRANCIS, J. *Advanced Chinese.* New Haven, Yale University Press, 1966. xvi, 574 pp. £3.25. Tapes, £82.

Continuation of *Intermediate Chinese*, with the same format. The general outline of each lesson is dialogue, vocabulary, illustrative sentences, vocabulary list, grammar drill, lecture, recapitulation, review, questions, English translation of illustrative sentences, and notes. Particular emphasis on language of classroom discussion and lectures on Chinese cultural and academic subjects. Glossary of new vocabulary (*c.* 2,000 items).

DE FRANCIS, J. *Character text for advanced Chinese.* New Haven, Yale University Press, 1966. 721 pp. £5.

DE FRANCIS, J. *Advanced Chinese reader.* New Haven, Yale University Press, 1969. xvi, 713 pp. £5. Tapes, £75.

A further 400 characters, bringing the total for the three readers up to 1,200.

DE FRANCIS, J. *Index volume: beginning, intermediate and advanced texts in spoken and written Chinese.* New Haven, Yale University Press, 1970. xviii, 424 pp. £4.50.

A comprehensive index to the preceding nine titles. Primary arrangement is alphabetical by romanisation, with characters (Traditional, but with the addition of the simplified form for individual-character entries), English equivalent, and at least one reference, enabling at least one exemplary sentence to be found. 11,000 entries including both individual characters and compounds. Three cross-indexes: (1) stroke and radical numbers of characters (character, romanisation, total stroke count and serial radical number), (2) stroke-radical index of characters (stroke number, radical number, character, romanisation), (3) stroke index of variant forms (stroke count, simplified character, traditional character, romanisation).

OTHER MODERN TEXTBOOKS, ETC.

CHAO, Y. R. *A grammar of spoken Chinese.* Berkeley and Los Angeles, California University Press, 1968. xxxi, 847 pp. £10.75.

Arranged systematically, with three-figure paragraphing and a subject index. The most complete reference of the spoken language, though it omits mention of everyday written usages if they are not familiar to the author in spoken form, so it is not always helpful for reading written 'colloquial' Chinese. The two main disadvantages for the student are that (*a*) it uses G.R. romanisation instead of the now usual Pinyin. and (*b*) not only official but also unofficial simplified characters are used, so that the spelling conforms neither to the traditional nor to the modern standard. More thorough indexing and cross-referencing would have made it easier to use for practical reference purposes. Despite these shortcomings, it is a monumental contribution to the study of Chinese grammar.

CHI, W. S. *Readings in Chinese Communist documents. A manual for students of the Chinese language.* Berkeley and Los Angeles, California University Press, 1963. xvi, 478 pp. £7.15.

Consists of 15 texts (policy documents, etc.) arranged in chronological order and covering the period 1949 to 1959. The texts are photographically reproduced from printed sources with some loss of legibility, and each text is provided with an introduction and with a vocabulary legibly brush-written. The romanisation used in the vocabularies is Wade-Giles and great care has clearly gone into the selection of English equivalents. Two glossaries are appended, one arranged by romanisation, with references to number of lesson and serial number within lesson-vocabulary, and the second by radicals. This work provides an excellent stepping-stone from the general run of textbooks to the reading of current newspapers and political writing in general and it can be unreservedly recommended for this purpose.

CHI, W. S. *Readings in Chinese Communist ideology*. Berkeley and Los Angeles, California University Press, 1968, xi, 440 pp. £10.20.

Sequel to the preceding title. Extracts from the writings of Mao Tse-tung, Liu Shao-ch'i, Fan Wen-lan and others, arranged thematically to show various aspects of the development of Chinese Communist thought (ideology, law, history, the economy) from 1930 to the time of publication. Consists of (1) 10 lessons each containing an introduction in English, a very legible printed (re-set) Chinese text with numbered lines, vocabulary (characters, Wade-Giles romanisation, English equivalent, page and line reference); (2) alphabetically arranged glossary of compounds (romanisation, traditional characters, reference); (3) glossary arranged by radical number, characters, reference; (4) converstion table (Wade-Giles, G.R., Yale, Pinyin); (5) conversion table of simplified characters.

CHI, W. S. *Readings in the Chinese Communist Cultural Revolution*. Berkely and Los Angeles, California University Press, 1971. xi, 530 pp. £8.40

Same format as preceding title. 21 lessons, with glossaries and conversion tables. Texts arranged in chronological order, not in order of difficulty. Texts are from official publications during the period 1965–8, covering a wide range of subjects. Particularly useful since dictionaries have not yet caught up with the peculiar vocabulary innovations and difficulties of this very significant period of modern Chinese writing.

CHIH, Y. J. *A primer of newspaper Chinese*. New Haven, Yale University Press, 1956 ix, 219 pp. (Mirror Series, No. A/12). £2.50.

A knowledge of about 800 characters is assumed. Legibly pen-written throughout. The 23 passages included are news-items from the Chinese press, each accompanied by a vocabulary, grammar notes and exercises in Chinese-to-English translation. Appendices include common surnames, the transliteration of foreign names, the organisation of the Governments of China and Taiwan, correspondences between literary and colloquial vocabulary, and a list of 800 basic characters arranged by radical.

CHIH, Y. J. *Advanced Chinese newspaper readings*. New Haven, Yale University Press, 1960. iii, 161 pp. (Mirror Series No. B/32). £2.05.

Intended to follow the preceding work. The 12 selections from the

Chinese press consist of editorial matter reproduced photographically, each accompanied by notes, mainly on vocabulary, legibly pen-written. Since the texts are photographically reproduced, simplified characters occurring in them are inevitably kept, though their traditional counterparts are also given. A glossary arranged by stroke-order is appended.

DE FRANCIS, J. *Annotated quotations from Chairman Mao*. New Haven, Yale University Press, 1975. xi, 314 pp. £5.25.

Annotated edition of *Mao Zhuxi Yulu* (*Quotations from Chairman Mao*), popularly known as the 'little red book'. The slightly reduced but still clearly legible character text (50,700 characters of running text using 1,600 different characters) is printed in parallel with a romanised version. It is followed by a vocabulary in order of occurrence, restricted to items (460 characters and 1,400 compounds) not included in the author's *Index volume* (see above). New characters are given both in traditional and in simplified form. Literary and bound forms are indicated. The vocabulary is followed by a few pages of brief notes, mainly on syntax, in order of occurrence. There is a stroke-index of variant forms (from simplified to traditional) and an alphabetical index (romanisation, characters, English equivalent, reference) to the vocabulary items not included in the *Index volume*.

MILLS, H. C. & NI, P. S. *Intermediate reader in modern Chinese*. Ithaca, N.Y., Cornell University Press, 1967. 3 v. (xx, xcv, 175 pp.; xx, 366 pp.; xi, 375 pp.). £14.65.

Texts from 1918 to 1959 on economics, demography, political theory, history, etc., representing 60,000 characters of running text. Assumes a knowledge of a basic 1,000 characters and concentrates on teaching a further 1,000, together with several thousand new compounds. V. 1 contains (*a*) the indexes and (*b*) the text. The indexes are five in number: (1) alphabetical index by Yale romanisation of the 1,000 new characters introduced, (2) radical and stroke index to the same, (3) a list of structure items in order of appearance, (4) index by Yale romanisation of the basic 1,010 characters of which a knowledge is assumed, and (5) table of romanisations – Wade-Giles, Yale and Pinyin. The text is printed in vertical columns in traditional characters. V. 2 and 3 contain the notes and exercises: each lesson consists of (1) a vocabulary (characters, romanisation of new characters only, part of speech, English equivalent), (2) a list of characters to be learned with exemplary compounds and a few exemplary sentences, (3) structure notes, and (4) exercises – translation in both directions involving new structures and vocabulary.

TENG, S. Y. *Conversational Chinese, with grammatical notes.* Chicago, Chicago University Press, 1947 (9th impression, 1973). ix, 441 pp. £7.80.

Traditional characters and Wade-Giles romanisation. The 47 lessons contain vocabulary, text in both characters and romanisation, notes on the text, exercises involving translation in both directions, and grammar notes with examples. A romanised character index and a general index are appended. This is a very solid textbook, but the romanisation in places leaves something to be desired and the language and contents are naturally somewhat dated.

TENG, S. Y. *Advanced conversational Chinese,* Chicago, Chicago University Press, 1965. xv, 293, pp. £5.40.

Follows the pattern of the preceding work. It consists of 'Part I, five lessons dealing with political and geographical terms; Part II, five lessons on religious and historical terms; Part III, two short plays.' Again a romanised character index is provided. Despite its more recent appearance this work is dated in its language and contents, as its predecessor was. Translation is very literal; while this is not out of place in an elementary work, a freer translation would seem more appropriate at this stage.

TEXTBOOKS, GRAMMARS AND READERS OF THE CLASSICAL LANGUAGE

DAWSON, R. *An introduction to classical Chinese.* Oxford, Oxford University Press, 1968. vii, 127 pp. £3.95.

A reader consisting of 11 short Warring States period texts (3,628 characters of running text) with the addition of sufficient apparatus to permit its use as a first Chinese text. This apparatus consists of (1) a general introduction to the principles of Chinese grammar and script, (2) a rough guide to the pronunciation of Wade-Giles romanisation, (3) notes especially on grammatical words (conjunctions, adverbs, particles) in order of occurrence in the text, with an appendix on common grammatical usages of such words not occurring in the texts, (4) translations of the first five texts, (5) a vocabulary arranged by radicals and giving the number of occurrences, romanisation, part of speech, English equivalent, and references which provide a complete index to the grammar notes. While the texts and apparatus are sound and unexceptionable, its traditional approach of piecemeal explanation of grammatical features without reference to a theoretical framework or systematic exercises has less to recommend it than Wang's or Shadick's approach (see below).

GABELENTZ, G. von der. *Chinesische Grammatik, mit Ausschluss des niederen Stiles und der heutigen Umgangssprache.* 4th ed. Halle, Niemeyer, 1960. xxviii, 549 pp. About £13.

First published 1881. All materials are given both in characters and in romanisation, which is the author's own system, basically Mandarin but including certain sound-distinctions obtaining in earlier stages of the langauge and in other dialects. This is a systematic treatment of the grammar of the classical language, not a textbook with exercises. Parts of it have become outdated by subsequent research, but it still remains a useful tool.

HAWKES, D. *A little primer of Tu Fu.* Oxford, Oxford University press, 1967. xii, 243 pp. £3.

35 poems by Tu Fu (712–770). For each poem the following is given: (1) Chinese character text with interlinear Pinyin romanisation, (2) notes on form and subject-matter, (3) romanised version with interlinear English glosses (word-for-word translation) and textual notes, and (4) free prose translation in English. A general vocabulary (est. 1,600 entries) is appended, giving romanisation (but no characters), contextual English equivalents, and references to poem and line numbers. There is also an index to proper names. This work provides a rapid approach to the study of T'ang verse. Although there is room for criticism in matters of detail, the overall approach is admirable. For beginners who wish to approach Chinese verse by the least circuitous route, this work is undoubtedly the best introduction, preferably after acquiring a basic familiarity with the principles of Chinese script and grammar, though it can also be warmly recommended to the general reader who wishes to gain an insight into the workings of Chinese verse without learning the language.

LIU, Y. C. *Fifty Chinese stories.* London, Lund Humphries, 1960. xxii, 233 pp. £2.50.

Consists of an introduction by W. Simon, 50 lessons, vocabularies and notes to the first 10 lessons, and lists of references for the texts and for translations of them. Each lesson contains a passage of classical Chinese (an anecdote from Warring States or Han literature), a G.R. romanised version, and a romanised literary Japanese version, faced on the opposite page by a modern Chinese translation in traditional characters and a G.R. version of this. The texts are well-chosen (even contriving some re-use of vocabulary) and the modern Chinese translation provides useful raw material for a comparison of classical and modern Chinese. On the other hand the Japanese version is of limited usefulness and the romanised versions would seem of limited value to a student who is proficient enough to use a modern Chinese translation as effectively as an English one; the space devoted to these could perhaps have been more profitably used for a complete vocabulary or exercises. Nevertheless it has proved its worth as a very useful reader in wide use.

SHADICK, H. *A first course in literary Chinese*. Ithaca, N.Y., Cornell University Press, 1968. 3 v. (xv, 196; xi, 297; xi, 392 pp.). £15.60.

An elementary knowledge of modern Chinese (including the script) is assumed. V. 1 contains 34 texts. Texts 1–6 were 'specially written or adapted to illustrate the most basic syntactic patterns'; texts 7–22 are mainly original Warring States texts, and these together with 1–6 form the core of the course; texts 23–34 cover a wider spectrum, including the 20th century, and are intended for the student who wishes to specialise in particular categories of texts. V. 1 also contains exercises: translations both ways, 14 passages for 'unseen' practice, and a character index arranged by radicals. V. 2 contains complete vocabularies to the text in order of occurrence. The first half of v. 3 is devoted to very full commentaries on the texts, dealing mainly with syntax; the second half is a systematic outline of grammar in 12 chapters using quotations from the texts for illustration, followed by an index of function-words. The romanisation used is Wade-Giles.

WANG, F. F. *Introduction to literary Chinese*. South Orange, N.J., Seton Hall University Press, 1972. 2 v. (xiii, 346; v, 170 pp.). £4.30.

25 lessons of which 6, 12, 18, 24 and 25 are revision lessons. The method assumes a knowledge of modern Chinese (*e.g.* the De Francis readers). It consists throughout of 'transfers' (translation) from classical to colloquial, avoiding English versions. Each lesson con-

sists of (1) partial vocabularies (characters, Pinyin, part of speech) with colloquial equivalents in characters and Pinyin, plus English equivalents, (2) texts written within the scope of vocabulary and grammar introduced so far (v. 2 contains colloquial versions of these), and (3) detailed notes on structure, well-illustrated with reference to colloquial equivalents. The inspiration for much of the vocabulary and themes is Warring States anecdotes (cf. Liu above), but the language is basically *modern* classical and includes, for instance, the word for 'aeroplane'. Its main defect is that it presupposes a knowledge of modern Chinese, making it unusable for the beginner who is interested only in classical Chinese. The text is very legibly handwritten throughout.

DICTIONARIES

HIXSON, J. & MATHIAS, J. *A. compilation of Chinese dictionaries.* New Haven, Yale University Press, 1975. xii, 87, 37 pp. (Far East Publications), £4.55.

A preliminary listing of over 1,000 specialist and general Chinese dictionaries by CETA (Chinese English Translation Assistance).

CHAO, Y. R. and YANG, L. S. *Concise dictionary of spoken Chinese.* Cambridge Mass., Harvard University Press, 1947. xxxix, 292 pp. £6.80.

Chinese–English only. Arranged by radicals. Both G.R. (with extra indication of some ancient and dialect features) and Wade-Giles romanisations. This is a dictionary of morphemes (est. 5,000 character entries) with some polysyllabic words exemplifying them. It further indicates which morphemes are free and which are bound; in this respect this work is unique and marks a great advance on the traditional morpheme-dictionaries. This indication of bound and free refers only to the modern language. By its very nature this work will not be particularly useful for determining the meaning of polysyllabic words. A G.R. index and a list of measures are appended.

COUVREUR, S. *Dictionnaire classique de la langue chinoise.* Hokienfou, Imprimerie de la Mission Catholique, 1904. Facsimile reprint. Taipei, Book World Co., 1963. xii, 1,080 pp. £28.

The arrangement of the entries is by radical and stroke count. 21,400 entries, each consisting of a character (with variant forms), romanisation (the author's own system), French equivalents, quotations with romanisation illustrating the uses of the character, and compounds treated in the same way. Various appendices (cyclical signs, constellations, ancient capitals, provinces, dynasties, official ranks) and an index of characters whose radicals are difficult to identify. Compares favourably with Mathews in the number of characters included, but has far fewer compounds.

Dictionary of spoken Chinese. (Compiled by the staff of the Institute of Far Eastern Languages, Yale University). New Haven, Yale University Press, 1966. xxxix, 1,071 pp. £36.25.

Two main parts: (1) Chinese–English (295 pp.), est. 2,300 characters. Arranged by first syllable of entry, Yale romanisation with cross-references from Pinyin. Simplified characters are given in brackets and also in the index. Full pronunciation included, with stress indicated. Many examples (characters only). Indication of bound and free morphemes, parts of speech and appropriate measure-words. (2) English–Chinese (737 pp.), estimated 2,300 entry-words. Romanisation only. Copious examples. Appendices include weights and measures, radical index, conversion tables from Wade-Giles to Pinyin and Yale. Legibility excellent. This is a unique reference work for the colloquial language, though it does not reflect the changes that have taken place in Chinese since 1949.

DOBSON, W. A. C. H. *A dictionary of the Chinese particles.* Toronto, Toronto University Press, 1974. x, 908 pp. £21.

694 particles (conjunctions, adverbs, particles, etc.) arranged alphabetically by G.R. A summarisation of the author's series of individual works on particular stages of the development of Chinese grammar from the earliest books and bronze inscriptions (oracle-bones not included) up to and including Han Chinese, i.e. the first recorded 1,000 years of the Chinese literary language. Each entry includes Karlgren's reconstruction of the Archaic Chinese (Old Chinese) and Ancient Chinese (Middle Chinese) pronunciation, references to *Grammata serica recensa*, the Harvard-Yenching concordances and other important reference works, part of speech according to the author's own system, and illustrative quotations (very legibly handwritten). Apart from the main body of the work there is a 102-page treatment of particles in general, including dated lists of particles arranged thematically. There is a radical index, an index of characters difficult to find, and a Wade-Giles–G.R. conversion table.

DOOLIN, D. J. & RIDLEY, C. P. *A Chinese–English dictionary of Chinese Communist terminology*. Stanford, Hoover Institution Press, 1973. xiv, 570 pp. £14.

'This dictionary is intended for the reader or translator of current Chinese documents and is concerned primarily with words and phrases either coined or given new currency by the Chinese Communist Party and the Government of the People's Republic of China. The individual entries furnish, whenever possible, a translation or equivalent sanctioned by Communist Chinese usage in official translations. ... The dictionary covers the period from ... the early 1920's to the present.' Arranged by radicals. Estimated number of entries: 18,400. Each entry consists of the word in traditional characters, with Wade-Giles romanisation and an English equivalent. Index of radicals.

LIANG, S. C. *A new practical Chinese–English dictionary*. Taipei, Far East Book Co., 1971. xl, 1,384 pp. £7.30.

Character-entries arranged by radicals and stroke-number, compounds sub-arranged by Chuyin Tzumu. 7,331 character-entries (character, Chuyin Tzumu romanisation, Wade-Giles, G.R., English equivalents). 80,000 compound-entries (characters, Chuyin Tzumu, English equivalents). Traditional characters throughout. Emphasis on modern rather than classical usage, on Taiwan usage rather than that of Mainland China. Inferior to Mathews for classical Chinese, but still a reasonable 'buy'. Many proper names, Chinese and foreign.

LYN, Y. T. *Chinese–English dictionary of modern usage*. Hongkong, Chinese University of Hongkong, 1972. lxvi, 1,720 pp. End-papers (index-system). £16.

Arranged by author's own system (the Instant Index System) based on the shape of the character. Compounds sub-arranged by author's own system of romanisation (inspired by G.R.). Romanised index by same system. English index. Its main defect is that it lacks any of the usual indexes (radical system or existing romanisation systems): one perforce uses the author's own idiosyncratic systems or none at all. It is claimed that 'It includes all words and phrases that a modern reader is likely to encounter with (*sic*) in reading modern newspapers, magazines and books.' In actual fact it compares badly with Doolin & Ridley (see above) on modern terminology and lacks very many everyday terms. Nevertheless it does include many compounds that are not given in the general run of dictionaries. It has a number of useful appendices, including conversion tables of traditional and simplified characters.

MATHEWS, R. H. *A Chinese–English dictionary.* Rev. American ed. Cambridge, Mass., Harvard University Press, 1949. xxiv, 1,226 pp. £16.10.

The largest Chinese–English general dictionary currently available, with over 100,000 entries under 7,773 characters. The entries have been taken indiscriminately from all periods and styles of spoken and written Chinese without indication. No indication of whether a given syllable is a free or bound morpheme. Much current vocabulary is not included. All entries are serially numbered. The radical index refers to these, as does the separately published English–Chinese index (out of print). A number of useful tables are appended, and a full radical index. Legibility is good despite the small type.

MATHEWS, R. H. *A Chinese–English dictionary.* Reduced photo-reprint of preceding. Taipei, Wenhua T'ushu Kungszu, 1973. xxiv, 1,226 pp. £4.50.

Some loss of legibility, reducing its usefulness to the beginner though not to the advanced student.

New English–Chinese dictionary. 1st ed. Shanghai, Joint Publishing Co., 1974. Hongkong, 1975. xxi, 1,689 pp. Separate chart of simplified characters. Library ed. ($9\frac{1}{4}'' \times 6\frac{1}{4}''$) £7.50; compact ed. ($7\frac{1}{4}'' \times 5''$) £4.80; popular ed. ($7\frac{1}{4}'' \times 5''$, limp cover) £4.50.

Compiled by 70-odd compilers from various Shanghai institutions of higher education primarily for Chinese users: pronunciation of English entries in I.P.A., Chinese equivalents in simplified characters only, and abbreviations and other notes in Chinese only. Over 50,000 main entries comprising 80,000 entries including derivatives and compounds, together with over 14,000 idioms. Illustrative examples. Some useful appendices. A great improvement on existing dictionaries of this kind, but there is still too much dead wood and too many omissions of everyday phrases, compounds and meanings. Library edition is very legible but beginners could have difficulty with some characters in the reduced editions.

WANG, F. F. *Mandarin Chinese dictionary: Chinese–English.* South Orange, N.J., Seton Hall University Press, 1967. xix, 660 pp. £4.50.

A dictionary of the spoken language which limits the number of entries (*c.* 6,000) in order to give a fuller treatment of basic vocabulary, particularly by illustrating with exemplary sentences the syntactic environment of individual words. The arrangement is alphabetical and each entry includes (1) Pinyin romanised form, (2) a figure suggesting order of learning, (3) traditional characters legibly handwritten, (4) part of speech, (5) English equivalent, (6) (according to need) examples in romanisation and characters, with English equivalent. There is a grammatical introduction, comparative transcription tables (Pinyin, Yale, Wade-Giles), and a radical and stroke index. Compiled with the needs of the beginner in school or university in mind, and intended not merely as a reference work but also as a point of departure for language-practice.

WANG, F. F. *Mandarin Chinese dictionary: English–Chinese.* South Orange, N.J., Seton Hall University Press, 1971. xxi, 779 pp. £4.50.

The English–Chinese counterpart of the preceding title (*q.v.*), with the same approach and format. 4,000 entries with over 10,000 examples. One of the few English–Chinese dictionaries compiled with the problems of the English-speaking student in mind. Both volumes are strongly recommended.

INDEX